FRANKLIN DELANO ROOSEVELT, PRESERVER OF SPIRIT AND HOPE

(A VOLUME IN FIRST MEN, AMERICA'S PRESIDENTS SERIES)

OTHER BOOKS IN THE
FIRST MEN, AMERICA'S PRESIDENTS SERIES

Barbara Bennett Peterson, Editor

**Theodore Roosevelt:
A Political Life**
Tom Lansford
2004. ISBN 1-59033-990-8

Citizen Lincoln
Ward M. McAfee
2004. ISBN 1-59454-112-4

**George Washington, America's
Moral Exemplar**
Barbara Bennett Peterson
2005. ISBN 1-59454-230-9

**President James K. Polk: The Dark
Horse President**
Louise Mayo
2006. ISBN 1-59454-718-1

**Franklin Delano Roosevelt,
Preserver of Spirit and Hope**
Barbara Bennett Peterson
2006. ISBN 1-60021-117-8

**John Quincy Adams:
Yankee Nationalist**
Paul E. Teed
2006. ISBN 1-59454-797-1

President Herbert Hoover
Don W. Whisenhunt
2007. ISBN 978-1-60021-476-9

**Chester Alan Arthur: The Life of a
Gilded Age Politician and President**
Gregory J. Dehler
2007. 978-1-60021-079-2

**William Henry Harrison:
General and President**
Mary Jane Child Queen
2007. 978-1-60021-407-3

FRANKLIN DELANO ROOSEVELT, PRESERVER OF SPIRIT AND HOPE

(A VOLUME IN FIRST MEN, AMERICA'S PRESIDENTS SERIES)

BARBARA BENNETT PETERSON

Nova Science Publishers, Inc.
New York

Copyright © 2009 by Nova Science Publishers, Inc.

All rights reserved. No part of this book may be reproduced, stored in a retrieval system or transmitted in any form or by any means: electronic, electrostatic, magnetic, tape, mechanical photocopying, recording or otherwise without the written permission of the Publisher.

For permission to use material from this book please contact us:
Telephone 631-231-7269; Fax 631-231-8175
Web Site: http://www.novapublishers.com

NOTICE TO THE READER

The Publisher has taken reasonable care in the preparation of this book, but makes no expressed or implied warranty of any kind and assumes no responsibility for any errors or omissions. No liability is assumed for incidental or consequential damages in connection with or arising out of information contained in this book. The Publisher shall not be liable for any special, consequential, or exemplary damages resulting, in whole or in part, from the readers' use of, or reliance upon, this material.

This publication is designed to provide accurate and authoritative information with regard to the subject matter covered herein. It is sold with the clear understanding that the Publisher is not engaged in rendering legal or any other professional services. If legal or any other expert assistance is required, the services of a competent person should be sought. FROM A DECLARATION OF PARTICIPANTS JOINTLY ADOPTED BY A COMMITTEE OF THE AMERICAN BAR ASSOCIATION AND A COMMITTEE OF PUBLISHERS.

LIBRARY OF CONGRESS CATALOGING-IN-PUBLICATION DATA
Available upon request.

ISBN 978-1-60456-496-9

Published by Nova Science Publishers, Inc. ✢ New York

DEDICATION

This book is dedicated to the generation that experienced the Depression and won World War II.

And to my grandparents Rose Barclay and Carl Ernest Chatfield and Clarence and Ora Bennett, to my parents Colonel George W. and Hope H. Bennett, and to my husband's parents Burton and Elizabeth Peterson, each of whom lived heroic lives in those decades.

And to my husband Dr. Frank L. Peterson for his immeasurable assistance.

CONTENTS

Dedication		v
Foreword		ix
Preface		xvii
Chapter 1	FDR's Youth and Progressive Apprenticeship	1
Chapter 2	Postwar 1920s to Governor of New York	33
Chapter 3	From New York Governor to U.S. President	63
Chapter 4	FDR Launches the New Deal Reforms	93
Chapter 5	FDR and the Coming of World War II	127
Chapter 6	U.S. Leadership in World War II	159
Chapter 7	Home Front During World War II	195
Chapter 8	FDR Leads U.S. to Victory	235
Acknowledgements		273
Bibliography		277
About the Author and Series Editor		293
Index		297

FOREWORD

President of the United States of America is an official title sought by many and won by only a few individuals. Most American Presidents are of high merit and political acumen and reflect wisdom, leadership, and integrity. This series titled *First Men, America's Presidents* published by NOVA Science Publishers contains a book length biography of each President of the United States of America. Every book contains information on the President's early education, professional career, military service or political service prior to the presidency, interpretative discussion of both domestic and foreign policies during each presidency, and the conclusion of their political lives in public service. Every presidential biography in the NOVA series has been written by a professional historian or political scientist well versed in the field of presidential scholarship. The two major themes of this series are the character traits marking success in the presidency, and the changes in the office of the presidency through America's history. Character matters in all walks of life, but perhaps it matters most within the character of the President of the United States.

The duties of the President of the United States are delegated through Article II of the Constitution of the United States of America, and from the successive laws passed by Congress over time. Each president takes the Oath of Affirmation:--"I do solemnly swear (or affirm) that I will faithfully execute the Office of the President of the United States, and will to the best of my Ability, preserve, protect and defend the Constitution of the United States." The president's duties and responsibilities under the Constitution are to serve as "Commander in Chief of the Army and Navy of the United States, and the Militia of the several States, when called into actual Service of the United States." The president may invite the counsel and opinions of his various department heads upon any subject related to the execution of the duties of their offices, either in writing or orally as has become the custom within the president's Cabinet. The president "shall have the power to grant Reprieves and Pardons for Offenses against the United States, except in Cases of Impeachment." Every president has realized that each must administer through constitutional principles, as each was elected by the voting majority of the people to be their chief executive through the Electoral College. Each president of the United States "shall have Power, by and with the Advice and Consent of the Senate, to make Treaties, provided two thirds of the Senators present concur." As the president directs both the domestic and foreign activities of the government, he has the power to "nominate and by and with the Advice and Consent of the Senate....appoint Ambassadors, other public Ministers and Consuls, Judges of the Supreme Court, and all other Officers of the United States, whose Appointments are not herein otherwise provided for, and which shall be established by law." The president also receives foreign ambassadors and officials on behalf of the American people. The president "shall have the Power to fill up all Vacancies that may happen during the Recess of the Senate, by granting Commissions which shall expire at the End of their next Session." The president under the Constitution shall give Congress a State of the Union address every year to acquaint them with his policy agenda and plans for the future. Usually in this address to Congress he recommends "to their Consideration such Measures as he shall judge necessary and expedient." Above all, the president of the United States "shall take Care that the Laws be faithfully executed, and shall Commission all the Officers of the United States." A strong role for the President had been envisioned by the Founding Fathers who rejected the obsolete Articles of Confederation and replaced the framework of government with the Constitution of the United States. Article II of the Constitution outlining the powers of the presidency provided that the office of the President would be held by one individual. It provided the President with enumerated powers including the power of the veto. And stipulated that the president's election would be above the control of the Congress to ensure the separation of powers and the system of checks and balances. It stipulated that the president, vice president, and all civil officers of the United States *must govern in the name of the American people* lest they "be removed from Office on Impeachment for, and Conviction of Treason, Bribery, or other high Crimes and Misdemeanors."

From Presidents George Washington through John Quincy Adams candidates for the presidency were selected in caucuses of senators and congressmen and then the state legislatures indirectly chose the president through the selection of Electors to the Electoral College. This system had worked for Washington, Adams, Jefferson, Madison and Monroe—they were statesmen who held wide appeal within Congress and the state legislatures and claimed to represent the people. But as demands for greater democracy in the election process were heard, the process was changed. In the outcome of the election of 1824, John Quincy Adams was chosen president by the Congressional House of Representatives under constitutional law after no candidate had received a majority of the electoral ballots in the Electoral College. Jackson, the candidate who had received the most popular votes was not chosen president and his supporters called for more direct popular participation and worked to introduce changes. Hence, the voting process was altered in the name of democracy. In the election of 1828 President Andrew Jackson triumphed after voting had been given directly to the people and removed from the state legislatures. Democracy further triumphed by the elimination of the congressional caucuses in naming presidential candidates and the holding of national political party conventions to name them instead, allowing greater voice and participation of the people. The institution of the party convention to nominate presidential candidates remains, although winners in various state primaries command party delegates to vote the choice of the people. The Presidency, molded by the character and designs of each president, oversees command, administration, diplomacy, ceremony, legislation, and public opinion. The modern strength of the Presidency is a reflection of the mighty power of the United States within a global world.

The majority of America's presidents have served for one four-year term or less as some died in office. Four presidents served out part of their predecessor's term and won subsequent re-election in their own right: Theodore Roosevelt, Calvin Coolidge, Harry S. Truman, and Lyndon Baines Johnson. Only one president, Grover Cleveland, was elected to two discontinuous terms of office and thus was both the twenty-second and the twenty-fourth president of the United States. Several outstanding presidents have been elected to two four-year terms or more. They were: George Washington, Thomas Jefferson, James Madison, James Monroe, Andrew Jackson, Abraham Lincoln, Ulysses S. Grant, Grover Cleveland, William McKinley, Woodrow Wilson, Franklin D. Roosevelt, Dwight D. Eisenhower, Richard Nixon, Ronald Reagan, and William Jefferson ("Bill") Clinton. Only one president, Franklin D. Roosevelt, was elected for a third and fourth term. Eight presidents have achieved their office as a result of being the vice-president of a preceding president who died in office or resigned: John Tyler, Millard Fillmore, Andrew Johnson, Chester Arthur, Theodore Roosevelt, Calvin Coolidge, Harry S. Truman, Lyndon Baines Johnson, and Gerald R. Ford. Additionally, John Adams, Thomas Jefferson, Martin Van Buren, Richard M. Nixon and George H.W. Bush also rose from the office of vice-president to president. Besides the vice-presidency as a stepping stone to the presidency, two thirds of the presidents elected had held congressional office earlier in their political careers. Twenty presidents had served as Governors of states or territories before being elected. They were: Thomas Jefferson (Virginia), James Monroe (Virginia), Andrew Jackson (Florida), Martin Van Buren (New York), William Henry Harrison (Indiana), John Tyler (Virginia), James K. Polk (Tennessee), Andrew Johnson (Tennessee), Rutherford B. Hayes (Ohio), Grover Cleveland (New York), William McKinley (Ohio), Theodore Roosevelt (New York), William Howard Taft (The Philippines), Woodrow Wilson (New Jersey), Calvin Coolidge (Massachusetts), Franklin D. Roosevelt (New York), Jimmy Carter (Georgia), Ronald Reagan (California), William Jefferson Clinton (Arkansas), and George W. Bush (Texas). Some states with larger voting populations and hence more electoral votes have seen their native sons rise to the presidency of the United States. The American Presidents have come from both coasts, east and west, and from both the upper tier and the lower tier of states geographically, north and south. When elected, the president becomes the president of 'all the people', not just those of his political party. Since the president acts as America's commander in chief, the majority of the presidents of the United States have served in the U.S. military. George Washington, Andrew Jackson, William Henry Harrison, Zachary Taylor, Franklin Pierce, Ulysses S. Grant, Rutherford B. Hayes, James Garfield, Chester Arthur, Benjamin Harrison, and Dwight David Eisenhower served in the capacity of generals. James Monroe, John Tyler, Abraham Lincoln, William McKinley, Theodore Roosevelt, Harry Truman, John F. Kennedy, Lyndon Baines Johnson, Richard Nixon, Gerald R. Ford, Jimmy Carter, Ronald Reagan, George Herbert Walker Bush, and George W. Bush also served their country in military service at various ranks, and always with dedication. The youngest elected president was John F. Kennedy (1960) at forty-three. The youngest man to ever serve as president was Theodore Roosevelt who at forty-two assumed the office following William McKinley's assassination. The average age for an elected president was fifty-four. The oldest elected president was Ronald Reagan at sixty-nine (1980) and seventy-three (1984).[1]

One of the major features of American constitutional development has been the growth of the presidency both in power and prestige as well as in new Cabinet positions, departments and agencies under the control of the president. The Federal government has grown mightily in comparison with the States' governments since the inception of the Constitution. Increases in presidential powers have been occasioned by wars, depressions, foreign relations, and the agenda of the presidents themselves. Henry F. Graff, Emeritus Professor at

---

[1] David C. Whitney and Robin Vaughn Whitney, *The American Presidents,* Garden City, New York: Doubleday, 1993, pp. v-ix.

Columbia University, described the office of the president as "the most powerful office in the world" in *The Presidents*. The Executive Office of the President (EOP) was created during the administration of President Franklin D. Roosevelt upon passage by Congress of the Reorganization Act of 1939. The EOP originally included the White House Office (WHO), the Bureau of the Budget, the Office of Government Reports, the National Resources Planning Board, and the Liaison Office for Personnel Management. In addition, wrote Henry F. Graff, the 1939 Act provided that an "office for emergency management" may be formed "in the event of a national emergency, or threat of a national emergency."[2] Today the White House Office has become "the political as well as policy arm of the chief executive." The larger, all encompassing Executive Office of the President has expanded through time to include a myriad number of departments in addition to the first five listed above and the president is advised by nearly 60 active boards, committees and commissions. During and immediately after World War II the following additional departments within the purview of the EOP were organized: Committee for Congested Production Areas, 1943-1944, War Refugee Board, 1944-1945, Council of Economic Advisers, 1946-, National Security Council, 1947-, and National Security Resources Board, 1947-1953. During the Cold War, additions to the EOP were made adding the following departments: Telecommunications Adviser to the President, 1951-1953, Office of the Director for Mutual Security, 1951-1954, Office of Defense Mobilization, 1952-1958, President's Advisory Committee on Government Organization, 1953-1961, Operations Coordinating Board, 1953-1961, President's Board of Consultants on Foreign Intelligence Activities, 1956-1961, Office of Civil and Defense Mobilization, 1958-1962, and National Aeronautics and Space Council, 1958-1993. By the Sixties, some of the earlier departments organized in the 1939 to 1960 decades were allowed to close, with newer agencies with a new focus and expanded technology taking their place. These newer agencies included: President's Foreign Intelligence Advisory Board, 1961-1977, Office of Emergency Planning, 1962-1969, Office of Science and Technology, 1962-1973, Office of Economic Opportunity, 1964-1975, Office of Emergency Preparedness, 1965-1973, National Council on Marine Resources and Engineering Development, 1966-1971, Council on Environmental Quality, 1969-, Council for Urban Affairs, 1969-1970, and Office of Intergovernmental Relations, 1969-1973. By the mid-Seventies, once again there was a general reorganization with some of the earlier departments and offices being swept away and replaced by newer

---

[2] Henry F. Graff, Editor, *The Presidents,* New York: Charles Scribner's Sons, Simon and Schuster Macmillan, 2nd edition, 1996, Appendix C pp. 743-745.

agencies reflecting new presidential agendas. Many of the new agencies reflected the urgencies in domestic policies and included: the Domestic Council, 1970-1978, Office of Management and Budget, 1970-, Office of Telecommunications Policy, 1970-1977, Council on International Economic Policy, 1971-1977, Office of Consumer Affairs, 1971-1973, Special Action Office for Drug Abuse Prevention, 1971-1975, Federal Property Council, 1973-1977, Council on Economic Policy, 1973-1974, Energy Policy Office, 1973-1974, Council on Wage and Price Stability, 1974-1981, Energy Resource Council, 1974-1977, Office of Special Representative for Trade Negotiations, 1974-, Presidential Clemency Board, 1974-1975, Office of Science and Technology Policy, 1976-, Office of Administration, 1977-, and Domestic Policy Staff, 1978-1981. Many of the departments, councils and agencies organized as part of the Executive Office of the President by the late Seventies and early Eighties included: Office of Policy Development, 1981-, Office of the U.S. Trade Representative, 1981-, National Critical Materials Council, 1984-, Office of National Drug Control Policy, 1988-, National Economic Council, 1993-. By the 21st Century the EOP continued several effective agencies started earlier: Council of Economic Advisers 1946-, National Security Council 1947-, Council on Environmental Quality 1964-, Office of Management and Budget 1970-, Office of Science and Technology Policy 1976-, Office of Administration 1977-, Office of the U.S. Trade Representative 1981-, Office of Policy Development 1981-, and the Office of National Drug Control Policy 1988-. In addition to the White House Office of the president, the Office of the Vice President functions and is administered as part of the EOP.[3] At the turn of the millennium the department of Homeland Security 2001- was established by presidential Executive Order and administered by the Executive Office of the President that continues to be evolutionary in response to new issues, demands, and events.

Capable presidents have responded to America's changing needs and responsibilities by retooling their administrations to meet new crises, opportunities, and challenges. This series *First Men, America's Presidents* published by NOVA explains the personal and public life of each President of the United States. Their qualities of character and leadership are aptly interpreted and offer strong role models for all citizens. Presidential successes are recorded for posterity, as are the pitfalls that should be guarded against in the future. This series also explains the domestic reasons and world backdrop for the expansion of the Executive Office of the President. The President of the United States is

---

[3] Henry F. Graff, Editor, *The Presidents,* New York: Charles Scribner's Sons, Simon and Schuster Macmillan, 3rd edition, 2002, Appendix C pp. 743-747.

perhaps the most coveted position in the world and this series reveals the lives of all those successfully elected, how each performed as president, and how each is to be measured in history. The collective life stories of the presidents reveal the greatness that America represents in the world.

Dr. Barbara Bennett Peterson
First Men, America's Presidents NOVA Series Editor
Professor of History, Oregon State University (retired)
Emeritus Professor University of Hawaii
Former Adjunct Fellow East-West Center
Professor of History, California State University San Bernardino, Palm Desert

PREFACE

Franklin Delano Roosevelt, thirty-second president of the United States, served four consecutive terms, the longest presidential administration in American history. His resilience, forbearance, and superb political abilities establish Roosevelt as one of America's greatest leaders and he has been called the greatest president of the twentieth century for restoring confidence following the onset of the Great Depression and for winning World War II. In both domestic and foreign policy FDR was an improviser rather than an ideologue. Politically skilled from his days as a member of the New York senate and then as the Empire state's Governor, he was elected to the presidency in 1932, 1936, 1940 and 1944 a testament to how his personal charm and astute New Deal programs resonated with Americans. FDR was truly a national president who became an international leader and did not succumb to regionalism but united the continent. President Roosevelt became the most influential leader in the world in his lifetime. His death near the end of World War II at the heights of his prestige and power allowed all of his accomplishments to be well remembered in history ever memorialized. FDR was a Good Neighbor, improved America's trade position, and was an architect of the strategies to win the war. He was a leader with a program launching the New Deal's multitude of programs for relief, recovery, and reform. As a Christian youth at Groton he had carried coal to a poor women's winter door, never forgetting the school motto *Cui servire est regnare, To Serve Him is to Rule,* a notion that he applied all his political life in helping the disadvantaged. FDR and the New Deal set America upon the ideal that America would be a better place if every citizen regardless of race, color, or creed participated in its wealth and opportunities. The government he believed must take responsibility for the general welfare of its citizens just as it is stated in the U.S. Constitution. Americans responded to Franklin Delano Roosevelt with an outpouring of affection and dedication to task when he roused them to fight against moral injustice and foreign tyranny. He was a U.S. president that came just in time to save the U.S. economy for capitalism and the world from fascism and Nazism. FDR was the greatest of 'the greatest generation'. FDR was remarkably in rhythm with the heartbeat of America preserving those sacred fires of spirit and hope as the story is revealed herein.

Dr. Barbara Bennett Peterson
Professor of History (retired) Oregon State University
Emeritus Professor University of Hawaii
Former Adjunct Fellow East-West Center
Professor of History California State San Bernardino,
Palm Desert

Chapter 1

FDR'S YOUTH AND PROGRESSIVE APPRENTICESHIP

Franklin Delano Roosevelt was born in his family's home, Springwood, at Hyde Park on January 30, 1882, and grew up to be the most inspirational man of his times. As thirty-second president he would lead the United States through the Great Depression and World War II, two monumental accomplishments. Born in New York's Dutchess County on his family's estate to wealth and refinement, he would use his position for the betterment of all man-kind. The Roosevelt's Dutch ancestors, headed by Claes Van Rosenvelt [meaning from the rose field], had arrived in America in the 17th Century, settling in New Amsterdam. His son Nicholas witnessed the change over to British control of New York in 1664. Nicholas was a fur trapper on the Hudson River but made his fortune through his flour-mill in New York City, where he was elected an alderman in 1719. By the time of the American Revolution the family name had become Roosevelt. A descendant from each of Nicholas' two sons Johannes and Jacobus would five generations later become a president of the United States, Theodore Roosevelt and Franklin Delano Roosevelt respectively. Johannes Roosevelt's branch of the family settled in Oyster Bay and became Republicans while Jacobus Roosevelt's branch settled on the Hudson and became Democrats. FDR liked to emphasize his Dutch ancestry and was proud of his forebears. Among the direct forerunners of FDR, a son of Jacobus, Issac Roosevelt (1726-1794), made his fortune in the sugar refinery business in New York, importing raw sugar from the West Indies. He opposed the Sugar Act passed by George III and agitated for independence. Known as 'Issac-the-Patriot', he voted for America's Declaration of Independence and moved his family to Dutchess County after the British occupied New York during the Revolutionary War. Issac Roosevelt assisted in drafting New York's first state constitution of 1788, and with Alexander Hamilton formed the Bank of New York. Gilbert Stuart painted his portrait and this painting was passed own through generations to hang at Hyde Park. Issac's son James, a graduate of Princeton, had established a landed country estate of Mount Hope in Dutchess County near Poughkeepsie. James' son Issac, Franklin's grandfather, was a doctor who had trained at Princeton and Columbia universities and lived at Mount Hope. Franklin's father was James Roosevelt, the great grandson of 'Issac-the Patriot' who also made his money in property investments, and his mother was Sara Delano, hence his middle name. Sara Delano traced her ancestry back to Philippe de la Noye, a French Huguenot who had immigrated to Plymouth colony in 1621 and whose descendants, including her father Warren Delano II, earned their fortunes in the shipping trade with China.[4] The Delano family home, Algonac, was twenty miles south of Hyde Park so the families had been friends for years when James and Sara were married.

James, respectfully called Mr. James, and Sara Roosevelt were among the first fifty families of New York who had "commodious estates along (mainly) the eastern bank of the majestic Hudson, where it flowed slowly by Westchester and Dutchess counties, especially from Rhinebeck to Tarrytown—from seventy-five down to fifteen miles north of New York City."[5] The original family home at Mount Hope had burned down and James purchased a new estate two miles north on the Hudson called Springwood where Franklin would grow up. They also owned a home in New York City and were members of the Knickerbocker society. Mr. James was a St. James Episcopal Church warden, served on the board of governors for the local St. Francis Hospital in Poughkeepsie, and was town manager of Hyde Park. Following Harvard Law School, James worked in a distinguished law firm in New York, served as director of the Consolidated Coal Company, was retained as general manager of the Cumberland and Pennsylvania Railroad, was vice-president of the Delaware & Hudson Railroad, and after 1872 served as president of the Southern Railway Securities Company.[6] Desiring that his young son Franklin should enjoy the finer things in life and receive the broadest education possible, the family toured Europe with Franklin when he was three and his formal portrait was taken in England in June 1885. Annual trips to the continent followed. The first letter young Franklin wrote was sent to his

---

[4] Ted Morgan, FDR, A Biography (New York: Simon and Schuster, 1985), p. 25; Conrad Black, Franklin Delano Roosevelt, Champion of Freedom (New York: Public Affairs, Perseus Book Group, 2003), pp. 4-6; Eleanor Roosevelt, On My Own (New York: Curtis, 1958), p. 31.

[5] Clara Steeholm and Hardy Steeholm, The House at Hyde Park (New York: Viking, 1950); Black, Franklin Delano Roosevelt, Champion of Freedom, p. 3; Morgan, FDR, A Biography, p. 31.

[6] Black, Franklin Delano Roosevelt, Champion of Freedom, pp. 6-7.

mother and illustrated with sailboats. He would become a first class sailor. Franklin learned boating from his father who served as Commodore of the local yacht club. They shared a similar passion for breeding horses and Franklin became an excellent rider and later won several prizes with his father's favorite trotters.

Springwood was actually a gentleman farm covering a thousand acres producing apples, running horses and selling hay. During the winter Franklin and his father enjoyed ice-boating, sledding and fishing on the Hudson River. Franklin took up the new skill of photography and loved to take pictures of his family's gatherings and reunions with an early Kodak camera. He read rapidly, devouring books on all sorts of topics. His nannies, Miss McRorie and Mlle. Sandoz, nursed and educated the young Franklin and from them he learned German and French. He grew up among adults both at Hyde Park and another Delano compound known as Fairhaven in Massachusetts. Young Franklin was very much at ease in social affairs, never becoming precocious, and cultivated a charm that endeared him to people of all walks of life.[7] From an early age he enjoyed the luxury of an education through Swiss tutors and was raised in the manner of English aristocracy. Franklin spoke with exceptional ease, honed his manners, and projected an image of a bright young man who would accomplish great things in his life. He learned the skills of a successful landowner and gentleman from his father, as he was taught land management and orchard crop production. During the Roosevelt stays on the Continent, Franklin attended various European grammar schools, most notably in a *Volkschule* in Bad Nauheim in 1891 in Germany. Raised as an only child, Franklin developed strong self-esteem and self-assurance, traits he exhibited throughout his life. He read for pleasure Alfred Mahan's *The Influence of Sea Power Upon History* and Francis Parkman's *Montcalm and Wolfe,* both books on manly arts of peace and war.

Believing morality to be in league with wealth, James Roosevelt had attended Hyde School in the Berkshire Mountains of Massachusetts and determined that Franklin would also profit from a strict and pious education. Franklin's father was considerably older than his mother and had married her after the death of his first wife Rebecca Brien Howland. Mr. James had been fifty-two and Sara twenty-six at their wedding in October 1880. By his first marriage FDR's father had an older

---

[7] Geoffrey Ward, Before The Trumpet: Young Franklin Roosevelt, 1882-1905 (New York: Harper and Row, 1985), Vol. I pp. 35, 38, 41. Alan Brinkley, "Franklin Delano Roosevelt," in American National Biography. Edited by John A. Garraty and Mark C. Carnes, Vol. 18 (New York: Oxford University Press, 1999), pp. 816-826; Sara Delano Roosevelt (as told to Isabel Leighton and Gabriel Forbush), My Boy Franklin (New York: Crown, 1933); Morgan, FDR, A Biography, p. 49-53.

son, James Roosevelt Roosevelt, nicknamed Rosy, who was twenty-seven when young Franklin was born. Rosy's own son James Roosevelt Roosevelt, Jr., nicknamed Taddy, would enter Groton in 1894 ahead of Franklin and pave the way for him. Franklin followed in 1896 at Groton in Massachusetts at age fourteen as a ninth grader, also called a Third Former. This relatively new boarding school molded the proper character in boys of position and breeding. His father had begun to have a series of small heart attacks in 1891 and Franklin endeavored to do exceptionally well in school to please his parents and produce no stress. Groton School had been established by Rector Endicott Peabody upon the British educational model. Peabody encouraged both high level academic lessons and sports to build 'manly character'. The school was endowed by financier J.P. Morgan, who sent his own children to Groton, and by additional wealthy New Yorkers like the Harrimans, Whitneys and Stillmans. Groton's motto was *Cui servire est regnare* [To Serve Him is to Rule] that expressed its dedication to Christian leadership. Its daily routine was Spartan to inculcate strict discipline. "All students except seniors lived in cubicles six by nine feet, and the cubicles had a curtain for a door and walls that left a three foot gap between the ceiling and the wall, perfect for throwing things at your neighbor….There was no closet, just pegs on the wall and a bureau, desk, and chair. The daily schedule also left little time for the boys to spend time alone or engage in unproductive pursuits. A bell rang at 6:45 a.m. to wake the students who were then expected to take a cold shower. A bell at 7:30 a.m. told the boys to attend breakfast in coats and ties. Then there was chapel for half an hour at 8:00 a.m. and classes until about 2 p.m."[8] Following classes, the boys were free to engage in all types of rough and tough sports until 4:00 p.m. when they showered and dressed for dinner. Study followed the formal dinner and bed and lights out were at 10:00 p.m. Franklin enjoyed having long academic conversations with his teachers and impressed them with his intellectual prowess and sense of humor. And from his classmates he learned the art of give and take and sharing so necessary to him growing up in the family environment of an only child.

At school Franklin became wise beyond his years. He joined the Groton Missionary Society and played the organ at religious services given throughout the community as a public service. Through the Society he helped care for an indigent Afro-American women named Mrs. Freeman who lived near the school. His public service and assisting others broadened his perspective, laying the groundwork for later political life. He played football, became the manager of the

---

[8] Tom Lamont, "From High School to the White House: FDR as a Student" paper presented at the National Council for History Education (NCHE) conference October 2003, p. 4 used by permission; Morgan, FDR, A Biography, p. 56-71.

school baseball team, and appeared in the school play, his senior year. These activities were in addition to his golf and tennis that he enjoyed immensely for pure social pleasure. Leadership came naturally to him. Franklin was good at his studies, was proficient in French and German from his European travels and mastered Latin and Greek plus the Classics. He warmed his cool gray eyes with the widest of grins and was a tall, lean, good-looking chap who easily attracted girls with his charm and teasing. He served as a prefect in a Groton dormitory supervising the younger boys who all looked up to him. His parents sent him *Punch* and the *Spectator* to keep him abreast of current events. His fifth cousin Theodore Roosevelt often came to Groton to speak of his experiences on the Police Board and as New York Police Commissioner, and in one graduation address so impressed the young Franklin that he determined to follow in TR's political footsteps of assisting the New York community. He often employed TR's favorite phrases of 'Bully', 'Ripping', and 'Delighted,' realizing the value of positive, enthusiastic and sunny attitudes. He was invited by TR to spend the Fourth of July at Oyster Bay. Following graduation Franklin worked as a Missionary Society camp counselor for two summers in New Hampshire supervising disadvantaged youth. Much later in a 1932 letter Peabody described Franklin Delano Roosevelt as "a quiet satisfactory boy....We all liked him so far as I know." Peabody confided upon graduation that he found Franklin a "thoroughly faithful scholar and most satisfactory member of this school...I part with Franklin with reluctance."[9] From Groton, Franklin had gained vast intellectual knowledge, lessons in human kindness, and devotion to public service. Groton had been a success for the young Franklin who truly enjoyed school and his lessons in Roman History, Greek and Latin plus German, daily English theme writing, and applied mathematics like algebra and geometry. He admired vast knowledge and determined to acquire much more of his own, knowing that through knowledge came power and position. He had completed his lower level examinations early enough to take fifteen hours of Harvard classes before he had graduated from Groton. Franklin was committed to the Groton motto and took Bible study to be confirmed for membership in the church in 1898. Endicott Peabody's tutelage of young Franklin was nurturing and caring and later the Rector was asked to preside at his wedding ceremony. FDR would send several of his own sons to Groton at age twelve.

    His father Mr. James had been a long time Democrat reaching back to friendships with presidents James Buchanan and Grover Cleveland, and running as a Democrat, had been elected Hyde Park town manager in 1871. He had

---

[9] Black, *Franklin Delano Roosevelt, Champion of Freedom*, p. 26.

approached this post as a civic duty incumbent upon his patrician station. James, like Groton, instilled in Franklin a social conscience as he was concerned with class divisions in America, and said: "We must furnish work to do away with pauperism," a notion FDR certainly remembered and practiced during the New Deal.[10] James Roosevelt, Sr. had declined President Grover Cleveland's offer of ambassadorial positions abroad following the Democratic victory in 1884. Earlier Cleveland had been governor of New York and Franklin met him when he was just five years old. Franklin's half brother Rosy, however, was pleased to accept President Cleveland's appointment as first secretary in the American embassy in Vienna, and later in the same position in London. FDR would later accept the best elements from Grover Cleveland's and Theodore Roosevelt's progressivism and considered both to have been valuable mentors. This would be part of the FDR magic that he blended the best ideas from all those surrounding him, recasting them in palatable forms and blending just the right amount of sugar and spice.

Franklin Roosevelt's formative years were the political Progressive years. The late 19th Century was a time of Christian conscience as both Democrats and Republicans cared deeply about the disadvantaged in the U.S., offering new solutions to their problems. Americans by 1900 welcomed the twentieth century with confidence that America was a wonderful country that offered splendid opportunities. "The will to grow was everywhere written large," said Henry James, "and to grow at no matter what or whose expense."[11] Puffed from victories in the Spanish-American War of 1898, peace, prosperity, and progress were heralded as the century's signposts. Franklin and a Groton school chum had actually tried to enlist for military service in the Navy during this war but were foiled by falling ill with scarlet fever. "There is not a man here who does not feel 400 percent bigger in 1900 than he did in 1896," stated Senator Chauncey Depew of New York, "bigger intellectually, bigger hopefully, bigger patriotically." Thus opened the period that has been given several titles, The Cocksure Era, The Age of Innocence, The Age of Optimism, The Age of Confidence—the beginning of the American Century. Americans not only hoped for the best, they expected it and believed that the numerous problems that beset the nation of immigrant slums, child labor, political corruption, and greedy trusts, could be corrected. The inevitable faith of Americans in progress could not be shaken. The system in America could be made to work, the youth of America could get ahead; as a nation and as individuals, progress was inevitable. This was the spirit that formed

---

[10] Ward, Before The Trumpet, p. 154; Black, Franklin Delano Roosevelt, Champion of Freedom, p. 16.

[11] Ezra Bowen, ed., This Fabulous Century, 1900-1910, Vol. 1 (New York: Time-Life Books, 1969), p. 29.

the core of the Progressive reform movement of the early 1900s and Franklin's youth.

In 1900 America's population was 76 million. In the thirty-five years after the Civil War the United States had jumped from fourth place to first among industrial nations as measured in productivity.[12] The population of New York, Chicago, and Philadelphia surged over the million mark by 1900. Despite growth, there were disturbing statistics: the average annual earnings of industrial workers in 1900 were merely a subsistence wage of less than $490. Some 1.7 million children labored for as little as 25 cents a day. One citizen out of eight lived in the festering slums and perished of disease at twice the rate of modest income groups. Nine million immigrants came to America between 1900 and 1910, some barely scraping together the meager sums for passage, $12.00 steerage from Italy.[13] In 1907, the climatic high-water mark of immigration, a million immigrants poured through Ellis Island's facilities and took jobs which averaged less than $12.50 per week. And they worked 12-hour days, six or seven days a week in the coal mines of Pennsylvania, the textile mills of New England, the slaughterhouses of Chicago, and the garment industry's sweat-shops in New York. One American in three was foreign born. The immigrants had been welcomed by the inscription on the Statue of Liberty "Give me your tired, your poor, your huddled masses yearning to breath free. Send …the homeless, tempest-tossed, to me, I lift my lamp beside the golden door!" Thousands of foreign-born immigrants poured onto America's shores believing in the American dream and that America was truly a 'City Upon the hill, a beacon to the world'.[14] "The ideals," stated sociologist Charles B. Spahr, and "the opportunities of our democracy change the immigrants into a new order of men."[15]

But the cutting edge of poverty whittled hopes as immigrants huddled in their ethnic enclaves in larger cities, German towns, and Little Italys. One immigrant from Denmark, Jacob Riis, went into the slums as a reporter, documented disease-ridden conditions, and photographed them. As a result he wrote *How The Other Half Lives* which stimulated a new awareness of the urban poor. The Rich said very little, but one plutocrat remarked: "We own America; we got it, God knows

---

[12] Bowen, This Fabulous Century, 1900-1910 Vol. 1, p. 30-31; James R. Arnold and Roberta Weiner, Industrial Revolution (New York: Grolier, 2005)
[13] Bowen, This Fabulous Century, 1900-1910, Vol. 1, pp. 72-85; Peter Lane, Industrial Revolution: The Birth of the Modern Age (New York: Barnes and Noble, 1978); Charles Moore, Understanding the Industrial Revolution (London and New York: Routledge, 2000).
[14] Barbara Bennett Peterson, America In British Eyes, (Honolulu: Hawaii Chapter Fulbright Association, 1988), pp. 29-37.
[15] Bowen, This Fabulous Century, 1900-1910 Vol. 1, pp. 72-76.

how, but we intend to keep it."[16] Squalor met only contempt; indifference created rage. Along these lines was drawn the battle line which pricked the progressive's social conscience. America's sense of justice and humanity, its equality for all, had been called into question. Progressive reformers were moved to act to end discrepancies between lofty ideals and expedient practices. Progressivism was essentially a reform movement in which thousands of public-spirited Americans tried to bring under control the excesses of industrialization and urbanization that burgeoned in post-Civil War decades. The Progressives sought to redirect the course of American life along more equitable lines. They hoped to return political control to the majority of Americans by curtailing the influences of city bosses who manipulated immigrant votes. And by regulating systems and institutions which sought to serve the public such as utilities and all forms of transportation, by bringing to heel the powerful money trust, and by introducing democratic political tools such as the initiative, referendum and the recall. Progressivism as a political movement was supported by an emergent citizenry that was becoming increasingly well-educated, reading scores of new magazines and newspapers, and enjoying a rising standard of living. America's literate society turned its attention to reforming social ills. Franklin and Eleanor Roosevelt fit the progressive profile perfectly. Like the former reform movement of the 1880s and 1890s, the populists, the aim of the Progressives was to equalize opportunities and further democratic practices, laying the foundation stones of New Deal legislation for the 1930s. With their sensibilities and statistics, the Progressives, including FDR, set about to hit the line of American injustice hard.[17]

Part of the force that galvanized the Progressives to act was the new realism in literature as William Dean Howells led the way to expose the shabby, false and shocking aspects of American life in *A Hazard of New Fortunes* (1890) focused on the inhumanities of urban-industrial life and the greed of capitalists. Helen Stuart Campbell described the slums of New York in *Problems of the Poor: A Record of Quiet Work in Unquiet Place's* (1882) as did reporter Jacob Riis in *How the Other Half Lives*. FDR read these eagerly placing them in his ever-growing personal library that totaled over 15,000 books by the time he was elected President. He often sought to impress his mother "by repeating back to her

---

[16] Bowen, This Fabulous Century, 1900-1910 Vol. 1, p. 34; Peter N. Stearns, Industrial Revolution in World History (Boulder, Colorado: Westview Press, 1998); Robert B. Marks, Origins of the Modern World: A Global and Ecological Narrative (Lanham, MD: Rowman and Littlefield, 2002).

[17] Theodore Roosevelt, Theodore Roosevelt: An Autobiography (New York: Scribner's, 1924); Roy Jenkins, Franklin Delano Roosevelt (New York: Times Books, Henry Holt and Company, 2003), pp.9-10.

verbatim tracts of books she read to him."[18] Washington Gladden, pastor of a Congregational church in Cleveland, Ohio from 1882 to 1918, believed the wage system based solely on competition was anti-social and anti-Christian, and class welfare was viewed as brutal and barbarous. Walter Rauschenbusch was pastor from 1886 to 1897 of a small German Baptist church in Hell's Kitchen, one of New York's most hideous slums, and then joined the faculty of Rochester Theological Seminary in 1897. There he wrote *Christianity and the Social Crisis* (1907), *Christianizing the Social Order* (1912) and *A Theology for the Social Gospel* (1917). Religious faith and moral strength should be made to break the bonds of injustice.[19] For FDR his motto learned at Groton 'To Serve Him is to Rule' meshed perfectly with these Christian social conscience writers attacking the greed and corruption of the trusts and financial leaders' insensitivity to the less fortunate. The implication was clear. Someone [progressive reformer] or something [progressive, far-sighted government] must intercede on behalf of the downtrodden and exploited. FDR firmly believed these ideals when he would work as a state senator, Governor of New York, and President of the United States. Those who reached the greatest numbers of readers and therefore had the greatest impact on mobilizing the public to encourage reform from their politicians were the muckrakers, journalists who wrote about political and corporate corruption and supported their accusations with documented evidence.[20]

Amidst this Progressive hustle and bustle, Franklin Roosevelt entered Harvard in 1900 as the Progressives were widely heralded as about to produce a new day. His fathered had attended Harvard Law School and it was natural that Franklin would follow him. A letter of recommendation written by Reverend Sherrard Billings to Admissions Officer Richard Cobb at Harvard had vaunted his candidacy: "F.D. Roosevelt is a fellow of *exceptional ability* and *high character*.... He hopes to go into public life, and will shape his work at Cambridge with that end in view." At Harvard Franklin enjoyed social successes and adopted a winning way of making numerous friends. He lived in the Westmorly University Residence. In his freshman year he joined the staff of the student daily newspaper, *The Harvard Crimson*, and by his senior year had worked his way up to managing editor. In this role Franklin D. Roosevelt displayed his powerful intellect and powers of political persuasion. He was elected the *Crimson's* president and editor-in-chief in 1904 and his name appeared

---

[18] Black, Franklin Delano Roosevelt, Champion of Freedom, p. 20.
[19] Walter Rauschenbusch, Christianity and the Social Crisis (New York: Macmillan, 1907).
[20] Theodore Roosevelt, Theodore Roosevelt: An Autobiography; Harold Howland, Theodore Roosevelt and His Times: A Chronicle of the Progressive Movement (New York: Yale University Press, 1921), pp. 84-104.

on the paper's masthead. A successor quipped of Franklin's stint on the paper that he "liked people and having made them instinctively like him...In his geniality there was a kind of frictionless command."[21] He had also found time to play football, serve as secretary of the glee club, and captain the second Newell crew rowing club, all the while pursuing his academic degree. Franklin Roosevelt, in addition to being a great wit, was something of a fashion plate and often dressed in stripped shirts and straw boater hats, flashing his famous smile. He was a popular campus leader attending numerous social functions, and had broadened his political skills. During moments of carefree relaxation from his studies he sailed the family yacht, the *Half Moon II,* with members of the Roosevelt and Delano clans after practicing on his personal sloop the *New Moon*. Franklin collected books on seafaring, navigation, and historical ocean maps and discussed intricate details of sailing and shipbuilding. He was a handsome, articulate, charming and capable man.

On December 8, 1900 during his freshman year at Harvard, Franklin's father passed away and he had to step to the head of the family. During this time he was protective and understanding of his mother Sara when she moved to Boston to be closer to him following the death of his father. Plus her relatives and friends in the Boston area served as a fresh tonic after losing James. FDR strove to become like his father: "generous, stylish, Christian," to serve the community as a "noblesse oblige gentleman" and to accomplish this selflessly. FDR had inherited $120,000 from his father in a trust while Sara inherited several million from the combined bequests of her husband James Roosevelt and her father Warren Delano who had died in 1898.

The summer following his father's death, Franklin took his mother and friends cruising up the Norwegian coast on the yacht *Prinzessin Victoria Luisa,* where they happened to entertain Kaiser Wilhelm II who was also vacationing in the area. Upon their return to New York, they heard that cousin Theodore was president following McKinley's assassination. Thus FDR, while working at *The Harvard Crimson,* invited TR to speak on campus and the new president showed him respect at this gathering. Franklin was often mentioned in the newspapers as TR's fifth cousin and he basked in this limelight. He determined to follow in his uncle's political footsteps. In January 1902 Franklin attended the coming out party for TR's daughter, Alice Roosevelt, the social event of the year at the White House. Yet despite the famous Roosevelt name, both TR and FDR tried to be 'thoroughly democratic'.

---

[21] Black, Franklin Delano Roosevelt, Champion of Freedom, pp. 30-31, 28.

While at Harvard Franklin was invited to membership in numerous prestigious clubs including the Hasty Pudding Society, serving as its librarian, the Signet Literary Society, the Memorial Society, and the famed Delta Kappa Epsilon or the 'Dickey' that included the Who's Who on campus. He missed the Porcellian Club, but joined Alpha Delta Phi or the 'Fly Club'. He graduated June 24, with the class of 1903 and received an B.A. degree, but he chose to attend the graduation ceremonies in 1904 because of his work on the *Crimson*. And during the academic year of 1904 he had worked on the newspaper, having reached the zenith of his Harvard days. During the summer of 1903 FDR had journeyed to Europe, staying in London and on the continent seeing family friends and solidifying alliances in his own right, preserving the friendships of his father.

While at Harvard, Franklin courted and fell in love with his sixth cousin Anna Eleanor Roosevelt, who was three years younger than himself. She was the daughter of Elliott Roosevelt, President Theodore Roosevelt's younger brother, and Anna Hall Roosevelt, and had been born in New York City October 11, 1884. Her mother died when Eleanor was eight and hence Eleanor was schooled in Paris at a convent briefly, then in London at age fifteen at the Allenswood School under the careful tutelage of Frenchwoman Mlle. Marie Souvestre, the daughter of French liberal philosopher Emil Souvestre. In this academic atmosphere she excelled displaying "kindliness, sincerity, and intelligence," and learned to aid others.[22] Eleanor, like Franklin, spoke French fluently as a result of her European sojourns and learned to appreciate the arts and humanities. Her father had died when she was ten and she and her brother Hall had been left in the care of relatives, but while in England Eleanor had blossomed. She returned to New York at age eighteen for her coming out party in 1903, making a formal debut in New York society, and by November she and Franklin were engaged. They attended President Theodore Roosevelt's New Year's celebration in 1903 and joined TR's family for outings to the theater. Eleanor and Franklin were members of the president's inner circle of close elite relatives and they attached great importance to TR's opinions and policies. They continued to meet for activities at Harvard such as the Harvard-Yale football game and Franklin even entertained her as one of the socially prominent young men selected as cheerleaders for the Harvard-Brown game. Eleanor continued to work in New York with the Junior League on various philanthropic projects and taught healthful exercise and dancing to immigrant children on Manhattan's Lower East Side at Rivington Street Settlement House. Franklin would often accompany her home from her settlement

---

[22] Black, Franklin Delano Roosevelt, Champion of Freedom, p. 38; Joseph P. Lash, Eleanor and Franklin, The Story of Their Relationship, Based on Eleanor Roosevelt's Private Papers (New York: W.W. Norton and Company, 1971), pp. 74-87.

duties while courting, observing the harsh slum conditions in the tenements. They both determined to do something to improve the lot of the poor. It was their social responsibility to remove social sins of exploitation and poverty. She joined the National Consumer's League and campaigned for improvements in working conditions for the laboring classes. Franklin supported her endeavors with cheerful pride. In Franklin's company she became confident. Elenor's excellent breeding showed and she dressed in the latest fashions of the Gibson Girl. Franklin and his mother Sara invited Eleanor to join the family at their summer home on Campobello, a Canadian island between Maine and New Brunswick in the Bay of Fundy. Eleanor and Franklin had both lost their fathers and had stepped up to aid their respective families. They were both serious and understood their responsibilities, and shared philosophies of aiding the disadvantaged. At a party at Hyde Park, the young couple shared a hay-ride, sailing, and walks alone along the river to discuss marriage plans. Just before their wedding, the couple attended Theodore Roosevelt's presidential inauguration on March 4, 1905, and were seated on the steps of the Capitol just behind the presidential family. FDR had voted for TR in the November election of 1904, saying he was more 'democratic' than his opponent. As this was his first vote cast in a presidential race, FDR realized that TR had won on the basis of progressive reforms that aided the citizenry. Earlier FDR had joined the Harvard Republican Club to campaign for TR when he ran for vice-president with McKinley. Even earlier all the Hyde Park Roosevelts had supported their cousin TR for Governor of New York in 1896 and again these experiences taught FDR much about the political process. Eleanor and Franklin appreciated the honor shown them at TR's presidential inauguration and remained close friends with TR's family throughout the president's life.

Franklin and Eleanor were married in New York City at the home of Mrs. Henry Parish on East 76th Street on March 17, 1905 according to the rites of the Episcopal Church. Since her own father was deceased, her uncle, President Theodore Roosevelt came up from Washington to give the bride away and signed the marriage certificate as a witness to the ceremony. President Theodore told Franklin on his wedding day "there's nothing like keeping the name in the family."[23] Eleanor Roosevelt's "bridesmaids at the wedding all had to wear three Prince of Wales feathers nodding on their heads" because this resembled the Roosevelt family crest, and "the ushers were given Prince of Wales feathers stickpins."[24] Alice Roosevelt, TR's eldest daughter was Eleanor's maid of honor.

---

[23] Black, Franklin Delano Roosevelt, Champion of Freedom, p. 40.
[24] Joseph Alsop, FDR, A Centenary Remembrance (New York: The Viking Press, 1982), p. 31; Lash, Eleanor and Franklin, pp. 138-141.

Franklin had received a congratulatory letter from the President shortly before his wedding. "I am as fond of Eleanor," confided TR, "as if she were my daughter, and I like you, and trust you, and believe in you…You and Eleanor are true and brave, and I believe you love each other unselfishly; and golden years open before you. May all good fortune attend to you both, ever…Your affectionate cousin."[25]

Franklin was a well-positioned gentleman who had politically married well. After their marriage the newlyweds had honeymooned at Hyde Park then went to live in New York City where Franklin was attending Columbia Law School. In June following the spring academic term the young couple took a longer honeymoon abroad in Britain, France and Italy where one of their favorite destinations was Venice. In London family friends had arranged a lunch for them with Sidney and Beatrice Webb and George Bernard Shaw. Returning home to New York, Franklin and Eleanor had amalgamated old-money credentials, as people referred to Franklin as 'the Hyde Park lot, you know' and to Eleanor as 'Oyster Bay, of course'.[26] The Roosevelts remained social blue bloods and their progressive friends and social circle occupied the boards of major universities, churches, businesses, and charitable institutions.

Franklin and Eleanor lived in central New York in a home at 125 East 36th Street near Columbia until he graduated from law school. Then they soon built a large home that adjoined to a similar home for Sara Roosevelt at 47 and 49 65th Street in New York. Franklin and Eleanor also acquired a separate summer home on Campobello where they could swim, ride, play golf and sail. It gave them immense pleasure and private time together with the children. Franklin was very generous to his widowed mother, granting her unlimited access to their married life, and Eleanor was generous too, allowing her mother-in-law to care for and spoil their children—Anna (1906), James (1907), Franklin, Jr.(b.1909-d.1909), Elliott (1910), Franklin, Jr. (1914), and John (1916). Eleanor and Sara became close confidants especially in the early years of the marriage. Franklin had passed the bar examination in 1906 and joined the law firm of Carter, Ledyard, and Milburn at 54 Wall Street in 1907 as a Counsellor at Law. He advertised his abilities as "unexcelled facilities for carrying on every description of legal business."[27] Here he began to make political contacts and became interested in running for office largely in order to serve the public.

Surveying the New York horizon, FDR felt he had much to do. It was at the local municipal level that corruption could be viewed close at hand and judged appalling. George Washington Plunkitt, a veteran ward boss for Tammany Hall in

---

[25] Black, Franklin Delano Roosevelt, Champion of Freedom, p. 42-46.
[26] Alsop, FDR, A Centenary Remembrance, p. 29.
[27] Alsop, FDR, A Centenary Remembrance, p.44.

New York City, unabashedly told an interviewer in 1905 that he engaged in "honest graft," shocking progressive reformers like FDR. In various ways, the Progressives set about to bring graft, honest or dishonest, and the myrid of other political abuses under control. In state after state reforms were adopted to break the power of party bosses. Initially FDR would consider cleaning up Tammany Hall as one of his most important progressive platforms. First he needed to consider the needs of potential voters. The Democratic Party approached Roosevelt in 1910 with an offer to support his candidacy for State Senator from Dutchess County. Even the Republican TR supported his candidacy and urged him to enter the race. Young Franklin Roosevelt plunged into the political contest, circulating through the entire county and covering 25,000 square miles with Eleanor by car and train. Eleanor was a natural campaigner and her warm maternal smile and handshaking complimented Franklin's enthusiasm to serve. They were best as a couple 'up close and personal' where Franklin used his charm plus keen knowledge of the issues to gather votes. The Roosevelts were delighted with Franklin's victory in the 1910 election. The FDR charisma spread as he worked hard in his new office in upstate New York in Albany where they had taken a small apartment during the legislative session. Sara Roosevelt was a tremendous aide in maintaining their large New York home when they were away. During summers they returned to enjoy their retreat at Campobello. Franklin was re-elected in 1912 to the state legislature and continued to pursue progressive politics.

It was at the municipal and state levels that the New York progressives made their most rapid and permanent gains, even encouraging woman's suffrage and causes of interest to women to broaden their base. FDR advocated women's suffrage in 1912 before Eleanor and his mother had embraced the idea to gain new moral reforming voters. Physicians confronted by slum disease demanded nothing less than the reorganization of entire cities to establish well-run public health departments. Social workers demanded nothing less than public welfare agencies, settlement houses, and free health care to the aged and indigent. Whether it was the creation of centralized systems of city government to combat urban corruption or the agencies, the urge was to establish order. The new middle-class—the college trained engineer, economist, lawyer, doctor—all wanted to bring confusion under control; their inclination was to think in terms of central planning and efficient management and their knowledge braced them to undertake bold programs. During FDR's legislative sessions in Albany he with colleagues strove to modernize the state's government to make it more responsive to the people, introducing new progressive legislation of all types. FDR and Eleanor had numerous role models on the municipal, state, and national level and counted many of the reformers as personal friends.

Tom Johnson, the benevolent mayor of Cleveland, Ohio introduced cheap public transportation and built parks, playgrounds, and public baths to help brighten the dreariness of slum life. Johnson was to directly influence the career of Raymond Moley who had been born in Berea, Ohio and later did a Cleveland Crime Study in 1922 and would become a member of the Brains Trust that advised FDR's 1932 campaign for the presidency. Moley firmly believed like Johnson in the government regulation of public utilities and he had become involved with the New York Bureau of Municipal Research that published his *The State Movement for Efficiency and Economy* in 1918. In his crime study he had employed the assistance of Roscoe Pound and Felix Frankfurter and it served as a model for other cities for decades. Harold Ickes, FDR's later Secretary of the Interior, was influenced by reform movements in Chicago. He worked for change with Jane Addams of Hull House, Raymond Robbins of Northwestern University Settlement House, Margaret Dreier Robins co-founder of the National Women's Trade Union League, and Charles E. Merriam a political scientist speaking out for social reforms at the University of Chicago. These social progressive concerns would later be translated into New Deal policies. Women involved in the local progressive movement encouraged city government to take responsibility for relief of the poor, improve public streets and garbage collection and organized themselves into numerous organizations of civic betterment. They were especially concerned about the health of the family and America's children and advocated free milk in schools, school health programs, public parks, libraries, laws limiting child labor, restricting the hours of work for women and children, and lobbied for safety measures and workmen's compensation in industry. FDR and Eleanor lobbied hard for the school milk program after the death of their son, the first Franklin D. Roosevelt, Jr., in 1909. Jane Addams remained the most prominent social worker of her time and befriended Progressive politicians to assist her work. "It was quite settled in my mind, she later wrote in *Twenty Years at Hull House*, "that I should study medicine and 'live with the poor'."[28] Jane Addams came to be recognized as the pioneer of the American settlement house. Describing what had attracted her to her calling, she wrote: "The settlement then, is an experimental effort to aid in the solution of the social and industrial problems which are engendered by the modern conditions of life in a great city." "It is an attempt to relieve, at the same time, the over accumulation at one end of society and destitution at the other." "It must be grounded in a philosophy whose

---

[28] Jane Addams, Twenty Years At Hull House (New York: Macmillan, 1910), pp. i-xii.

foundation is on the solidarity of the human race."[29] Lillian Wald directed the Henry Street Settlement House in New York City and attracted a significant number of young people as volunteers. Among them were most notably Henry Morgenthau, Jr. who later served as Secretary of the Treasury for FDR's New Deal, and Adolf A. Berle who offered Wald's Settlement his legal services and later served FDR as assistant Secretary of State. Thus the thrust of many New Deal reforms came directly out of the older Progressive movement. It incorporated the old reforming drives of the Mugwump movement from the 1880s and the Populists, the call for purging government of corruption and cronyism, and the maintenance of a thriving laissez-faire capitalism that benefited all.

FDR had seen both Presidents Grover Cleveland and Theodore Roosevelt at close range to imbibe their politics and political techniques. TR believed in utilizing the constitutional powers of the presidency to accomplish Progressive ends such as preserving natural resources through conservation, regulating monopolies, ensuring social justice for the disadvantaged. The 'use' of political power to achieve progressive goals became the focus of FDR's dreams. Indeed he had learned well from TR, whom he called 'Uncle Ted,' and would endeavor to match his career and political clout to serve similar ends. TR aided FDR's political plans even though his protégé was a Democrat, but admitted he wished FDR was a Republican. But blood was thicker than politics. These progressive activists were part of FDR's mileux. Franklin and Eleanor knew well these progressive personalities, their policies, their arguments and programs for family advancement. Eleanor joined the Women's Trade Union League in 1922, the organization co-founded by Jane Addams [with Margaret Dreier Robins] in 1903. This organization tried to secure better conditions for working women and Eleanor agreed with the League's goal to serve human needs.[30] FDR was deeply affected by these female reformers and their good works, especially in his impressionable and liberal college years. He desired to emulate their deeds on a larger scope. He read most of the muckraking books and articles because he supported their goals. Progressivism was in *vogue* and most young people like the Roosevelts embraced its causes and plans to improve society. He would decide to enter politics because of his desire to fix weaknesses in the social fabric and to achieve fame as a social reformer.[31] FDR was in his element as an athletic man's man who charmed people with his policies, smile, and caring. Eleanor and other female progressives desired to work with men like Franklin to help women and children.

---

[29] Addams, Twenty Year At Hull House, p. xii.
[30] Lash, Eleanor and Franklin, p. 280.
[31] Bowen, This Fabulous Century, 1900-1910 Vol. 1, p. 43.

The Progressive wave of reform rose up from the cities to the states in part because the cities learned that their problems could not be completely solved until they had been addressed on a state-wide basis. When Robert M. LaFollette became governor of Wisconsin in 1901, a chain reaction of state Progressive reforms began. LaFollette's Wisconsin Idea adopted the direct primary, created a railroad commission that had real power to regulate railway rates and practices, curbed lobbying, began to stress conservation of natural resources, established state regulation over state banks, raised taxes on corporations and railroads, and created a state civil service examination system. Wisconsin even enacted a state income tax law, and became known as 'the laboratory of democracy'.

Early in his career, on a national level, FDR had a successful mentor in Republican Theodore Roosevelt, 'Cousin Theodore', or 'Uncle Ted' during his presidential years. Progressive reformers had wisely turned to Washington D.C. and the presidency to solve the nation's larger problems. Controlling trusts, the railroad system, the protective tariff, the banking network, and the issue of conservation all were national in scope. National reform had found its national spokesman in Theodore Roosevelt, FDR's foremost role model. It was the dynamic force of TR's personality, together with tremendous energy that made the ebullient Teddy stand larger in people's minds than any other man of his times. "His personality so crowds the room," said a friend, "that the walls are worn thin and threatened to burst outward."[32] Grinning from beneath a walrus mustache and twinkling, spectacled eyes, he exuded confidence and when he spoke he became a "human volcano, roaring as only a human volcano can roar!, leading the laughter and singing and shouting, like a boy out of school, pounding the table with both noisy fists." "I always believe in going hard at everything," he wrote his son Kermit, and this vitality had driven Theodore Roosevelt into public life at age twenty-four when he became a crusading assemblyman from New York City, determined to clean up political abuses in both Democratic and Republican parties. As New York's police commissioner he had visited the slums with Jacob Riis, learning first hand of the misery, squalor and contempt that allowed political boss machines and ward-healers who frequented the ethnic kitchens to exploit the immigrants' vote and continue graft. With the outbreak of the Spanish-American War, he had resigned as assistant secretary of the Navy to join the Rough Riders. After the war TR was elected Governor of New York in 1898-1900 before joining William McKinley as his Republican vice-presidential running mate in the election of 1900. In September 1901, after an assassin took McKinley's life, Theodore Roosevelt had become the youngest president in history at 42. FDR was

---

[32] Theodore Roosevelt, Theodore Roosevelt, An Autobiography

nineteen years old when his fifth cousin and idol Theodore Roosevelt had ascended to the presidency of the United States. Since FDR had cast his first presidential vote for Theodore Roosevelt in 1904, he endeavored that his political path would mimic TR's to the White House.[33]

Upon assuming the presidency, one of the first crusades of Theodore Roosevelt had been conservation, and FDR would promote this same issue in New York as his first issue in the senate. [34] The husbanding of the nation's resources would ensure youth's future and the place of America among nations they believed. Gifford Pinchot, TR's chief of the federal forestry division, had set about to educate the public at the urging of the president about scientific forest management. Pinchot had been trained in French and German forestry practices and was inspired by the ideal of a continuous "sustained yield" and pursued this goal through the planned use of resources and controlled exploitation of the environment. The preservationist movement started by John Muir was inspired by the dictum of Henry David Thoreau, 'In Wilderness is the Preservation of the World'. Conservation areas, like America's small towns, represented pantheistic ideals amid brutalities breeding elsewhere; nature was seen as a restorative to jaded humanity. Muir spent years living in Yosemite Valley and hiking through the Sierra Nevada; due to his urgings Yosemite National park was established and Muir helped to found the Sierra Club. After his election in 1910 to the state senate as a Democrat, FDR's first state legislative chairmanship would be dedicated to reforestation in New York as he applied TR's policies to his home region. Harold Ickes, who would later work for FDR during the New Deal, often found himself too in the company of both TR and Gifford Pinchot as he had begun his career as a Republican reformer, and taught at the University of Chicago while assisting Jane Addams' social causes. Ickes actually delivered Chicago and Cook County to TR during the presidential campaign of 1912. Later in 1932 Ickes would be invited to organize Republicans for Franklin Delano Roosevelt. Ickes, during his later tenure in the 1930s as New Deal Secretary of Interior, would be in charge of the National Park System, the Geological Survey, and the Bureau of Reclamation, and would, with FDR, continue the conservation measures of TR. Ickes personified how former Republican progressives eventually became converts to the Democratic policies of FDR and the New Dealers through issues like conservation.

From TR's activities with trust-busting, Franklin Roosevelt also learned the value of government's entry directly into the economy. Theodore Roosevelt had

---

[33] Bowen, This Fabulous Century, 1900-1910 Vol. 1, p. 61.
[34] Bowen, This Fabulous Century, 1900-1910 Vol. 1, p. 62; Tom Lansford, Theodore Roosevelt, A Political Life (Hauppauge, NY: Nova Science Publishers, 2004), pp. 49, 93, 112.

applied the Sherman Anti-Trust Act to break up trusts such as the Northern Securities Company, controlled by financier J.P. Morgan, which controlled the railroad corporations which served the Northwestern United States. In 1902 while Franklin had watched the national political scene from Harvard, the president had won his case against Northern Securities and the company was dissolved. In 1911, when FDR was a New York state senator, the courts further upheld the federal government's power to break up monopolies engaged in "an unreasonable restraint of trade." FDR watched this lesson in politics as he sat in the New York legislature and determined that business and industry should not be above the people but should serve their interests to the profit of all. TR's administration had brought suit against over forty trusts and the administration of his successor William Howard Taft brought many more. The government showed that it was above the plutocrats, despite their yachts, tennis matches at Newport Casino, and marble summer homes at Newport Beach. Further FDR had originally entered New York politics as a state senator partially to curtail the fat plutocrats who held little interest in social reforms, believing it was his patrician duty to protect and legislate for the public.

Too FDR had learned to court labor as TR had sought to curtail privilege again in 1902 when the president intervened in a crucial labor-management dispute, the Anthracite Coal Strike in Pennsylvania. The United Mine Workers led by John Mitchell had gone on strike seeking higher wages, shorter hours and safety measures, but the mine owner refused to bargain. With the mines shut down, there was a shortage of coal as winter began and in October a number of schools began to close due to the lack of fuel. The public clamored for resolution and TR threatened to have the U.S. Army operate the mines unless a settlement could be reached. [35] TR illustrated for his twenty year-old protégé FDR how to wield governmental authority over big business, and FDR learned to practice fairness regardless of class. FDR never forgot TR's actions in the coal strike as during World War II FDR would also threaten to nationalize the coal mines unless labor and mine owners could reach an accord. FDR also learned from TR's regulation of the railroads with Elkins Act of 1903 aimed at stopping rebates, and the Hepburn Act of 1906 which empowered the Interstate Commerce Commission to set "reasonable rates" charged by the railroads and made railroad accounts subject to governmental inspection. Four years later in 1910, following FDR's election to the state legislature at age twenty-eight, Americans realized that government had become an umpire between economic interests and that the public good should be paramount. FDR had come to understand TR's approach to

---

35 Bowen, This Fabulous Century, 1900-1910 Vol. 1, p. 31.

power with social conscience, since it meshed with his own values learned from family, Groton, and Harvard. To make New York's agricultural products safer, in January 1907 FDR encouraged state legislation which emulated the Pure Food and Drug Act passed earlier nationally by TR's administration in response to the scandals in the meat-packing industries.[36] Again what TR was doing for the nation, FDR would promote in the New York Senate, likewise broadening his bi-partisan appeal.

Additionally, race relations of the day offered object lessons to FDR, who recalled himself as the young Groton boy who had helped the indigent black woman Mrs. Freeman by bringing coal to her door during the winter. Theodore Roosevelt had wanted a Square Deal for all Americans, not just white Americans. TR had invited Booker Taliaferro Washington to the White House for dinner and asked him about the plight of Afro-Americans. Washington had graduated from Hampton Institute founded by Samuel C. Armstrong, a son of missionaries to Hawaii; Washington had proceeded to found his own school based on the Hampton model, Tuskegee Institute in Alabama, America's first college for black teachers. Publicly, Booker T. Washington urged blacks to stay in the South, strive for economic prosperity which largely meant agricultural land owning to develop an independent Afro-American group of yeoman farmers. He stressed the doctrine of "self-help," suggesting blacks learn trades and skills in order to better their race and compete with whites. While he strove for social equality, a careful reading of his works, especially his Atlanta Exposition speech, indicates his words could be interpreted to include ultimate goals much more advanced than white southerners at the time could possibly accept. Yet his conciliatory approach was an important factor in his gaining eminence. He emphasized racial pride, solidarity, and economic nationalism, but he was criticized as an accommodationist for working within the framework of white prejudice and accommodating 'the Negro program' to this reality. His central critic was W.E.B. DuBois, who advocated a liberal integrationist policy as the only way to combat lynching, poverty and the color line. Educated at Fisk and Harvard universities, DuBois gained distinction as a professor at Atlanta University. He urged a "talented-tenth" to emerge from black ranks to pursue remedial civil rights legislation, and led the founding of the Niagara Movement that demanded immediate economic and political equality for blacks. This movement led to the foundation of the NAACP which was organized in 1909 when the Niagara group was joined by other organizations such as the National Association of Colored Women (1896) and the National Negro Business League (1900). DuBois's articles in *The Crisis,* the official organ of the NAACP,

---

36 Upton Sinclair, The Jungle (New York: Signet Classic, 1906), pp. 136-137.

called for integrated housing, better education, integrated accommodations, racial pride and self-respect, equality, federal aid to education, and full political rights. DuBois attacked Washington's idea that the Afro-American should try to "measure up," calling this patronizing and a stain on liberalism. DuBois represented the black progressive's cry for human individuality and equality of opportunity. FDR was most certainly listening to his fellow Harvard alumni Dr. DuBois and aware of these racial issues. FDR supported opportunities for Jews, Blacks, Catholics—all races and all creeds in his New York politics. He knew how to carry New York City and courted minorities' votes. Warren Delano, FDR's mother's father, was "comprehensively generous to the poor and particularly concerned with the status of African-Americans. He supported the black educator Booker T. Washington financially and welcomed him to his house, where Sara met him. Franklin would be influenced by this view also, both directly and through his mother. His and his antecedents' concepts of public policy and private duty vastly transcended mere paternalism and were amplified by Mlle. Sandoz's advocacy of social Christianity. The roots of the New Deal were not in the factories or mines or union halls or universities or farmers' associations of America, but in Springwood and Algonac."[37]

Theodore Roosevelt, after the election of 1904, had said, "By no means will I become a candidate for a third term." This was a tactical blunder as his influence waned when politicians understood that within four years he would be gone from office. FDR would remember this and always left the door open for a presidential re-election bid that would earn him an unprecedented election to four presidential terms. In 1908 TR could easily have won the bid for a third term, but felt compelled to stand by his statement. TR had hand picked his successor, William Howard Taft, and was confident that Taft would follow his policies. Taft was a party man who followed the party line and had served in the Roosevelt Cabinet as Secretary of War. He was nominated on the first ballot at the convention in Chicago and would go on to defeat Democratic nominee William J. Bryan who had been defeated twice by McKinley in 1896 and 1900. Ex-President Roosevelt graciously took leave to go on a safari in Africa, allowing Taft to hold the spotlight.

William Howard Taft already had a long career of public service when he was elected president in 1908. From a prominent family in Cincinnati, Ohio, his father was Judge Alphonso Taft who had been a member of Grant's Cabinet. Taft had risen through appointments, having served as a judge in the superior court in Ohio, a solicitor-general in the Department of Justice, a Governor-General of the

---

[37] Black, *Franklin Delano Roosevelt, Champion of Freedom*, p. 16.

Philippines and Secretary of War under TR. During the election, the Taft Republicans had promised a reduction in the tariff, so, true to his word, Taft called a special session of Congress to accomplish this. After wrangling, the Payne-Aldrich Bill finally passed the Senate, offering only minor tariff reductions, yet Taft felt compelled to sign the bill lest he break his campaign promise. A group of mid-westerners led by LaFollette had challenged the tariff bill as an insufficient reduction and the president's signature authorizing the bill began to split the Republican Party wide open. FDR had first been elected to the New York state senate in 1910 at the end of Taft's second year as president, just as the Republicans broke apart offering new opportunities to Democrats. FDR had ridden on the wave of discontent with Taft. The divergence widened nationally when the liberal Republicans and the dissatisfied Democrats joined together to curtail the power of the Speaker of the House, Joe Cannon, by changing the composition of the Rules Committee, making it an elective body rather than a hand picked group selected by Speaker Cannon. The revolt in the House was led by George W. Norris of Nebraska and Victor Murdock of Kansas, and in the Senate by Beveridge of Indiana, Cummins of Iowa, and LaFollette of Wisconsin. A National Republican Progressive League was formed on January 21, 1911, at the Washington residence of LaFollette, and a program of progressive reforms was agreed upon. Leaders in Washington society now competed to out "progressive" President Taft and LaFollette was to be brought out as the progressive candidate against Taft for the Republican nomination in 1912. But LaFollette would soon be shelved and Taft would win an easy bid for re-nomination as he controlled Republican Party machinery. This split within the Republican Party originating over the Payne-Aldrich tariff bill and the fight over the Rules Committee and the quarrel between Secretary of Interior Ballinger and head of the U.S. Forest Service Pinchot over private development of government natural resources, gave an easy victory to the Democratic Party in 1912. Democrats also promised to continue progressive ideals under Woodrow Wilson. Hence, FDR entered New York politics in 1910 when Taft was still president and attempted to continue the progressive ambitions for reform dictated by TR's agenda, *but within the Democratic Party.* TR had actually aided FDR in his first Democratic bid into politics because of his growing dissatisfaction with the administration of Taft and his fellow Republicans. In 1910 farmers and Progressives in New York saw in the candidacy of FDR their new champion, and he had the name *Roosevelt.* The old Republican bosses in New York had been in some respects discredited by Taft's policies, especially in conservation. And even though they elected a Republican Governor Henry L. Stimson, FDR had been able to win a state senate seat as a Democrat. His name and links to TR had obviously assisted his quest as he had campaigned notably on the issues of honesty, efficiency, and economy to gain his seat again in the State Senate. The rising reputation of Democrat Woodrow Wilson and the defections from Taft after 1910 also aided FDR's successful bid for re-election in 1912.

The festering schism among progressives seeking leadership had been accelerated in February 1912, when Theodore Roosevelt wrote to seven state governors saying that he would accept a draft for the presidential nomination; he explained that by no third term, he had meant no third term in a row. LaFollette was hustled aside and TR's 'hat was in the ring' as he bolted from the Republicans to run as the Progressive Party's nominee. FDR meanwhile was running successfully for another term in the New York senate in 1912 aided by a marathon letter writing campaign to his Democratic supporters. He hoped to use this vast correspondence network to revitalize the Democratic Party on a national level since the Taft Republicans were in trouble and TR now appeared as a maverick. During the three-way national campaign of 1912, TR called for a national initiative, referendum and recall and even the recall of judicial decisions which alienated many moderate reformers. The *New York World* denounced: "This (recall of judicial decisions) is a frank repudiation of the principles upon which American institutions were established. It is another way of saying that the power of the majority ought always to be absolute, and that the minority has no rights which the majority is bound to respect....According to his [TR's] scheme of a Constitution, if the majority happens to think it better...to take away the minority's property without due process of law, it should have that power....To carry out his theory of government, Mr. Roosevelt would not only destroy constitutional guarantees but he would destroy the Constitution as well."[38] FDR later as U.S. president himself would attempt to control the judiciary through the 'court-packing' scheme.

The Democratic nominee in the 1912 presidential race was Woodrow Wilson, who FDR supported and for whom he campaigned. Wilson had been a brilliant academic lecturer in political science and history at Princeton in the 1890s, in 1902 being elevated to the university's presidency. In 1910, just as FDR had been elected to the Senate in New York, Woodrow Wilson had been selected as the Democratic candidate for governor of New Jersey. Refreshingly ethical, Wilson

---

[38] Roy Jenkins, Franklin Delano Roosevelt (New York: Times Books Henry Holt and Company, 2003), p. 18 explained TR's idea for a public referendum on judicial decisions; Theodore Roosevelt, Theodore Roosevelt, An Autobiography; Harold Howland, Theodore Roosevelt and His Times: A Chronicle of the Progressive Movement (New Haven: Yale University Press, 1921); Kathleen Dalton, Theodore Roosevelt: A Strenuous Life (New York: Alfred A. Knopf, 2002).

was elected and immediately took control of the political machine that had believed it could control him. After overturning boss rule, Wilson had created strict controls over utilities and established the initiative and the referendum. FDR agreed with Wilson's anti-bossism and his progressive reforming outlook, seeing him as another political mentor. The 1912 election pitted TR's New Nationalism against Woodrow Wilson's New Freedom. A strong federal government should regulate monopolies in the interest of the populace said TR, while Wilson opposed stronger centralized government, viewing it as a "foster-child" of big business, and preferred to leave a large measure of authority to the states. Woodrow Wilson captured the presidency with 41.8% of the popular vote, but in the electoral balloting the Democrats were more overwhelming: 8 electoral votes for Taft, 88 for Roosevelt and 435 for Wilson. The son of a Presbyterian minister, Woodrow Wilson used the White House in much the same manner as had Theodore Roosevelt—as a pulpit and crusading forum for national Progressivism. FDR learned much from this rich tapestry of state, municipal and national politicians and had made the progressive's crusade his own through his Democrat politicking in the New York legislature.

During his terms as state senator in New York in 1910-1912 FDR had challenged Tammany boss Charles F. Murphy. In 1910 he led the 'Roosevelt Renegades' in opposing William F. Sheehan for election by the state legislature to become a U.S. Senator from New York. Sheehan was seen by the Roosevelt reformers as corrupt, and FDR wielded great prowess in securing the aid of Al Smith and Robert Wagner among other reformers to support an alternative candidate, James A. O'Gorman, who was chosen. In his debut FDR had won immense prestige in the legislature for standing up for reform against Murphy and Tammany Hall and securing the 'Murphy surrender'.[39] He had boldly declared: "C.F. Murphy and his kind must, like the noxious weed, be plucked out." This ringing phrase played well in upstate New York where the farmers held sway. FDR was one of the spearheads for the 17th amendment to the U.S. Constitution that provided for the direct election of U.S. Senators by the people rather than state legislatures. This brought the young Franklin to the attention of national voters. TR and his former Groton mentors quickly congratulated FDR on his progressive lobbying success for the direct election of senators that they considered a progressive 'just cause'. In the New York State Senate Robert F. Wagner, soon to become a close political ally of FDR, served as president pro tempore, and Al Smith, another progressive ally served as majority leader of the

---

[39] Black, Franklin Delano Roosevelt, Champion of Freedom, pp. 56-57; Frank Freidel, Franklin D. Roosevelt, A Rendezvous with Destiny (Boston: Little, Brown and Company, 1990), p. 19-20.

assembly. FDR had found his niche in politics and made powerful friends to assist his agenda for progressive reform. He became the chairman of New York's Forest, Fish, and Game Commission committed to conservation and reforestation. He hoped to find solutions to the Ballinger-Pinchot controversy at the state level, and FDR was advised by Pinchot in drafting his New York state bill for the Protection of Lands, Forest, and Public Parks. Implementing Progressivism was their shared political bent. Franklin also supported public production of electricity, and later served as chairman of the Agricultural Commission. He firmly believed in using government intervention to ease the problems of farmers and sought support from Cornell University's agricultural expert Liberty Hyde Bailey and the State Grange to mold legislation. FDR assisted New York farmers with tax relief, cooperative marketing programs, and loans for agricultural improvements. This legislation opened upstate New York to further inroads by the Democratic Party. All of this experience prepared FDR for his later New Deal legislation of the 1930s.

While working in the New York legislature FDR won the applause and lasting friendship of Louis McHenry Howe, a reporter for the *New York Herald* who became his campaign manager committed to taking him all the way to the White House as a Democratic reformer. Howe had a series of aliments, including asthma, and suffered from severe bronchitis, but his frailty never kept him from attending to FDR's best public image and political ambitions. Howe, as a newspaperman for the New York *Herald* had covered the political news in the New York State legislature beginning in 1906. In FDR Howe found a political candidate in 1910 that he admired because FDR was willing to challenge Tammany Hall. Though married with children, Howe put the needs of FDR before his own and often answered the phone while working for FDR with the diminutive 'Medieval Gnome Here'. Following the disastrous Triangle Shirtwaist Company fire of March 25, 1911 in New York City which produced 146 dead, FDR and the progressive reformers created the New York Factory Commission headed by Al Smith, Robert Wagner and Frances Perkins. "This commission poured forth reform bills over the next several years governing wages and hours, safety provisions in workplaces, improved building codes, the banning of child labor, and categories of workmen's compensation. One of the pivotal measures was a bill limiting women's and children's working hours to fifty-four per week."[40] FDR voted in support of all these reform measures, making lifetime political alliances. Frances Perkins (1880-1965) had been born Fannie Coralie Perkins in Boston but had changed her name in 1905 to Frances. She was a 1902

---

[40] Black, Franklin Delano Roosevelt, Champion of Freedom, pp. 58-59.

graduate of Mount Holyoke in chemistry and physics where she had joined the National Consumers' League, becoming dedicated to the abolition of child labor and poor working conditions. Upon graduation Frances had taught at Monson Academy in Massachusetts and at Ferry Hall in Illinois where she identified with the goals of Jane Addams' Hull House Settlement in Chicago. Drawn to social work she took a position as general secretary of the Philadelphia Research and Protective Association an organization devoted to aiding young immigrant women and southern blacks that had migrated north from the south. At the University of Pennsylvania she studied economics and sociology, broadening her credentials for future government service. Perkins arrived in New York in 1909 with a fellowship from the Russell Sage Foundation to enroll in the New York School of Philanthropy. By 1910 she received an M.A. in sociology and economics from Columbia University, having written her thesis on malnourished children in New York's district of Hell's Kitchen. She took a post as executive secretary of the New York City Consumer's League where she shared interests with Eleanor and Franklin in fire prevention, safe factory conditions and sanitation in food production. She taught sociology part-time at Adelphi College. Following the Triangle Shirtwaist Company fire she had resigned her former positions to serve as the executive secretary on the State Factory Investigating Commission. As a result of this investigation she became an experienced lobbyist working for industrial regulation and benefits to workers, especially women and children. Her protective supporters were Robert F. Wagner, Samuel Gompers, and Franklin Roosevelt. She married Paul Caldwell Wilson in 1913 and had two children, but her husband's ill health forced her to continue to work. When Al Smith had served as Governor of New York he had named her to the Industrial Commission in 1919 and she became its chairman by 1926.

Both Frances Perkins and Robert F. Wagner would later work with FDR again to pursue progressive political goals. Wagner's family had migrated to the U.S. from Germany in 1886, and as an immigrant he knew the value of an education and graduated from City College of New York in 1898. He took a law degree from New York Law School and became a practicing attorney in New York. He married in 1908 and his son Robert Ferdinand Wagner Jr. later became Mayor of New York. Politically active in the Democratic Party, he was elected to the New York State Assembly in 1904 and to the New York Senate by 1908 where he served as president pro tempore while Al Smith had served as the Assembly's majority leader. Franklin Roosevelt worked well with them while he was in the New York legislature. FDR and Wagner had encouraged the direct election of senators, public control over utilities, and improvements in industrial working conditions. New York was to lead the nation in public service commissions that regulated public transportation, electricity and gas, laws offering workmen's compensation, and new safety codes for factories after the 1911 fire and the Investigating Commission's work that Wagner had chaired. In New York FDR and his progressives friends had pioneered industrial regulatory legislation that would be implemented on the national level during the New Deal. Elected a Senator from New York to the national Congress in 1926, Wagner would be seen later as FDR's champion for New Deal policies in the U.S. Senate. About the time that FDR had been elected to the New York legislature, the Democrats had been able to take the mantle as Progressive reformers away from the Republicans within the state. FDR had become one of the best known Democratic progressive reformers in Albany who was willing to challenge Tammany Hall to secure needed social change. Late in 1911 FDR had visited Governor Woodrow Wilson in New Jersey and offered his services to his presidential campaign, saying he supported his progressive state politics. By 1912 FDR had organized the New York State Wilson Conference to win delegates for Wilson in upstate and organized the Empire State Democrats in New York City as a 'Wilson-man'.

Following the investigative work of the Investigating Commission after the Triangle Shirtwaist Factory fire, in the spring of 1912 FDR had testified at a hearing in support of all thirty-two legislative bills promoting fire safety. Afterwards he set out to visit the Panama Canal construction site at the request of Theodore Roosevelt and returned fully convinced of the project's great success. FDR had been an ardent supporter of an Isthmian canal as his father Mr. James had proposed such a canal through Nicaragua to join the U.S. Pacific and Atlantic fleets. The fact that TR had asked him to go illustrated FDR's bi-partisan appeal and TR's generous mentoring. But prior to his own re-election to the New York state legislature in 1912, FDR had openly endorsed Woodrow Wilson in the fall of 1911 even before the former president of Princeton and then Governor of New Jersey had won the Democratic Party's nomination. FDR paid his own way to the Democratic convention in Baltimore in June 1912 and campaigned for a ticket headed by Wilson. FDR was soon to be rewarded following Wilson's election. But a life threatening illness, typhoid fever, nearly forced FDR from politics during his re-election campaign in 1912. FDR was bed-ridden but his faithful Sancho Panza figure Louis Howe boldly took charge of the campaign and FDR won. Howe had organized huge publicity posters and circulated flyers, letters, handbills, and press releases discussing FDR's policies and programs while in the senate. Howe addressed FDR during this whirlwind effort as 'Beloved and Revered Future President'. Happily, FDR would be able to follow the path laid out by TR upon the invitation of newly elected President Wilson as interestingly

FDR had the ability to attract support from both Republicans and Democrats. By the time of the New Deal FDR had been able to make Democrats of many of his good Republican friends.

In March 1913 FDR was offered the opportunity to become the Assistant Secretary of the Navy by President Wilson and he accepted. Louis Howe went to Washington as FDR's chief of staff where personnel called him 'Roosevelt's Gumshoe'. FDR eagerly sought the political capital that his new position would bring. The U.S. fleet ranked third in the world behind that of Britain and Germany. Resigning his state senate seat, Franklin and Eleanor lived in Washington, D.C. for the next seven years. FDR was naturally well suited for this position. No other person had entered this post with as much preparation and as much knowledge of the sea, ship technology, and sea power. His knowledge of sailing and love of ships allowed him to understand and appreciate the work done at naval yards that he frequented on inspections. "A yachtsman himself, FDR spoke the nautical terms of the sailor, mixed readily with admirals, appreciated the seventeen-gun salute, and was so dedicated to his job that he had a special flag designed to be flown whenever he was aboard a ship."[41] He traveled the nation visiting shipyards from Pensacola to San Diego. "He administered an enormous budget and dispersed contracts and supplies to shipyards with consummate skill and diplomacy." Working well with his boss, Josephus Daniels, Secretary of the Navy, Franklin Roosevelt became a major force for preparedness as World War I hung on the horizon. He supervised labor relations, purchasing, and personnel, and to his credit there was never a strike in the shipyards. FDR was 'their man' in public administration fighting for their needs and their jobs as he supervised 50,000 to 100,000 employees. He expanded naval production to prevent layoffs, thus building the U.S. fleet to safety levels in case of war and pleasing union leaders. FDR managed the public funds allotted to the naval building program carefully as if they were his own, thus securing a solid reputation as a first class administrator. He paid attention to people's needs. "For the benefit of U.S. seamen, he encouraged that each ship be assigned a home yard for port repairs." "He authorized the installation of safety devices on machines and encouraged recreation rooms for employees." FDR adopted new skills of scientific management. He further endeared himself to labor organizations when he fixed the wages of shipyard workers at the Brooklyn Naval Yard and then raised them to keep pace with inflation following the eruption of World War I in 1914.

---

[41] Barbara Bennett Peterson, "Franklin Delano Roosevelt (1882-1945)," in The United States in the First World War. Edited by Anne Cipriano Venzon (New York and London: Garland Press, 1995), pp. 502-503; Nathan Miller, F.D.R. An Intimate Portrait (New York: Doubleday and Company, 1983), pp. 127-129.

Briefly in 1914 FDR took time to run for the U.S. Senate from New York but was defeated largely due to his anti-Tammany Hall promises. He was defeated in the New York primary by the Tammany and Charles F. Murphy backed candidate James W. Gerard who had served as ambassador to Germany. FDR learned never to oppose Tammany Hall again, made his peace with Boss Murphy, and this campaign had little effect on his larger career with the Navy Department or his future political races. Gerard lost the election to the Republican candidate and Boss Murphy realized that perhaps after all he needed an alliance with FDR and his upstate Democratic farming friends. FDR made working in the shipyards enormously attractive due to good working relations and relatively high pay. His labor friends never forgot him and he was cooperative in expanding the Brooklyn Navy Yard that pleased Tammany Hall. He re-opened the naval yards at Pensacola and New Orleans by attaching squadrons of aviators to the bases. He also built relations with naval officers that never faltered either. FDR insisted that the assistant chiefs of the Bureau of Construction and Repair of Yards and Docks be naval officers with detailed experience rather than mere desk clerks. Further he made it mandatory that highly trained engineers supervise all ship construction and that they have fluency in ship mechanics. FDR demanded the best men for these positions and paid them what they were worth to safeguard American troops and merchant-men at sea. By April 1917 when President Wilson asked Congress for a declaration of war against Germany, the American Navy was battle ready. Earlier FDR had asked Daniels if he could bring the U.S. fleet at Guantanamo Bay, Cuba northward to protect America's coastline given the circumstances of Germany's resumption of unlimited and unrestricted submarine warfare declaration February 2, 1917. The fleet in the Caribbean remained there but the decision was made to arm merchant vessels to protect American shipping. FDR had seen the war coming for the U.S. and placed the nation in readiness by enlarging its sea power. Senator Elihu Root evaluated FDR's ambition correctly when he stated: 'Whenever a Roosevelt rides, he wishes to ride in front' explaining his desire to be the real leader of the Navy Department. FDR worked well with the pair dubbed 'the Heavenly Twins'—Samuel McGowan and Christian Peoples who saved the Navy department money through greater efficiency while administering the Bureau of Supplies and Accounts. Herein was another of FDR's successes—greater government efficiency. He had continuously lobbied for a Navy Department budget second to none in the world. He agreed with Wilson's policies in Mexico and in the Caribbean and had encouraged Wilson's establishment of a Council of National Defense before the U.S. had been drawn into the war against Germany. FDR understood history and had given a copy of James Monroe's 'appeal to the sword' memo justifying war to the president when national honor was at stake. FDR had also discovered and forwarded to Wilson the legal justifications for arming merchant vessels before Germany's unrestricted submarine warfare declaration. FDR had been encouraged to actually join the armed services in uniform, but Wilson and Daniels pressed the fact that he was needed at home in the Navy Department.

Having supported Wilson in his re-election bid in 1916, FDR appeared along side President Wilson in ceremonious events like the Flag Day celebrations and remained a presidential confidante through 1918. FDR assisted in mobilization of forces for the conduct of the naval war, enlarged the militia and reserves, and purchased naval stores. "His greatest task was to bring the German submarines under control. To that end, FDR had a hand in running the Atlantic convoy system, increasing the number of destroyers and sub-chasers under construction in American shipyards. He also supported the North Sea Mine Barrage to counter German submarines, which was laid with newly developed mines in the spring of 1918."[42] FDR was in his element, rising to wartime challenges. His celebrity status increased as he stood beside Mary Pickford and Douglas Fairbanks, Marie Dressler and Charlie Chaplin raising money for the war effort through the sale of war bonds. In Washington he participated in the Liberty Loan Rally of April 14, 1918 and was recognized around the country through photos of this event. His star had risen. He had also kept his hand in state politics of New York, having accepted a position as vice president of the State Forestry Association.

During the war, FDR developed a relationship with Lucy Mercer who worked as Eleanor's social secretary and then in the Navy Department. She was from a fine Mercerburg, Maryland family and in Washington, when Eleanor was away with the children at Campobello, FDR attended parties, dances and other social functions where he saw Lucy. They became close friends who enjoyed each other's company, especially after Lucy began working in the Navy Department close to his office where he enjoyed her admiration bordering on hero-worship. Eleanor offered FDR a divorce when she found out about their close attachment which was revealed by fawning letters written to Franklin by Lucy when he was in Europe on war business. Franklin, when confronted, told Eleanor not to be a 'Goose' and down-played his friendship with Lucy. Alice Roosevelt Longworth, TR's daughter and maid of honor at Eleanor and Franklin's wedding, "never regarded it as an adulterous relationship."[43] It was simply a "carefree friendship of

---

[42] Barbara Bennett Peterson, "Franklin Delano Roosevelt (1882-1945)", in The United States in the First World War, p. 503.
[43] Lash, Eleanor and Franklin, pp. 220-236; Frank Freidel, Franklin D. Roosevelt, A Rendezvous With Destiny (Boston: Little, Brown and Company, 1990), pp. 35-36; Alsop, FDR, A Centenary

the sort Franklin had always enjoyed with female friends and relatives—and always was to enjoy in the future." Indeed Eleanor herself denied that there had been any intimate relationship between Franklin and Lucy to FDR's biographer Frank Freidel who was convinced of Franklin's innocence. It was simply an admiring friendship. Mother Sara Roosevelt emerged as a heroine in the crisis between Franklin and Eleanor, and stepped in and threatened to cut off FDR without a dollar should he accept Eleanor's offer of a divorce. Lucy Mercer, a good Catholic girl, could never marry a divorced FDR anyway while Eleanor was still alive, hence the matter closed. FDR and Lucy broke off their friendly relationship in late 1918. Lucy went on to marry the socially prominent and widowed Winthrop Rutherford. Staying by his side, Eleanor preserved her dignity, her marriage, and went on to remain the most significant person and aide in FDR's life. Lucy Mercer Rutherford later appeared at FDR's inaugurations and at receptions at the White House escorted by others, underlining the fact that theirs was only a friendship. FDR's character matured and he moved on to larger goals. To her credit Sara Roosevelt had sided with her daughter-in-law and the Roosevelt children over the letters issue to effect the story's happier ending.

In July 1918 FDR had been sent on a mission to Europe to inspect the front and Lucy had written him the letters that were later uncovered. FDR had witnessed the Allied shelling of the German lines, visited the Naval Air Station at Pauillac, France, and stated "it is hard for me to go back to a dull office job in Washington after having visited the lines where our boys are making history."[44] At home, from Daniels, FDR learned how the federal departments interacted with each other and with the president—invaluable knowledge for FDR in World War II. Abroad, FDR made friends with all of the leaders of the Allied countries, a network that proved priceless in his future diplomacy. At age thirty-six FDR had matured, overcome personal and professional challenges, and joined forces with the progressive politicians. Wilson was "the second of the progressive presidents who made a deep impression upon him. Theodore Roosevelt had been a flamboyant relative, beckoning young Franklin to an exciting life of political strenuosity; Wilson was an austere, revered schoolmaster, like Peabody of Groton, teaching the uses and responsibilities of power."[45] FDR felt ready to achieve greater heights after this apprenticeship with progressive politicians of both political parties.

Remembrance, pp. 65-74; Black, Franklin Delano Roosevelt, Champion of Freedom, pp. 96-101.
[44] Alsop, FDR, A Centenary Remembrance, p. 53.
[45] Freidel, Franklin D. Roosevelt, A Rendezvous with Destiny, p. 23.

Figure 1. President Franklin Delano Roosevelt an official portrait from the mid-Thirties in the Library of Congress. Reproduced from the Collection of the Library of Congress, LC-USZ62-117121

Chapter 2

POSTWAR 1920S TO GOVERNOR OF NEW YORK

During his visit to Europe during World War I, Franklin Roosevelt had met King George V on July 29, 1918 in an audience in London and attended a dinner for allied war ministers at Gray's Inn where he gave an address. Franklin discussed the war with General Jan Christian Smuts from South Africa, commanding the British Royal Air Force, and Winston Spencer Churchill who served as Britain's minister of munitions. David Lloyd George, leading England's effort as Prime Minister, and Arthur Balfour the foreign secretary met Franklin the next day at Parliament. FDR wrote of this encounter: "What has pleased me more than anything else is the...determination of the British Cabinet to go through with the war to a definitely successful end."[46] On July 31 Franklin had set out from Dover to Dunkirk on a British destroyer and had flown his own flag as Assistant Secretary of the U.S. Navy. He had designed his own flag, after all the president and the Secretary of the Navy had their own flags, and FDR would have one too, even receiving a seventeen guns salute and a ruffle of drums as he set foot on naval vessels under inspection. He understood the value of ceremony and rank. It was all part of developing a national following. Driving on to Paris, his party visited Theodore Roosevelt, Jr. and Archie Roosevelt in a hospital, both recovering from war wounds. Later Franklin met with George Leygues, French Navy minister, Andre Tardieu, liaison officer with the U.S., Marshall Joffre, key military leader, Georges Clemenceau the French Premier, and Raymond Poincare, President of the French Republic. Joffre was indebted to FDR for their earlier

---

[46] Elliott Roosevelt, ed., FDR: His Personal Letters, II (New York: Duell, Sloan and Pearce, 1948), p. 393.

meeting in Washington in May 1917. "He kept insisting that the friendly advice I had given him from the very first day when I met him," recorded Franklin, "at Hampton Roads had in the end enabled him to obtain the answers for which he had come to America...I think he felt, and rightly so, that only a small part of the million and a quarter Americans now in France would be there had it not been for his mission."[47] FDR toured Verdun and along the roadsides witnessed "huge numbers of wounded, utter devastation of the countryside, and the pathetic spectacle of refugees returning to rebuild their homes and lives." Upon discussing with Sir Eric Geddes a unified military command led by the British in the Mediterranean, FDR embarked for Italy to bring the Italians more closely into agreement. Here he met Baron Sidney Sonnino, the foreign minister, his opposite number in the naval department, and Prime Minister Orlando. But the Italians wished to keep control of the Adriatic and these discussions ascended to higher levels. FDR drew from these experiences a formidable knowledge of geography, topography, allied strategies, and the intricacies of European diplomacy. Franklin returned to Paris for meetings with General Pershing and Marshal Foch where he discussed "coordinating the American Marine railroad artillery batteries with the French high command."[48]

Franklin had returned to the U.S. with pneumonia caused partially by over work. Yet he produced a brilliant report for Secretary Daniels who sent it on to President Wilson as coming from "the clear-headed and able" FDR. The praise for FDR's successful foreign mission was bipartisan as Theodore Roosevelt wrote: "Dear Franklin, We are deeply concerned about your sickness, and trust you will soon be well. We are very proud of you. With love, affectionately yours, Theodore Roosevelt."[49] It had been upon his return from Europe that the Lucy Mercer episode had erupted, but it blew over and Franklin's career was elevated immeasurably by his overseas diplomacy. Eleanor and Franklin endeavored to spend more time together, he going to church with her and she going out dancing to please him. Her fears were put to rest and soon their personal agendas reconverged on Franklin's mission overseas again. Oswald Garrison Villard had written that he hoped FDR would quickly follow in TR's footsteps toward the presidency, but *not* by means of a future war. Franklin and Eleanor hoped so too.

---

[47] Conrad Black, Franklin Delano Roosevelt, Champion of Freedom (New York: Public Affairs, The Perseus Book Group, 2003), p. 92-93; Elliott Roosevelt, FDR: His Personal Letters, II, p. 411.

[48] Black, Franklin Delano Roosevelt, Champion of Freedom, p. 96; Kenneth S. Davis, Vol. I, FDR, The Beckoning of Destiny, 1882-1928 (New York: Putnam, 1972), pp. 527-528; Samuel I. Rosenman, ed., Public Papers and Addresses of Franklin D. Roosevelt 13 Vols. (New York: Random House, 1938), Vol. I, pp. 249-252.

[49] Frank Freidel, FDR, The Apprenticeship (Boston: Little, Brown, 1952), Vol. I, p. 369.

In the post World War I period FDR, accompanied by Eleanor, went to Europe and the Paris peace conference to reclaim or dispose of wartime U.S. military property. Their Atlantic crossing on the *George Washington* was only marred by the news of Theodore Roosevelt's death. In 1915 Jane Addams had led an international women's congress at The Hague and produced an outline for peace that was reflected in Wilson's Fourteen Points. She too represented a bipartisan nature as she had earlier supported TR and the party of Lincoln but had entered her pacifist stage and moved to support the peacetime policies of Wilson. Germany had signed an armistice based upon the Fourteen Points and the nations gathered at Versailles to draft the peace treaty and discuss the League of Nations. An era had ended. "The Roosevelts had a fine suite in the Ritz, and Paris was an unforgettable sight, crowded with prizes of war along the great boulevards, as elegant as ever, but with a great number of war widows and wounded men, and colorful peace conference delegations from vitually every ethnic group in Europe, Asia, and the Middle East, all pressing their claims as Wilson, Clemenceau, Lloyd George, and Orlando set out to redraw the map of much of the world."[50] In cleaning up European war theaters nothing was left to waste. Salvage and scrap were secured for recycling and FDR saw to the disposal of U.S. naval properties at a fair price. FDR was invited to all the political and social inner circles. He skillfully negotiated the end to wartime contracts and subsidies while maintaining friendships with the Allies. "The highlight of Roosevelt's activities in France was his negotiation with Andre Tardieu…who was now in charge of inter-allied relations, over the fate of a naval radio station at Bordeaux. The French were hoping the Americans would leave it behind, but when Roosevelt threatened to pack it up and transport it, Tardieu agreed to pay a fair price for it."[51] FDR's industrial naval management and postwar diplomacy made headlines around the world and the phrase 'see young Roosevelt about it' was a common political phrase. His reassuring manner closed many a deal with a handshake and his word solidified European postwar alliances. The Roosevelts returned to America with President Wilson on the *George Washington* with the peace treaty and the provision for the League of Nations that Americans would be asked to support in the coming election. FDR promised Wilson that he would support the treaty of Versailles and the League of Nations that were so vitally important to the president. FDR resigned his Assistant Secretary of the Navy post in 1920 but was given a warm farewell sendoff by 2,000 employees of the Navy Department that

---

[50] Black, Franklin Delano Roosevelt, Champion of Freedom, p. 103.
[51] Elliott Roosevelt, FDR: His Personal Letters, II, pp. 435-455.

included a silver cup presented by Secretary Daniels as a congratulatory gift for a job well done.

Progressivism would continue in the postwar America and ultimately be highly regarded during the future New Deal era. Domestically, like TR, Wilson had laid presidential road maps that could be followed by successors. All of his progressive reform policies adopted during his two terms would remain in effect throughout the 1920s and FDR would build upon them after 1932. The first successful domestic measure of the Wilson administration had been the provision for tariff reduction. The Underwood tariff of 1913 had reduced rates from 44% to 29% and this represented the first real tariff reduction since the Civil War and redeemed Democratic pledges to accomplish this feat. The tariff bill was also a benchmark in tax legislation as it authorized Congress under the newly ratified 16th amendment to levy a progressive graduated income tax on incomes above $3,000 for single people and $4,000 for a married couple. A married man in 1913 who earned $5,000 a year paid only about $10.00 in income tax. But it was a beginning and was originally aimed at equaling federal revenues that would be lost due to the tariff's reduction. Congress had been forced to stay in session during the summer and autumn of 1913 to tackle another issue—the reform of the banking system. Untrammeled and triumphant, at the heart of the economy lay private control over the money system. No public agency had previously any voice in settling such critical issues as when and how to expand the money supply, the location of banking facilities, their terms of lending, and what type of links between banks and business corporations were ethical. Progressives insisted that the control over money be taken out of private hands and put into those of a public agency. Farmers wished the money supply to be responsive to special circumstances such as droughts or depressions and small businesses wanted the conditions for lending money more closely regulated by a disinterested authority. Woodrow Wilson had had no intention of dismantling private banking but he had wanted to establish public supervision. Before the war, in June 1913, he had called for the creation of the Federal Reserve Board that would supervise the banking system. Its membership would be appointed by the president and confirmed by the Senate. The country was divided into twelve federal reserve districts, each with its central federal reserve bank. The Federal Reserve System had been perhaps the crowning achievement of the Wilson administration and FDR would be able to use this system to regulate the depression's monetary security and solve the national banking crisis of 1932-33.

Another major holdover in the 1920s from Wilson's two terms was the Federal Trade Commission established in 1914 as the agency through which Wilson had sought to regulate the trusts. Modeled on the Interstate Commerce

Commission, the FTC was composed of five members appointed by the President with the Senate's consent and each member would serve for seven years. Its purpose was to eliminate unfair business practices and restore lawful competition by empowering the commission to issue "cease and desist" orders. Over two thousand malpractice complaints were heard by the FTC, and it ordered 379 cease and desist orders after investigations of such firms as light and power production companies, and private municipal transportation firms. Accompanying the FTC was the Clayton Anti-Trust Bill which prohibited price discrimination harmful to competition and beneficial to monopolies, eliminated interlocking directories (except those that did not impair free competition) and made corporation officers personally liable for illegal corporate acts. At the time, although later much less so, it appeared also to be a boon for labor because the Clayton Anti-Trust Act limited the use of government injunctions used to break strikes and exempted labor unions from being considered monopolies in restraint of trade. President Wilson's appointment of Louis Brandeis known as 'the people's attorney' for his liberal views to the Supreme Court had further demonstrated to the public his commitment to further yet the progressive goals. But events leading to America's involvement in the World War I had been the increasing focus of administrative attentions after Wilson's re-election in 1916. FDR would rely similarly upon Felix Frankfurter in the 1930s. Evidence showed that Wilson desired to continue the progressive movement toward the left as he pushed through a bill in Congress that established twelve farm loan banks, each of them with $500,000 provided by the federal government. He also personally lobbied for a child labor law that prohibited the shipment of goods in interstate commerce that were made by children under 14 or children under 16 if they worked more than an 8-hour day. This was one of the first attempts to regulate business practices directly. FDR, then working in the Navy Department, learned first hand how government involved itself in business for progressive ends from Wilson just as he had from TR. It was once again a model to be followed in the future. FDR's progressive policies would be further advanced through the New Deal with the government's continued concern for banking regulations, restrictions on business, improvements to transportation and public utilities, working conditions for labor, and public health standards, especially for women and children. Echoing Franklin's progressive concerns, Eleanor during the war had worked in the Washington Red Cross canteen.

When World War I had ended the government had no plan for demobilization. It simply lifted wartime controls, believing business would absorb the tremendous volume of workers who had worked in industries essential to the war effort. This had caused serious dislocations in some parts of the country where unemployed workers competed with returning soldiers for jobs. But postwar demand expanded the U.S. market as the demand for automobiles and homes skyrocketed generated by inflation. In 1919 the cost-of-living index rose 77% above the prewar level and in 1920 it rose another 28%. Some groups lost their strong position they had held during the war. One such group was the railway brotherhood that had found that governmental regulation of the railroads during the war had been more fair and efficient than private management. An attorney for the brotherhood, Glenn Plumb, wanted the government to nationalize the railways and the American Federation of Labor supported this concept. The railroads were finally returned to private ownership but the federal government applied tighter control of them through the Transportation Act of 1920. This gave the Interstate Commerce Commission control over the issue of railway securities and gave the commission some control over the rates charged by the lines for shipping goods. This whole discussion elicited arguments that FDR would later use to promote state owned public power.

America's favorite pastimes also reflected progressive ideals pursued by both parties. FDR had made a name for himself as a progressive reformer, big navy man, a Wilson man, and a proponent of the League of Nations and internationalism. Franklin Roosevelt was seen as a man with a future based on his ability and ambition. The times matched the man perfectly. The tone of the first decade of the 20th Century had been one of optimism in the success of Progressive reforms, and leisure time pursuits were in perfect congruence with America's happy postwar hopefulness. These sentiments were re-echoed during the 1920s. The "automobility" had become a craze. America had only 8,000 cars in 1900, but 460,000 cars were purchased between 1900 and 1910.[52] Cars took some getting used to as in 1902 Vermont had "required every auto to be proceeded by a mature individual waving a red flag." "In Tennessee, motorists had to post a week's notice before they could legally start out on a trip." This newness and awe over the automobile produced several laughable, but at the time serious articles. *Everyday Etiquette* (1905) advised the parvenue: "Do not stare at another's car, nor if at a standstill, examine the mechanism. This is the height of rudeness."[53] At the time, it would have been difficult not to stare in admiration of the new models of the Great Arrow, the Pierce Arrow, the Peerless or a Baker Electric Vehicle, and the Model T. Pedestrians were not so much angered as envious as millionaires

---

[52] Ezra Bowen, ed., This Fabulous Century, 1900-1910 Vol. 1 (New York: Time-Life Books, 1969), p. 228.
[53] Bowen, ed., This Fabulous Century, pp. 228-229; Ernest Kidder Lindley, Franklin D. Roosevelt: A Career in Progressive Democracy (New York: Da Capo Press, 1974 originally published in 1931).

like Alfred Gwynne Vanderbilt raced his red touring car through New York at reckless speeds of more than 10 miles per hour.[54] The auto bespoke the virtues of capitalism with every model; the car became the symbol of success, inexpensive models within the reach of almost everyman. FDR purchased his first car in 1908. Rather than a symbol of resentment, the automobile triumphed as the very symbol of the good life open to so many. Taming the automobile however took some instruction, as every new motorist was urged to equip his car with a basic outfit of tools including, "one blowout patch, one package assorted cement patches, one tube self-vulcanizing cement, two extra tail-light bulbs....and for emergencies 2 pounds chocolate and 4 half-pound cans of meat."[55] No woman should be without her touring outfit and Saks and Co. of New York offered her a 270-page catalogue on motoring apparel.[56] For men, goggles, cap, wind breaker, and tool kit were quintessential for motoring as beyond the city limits only a small number of roads were paved and offered thick mud, potholes and blinding dust, in a period of time that had never seen as yet a "rural gas station." The "automobility" craze led to songs like "Toot Your Horn, Kid," and "You're In A Fog," and the Very Rich emblazoned their cars with gold plated headlights dotted with rubies.[57] Races such as the Indianapolis race of 1909 won by Louis Strong with an average speed of 64 miles per hour had glamorized the automobile.[58] Closer to home, the Sunday drive became a Roosevelt family past time. FDR and Eleanor had campaigned in 1910 to gain the state senate seat across New York in a rented "red-two-cylinder Maxwell" car and paid $20.00 a day.[59] To save expenses "Franklin had teamed up with Assembly candidate Ferdinand A. Hoyt and Richard E. Connell, candidate for the twenty-first U.S. congressional district....Together they chugged down country roads at twenty-two miles an hour, stopping and cutting the engine whenever they met a horse and team. The car had no top and no windshield, and they wore raincoats when it rained and dusters on dirt roads." Early cars were a luxury. After World War I car production sky-rocketed and families of the middle class came to boast of their own automobiles. In 1918 there had been nine million cars on the road, in 1929 there were 26 million. In 1921 President Warren Harding

---

[54] Bowen, ed., This Fabulous Century, p. 236; James Rood Doolittle, Romance of the Automobile Industry, Being the Story of Its Development, Its Contribution to Health and Prosperity, Its Influence on Eugenics, Its Effects on Personal Efficiency, and Its Service and Mission to Humanity as the Latest and Greatest Phase of Transportation (New York: Klebold Press, 1916).

[55] Bowen, ed., This Fabulous Century, 1900-1910 Vol. 1, p. 233.

[56] Bowen, ed., This Fabulous Century, 1900-1910 Vol. 1, p. 232;

[57] Bowen, ed., This Fabulous Century, 1900-1910 Vol. 1, pp. 231-236; Howard Teichman, Alice: The Life and Times of Alice Roosevelt Longworth (Englewood Cliffs, Prentice Hall, 1979).

[58] Bowen, ed., This Fabulous Century, 1900-1910 Vol. 1, p. 241; Geoffrey Ward, A First-Class Temperament: The Emergence of Franklin Roosevelt (New York: Harper and Row, 1989).

[59] Ted Morgan, FDR, A Biography (New York: Simon and Schuster, 1985), pp. 114-115.

successor to President Wilson arrived in style at his inauguration on March 4 in a Pierce Arrow touring car. By this time both Franklin and Eleanor each had their own automobiles. In 1928 when he was Governor of New York FDR had a large car with a driver that accompanied him on all his inspection tours whether he traveled by rail or by boat. Eleanor would take her own personal car on European excursions, placing it in the hold of their passenger ship. The Roosevelts made continuous road trips from Hyde Park to Campobello with the children during the summers. They made motoring tours family excursions especially after hard surfaced roads became a reality through the Federal Highway Act of 1921 and the Holland Tunnel was completed in 1927. During the summer of 1929 Eleanor and the children were driven around Europe in a chauffeur driven Daimler, and Eleanor's friends accompanied them in their own Buick.

The "flickering flicks" as the early movies were called, were a close second in the pursuit of pleasure with the auto and had rivals in the circuses that traveled from city to city, and the legitimate stage and vaudeville that continued after the war as entertainment became even a bigger industry.[60] More than four hundred stock and touring theater groups carried drama to the nation, with four or five plays opening on Broadway on an ordinary night. But vaudeville was both the family's and the nation's favorite entertainment—jugglers, acrobats, singers, dancers, ventriloquists, animal acts, and magicians—all came together to thrill packed houses and noisy throngs eager to laugh. In the 1920s the public watched Al Jolson in *The Jazz Singer* when movies began to have sound and their favorite heroes and heroines like Greta Garbo, Clara Bow, Gloria Swanson, Pola Negri, Rudolph Valentino, John Gilbert and Douglas Fairbanks. The earliest silent "flickering flicks" within five years had inspired the establishment of hundreds of nickelodeons or small theaters where for 5 cents a short movie could be viewed by a public ravenous for this form of entertainment. While the flicks wowed the masses, millions responded joyously with their nickels when a nickel also bought a root beer float but an ice cream sundae cost 10 cents. Soon Charlie Chaplin, Lon Chaney and Buster Keaton replaced these movie shorts on the big screen. These entertainers competed for public attention with Chautauqua programs, Broadway shows, the Ziegfeld Follies, the music of Irving Berlin and the comedy of Fanny Brice, W.C. Fields, and Will Rogers. Youth were attracted to the Boy Scouts of America, founded in 1910, and to the Girl Scouts or Camp Fire Girls both founded in 1912. FDR would heartily support the Boy Scout Foundation in New York following the 1920 election. The first Miss America Pageant was held in 1921 largely to promote Atlantic City and it was held on the Boardwalk.

---

[60] Bowen, ed., This Fabulous Century, 1900-1910 Vol. 1, pp. 244-261.

Prohibition was another significant 1920s social characteristic. The 18th amendment to the U.S. Constitution had prohibited the sale and consumption of alcoholic beverages and had passed in January 1920. America went 'dry' by law but not in practice. FDR believed prohibition to be impractical and unenforceable. But the measure had gained ground before the war's end to conserve grains for food consumption at home and in Allied Europe and meshed with progressive ideals to cleanup corruption and vice. At official functions FDR, when a host, did not provide liquor but was present at events where others had brought in supplies to be imbibed.

Another of the victories for social justice accomplished by the presidency of Woodrow Wilson had been the passage of the 19th amendment that empowered women to vote. Before the World War I women's organizations proliferated concerned with women's causes, especially to aid children, and assisted the advancement of Progressivism. By 1914 all the segments of the women's movement had come together around a commitment to suffrage as their main goal. And this fusion of interests had not been accomplished easily. In 1890 the National American Woman Suffrage Association was formed by the unification of the National Woman's Suffrage Association led by Elizabeth Cady Stanton and Susan B. Anthony and the rival group, the American Woman's Suffrage Association, which had been led by Lucy Stone and Julia Ward Howe, author of the *Battle Hymn of the Republic*. This early period of the suffrage movement from the 1870s to 1890 had been a period in which women claimed the right to vote using the "justice" argument. Equality was a natural right. After 1890, after the re-unification of the suffrage groups under the banner of the NAWSA, the argument for equality and woman's autonomy changed to the argument of "expediency." The expediency argument linked the vote for women with social reform, enabled women to capitalize on the Progressive momentum and, ultimately, women's suffrage became part of the Progressive Party platform of 1912. Women were saying 'double your political power by enfranchising us.' 'Give the women the vote and they will reform society' proved a powerful propelling force as suffrage groups were supported by the Women's Christian Temperance Union (1874), by the Consumers' League (1890), by the General Federation of Women's Clubs (1893) and by the Women's Trade Union League (1903). As elsewhere in the Progressive Era, the influence of the new college-educated middle class was significant. In 1910 almost 8,500 women received baccalaureate degrees, as compared with approximately 29,000 men. Carrie Chapman Catt, college trained and an experienced organizer of the International Woman Suffrage Alliance that had been founded in Germany in 1904, served as president of the NAWSA from 1915 to 1920. She spearheaded the successful move for the passage of the 19th

amendment enfranchising women with the vote by 1920. Catt would later introduce Eleanor Roosevelt as 'a woman in the White House who is one of us'. During the 1920 election Catt would urge newly enfranchised women to vote for the Cox-Roosevelt ticket to ensure peace through the League of Nations and applauded the Democratic administration of Wilson who had given them the vote.

Earlier as a New York state senator from 1910 to 1912, FDR had firmly committed himself to advocating votes for women as he liberally supported women's suffrage even before his wife and mother. Inez Mulholland had campaigned for women's suffrage in Poughkeepsie, New York in May 1911 and met with FDR and the Dutchess County membership of the Equal Suffrage League. As Senator, FDR had become convinced that supporting women's suffrage was taking 'the correct stance'. He saw the value of harnessing female moral concerns to effect progressive policy. Likewise he later supported Frances Perkins and her lobbying campaign for the fifty-four hour work week bill for women passed by the New York legislature in Albany. Suffrage money was raised, speakers lobbied, strikes, pickets, and hunger strikes were begun and Wilson was wooed in his re-election campaign of 1916. On one occasion, as Wilson spoke before the NAWSA, Anna Howard Shaw had said to him: 'We have waited so long, Mr. President, for the vote—we had hoped it might come in your administration'. At which point the immense audience of women rose silently and stood quietly looking at the president. Within a year, Wilson came out in support of women's suffrage. In January 1918, it passed the House of Representatives and in 1919 the Senate followed and in August 1920 the amendment was ratified by the states. Twenty-six million women could now go to vote and the electorate was almost doubled. The urge to reform that had been launched so successfully during the Progressive Era would begin anew after World War I when attentions could again be focused on domestic challenges. By 1920 Eleanor joined the League of Women Voters and became a leader in advocacy for women and enrolled women to vote. Alice Paul's Woman's Party, founded in 1916, continued to promote the Equal Rights Amendment (ERA) that was first introduced into Congress in 1923. The League of Women Voters was more broadly based and was an advocacy lobby for municipal reform, conservation, laws to protect children, tighter consumer laws, and public support for indigent mothers. Eleanor was supported by Franklin as he saw the League as continuing progressive gains and as being composed of wives and mothers who primarily lobbied for benefits for women and children. They were high-class philanthropists who were willing to use their largess to benefit the under privileged. The League members encouraged women to run for public office and on the state and local levels were successful in whittling down discriminatory marriage and property laws and in fighting for the repeal of statutes that prohibited women from serving on juries. FDR had numerous friends in the League who were some of his strongest political supporters and campaigners, helping to get out the Democratic vote. The causes for which the League lobbied were mainstream political goals supported by both men and women, and were reforming progressive causes espoused by FDR. Frances Perkins converted from the Republican party to the Democratic Party largely because the Democrats had embraced social reform and promoted votes for women.

In the postwar period, Progressives had been aware, even amidst political battles, that there was something distinctive about the social and political attitudes and accomplishments of their time that set it off from the proceeding era of corruption, materialism, and competitive struggle. The distinctiveness of the Progressive period lies in its *morality* and both political parties had shared in its accomplishments. From the end of the Civil War to the end of the 19th Century, Americans had mobilized for a remarkable burst of physical industrialization and by quantum leaps had by passed other countries of the world. In the Progressive era, America's conscience had been called into question, asking, 'on whose backs have we made millions of dollars and stunning industrial progress'? And the era set about to make amends. This self-righting mechanism was a virtuous and re-occurring theme in American history; when the tilt is too far left or right a group arises to balance America's social groups. Such is the way of encouraging equality and adherence to Christian conscience. In the Progressive era, the equivalent of a moral crusade had been launched; it was as though Americans were fire-hardened anew to take up the crusades that first launched the founding religious settlements in the New World. For the future, the national government's very responsiveness to change, indeed its willingness to facilitate change, was the important foundation that Progressivism laid for the New Deal.

In the national election of 1920 FDR was selected to run as the Democratic Party's nominee for Vice President of the United States on the ticket headed by Ohio Governor James M. Cox as the candidate for President. They would campaign against the Republican nominee Warren G. Harding and his running mate Calvin Coolidge. FDR gave a resounding progressive speech at the Democratic Party's national convention and drew attention to himself as a wise and candid leader. His speech was noticed by Cox who lobbied hard to have Franklin Roosevelt on the ticket with him. FDR's convention speech had contrasted sharply with that of Wilson's former Attorney-General A. Mitchell Palmer who had hoped to secure the party's nomination himself using the 'fear of reds' or Bolsheviks in America with his red-baiting speeches. But Palmer's negativity had not worked and Franklin won the day as the Vice-presidential nominee. FDR pledged in his acceptance speech to party and public that "our eyes are trained ahead—forward to better days," pledging the Democratic Party to continue as a "progressive democracy."[61] He understood that America really could never retreat into isolationism again as it was "impossible to be in this world and not of it." "The League will not die. An idea does not die which meets the call of the hearts of our mothers." Shrewdly this was mentioned to appeal to women voters. Peace was to be "established by mutual consent." "We cannot anchor our ship of state in this world tempest, nor can we return to the placid harbor of long years ago."[62] FDR attempted to preserve progressive gains made by the previous Democratic administration of Wilson. "We oppose money in politics, we oppose private control of national finances. We oppose the treatment of human beings as commodities, we oppose the saloon-bossed city, we oppose starvation wages, we oppose rule by groups or cliques....We oppose a mere period of coma in our national life."[63] Wilson had been incapacitated by a stroke and the leadership torch had passed to Cox and FDR, both of whom attempted to internationalize progressivism. During their campaign, Cox and FDR had made membership in the League of Nations a cornerstone promise, but voters were reluctant to shoulder European involvement and further burdens, especially any military commitment to protect the League and the Treaty of Versailles that had ended the war with Germany. As a result of the election, FDR earned national exposure, a wider circle of political friends and contacts, experience at the national podium, and kept his promises to Woodrow Wilson. Traveling 8,000 miles largely by train and car, FDR "got to know the country as only a candidate for office or a traveling salesman can get to know it."[64] Eleanor was interviewed by the *Poughkeepsie Eagle News* on July 16, 1920 and she stated:"My politics? Oh yes, I am a Democrat, but I was brought up a staunch Republican, and turned Democrat. I believe the best interests of the country are in the hands of the Democratic Party, for I believe they are the most progressive. The Republicans are, well, they are more conservative, you know, and can't be too conservative and accomplish things." Steve Early was his highly disciplined press secretary

---

[61] Joseph Alsop, FDR, A Centenary Remembrance (New York: The Viking Press, 1982), p. 93.

[62] Black, Franklin Delano Roosevelt, Champion of Freedom, p. 103; Elliott Roosevelt, FDR: His Personal Letters, II, pp. 495-508.

[63] Franklin D. Roosevelt Campaign Papers, Franklin D. Roosevelt Library, Hyde Park, New York, FDR to Willard Saulsbury 9/12/1924; Stephen Hess, America's Political Dynasties (New Brunswick, NJ: Transaction Publishers, 1997).

[64] Black, Franklin Delano Roosevelt, Champion of Freedom, p. 127; Geoffrey Ward, A First Class Temperament, The Emergence of Franklin Roosevelt (New York: Harper and Row, 1989), p. 520; Eleanor's interview with the Poughkeepsie Eagle News is quoted in Joseph P. Lash, Eleanor and Franklin (New York: W.W. Norton and Company, 1971), p. 252.

who tooted FDR's horn regarding his diplomacy in Europe during the war. Marvin McIntyre handled public relations for FDR's campaign. Both Early and McIntyre had previously worked with FDR during the war, Early as journalist for the armed services *Stars and Stripes* and McIntyre had worked in the Navy department.[65] FDR was an elegant seasoned veteran campaigner, rich deep voiced and immensely likable as a person. Louis Howe accompanied FDR throughout his campaign across the country and realized the importance of Eleanor to FDR's political success and began inviting her to participate in the campaign. She often traveled with Franklin and her views were sought on issues of significance to the public, especially women. Handsome robust FDR charmed female voters and they voted for him in droves because he concerned himself intelligently with their issues and had helped secure their enfranchisement.

But his defeat and the election of Harding and Coolidge returned FDR to New York where he established his own law firm. Many voters told him they had liked his campaign but could not support 'Mr. Wilson's League'. He and Eleanor returned to their big home on 65th Street connected to the home of Sara Roosevelt that they so enjoyed. FDR started the Cuff Links Club at Christmas time, so named because he gave gifts to all his campaign workers of gold cufflinks with his and the recipient's names inscribed. This thoughtfulness was repeated following all future campaigns and hence the 'club'. His popularity continued along with his renown for leading the naval charge during the war. America had returned to Harding's promised 'normalcy' in 1920 and selected not to join the League of Nations, ultimately signing a separate peace treaty with defeated Germany. But FDR would, as promised, keep his eyes trained ahead for better days. He remained in good spirits and high minded. Ultimately the high road and integrity would win the day for FDR when the scandals of the Harding administration involved with the leasing of government oil reserves at Elk Hills, California and Teapot Dome, Wyoming and improprieties in the Alien Property department and the Veteran's Bureau caused Republicans to lose control of various states like New York to the Democrats. The major accomplishment of Harding's time as president was the Washington Naval Conference in November 1921. Harding's Secretary of State Charles Evans Hughes had sent a circular to eight countries—Britain, France, Japan, Italy, Belgium, China, Portugal, and The Netherlands—inviting them to join with the United States in a series of agreements. These accords would all focus on the ultimate objective of disarmament and international discussion of potential disputes. There were three treaties that came out of this conference—the Nine-Power Pact, the Five-Power

---

[65] Black, *Franklin Delano Roosevelt, Champion of Freedom*, p. 127.

Pact, and the Four-Power Pact. The Nine-Power Pact guaranteed "the sovereignty, the independence, and the territorial and administrative integrity of China." This was an extension of American ideas behind the Open Door policies of the early 1900s. The Five-Power Pact established naval parity in capital ships by fixing a ratio of 5-5-3-1.75-1.75 for the largest seafaring powers respectively Britain, United States, Japan, France and Italy. These treaties were heralded throughout America as pacts to prevent or limit war. The Four-Power Pact preserved the status quo in the Pacific and was signed by Britain, United States, Japan, and France. The signatories agreed to respect each other's possessions and interests in the Far East and the island mandates. The rationale behind these pacts was that in limiting armaments, wars could be limited or avoided. FDR remained involved in Democratic politics often speaking about the need for government efficiency. This was a topic that attracted wide audiences as the 1920s were years of the businessman and burgeoning businesses. Progressive themes still played well especially with the Democrats speaking the lines. FDR often traveled by private railroad car this remained his favorite mode of traveling and future campaigning as he moved coast to coast.

FDR formed a law partnership with old friends, Grenville T. Emmett and Langdon P. Martin. The twenties of America were booming. In 1920 FDR accepted a position as vice president of Fidelity and Deposit Company of Maryland with a salary of $25,000 per year as head of the firm's New York office. Here he applied his knowledge of the Federal Reserve System learned in the Wilson administration to the world of banking and finance. He employed Marguerite LeHand called 'Missy' as his private secretary and she continued to work for FDR throughout most of his future career. He became friends with Van Lear Black who controlled the company and they sailed together on Lear's yacht, *Sabalo*. FDR invited Lear and friends to fish with him at his summer home on Campobello. The week before, FDR and Boy Scout Foundation supporters had journeyed on July 28, 1921 to Bear Mountain to visit the scout summer camp at Lake Kanowahke that had been erected there. "Roosevelt always enjoyed this sort of outing and encouraged many of the transplanted city boys as they displayed their newly acquired skills in the manly outdoors."[66] It was either at Bear Mountain or at Campobello that FDR contracted a dread disease that altered his life.

During the working vacation with Van Lear Black at Campobello that began on August 5, Franklin overworked as host. As his children and Eleanor were

---

[66] Black, *Franklin Delano Roosevelt, Champion of Freedom*, p. 135; Karl Schriftgiesser, *The Amazing Roosevelt Family, 1613-1942* (New York: W. Funk, 1942).

there, he spent extra time with the family swimming in cold waters of the Bay of Fundy. It was an exhausting experience and in a weakened condition, FDR contracted polio by August 9. His left leg seemed lax and limp. "I sat reading for a while, too tired to even dress….I tried to persuade myself that the trouble with my leg was muscular, that it would disappear as I used it. But presently it refused to work, and then the other," he confided. FDR's will and inner strength would be severely tested. There was "the grim moment when Roosevelt had to face the fact that he might be paralyzed for life."[67] There was "acute pain long after the actual infection passed." "The parts of his body that were mainly affected remained inflamed for months, and the inflammation and the inevitable muscular adjustments and distortions at first made even bed bound passivity near torture for him." When his own father James Roosevelt had been ill with heart problems, the young Franklin had always been careful to put on a smiling face, lest he disturb his father's health. Now FDR put on an ever-smiling face to ward off this catastrophe. As "from first to last and whether in public or in private—even with his wife and mother, his children and his nurses and doctors—he never failed to put a smiling, gallant front on his plight. In short, the disease revealed that he possessed a supply of sheer guts so large that even those closest to him were surprised and admiring." Eleanor called this period of his life his 'trial by fire'.[68] The whole experience she confided "gave him a strength and courage he had not had before" and he gathered "infinite patience and never-ending perseverance."[69] He had been diagnosed by Dr. Robert W. Lovett of Boston and Dr. George Draper treated FDR in New York. Franklin's friend from his legislative days Frances Perkins noted a "spiritual transformation" from which FDR "emerged completely warm-hearted, with humility of spirit and deeper philosophy." His political aide Louis Howe stuck with FDR as his choice of the man most worthy of becoming U.S. President.

Franklin, now forty, took health treatments at Warm Springs, Georgia and believed he might learn to walk again after the infantile paralysis had left his legs paralyzed. Exercise, spa treatments, and special diet all were used to improve his health. He bought an old hotel-spa and expanded it as a center to treat polio victims as well as himself. While swimming in the hot natural pools of Warm Springs he could slightly move his own legs due to the water's buoyancy supporting his upper body weight. The sailor, horseman, hiker now came to

---

[67] Frank Freidel, Franklin D. Roosevelt, A Rendezvous with Destiny, p. 41; Alsop, FDR, A Centenary Remembrance, p. 95.
[68] Eleanor Roosevelt, This is My Story (New York: Harper and Brothers, 1937), chapter 12.
[69] James Roosevelt and Sidney Shalett, Affectionately, FDR: A Son's Story of a Lonely Man (New York: Harcourt Brace, 1959), p. 158.

depend on others. He had a special car designed so he could drive without using pedals, using hand controls to work both the brake and the accelerator. This automobile gave him a degree of independence from his caretakers and he often drove friends on special rides. A light-weight wheel chair afforded him mobility around his home and offices. He invested $200,000 of his own money in renovating his Warm Springs hotel-spa facilities and visited them whenever he could. Later during his presidency the March of Dimes campaign would be established to fund polio research and support treatment facilities like the Warm Springs Foundation. Much later following his death his empty wheel chair was always present at the Foundation's meetings to remind people of the president's battle with polio. Yet his inner strength kept a smile on his face as he desired to move forward beyond his handicap and still achieve his dreams. Eleanor was a great aid and comfort to him as were the children. "Hence guts, rational optimism, and tough obstinacy about accepting defeat were added in full measure to Roosevelt's wiliness, his magical sense of political timing, and his remarkable astuteness" in dealing with life.[70] "Eventually he became at least partially reconciled to his continuing paralysis and learned to disguise it for public purposes by wearing heavy leg braces, supporting himself with a cane and the arm of a companion (usually a son), and using his hips to swing his inert legs forward. So effective was this deception (and so cooperative was the press in preserving it) that few Americans knew during his lifetime that he was largely confined to a wheelchair."[71] He adopted "an aggressive public geniality" and revealed only outward buoyancy. He strove mightily to regain the use of his legs now supported by fourteen pounds of steel braces that were clicked into place when he stood.

Polio made FDR pace himself. Eleanor and Louis Howe supported FDR's own resolve to resume his normal political career. Politics would sustain FDR in this crisis and boost his morale. Howe conducted a massive letter writing campaign to further develop FDR's political network, a strategy that had worked earlier during the 1912 campaign for re-election to the New York state senate. Eleanor joined the women's division of the state Democratic Party and soon became its leader, keeping the Roosevelt name before the public. After October 1922, FDR continued working at the Fidelity and Deposit firm through the goodwill of Van Lear Black to pay the bills. In 1923 he formed a law practice with Basil O'Connor in a building close to Fidelity and Deposit. He made several business investments in the 1920s most notably in a helium dirigible business flying between New York and Chicago, oil drilling, resort hotels, advertising in

---

[70] Alsop, FDR, A Centenary Remembrance, p. 96.
[71] Alan Brinkley, "Franklin Delano Roosevelt," in American National Biography. Edited by John A. Garraty and Mark C. Carnes, Vol. 18 (New York: Oxford University Press, 1999), p. 818.

taxicabs, selling products in vending machines, and operating fleets of coastal vessels. FDR remained interested in politics but was in no position to challenge Alfred E. Smith for the Governorship of New York in 1922 and hence made a virtue out of supporting his good friend and retaining the confidence and support of the New York Democrats. FDR served as president of the American Construction Council that worked as a trade association striving to promote efficiency. And the Roosevelt family continued its philanthropy with FDR serving on various charitable boards. When he could take the time away from the office, FDR had rented a houseboat in Florida in 1923, the *Weona II,* to restore his health and enjoy fishing before he bought the Warm Springs property. Here he began to build up his upper body so that he could catch fish from a revolving fishing chair without the use of a harness strap. From 1924-26 he fished and swam in the warm waters from his own houseboat, the *Larooco* purchased with business associate John S. Lawrence, but by 1927 had established the Warm Springs Foundation.

From 1922 to 1924 significant national events were to take place. The Republicans had cut taxes through the efforts of Andrew Mellon who believed high taxes sapped business incentives to expand production and create jobs. But with less tax revenues the federal government drastically cut social services and needed social programs. The tariff was raised in 1922 with the Fordney-McCumber Act protecting aluminum, chemicals, steel, machinery, locomotives, and hides and wool. When the economy would slow down, this high tariff policy restricted trade with disastrous consequences. Military budgets were reduced under Harding and his vice-president Coolidge, and veterans began to feel disenfranchised. The veterans had formed themselves into two powerful lobbies at the end of World War I—the Veterans' Administration and the American Legion. The Veterans' Administration was founded in 1921 and was devoted to vocational rehabilitation of wounded veterans. The American Legion had been formed in Paris in 1919 by Theodore Roosevelt, Jr. initially as a friendship society for all veterans who had fought for the Allies in World War I. The Legion lobbied in the 1920s for a bonus that was to represent the difference in wage they had received as combat soldiers and what they might have earned had they stayed at home and worked in wartime industries. This bonus was called 'adjusted compensation'. The Bonus Bill passed Congress in 1922 but was vetoed by Harding. It would have granted a veteran fifty dollars for each month of service. Another Bonus Bill, known as the Adjusted Compensation Act under which each soldier was to receive a paid-up insurance policy due in twenty years, was passed in 1924. This represented $1.25 for every day spent overseas and $1.00 for every day spent in home service. This was small compensation and would appear even niggardly by the Depression.

Another group who lost ground due to Harding's policies was the immigrant class. At war's end the U.S. had become isolationistic with the failure to ratify the Treaty of Versailles and non-entry into the League of Nations. In 1921 800,000 immigrants came to America seeking a better life from war torn Europe causing an outcry against 'alien' immigration. The Emergency Quota Act of 1921 regulated immigrants and stipulated that the number of new entries could total only 3% of their nationals living in the U.S. in 1920. Later the Immigration Act of 1924 cut the quota based on national origins to 2% and altered the year to 1890. This favored immigrants from northern Europe. All of these groups would continue to seek redress.

Calvin Coolidge became president upon the death of Harding on August 2, 1923. A former Governor of Massachusetts, Coolidge believed as president that "the business of America is business," and buoyed the materialism of the 1920s, pursuing it almost as a religious cult. From 1921 to 1929 the gross national product jumped from $74 billion to $104 billion and the buying power of wages rose by 50% between 1913 and 1927. Huge chain conglomerates replaced the Mom and Pop stores and Americans enjoyed themselves in the age of 'fords, flappers, and fanatics'. 'Pay as you ride', 'Pay as you go' blared the radio advertising. 'Installment buying' allowed consumers to 'enjoy as you pay' as it reached the six billion dollar per year level by 1929. Purchases on time accounted for 60 per cent of all auto sales by 1929, 70 per cent of all furniture sales, 80 per cent of all vacuum cleaners, radio, and refrigerator sales, and 90 per cent of all piano, sewing machine and washing machine sales. The output per man-hour in manufacturing industries almost doubled from 1909 to 1929, indicating growing efficiency. Capital accumulation was supported by reducing the public debt, lowering tax rates, raising a protective tariff, the fostering of trade associations within industry to enhance profit margins, and making foreign investments abroad. The Harding-Coolidge era would promote 'less government in business and more business in government' and attempted to turn back the clock on progressive reforms like trust-busting, conservation, and promoting social advances for workers. The Democrats and Republicans began to break apart on social philosophies with the Democrats retaining the mantle of the true reforming Progressives.

World War I had produced a crisis of rising expectations for American blacks. Between 1916 and 1923 approximately one million blacks migrated from the South to the North. In 1900 45% of Alabama's population was black; by 1930 blacks composed only 30% of the population in that state. During the war, blacks had entered the major industrial cities of New York, Detroit, Akron, Pittsburgh, and Chicago, attracted by expanded employment opportunities. As blacks left the

South there seemed to be a gradual relaxation of some of the black codes, but as they entered northern cities racial tensions increased. However, out of these conditions came a firm base for black nationalism and racial pride that emerged in the Harlem Renaissance of the 1920s. New York remained the most progressive state throughout the period between the wars.

Al Smith had won the Governorship of New York in 1922 with FDR's assistance and went on to seek the presidential nomination from the Democratic Party in 1924. At the Democratic Party's convention for the presidency at Madison Square Garden in New York FDR gave his famed nominating speech calling Al Smith the 'Happy Warrior'. Franklin Roosevelt had walked through the main floor of the convention on crutches, reached the podium, and faced the thunderous applause with his handsome smile, robust upper body, and keen political finesse. Al Smith as a 'wet', a Tammany Hall candidate, a Catholic, and reforming Governor of New York was challenged by William McAdoo, a 'dry', an anti-Tammany Hall candidate, a Protestant, and former Secretary of the Treasury under Woodrow Wilson. Neither of the two potential candidates could win the necessary two-thirds of the votes to secure the nomination and a compromise candidate, John W. Davis, a Wall Street lawyer and former ambassador to Great Britain, was selected. But the 'Happy Warrior' speech established FDR as a still shining star despite his polio. He had built secure bridges to both factions, the Smith and McAdoo groups, of the Democratic Party. He had shown that he could bring together white Anglo-Saxon Protestants, Jews, blacks, and Roman Catholics and spoke often of how bigotry was un-American. In the 1924 election, John W. Davis was defeated by Calvin Coolidge. Nevertheless, the Roosevelts had re-entered politics in a big way. The resplendent FDR was often mentioned as a future presidential contender. Eleanor had "turned the women's division of the New York Democratic Party into a powerhouse and, with Smith's assistance, secured the ability for the women to name their own delegates to the state convention."[72]

FDR had been chairman of the Citizens for Smith organization during the election and he had ably co-opted this organization. He had garnered the position as the "state's second most powerful Democrat" after Al Smith, who ran for a third term for the New York governorship in 1924 after he failed to receive the presidential nomination. Smith won the governorship over Eleanor's first cousin Ted Roosevelt, Jr. and Eleanor and some of her League friends had campaigned vigorously for Smith in a touring car decorated with a huge 'teapot' to remind voters of the Republican-Harding scandal involving the lease of public oil

---

[72] Black, Franklin Delano Roosevelt, Champion of Freedom, p. 161;

reserves at Teapot Dome, Wyoming. Both Roosevelts were riding high at the front of the Democratic Party. And instinctively Tom Pendergast, city boss of Kansas City, remarked after FDR's stellar performance at the 1924 nominating convention: "I predict he will be the candidate…in 1928," after labeling Franklin "the most magnetic personality of any individual I have ever met."[73] In 1924 Roosevelt's speech nominating Al Smith had been broadcast over the radio and his genial, beguiling, baritone voice reached out to people. He never relied upon his aristocratic Hyde Park background to communicate as he talked to people in words they could readily understand. "By the time he became president," in 1932, "it is arguable that Franklin Roosevelt understood the essence of the medium better than any political figure."[74] The radio and FDR as a seasoned politician came of age together. By the mid-twenties there were over six hundred radio stations throughout the country and three million radios sold.

From 1924 to 1928 FDR continued to gain greater strength both physically and politically. Franklin was named by Governor Smith to become chairman of the Taconic State Park Commission. Eleanor continued her League activities and the Roosevelts built a small cottage at Val Kill near Springwood that she could call her own. It was located on a creek and was dammed producing a pool for Franklin's swimming exercise. America saw a royal visit from the Prince of Wales in 1924 and FDR participated in the festivities. In 1925 the Scopes Trial in Dayton, Tennessee sparked the public's interest in the theory of evolution vs. religious fundamentalism. And Americans witnessed the first trans-Atlantic flight of Charles Lindbergh from New York to Paris in 1927, wildly cheered in both cities. Rosy Roosevelt, FDR's half brother, died in 1927 leaving Franklin a substantial inheritance that was used to improve the facilities at Warm Springs and educate his children. FDR had declined an invitation to run for the U.S. Senate from New York in 1926, preferring to wait for a bigger executive prize.

His prize would soon come. In 1928 Al Smith took up the banner once again to run for the presidency and this time won the Democratic nomination. Once again FDR spoke at this Democratic convention and nominated Al Smith after walking to the speaker's rostrum with only a cane and the assistance of his son. He was back and had not been felled by infantile paralysis. His voice remained resonant. He and Howe had arranged with photographers and newsreel cameramen not to take pictures of FDR emerging from automobiles or other transport before he had stood up and his braces were locked into place. FDR would simple say, 'No movies of me getting out of the machine, boys' and his

---

[73] Black, *Franklin Delano Roosevelt, Champion of Freedom*, p. 166.
[74] Russell D. Buhite and David W. Levy, eds., *FDR's Fireside Chats* (New York: Penguin Books, 1992), p. xiv.

request was honored. The public saw only FDR's robust upper body and winning smile thanks to this journalist understanding. At the convention held in Houston, Texas, FDR called Al Smith "a pathfinder, a blazer of the trail to the high road that will avoid the bottomless morass of crass materialism." "I offer one who has the will to win, who not only deserves success but commands it. Victory is his habit—the happy warrior of the political battlefield—Alfred E. Smith."[75] Smiling FDR was back in the game. He was more appealing, riveting, and commanding than ever before as the *Chicago Tribune* called FDR the last of the 'silver tongues'. He could just as easily have been talking about himself as the 'Happy Warrior' and no doubt many listeners made the comparison. Doors opened to FDR as the Democrats begged him to now run for governor of New York, the post vacated by Al Smith in his bid for the presidency against Republican Herbert Hoover. Being governor was the job FDR had always wanted. He had maintained his friendships with peoples of all colors and religions and his close circle included Felix Frankfurter, Samuel I. Rosenman, Bernard Baruch, Joseph P. Kennedy, John L. Lewis, William Jennings Bryan, and James Michael Curley. Al Smith urged him to enter the race, believing FDR would continue his reform policies. Franklin and Eleanor were aided in their decision that Franklin should run for Governor of New York by the assistance of Smith's campaign manager John J. Raskob who had made a fortune with Du Pont and General Motors. Raskob made an offer to assist the Roosevelts with the development of Warm Springs, and Franklin accepted Smith's urging to enter the race. FDR plunged into the contest hopeful of winning the position that he coveted so much in his home state, knowing it to be a significant stepping stone on the way to the presidency. He had been nominated by acclamation, his Party showing their affection and enthusiastic support. While focusing on America's domestic scene and planning for the national convention and his own election, FDR never lost sight of foreign affairs. He had commented upon the Kellogg-Briand pact that outlawed war as an instrument of national policy in an article he wrote for *Foreign Affairs* that he widely circulated. This pact he wrote "leads to a false belief in America that we have taken a great step forward. It does not contribute in any way to settling matters of international controversy."[76]

Al Smith lost the presidential election to Herbert Hoover. But to the Roosevelts' delight, FDR became governor of New York, and could now forward progressive reforms. He was inaugurated on January 1, 1929 in the Assembly room of the state capitol, taking his oath of office on a Dutch Bible, a family

---

[75] Black, Franklin Delano Roosevelt, Champion of Freedom, p. 179.
[76] Foreign Affairs, VI (July 1928): 585.

heirloom.[77] Al Smith welcomed the Roosevelts to the Executive Mansion saying "A thousand welcomes. We've got the home fires burning and you'll find this a fine place to live." They celebrated over dinner with Smith pledging his support for the new governor. FDR had won over the Republican challenger Albert Ottinger who had served as Attorney General of New York. FDR had promised cleaner government, an end to corruption, lower tariffs, regulation of business, and efficient use of public revenues gathered through taxes. He wished to end the Poor Laws and Poor Houses in New York, introducing instead old-age pensions. Currying favor with Jews and Blacks, he promised everywhere to end bigotry, and lobbied for an eight-hour work-day and a forty-eight hour work week with safeguards for women and children in industry. His earlier campaign support for Al Smith brought most Catholics to the Democratic camp. Franklin's campaign team included all his old friends and many new ones. They included Edward J. Flynn, a political organizer from the Bronx, who served as secretary of state, Louis Howe his campaign organizer, and Raymond Moley a member of the National Crime Commission and Columbia political science professor. They were joined by James A. Farley, a top organizer of the Democratic State Committee, Henry Morgenthau, Jr., a long-time farmer friend from Hyde Park, and William Woodin a banker. His immediate team was rounded out with Samuel I. Rosenman who worked as a lawyer, and Maurice Bloch as a party leader in the New York Assembly. FDR's lieutenant governor was Herbert Lehman who would fill in when Roosevelt went to Warm Springs. He appointed his long-time friend from the settlement house days and the Investigating Commission that had looked into the Triangle Shirtwaist fire, Frances Perkins, as his industrial commissioner and head of the New York Labor Department. She, like FDR, pressed for workingmen's compensation, a shorter work-week, and a minimum wage level. Perkins reactivated the Bureau of Women in Industry and continued her fight for protective legislation to safeguard working women and children. She brought all the moral indignation from her investigative days to bear on social reform in New York. This team put together to assist the Governor of New York would continue with him later to the New Deal years of the presidency. Having secured his goal with his 1928 victory, Franklin and Eleanor determined to carve out their own political territory, breaking new ground in Albany rather than shadowing the former Smith administration. Franklin determined never to be a mere figurehead for the Smith interests on the state level. Showing his independence immediately, FDR let go two of Smith's closest advisors, Robert Moses and Mrs. Belle Moskowitz, and this move began a break between FDR and Smith. They

---

[77] Morgan, FDR, A Biography, p. 298.

gradually would become political rivals with FDR challenging his former mentor. But Smith was generous during the transition and advised Franklin "to devote that intelligent mind of yours to the problems of this state."[78] This FDR would certainly do, and Eleanor continued her work with the League of Women Voters and the Democratic State Committee. Eleanor worked with Frances Perkins, head the New York State Department of Labor, as like FDR they shared a social conscience and concern for the less fortunate.[79] FDR protectively supported women and their causes of reform, especially better working conditions for women and children. He also urged his wife to make political speeches and appearances on his behalf and had Howe coach her in delivery. On January 18, 1922, FDR realized the voting power of women and wrote Caroline O'Day, leader of the women's division of the New York Democratic Party, saying, "Get the right kind of women in every election district in the various rural counties....Democratic women...should let the world and their neighbors know they take great pride in their Party." Eleanor Roosevelt would mobilize women on FDR's behalf. She introduced him to the leading political women of the day including Rose Schneiderman, associated with the Women's Trade Union League and other progressive Democrats associated with the plight of urban workers. In addition to recruiting able women, FDR paid a great deal of attention to farming issues in upstate New York to build the Democratic Party north of the City.

The period of FDR as governor of New York encompassed the end of the Roaring Twenties and the first three and a half years of the Depression. But long before the bubble burst in the Stock Market, FDR was laying the groundwork for social progressive reforms throughout his state. He capitalized upon his farming roots in New York and sought to bind the upstate farmers firmly to his Democratic chariot. Working with his friend and neighbor Henry Morgenthau, Jr. Governor Franklin D. Roosevelt established an Agricultural Commission to recommend solutions to farming problems. He had paid attention to rural districts of New York because there were more farmers in his state than in Kansas and he readily identified with their concerns as a gentleman farmer himself at Springwood. As Governor he substituted a gasoline tax as a revenue source and reduced taxes on farming property by 20 per cent. He sought means to reduce electricity costs to the consumer and changed the tax laws to benefit the public. True to his earlier ideas involving the production of public power, he proposed that the state purchase properties and build power generating facilities. Moreover, "he specifically threatened that New York State would go into the power

---

[78] New York Times, New York Herald, and New York World, 2/1/1929.
[79] Morgan, FDR, A Biography, p. 127.

transmission business if the private sector tried to overcharge as a distributor of publicly owned and generated power."[80] He strove to lower prices for electricity at a time when the average family's electrical bill in New York City was $17.50 compared to $3.00 in Ontario, Canada. And his proposal was immensely popular with the average citizen. He might be 'high-bred' but he was a man of people.

FDR's initiatives attracted a wide non-partisan following including Senator George W. Norris of Nebraska. In *Forum* magazine FDR promoted the development of hydroelectric power in Colorado, Tennessee, and the St. Lawrence through a partnership between state and federal agencies. And his policies attempted to emulate the production of public power in Ontario, Canada and force a 'Republican surrender' on this question. Following up on a campaign promise, FDR established a commission on Old Age Pensions and allowed tax incentives for homes that cared for the elderly. He also promoted new hospital construction. He desired to develop Sarasota Springs in New York as a spa-health resort that would benefit the aged and infirm. "Public health…is a responsibility of the state," he said, "as was the duty to promote the general welfare."[81] He tried his hand at prison reform, encouraging smaller facilities and larger work programs on construction projects in the open air. FDR wished that prohibition would be rethought as its evasion obviously contributed to crime. From these policies, FDR earned the reputation of being a progressive and able administrator. He was rewarded with honorary degrees from Harvard, Dartmouth and Fordham. Will Rogers believed that FDR's efforts assured him a chance at the presidential bid in 1932.

True to his campaign pledge to sweep New York clean of corruption, FDR sought to control and bring Mayor of New York City James J. Walker into his reform camp. He placed Felix Frankfurter at the head of a Public Service Investigations Committee. Building on the successes of the early progressives in public utilities control, this committee was able to reduce telephone rates, a feat much applauded by New Yorkers. In both writing and speaking FDR was constantly promoting policies to benefit all citizens not just the advantaged. In a July 4th speech to Tammany Hall, he prophetically warned that the "liberty" of all needed protection against "highly centralized industrial control."[82] He feared the

---

[80] Black, Franklin Delano Roosevelt, Champion of Freedom, p. 191; Franklin D. Roosevelt Library, Hyde Park, New York, Governor Office File, letters to James C.. Bonbright (12/10/1929) and to L. David (5/12/1929). Samuel I. Rosenman, Public Papers and Addresses of Franklin D. Roosevelt (New York: Random House, 1938) Vol 1 "The Genesis of the New Deal" contains papers on FDR's relations as Governor of New York with the state's public utilities between 1928 and 1932, especially pages 233-263.

[81] New York Times, 30/12/1928.

[82] Black, Franklin Delano Roosevelt, Champion of Freedom, p. 194.

disparity between the rich and poor. He openly wondered at how high the stock market would go and whether or not it could continue to rise beyond its dizzy heights. His policies sought to bring everyone into the economic boom not just the feudalistic descendants of the robber barons. Building upon the TR-Wilson Progressive tradition, FDR sought to 'progress' through efficient channels, safeguarding the public's interest, and liberty and equality were to be protected by the state. Governor Franklin toured his state widely, making certain that he was well recognized and he showed concern for every constituency. During the summer of 1929 FDR toured New York's inland waterway aboard the *Inspector,* traveling from Albany to Buffalo, through Lake Ontario and into the St. Lawrence and eventually down the Hudson. Everywhere he was greeted by well-wishers as the Governor tapped into the public's needs, inspected facilities, and heard from local politicians. FDR immensely enjoyed these trips and his entourage was always greeted with his private car wherever he disembarked. Outside and inside the Governor's Albany office, he was an excellent listener, the mark of a truly genuine politician, and gave each person he met his undivided attention. Whenever FDR could not make these excursions due to his pressing work schedule he sent Eleanor who visited hospitals, schools and universities, philanthropic, political and civic organizations, old aged homes, and prisons with her security person Earl Miller.[83] Eleanor acted as his 'eyes and ears', reporting her findings and she began to immensely enjoy these political forays into the community. To garner support for his policies FDR cleverly used radio addresses to educate the public, appearing on a state-wide radio show once a month to discuss issues. The Democrats set up a special fund for a publicity bureau to further educate the public and counter the views of Republican controlled newspapers. In the capacity of governor FDR learned how to initiate policies and how to have them passed by the state legislature. On the national level, it was assumed that the Congress would initiate policies, but that would certainly change during the New Deal when FDR became "the proposer and maker of new laws— the formulator of public policy."[84]

FDR had met Woodrow Wilson in 1911 when Wilson was Governor of New Jersey and endeavored during his own period as New York Governor to emulate and surpass his political mentor. "They had much in common," FDR "thought— they had fought the political machines of their respective states, and they both wanted a reform in party nominating methods, a regulation of business abuses, and the conservation of natural resources." Wilson had secured as Governor "a

---

[83] Frank Freidel, FDR: The Triumph (Boston: Little, Brown, 1956), p. 80.
[84] Buhite and Levy, eds., FDR's Fireside Chats, p. ix.

direct primary law, a public utilities commission with rate-setting powers, a corrupt-practices law, an employer's liability law" that "was a lesson in leadership" that had propelled him toward the presidency.[85] FDR used the Governorship of New York in precisely the same manner and rose to even greater heights because of the challenges of the Depression. In true reforming style, FDR gained control of lump-sum appropriations in the state budget, allowing the governor rather than the legislature to determine how the money was spent in detail. He struggled with the New York legislature to wrest away control. "The difficulty which I constantly feel," wrote Roosevelt, "is that the moment I make any recommendation or even try to get together with them, they take the angle that to accede or even meet me half way would be to hand me some kind of political credit, and that in order to avoid this, the only method is to turn down every proposal which emanates from this Executive Chamber."[86] FDR won control over the budget through a decision in the Court of Appeals. "That is what I call batting one hundred percent," commented Maurice Bloch. Thus, FDR greatly extended the powers of the executive branch and had "gone to the mat for a principle." FDR had built Attica prison and changed penal laws to humanize prison reform. He had recommended new laws to offer security to the elderly, and with Frances Perkins passed workmen's compensation laws and drafted legislation to prohibit medical fraud and malpractice. The bi-partisan progressivism of both TR and Woodrow Wilson lived comfortably on through the energies of FDR as Governor of New York.

In 1928 as FDR had become governor of New York, nationally, Herbert Hoover had taken office on March 4, 1929 as president and the public expected his administration to be a notable one. After all he had entered the White House as a Quaker, Iowa born, orphaned at a young age but had made his own way in the world through 'rugged individualism' to become a graduate of Stanford University majoring in mining engineering. He worked internationally in Canada, Australia, Mexico, India, China and Russia, and amassed a modest fortune. During World War I he had worked with President Wilson as head of the American Relief Committee and later as chief of the Belgian Relief Committee. He had worked for both Democratic and Republican presidents serving as Secretary of Commerce for Wilson, Harding and Coolidge. His book *Rugged Individualism* had perfectly captured the spirit of the times and at one time he

---

[85] Morgan, FDR, A Biography, p. 137; Ray Stannard Baker, Woodrow Wilson: Life and Letters 8 vols. (New York: Doubleday, 1927-1939); Arthur S. Link, Wilson 5 vols. (Princeton, NJ: Princeton University Press, 1947-1965); John Milton Cooper, Jr., The Warrior and the Priest: Woodrow Wilson and Theodore Roosevelt (Cambridge, Mass: Harvard University Press, 1983).
[86] Morgan, FDR, A Biography, pp. 300-301.

could have been nominated for president from either party. He had won the presidency with 444 electoral votes to 37 for Al Smith. But with the onset of the Great Depression the Republicans led by Hoover suffered one of the greatest debacles in history and the reversal of political fortunes as he was blamed for a national economy that spiraled downward. FDR was fortunately there as a reform governor of New York to pick up the nation and lead America to new heights through the New Deal. Ironically FDR had predicted what was to happen politically, insisting that the Republicans would not be turned out of the presidency while wages remained high and business was booming. He believed the conservative 1920s were a natural cycle of history following a major war, but knew that when the economy turned downward the nation would again elect a Democrat to lead. As Governor he sensed that a period of depression and unemployment was coming.

The Great Depression had its roots in the agricultural recession that reduced the farmer's purchasing power and limited the demand for new farm machinery. This slow down in the mid-West was coupled with technological unemployment in urban areas. During the 1920s from two to four million individuals were willing and able to work but could not find jobs even in the years of peak prosperity. Like the farmer, this group obviously could not consume on such a high level as those who were employed. Over-production, the farm problem, under consumption, the urban unemployed problem, and the concentration of income and wealth were all aspects of the same essential dilemma in the 1920s. It pointed to an inadequate distribution of wealth. One percent of the population in America in 1929 controlled sixty percent of the wealth, and thirteen percent controlled ninety percent of the wealth. Twenty percent of the nation was composed of families earning less than $1,000 a year and without savings. The growth of monopolies in America further restricted flexibility in the price structure, as the conglomerates tended to keep the prices high and stable in spite of decreasing purchasing power within segments of the society. By 1929, two hundred corporations controlled nearly half of the nation's industrial assets. Four tobacco companies controlled the manufacture, distribution and sale of ninety percent of all cigarettes sold; and three automobile corporations, General Motors, Ford, and Chrysler, controlled ninety percent of the industry's production. Productivity raced ahead of buying power.

A concentration of capital and monopolistic control was also taking place on an international scale as America pioneered the international cartel. DuPont, U.S. Steel, Westinghouse, General Electric, and Anaconda Copper were some of the major American firms which had joined with firms in other nations, especially in Western Europe, for the erection of monopolies which controlled markets, divided the world market into areas wherein certain firms would hold a monopoly, and exchanged patent information to keep abreast of the latest inventions. These cartels kept prices and profits high at a time when domestic reduced buying power was becoming a serious problem. Mass consumption was being restricted in an era that had thrived on an expanding post World War I market. Within the total national income, too large a proportion was going to profits and dividends, and too little to farm income, wages, and salaries. Moreover, during the late 1920s income which accumulated in the coffers of the rich tended to be either saved (which restricted consumption) or used for speculation on the stock market (which inflated stock prices), rather than for the expansion of the industrial plant. Prosperity depended upon high levels of consumption that did not keep pace with ever increasing productivity or speculation. Even before 1929, inventories increased and goods began piling up in warehouses, not because households did not wish for them, but because they lacked the where-with-all to purchase them. These circumstances, coupled with the prevailing governmental policies, would serve to deepen the depression when it occurred. A final cause of the Great Depression, related to the immediate circumstance, the Stock Market Crash, which precipitated recession was the over-extension of credit. From 1920 to 1929, there was an increase in indebtedness in the economy from $76 to $126 billion. State and local governments had gone into debt promoting local improvements such as hard-surface roads, bridges, and public schools. There was an over expansion in public utilities as the career and pyramid structure of Samuel Insull illustrated. The real estate market was overextended as the Florida land booms and busts depicted. And participation of the general public in stock market speculation through the idea of buying on margin (which required only 10 percent of the value of the stock down for purchase) represented the fact that their financial success depended upon the continual upward advance of the economy and the advance of the stock market. Buying on margin was a system by which credit for the purchase of stocks was provided by stockbrokers. The investor could repay the loan from his profits as the stock price rose. But when the price of the stock went down, the small investor was often cut short and unable to make his payments. The total amount of broker's loans increased from $3 billion to $8.5 billion between 1927 and 1929. Historically, there seemed reason and justification for speculation, as in a period of eighteen months from March, 1928 to September, 1929 Westinghouse stock rose from 92 to 313, General Electric from 130 to 400, and American Telephone and Telegraph from 130 to 300. These blue-chip stocks were seen as measuring rods for continuing climb. Suddenly however the market turned downward on Thursday, October 24, 1929. Small traders whose margins were due lost their stock if they could not pay. Many began selling in fear. From 9 a.m. to noon U.S. radio fell 75 points and General Electric fell 32.

The New York Times described Black Thursday and then Tragic Tuesday, October 29, 1929:

> "WORST STOCK CRASH STEMMED BY BANKS, 12,894,650-Share Day Swamps Market, Leaders Confer, Find Conditions Sound- The most disastrous decline in the biggest and broadest stock market of history rocked the financial district yesterday. In the very midst of the collapse five of the country's most influential bankers hurried to the office of J.P. Morgan and Company, and after a brief conference gave out word that they believe the foundations of the market to be sound, that the market smash has been caused by technical rather than fundamental considerations, and that many sound stocks are selling too low . . . The break was one of the widest in the market's history . . . It carried down with it speculators, big and little, in every part of the country, wiping out thousands of accounts . . . The total losses were staggering. . . running into billions of dollars. . . ."[87]

The New York Times of October 30, 1929 ran an article on the downward spiral of the economy:

> "STOCKS COLLAPSE IN 16,410,030-Share Day, But Rally At Close Cheers Brokers. Stock prices virtually collapsed yesterday, swept downward with gigantic losses in the most disastrous trading day in the stock market's history. Billions of dollars in open market values were wiped out as prices crumbled under the pressure of liquidation of securities which had to be sold at any price...It was estimated that 880 issues, on the New York Stock Exchange, lost between $8,000,000,000 and $9,000,000,000 yesterday....Groups of men, with here and there a woman, stood about inverted glass bowls all over the city yesterday watching spools of ticker tape unwind and as the tenuous paper with its cryptic numerals grew longer at their feet their fortunes sank...."[88]

"Be a bull on America," people had cried before the stock market crash, "Never sell the United States short," they had heralded. But after the end of October 1929, the boom was over. Traditional financial policies still prevailed, and perhaps this is really what promoted the Great Depression—the refusal to change quickly those policies which had restricted mass consumption and those mechanisms which had artificially controlled the market, not allowing supply and

---

[87] New York Times, October 29, 1929, p. 1.
[88] New York Times, October 30, 1929, p. 1.

demand to set world prices. Farmer indebtedness, over production, under consumption, monopolistic tendencies, and the unequal distribution of wealth all combined in their effects to produce the quickest recession and worst depression the world had ever seen. "The country," Coolidge had conveyed to Congress in 1928, "can regard the present with satisfaction, and anticipate the future with optimism." Yet, at the end of the decade many Americans wondered what the light of a new day would bring. Many looked back upon the 1920s with a strange admixture of fond nostalgia and repentance. Whether or not America lost her vigor, idealism, and innocence when she tasted disaster remained to be seen. FDR as Governor of New York believed "that there is a duty on the part of the government to do something about this."[89] He began to initiate legislation that would correct some of the Depression's hardships and often appealed over the heads of recalcitrant lawmakers if they dragged their feet in passing needed bills. Frances Perkins became an ardent supporter of FDR to run for the U.S. presidency and openly criticized Hoover for his inept policies. She persuaded Governor Roosevelt to establish a Committee on the Stabilization of Industry for the Prevention of Unemployment and sought legislation to guarantee unemployment insurance. FDR had selected his administrators carefully and acted as a wise coach of his successful team. By the time FDR was elected president of the United States in 1932, Endicott Peabody at Groton wrote: "It is a great thing for our country to have before it the leadership of a man who cares primarily for spiritual things. At a time when the minds of men are distraught and their faith unsteady, a spiritual leader at the head of the nation brings fresh power to the individual and to the Cause of Christ and His Church." In his politics FDR would incorporate the ideals of the Social Gospel. While at Harvard President Eliot had addressed FDR's freshman class saying: "A course of study should be only long enough to win power; the sooner you begin to use it, the better."[90] By this Peabody meant gaining power through merit to do good. Franklin Delano Roosevelt would assume the mantle of the presidency and restore the themes of Christian charity and apply his political savvy learned from Groton, Harvard, and Progressive mentors.

---

[89] Brinkley, "Franklin Delano Roosevelt," in American National Biography, p. 818.
[90] Morgan, FDR, A Biography, p. 73.

Chapter 3

FROM NEW YORK GOVERNOR TO U.S. PRESIDENT

Banking was a serious matter to Franklin D. Roosevelt. During the summer before the Stock Market crash in October 1929 Governor Roosevelt had established an investigative commission to police New York banks. He appointed Joseph A. Broderick superintendent of banks and took measures to prop up the Bank of the United States' branches operating in New York. "Roosevelt's commission did recommend the regulation of private banks, which the 1930 legislative session put into law."[91] " 'The new legislation is wonderful,' Broderick wrote the governor, 'it gives us even greater responsibility than we dreamed of'." Following the Stock Market Crash FDR held a private meeting to save the Bank of the United States. " 'I reached out,' said FDR. 'I sent for Morgan and I sent for several of the other great bankers in this state and city. I told them, in the privacy of my own room, that this would be a frightful thing, that this was little people. I wanted them to come to the rescue of that bank. At that time my commissioner was ready to move in and close that bank, but each time he proposed it I got a statement that these men were considering saving the bank." But FDR's efforts could not save the bank and it failed. "It was the worst bank failure in the nation's history." On December 10, 1929 " there was a run on the bank, with 15,000 depositors lined up in the rain, and the next day Broderick closed it." Thousands lost their life savings. FDR pressed the legislature for more bank regulation. He was willing to compromise and make concessions to secure necessary ends.

---

[91] Ted Morgan, FDR: A Biography (New York: Simon and Schuster, 1985), p. 306; Clarence Cramer, American Enterprise: Free and Not So Free (Boston: Little, Brown and Company, 1972); William E. Leuchtenburg, Franklin D. Roosevelt and the New Deal (New York: Harper and Row, 1963).

Nationally 5,000 banks would collapse by 1933 and one wage earner in four lost their jobs. Yet FDR attacked the depression head on with winning solutions and bipartisan cures. He never ceased to attempt to make a political enemy a friend to achieve essential goals in his governorship. FDR's sunny confidence shone like a bright star during the harshest days of the depression. Securities sold on the New York Stock Exchange continued to plummet until 1933 when they had lost half their 1929 value. Additionally America's farming sector collapsed with piles of surplus crops left unsold. Workers by 1933 earned half of what they had collectively earned before October 1929. But FDR began finding workable programs by 1932-33.

His charm and savvy became legendary as he built Jones Beach and public parkways. He delved into hydroelectric power production, purged Republican chairman William A. Prendergast from his leadership of the Public Service Commission and appointed Milo Maltbie in February 1931 in his place. Maltbie became the "people's champion" and pursued FDR's dream of state produced public power. FDR urged more state government in this formerly private sector. "The state," he believed "had the absolute right not only to regulate [gas, electricity, and street cars]…but also to give or deny them the rights to charters except on terms laid down by the state. The Public Service Commission had been created to supervise the utilities, but gradually it began to see itself more as a court and the utilities as normal corporations." FDR believed the private power companies operating in New York gouged the public, and insisted "that New York State should return to the theory of granting only a reasonable return on investment."[92] "Roosevelt came to see the utilities magnates as selfish and unprincipled men." FDR appointed a state Power Authority to "study the feasibility of harnessing the waters of the St. Lawrence River for electric power. Water from the Great Lakes flowed into the St. Lawrence and escaped into Canada and emptied into the Gulf of St. Lawrence and the Atlantic Ocean. The thought of all this vast untapped and wasted power chafed at his constructivist side. It was a grandiose scheme." A successful project would involve a treaty with Canada "but President Hoover was not going to be rushed into a project that would benefit his chief political rival." FDR's national reputation was greatly enhanced by his proposal of this scheme to produce cheap public power. He became the champion of the people who challenged his own class. He articulated the desires of the populace during the Depression and sensed their dissatisfaction with Hoover. He wanted to be part of the great American destiny to achieve great

---

[92] Morgan, FDR: A Biography, pp. 313-314; Carl N. Degler, Out of Our Past, New York: Harper and Row, 1970; Caroline Bird, The Invisible Scar (New York: Pocket Books, 1967).

ends. He instilled hope amidst despair, attempting to work things out. Improvising was his tool; historical eminence his quest. "It was that the governor was seen as a savior, and that people constantly wrote him asking to be saved, from unemployment, from injustice, from deportation or jail or discharge, from all the disappointments of life."[93] "To the hundreds of requests for jobs a form letter replied that they could not be dealt with individually. For begging letters there was also a standard reply." The Hoover administration refused to establish a federal public works to provide jobs and income. In September 1930 England went off the gold standard. Numerous foreign investors sold their U.S. stocks and took money out of the country. Deposits became smaller and more banks failed. The world economy spiraled downward. "The new Empire State Building could not rent its offices and cut off elevator service between the forty-second and sixty-seventh floors."

Yet there was sunshine amidst the darkness of the early Depression in New York. "There was a unique atmosphere in Albany under Roosevelt, an 'elan, a sense of largess and potentiality. It radiated so strongly from his buoyant personality that it cast a kind of glow. People were affected by a man who was performing well in his position and also proceeding with seeming effortlessness toward a larger destiny." Everywhere he went he spread cheerfulness and confidence that solutions to economic problems would soon be found. The 'stiff upper lip', sense of fair play, and America's especial destiny were all trumpeted to good effect. He oversaw a New York state budget of $311 million and knew where every dollar was going. FDR used the press to persuade and cajole, spreading affable well being. Eleanor was a great help to him and remained in Albany in the executive mansion at least four days a week. On the other days she taught school at the Todhunter School, and oversaw her small furniture and weaving businesses administered out of Val Kill and Hyde Park. Louis Howe acted as chief of the governor's staff, and Missy LeHand and Samuel Rosenman assisted FDR greatly. FDR was able to place himself in the position of others and his generous sense of empathy drove him to achieve great ends as governor of New York.

Franklin Delano Roosevelt won re-election as Governor of New York in November 1930 defeating Republican Charles H. Tuttle who had served as New York City's district attorney. This election had proved to be a reaffirmation that FDR's policies were working to solve many of New York's problems started by the Depression. It also underscored that Governor Roosevelt, despite his physical

---

[93] Morgan, FDR: A Biography, pp. 315-318; John Kenneth Galbraith, The Great Crash (Boston: Houghton Mifflin, 1955); Eric Goldman, Rendezvous With Destiny (New York: Vintage, 1955).

infirmities, was eligible for higher political office, including a run for the presidency in the future. FDR focused on economic issues, especially on aid to farmers in upstate New York, and carried the majority of the voters who were concerned with securing a 'chicken in every pot' and an adequate dinner table spread. Hoover's secretaries Henry Stimson, Ogden Mills, and Patrick Hurley were sent to aid the Republican cause but FDR's rhetoric chased them back to Washington, D.C. "'I say to these gentlemen: we shall be grateful if you return to your posts in Washington, and bend your efforts and spend your time solving the problems which the whole Nation is bearing under your Administration. Rest assured that we of the Empire State can and will take care of ourselves and our problems'."[94] This election that FDR won by 725,000 votes validated his policies of state intervention in the economy to aid the indigent. Tuttle's Hooverism had proved unpopular and unbelievable to New Yorkers demanding that the economy be fixed first and foremost before all other issues. Carrying the upstate farmers would translate to farm support on the national level by 1932 as FDR remained their champion coming from a gentleman farming background himself. Through his farming friends he cultivated the South and the West, tapping additional political allies.

Meanwhile on the federal level President Herbert Hoover had great difficulty coping with the Depression. Rugged individualism, self reliance, and pulling one's self up by the bootstraps was the American way of life during the days of the frontier through the 1920s. Hoover believed that government interference in the economy was un-American and would destroy economic individualism. But by the winter of 1931 more than 25% of the U.S. work force had lost their jobs and people clamored for government relief. Hoovervilles appeared—"a community of shacks with walls made from grocery cartons smoothed flat, roofs of hammered-out tin cans, and door hinges cut from worn-out tires, rising in the excavations of unbuilt apartment houses."[95] America had entered the lean years. The Depression was a severely painful experience for millions of Americans in the 1930s. It threatened the very foundations of capitalism and democracy, uprooted families, and challenged the idealism long felt by Americans that America was somehow different from the rest of the world. A large part of the nation learned what it was like to be poor. Misery found its way into every ethnic group, every region, and every occupation. The chronic problem of under

---

[94] Morgan, FDR: A Biography, p. 327.
[95] Morgan, FDR: A Biography., p. 320; Robert S. McElvaine, The Depression and the New Deal: A History in Documents (New York: Oxford University Press, 2000); George T. McJimsey, Documentary History of the Franklin D. Roosevelt Presidency (Bethesda, MD: University Publications of America, 2001).

consumption spiraled the economy downward; industries found themselves with mounting inventories and in turn closed factories and laid off workers causing purchasing power to shrink further. Poverty became a way of life for 40 million Americans as laid off workers roamed the streets sleeping under Hoover 'blankets'- old newspapers. By 1933 the number of unemployed would mount to between 13 and 15 million and the unemployed had approximately 30 million mouths to feed besides their own. Automobile output shrank from 4.5 million units in 1929 to 1.1 million by 1933 and hourly wages had dropped 60 percent and white-collar salaries had dropped 40 percent. People lost their homes, their farms, their possessions, and wandered the streets in search of bread lines and soup kitchens. Farmers struggled to keep their feet as the price of cotton plummeted to 5 cents a pound, and 50 cents for a bushel of wheat, and were knocked down further by floods, droughts, plagues, and dust storms. Sharecroppers drifted north, plodding from city to city in search of a job or a bread line. Ragged bands of youths prowled the countryside sleeping in hobo jungles or riding trains west in search of meager work or handouts. "I remember lying in bed one night and thinking," said one depression victim in Chattanooga, Tennessee, "All at once I realized something. We were poor.... It was weeks before I could get over that."[96] As purchasing power dwindled, the financial system cracked as nationally 1,300 banks had closed their doors in 1930.

'Let the slump liquidate the unproductive farmers', said former Secretary of the Treasury Andrew Mellon, but President Hoover rejected this laissez-faire advice. Hoover tried to restore public confidence, saying the economy was basically healthy and that the depression was an aberration; prosperity was 'just around the corner'. Hoover's program for ending the depression evolved slowly from 1929 through 1932. In addition to cooperative action by businessmen to maintain prices and wages, Hoover called for tax cuts to increase consumption, for public works programs to stimulate production, lower interest rates to allow business to expand, and banking measures which would allow the farmers to borrow money at lower rates. Through the Agricultural Marketing Act of June 1929, Hoover had established the Federal Farm Board that was authorized to buy farm surpluses and therefore raise the prices that the farmer received for his crops. But the president refused to adopt policies that would limit production or establish acreage controls. The Federal Farm Board paid out hundreds of millions of dollars without halting sliding farm prices because the farmers increased production faster than the board could buy surpluses for disposal abroad. Farmers believed

---

[96] Ezra Bowen, ed, This Fabulous Century, 1930-1940, Vol. IV (New York: Time-Life Books, 1970), p. 46.

FDR understood their situation better than Hoover who had been a mining engineer.[97]

In 1932 Hoover's administration established the Reconstruction Finance Corporation which was an agency for making loans to banks, railroads, and insurance companies. But this money was to be repaid once businesses regained their strength; these loans were not gifts but commercial transactions and were restricted in their ability to promote recovery. Hoover believed in balancing the budget and governmental reduction in expenditures that made the Depression worse. Prosperity should not be restored by raids on the public Treasury, believed Hoover, as he voiced support for the rigors of rugged individualism rather than federal subsidies. Hoover advocated that the individual states should shoulder the burden of finding solutions and relief, and largely pay for their own programs. FDR as Governor of New York rose magnificently to this challenge and mandate to find workable solutions.

Hoover could be criticized however for not realizing that the Depression's domestic cures were tied to European economies. In 1930 Congress passed the Hawley-Smoot Tariff which raised duties on most European manufactured items to prohibitive levels. The effect of this tariff, which was protested by over a thousand leading economists, was to raise prices at a time when prices should have dropped, limited American exports at a time when the United States needed to sell inventories and farm products abroad, encouraged inefficient small businesses to stay in business, and generated reprisals from the European countries that raised their tariffs in retaliation. This tariff made it impossible for the European nations to earn the dollars needed to continue their World War I reparations and war debt payments. This United States policy helped to bring about a financial collapse in Europe in 1931 and Hoover was forced to issue a moratorium on all international debt obligations. The tariff also made currency devaluation almost inevitable in Europe and the depression itself curtailed foreign investment.

While Hoover's dire political course was proving inadequate, Governor FDR held a new vision. "'What is the state?' Roosevelt asked in his 1931 message to an extraordinary session of the legislature. 'It is the duly constituted representation of an organized society of human beings, created by them for their mutual protection and well-being.' 'The State or the Government is but the machinery through which such mutual aid and protection are achieved'." [98]"'In broad terms,' Roosevelt went on, 'I assert that modern society, acting through its government,

---

[97] Nathan Miller, F.D.R. An Intimate History (Garden City, NY: Doubleday and Company, 1983), p. 253.
[98] Morgan, FDR: A Biography, p. 321.

owes the definite obligation to prevent the starvation or the dire want of any of its fellow men and women who try to maintain themselves but cannot'." Here was the new vision—government must enter the economy to benefit the people. No more hands off policies but direct intervention in the name of the public welfare. FDR called the states "laboratories" and "was willing to experiment." "He authorized the use of National Guard armories to house the homeless. He set up a commission to study unemployment insurance—that was as far as the legislature was willing to go in 1931. Another commission, on stabilization of industry, studied ways to keep workers from being laid off. One method was the eight-hour day and the five-day week, which won him applause" from the poet Ezra Pound. The shortened work week had the effect of employing more people and FDR sought additional ways of doing so. To *experiment* became his watchword. In August 1931 FDR asked a special legislative session in New York to "consider unemployment relief." "He went in person to the capitol to deliver his request for a new state agency, the Temporary Emergency Relief Administration, which would distribute $25 million" and raised state income taxes to fund this agency, calling his actions a patriotic calling. FDR applied the old concepts of Christian conscience he learned while at Groton and imbibed as a young man listening to Washington Gladden. "'It is clear to me,' he said, 'that it is the duty of those who have benefited by our industrial and economic system to come to the front in such a grave emergency and assist in relieving those who under the same industrial and economic order are the losers and sufferers'."[99] The New York legislature approved $20 million for relief and public works projects within the state to aid the suffering and put people to work. Harry L. Hopkins, formerly an administrator with New York's Tuberculosis and Health Association, was appointed by Governor Roosevelt to oversee this program that by the spring of 1932 had placed 75,000 people on work relief. Men were employed in cutting brush, sewer construction, improving the city's water system and streets, building airports and playgrounds, and generally making New York a better place in which to live. Civic pride was invoked in all these manual labor positions and workers were grateful to be employed by the state. Hopkins would follow FDR into the New Deal and bring with him many progressive values instilled while he was a student

---

[99] Franklin D. Roosevelt, The Public Papers of Governor Franklin D. Roosevelt, 4 vols. (Albany, NY: J. Blyon Co., 1930-1939); Morgan, FDR: A Biography, pp.322-323; Richard Harrity and Ralph G. Martin, The Human Side of F.D.R. (New York: Duell, 1960); Harold Gosnell, Champion Campaigner (New York: Macmillan, 1952; George T. McJimsey, Harry Hopkins: Ally of the Poor and Defender of Democracy (Cambridge, Mass: Harvard University Press, 1987); George T. McJimsey, "Harry Lloyd Hopkins," in American National Biography. Edited by John A. Garraty and Mark C. Carnes, Vol. 11 (New York: Oxford University Press, 1999), pp. 172-174; Robert E. Sherwood, Roosevelt and Hopkins (New York: Harper and Row, 1948).

at Grinnell College in Iowa where he had grown up. Like FDR he worked for honest government, aid to the poor, and bureaucratic efficiency. He had been a social worker in New York City working with the Association for Improving the Conditions of the Poor and the city's first Board of Child Welfare, and the Red Cross. In 1922 Hopkins had been elected president of the American Association of Social Workers when he was invited to work for the Tuberculosis and Health Association and then FDR's state Temporary Emergency Relief Administration. It was a good fit and Hopkins made this agency a great success with FDR's guidance and direction.

FDR's effective policies were noticed on the national level and talk grew that he should run for the U.S. presidency. Franklin Roosevelt wanted to become president because he felt he knew how to cure the Depression, as his state laboratory had yielded successful results. "By readjusting the tax burden on the farmer, for instance, by providing state aid for rural education, by using the gasoline tax to finance the construction of farm-to-market roads," FDR "identified himself as a sympathetic spokesman for the rural voter, a position he could project on the national scene as the farmer's friend."[100] Taxes had been reduced for New York farmers, just as FDR had pleased urban voters by lowering utility rates and publicly developing electrical power. FDR and Louis Howe began to contact all their old political friends preserved since the 1920 election campaign, sounding them out on policy suggestions for the Democratic party in 1932. This network had grown into a viable political machine ready to launch his presidential candidacy, to his great pleasure. Howe had continued to make political friends for Roosevelt who he hoped to support for the Party's presidential nomination in 1932. Howe often coordinated his efforts with James Farley who had politically organized FDR's two successful gubernatorial campaigns in New York. In June 1931 Farley had made a wide circuit tour through eighteen states to line up delegate support for FDR at the nominating convention. Farley negotiated with numerous delegates in the mid-west, the Rocky Mountain regions, and the Western Pacific coastal states. And as the selection of the party's presidential front runner drew closer, FDR designed the strategy for the Democratic Party nominee that he hoped would be himself. Instinctively he knew that a first ballot

---

[100] Morgan, FDR: A Biography, p. 323; James A. Farley, Behind the Ballots, (New York: Harcourt Brace, 1938); James A. Farley, Jim Farley's Story, (New York: Whittlesey House, 1948); Henry L. Feingold, The Politics of Rescue, (New Brunswick, NJ: Rutgers University Press, 1970); Samuel I. Rosenman, Working with Roosevelt (New York: Harper and Row, 1952); Francis Russell, The President Makers (Boston: Little, Brown and Company, 1976); Franklin D. Roosevelt, The Happy Warrior (Boston: Houghton Mifflin, 1928).

win would be difficult to secure at the convention despite all the preliminary planning and delegate pledges.

Taking the bull by the horns, he urged that the economy be the single most important issue in the campaign. "Roosevelt urged a strategy that would emphasize Republican mishandling of the economy—it 'should bring out very forcibly the fact that Republican political leaders even up to the Secretary of the Treasury himself have joined with Republican bankers and Republican industrial and power company presidents for many months past in telling the country that everything was sound and that the speed of prosperity could not possibly slacken. They deliberately led the country to believe that it could pull itself up by the bootstraps, doubling its wealth and earning power every two or three years by simply pouring more money into new stock issues and mergers'."[101] Deception and deceit had prolonged the Depression supported by misguided federal policies. The Democrats must galvanize and act to save the nation. FDR had the courage to say what was wrong in America. " 'The point to be made,' he continued, 'is that the Republican leaders themselves are the people responsible for inflating the general prosperity bubble until like the Florida land boom it burst with a loud report'." FDR began to campaign behind the scenes for the Democratic presidential nomination in 1932. He increased his letter writing campaigns, enlarged state dinners, added political lunches, exchanged political courtesies and favors, supported other campaigning Democrats, and above all formulated a winning policy platform for reform. His ideals would carry him through to victory. He would protect America's vitality, hopes and dreams, and recapture prosperity for the multitudes. Voters were confident FDR would deliver on his promises. They seemed to agree with Senator Henry Ashurst who announced " 'Roosevelt is a Man of Destiny!…He will lift this country out of the depression and go down in history as one of our greatest Americans'." The basis for this statement Ashurst said was " 'When he was elected Governor of New York and couldn't walk. Providence doesn't drag a man back from the grave unless it has a great purpose to be served'."[102] Americans everywhere seemed to agree, as if FDR held up some sort of special light to be turned to for guidance.

The 18th amendment establishing Prohibition had always been a failure in FDR's eyes and in September 1930 he wrote a letter to Senator Robert F. Wagner

---

[101] David Bruner, Herbert Hoover: A Public Life (New York: Alfred A. Knopf, 1979); Morgan, FDR: A Biography, p. 324; Herbert Hoover, The Memoirs of Herbert Hoover, Vol. III (New York: Macmillan, 1952); Daniel R. Fusfeld, The Economic Thought of Franklin D. Roosevelt (New York: Columbia University Press, 1956).

[102] Morgan, FDR: A Biography, p. 325; Earle Looker, This Man Roosevelt (New York: Brewer, Warren and Putnam, 1932); John T. Flynn, Country Squire in the White House (Garden City, NY: Doubleday, 1940).

that was published in the *New York Times*. He called for the repeal of national Prohibition and the return to the states of the powers to control liquor sales. This won FDR additional support throughout America in the big cities and urban areas, and garnered additional praise from numerous state governors. FDR desired to control statewide liquor sales both as a source of revenue and as a means to end corruption. FDR also kept his reputation clean by launching an investigation of New York City's magistrates' courts accused of selling judgeships. Thus, he bound the urban regions to his policies and views as he had the farming sectors.

Nothing revealed so sharply Hoover's lack of rapport with the people than the inept handling of the Bonus Army. In June and July 1932, thousands of veterans marched on Washington to demand payment of their war bonuses they were due to receive in 1945. These veterans set up a large shanty-town at Anacostia Flats along the river near the capitol. At its height the Bonus Army numbered 20,000 as they sought to shake lose their promised bonus from Congress by the weight of their sheer numbers. By July 28, 1932 Hoover became alarmed, calling these veterans radicals and insurrectionists and the White House had been put under guard, the gates chained. It seemed that the president had shut himself off from the people. Brigadier General Pelham D. Glassford, chief of the Washington police, reinforced by General Douglas MacArthur and four troops of cavalry, were authorized to dislodge the veterans and in the process two individuals were killed. The shanty-town of their huts were burned. The newspapers lambasted Hoover across the country describing what a pitiful sight it was for the American government to chase unarmed men, women and children with Army tanks and burn their "shacks that had been home to the pitiful ragtags for more than a month." "A challenge to the authority of the United States government has been met," said Hoover. "But the episode cost him dearly."[103] Against this backdrop of federal government ineptitude, FDR was jubilantly nominated for the presidency by the Democrats in Chicago in June 1932.

By the spring of 1932, as the economy had hit bottom, thousands of Americans faced starvation. "We saw a crowd of some 50 men fighting over a barrel of garbage that had been set outside the back door of a restaurant," said a witness in Chicago.[104] In Philadelphia during a period when no relief funds were available, hundreds of families existed on stale bread and thin soup. The Depression, an English observer said, "outraged and baffled" the nation that took it as an article of faith that America somehow, was different from the rest of the world. Farmers blocked roads to dump milk cans in a desperate effort to force up

---

[103] Ezra Bowen, ed., This Fabulous Century, 1930-1940, Vol. IV, pp. 25-26.
[104] Ibid. p. 23.

the price of milk while starving children stood in the slums of New York with bloated bellies. Clearly something new was needed. Yet Hoover clung desperately to his policies of rugged individualism saying "economic depression cannot be cured by legislative action or executive pronouncement." "Federal feeding would set a most dangerous precedent," echoed the *Schenectady Union Star*. "It would be too dangerously like the dole, which paralyzed British labor."[105] Tragically the idea of a temporary dole to the disadvantaged received not sympathy from wealthy Americans but scorn. FDR's humanitarian policies were sorely needed to guide Americans to recover their own destiny and Christian conscience.

In his campaign for his party's nomination, FDR was successful in curbing the power of John J. Raskob, who attempted to control the Democratic National Committee and its platform. The New York State Democratic Committee supported FDR's political position that the party's platform should result from the national convention and only this body could declare its party nominee for the presidency. By this struggle of March 1932, it had been well understood that FDR had made himself a candidate for the party's nomination for the U.S. presidency. In June FDR wooed support from Democratic governors at their conference in French Lick, Indiana. FDR's star shown more brightly than his former mentor's Al Smith and the two began to drift apart, aided by untrue rumors that FDR had criticized Smith's leadership. FDR denied any spurious remarks having been made saying: "Any man who circulates a story of that kind is not only a liar but a contemptible liar."[106] Later Al Smith congratulated FDR on his fiftieth birthday and the two remained cordial even though now rivals. FDR first announced his candidacy for the presidency in North Dakota's primary and confided to relatives that he would "like to win it." He went to great lengths to tell the public that he was physically fit and strong to serve as U.S. President, even submitting to doctor's examinations and publishing the results. FDR traveled widely criticizing Hoover's economic policies and failure to balance the budget and inflating the government bureaucracy. Ever genial and buoyant and radiating confidence, he won converts to the Democrats. At a famed speech before the Commonwealth Club in San Francisco, FDR revealed his agenda for an 'enlightened administration' that would revive prosperity by directly involving the federal government in the economy to assume social responsibilities to distribute "wealth and products more equitably" to aid the disadvantaged. He emphasized the

---

[105] Ibid. p. 25.
[106] Morgan, FDR: A Biography, p. 329; Edgar E. Robinson, The Roosevelt Leadership 1933-1935 (Philadelphia: Lippincott, 1955); Warren Moscow, Politics in the Empire State (New York: Alfred A. Knopf, 1948); Benjamin Bellush, Franklin D. Roosevelt as Governor of New York (New York: Columbia University Press, 1956).

American belief in the Puritan work ethic and dismissed socialism as an alternative to capitalism, saying he would provide "everyone an avenue to possess himself of a portion of that plenty sufficient for his needs, through his own work." Capitalism would triumph when assisted by intelligent decisions in Washington, D.C. that he would bring to bear should he gain the presidency. FDR's reputation for being an ardent progressive reached back to his student days at Harvard. He had written an essay on the Dutch first families of New York, including the Roosevelts, and foretold of his dedication to reform and uplift: "They have never felt," he wrote, "that because they were born in a good position they could put their hands in their pockets and succeed. They have felt, rather, that being born in a good position, there was no excuse for them if they did not do their duty to the community."[107] As a politician FDR had committed himself to serving the community as a *moral duty*. It was a blessing he was so good at his profession. FDR was responsible for making the Democratic Party the party of the old Progressive policies. He cannily appropriated the goals of Theodore Roosevelt and made them his own. As early as 1924 FDR had stated "the Democratic Party is *the* Progressive Party of this country." By 1926 he reiterated his theme of a strong role of involvement for the state. "A nation or a State which is unwilling by governmental action to tackle the new problems, caused by immense increase of population and by the astounding strides of modern science, is headed for ultimate decline and ultimate death." He had sensed the mood of the nation early on and presented himself as the harbinger of change.

FDR was able to head off the challenge from Al Smith and his supporter John J. Raskob by placing Senator Alben Barkley of Kentucky as head of the Democratic national convention instead of Smith's man Jouett Shouse. FDR held the majority of delegates going into the convention in June in Chicago but did not have the necessary two-thirds to win the party nomination on the first ballot. Therefore Howe and Farley from their Roosevelt headquarters at the Congress Hotel brokered political deals to win over delegates pledged to John Nance Garner of Texas. In exchange for Garner's releasing delegates to FDR to win the nomination for the presidency, Garner was to receive the second spot on the ticket to run for the vice-presidency. While Howe and Farley planned campaign strategy, they were aided by Eleanor Roosevelt who worked constantly as her husband's 'legs, eyes and ears'. And by Marguerite "Missy" LeHand, Roosevelt's personal secretary since 1920, who appeared daily to coordinate the Governor's memos and correspondence, directing access to FDR and his inner circle of

---

[107] Henry F. Graff, ed., The Presidents, A Reference History (New York: Charles Scribner's Sons, 2nd ed., 1996), pp. 426-427.

advisers. The 'Brains Trust' of supporters writing speeches and position papers for FDR during the campaign had formed before the convention and continued their work to advise. They included Sam Rosenman before he moved on to take a seat in the New York State Supreme Court, Ray Moley a government professor at Columbia, Rexford Tugwell also a professor at Columbia in economics, and Adolf A. Berle, Jr. in Columbia's Law School.

As a professor of public law at Columbia University, Raymond Moley (1886-1975) held a Master's degree in political science from Oberlin College (1913) and a Ph.D. from Columbia (1918). He had taught earlier at Western Reserve University (1916-1919). He also later taught at Barnard (1923-1926). Moley's Democratic family had adhered to the principles of William Jennings Bryan and the frontier progressives and carried their sentiments into the future New Deal rhetoric. He greatly admired Tom Johnson the progressive mayor of Cleveland, Ohio and supported the idea of public regulation of utilities that he had championed. Like FDR, Moley had also been influenced by Woodrow Wilson, and like Wilson had focused on the study and teaching of political science, government, and law. They also shared sympathy for the farmers and endeavored to eradicate abuses from creditor sectors that exploited the farming sector. Moley had won admiration upon publication of his book *The State Movement for Efficiency and Economy* in 1918 under the auspices of the Bureau of Municipal Research in New York. He also earned stature as director of the Cleveland Foundation in 1919, "the nation's first community trust, a fact-finding agency and funnel for business-sponsored civic improvement projects" that "revived the reform spirit" for former mayor Tom Johnson.[108] In 1922, aided by Harvard law professors Felix Frankfurter and Roscoe Pound, he had produced the Cleveland Crime Survey. Two additional books researched by Moley—*Politics and Criminal Prosecution* published in 1928 and *Our Criminal Courts* that appeared in 1930 brought him to the attention of FDR's political colleague Louis Howe, who then served as the executive secretary of the National Crime Commission. Governor FDR had first employed Moley in New York City as part of his investigation team that looked into the functioning of the local magistrates' courts in regards to applying criminal laws and penalties. Moley also had been part of the Governor's investigative team evaluating the District Attorney's Office in New York. Moley's research and findings had elevated FDR's reputation for

---

[108] Elliot A. Rosen, "Raymond Moley" in American National Biography. Edited by John A. Garraty and Mark C. Carnes Vol. 15 (New York: Oxford University Press, 1999), pp. 665-667; Raymond Moley, After Seven Years (New York: Harper and Row, 1939); Raymond Moley, Realities and Illusions, 1886-1931: The Autobiography of Raymond Moley. Edited by Frank Freidel (New York: Garland Press, 1980).

being tough on crime and adhering to the strict enforcement of the law. A publication titled *Tribunes of the People* in 1932 offered Moley's investigative conclusions to the public and both Governor Roosevelt and Moley were praised for their diligence in ferreting out crime. During the presidential campaign, Moley assisted FDR in writing the 'Forgotten Man' speech of April 1932 that addressed the issue of rural poverty and the plight of the farmer across America.

FDR was introduced to Columbia professors Rexford Tugwell (1891-1979) and Adolf A. Berle (1895-1971) through his friendship-collaboration with Raymond Moley. Tugwell specialized in farming economics and Berle in corporation finance and organizational structure. Tugwell was born in New York but received all of his academic degrees, B.S. (1915) through Ph.D. (1922) from the Wharton School at the University of Pennsylvania. He became a professor at Columbia University, rising through the ranks between 1920 and 1931. "Throughout the 1920s, Tugwell's writings concentrated on the growing inequities in the American economic system, the economy's failure to achieve abundance, business's selfish commitment to laissez-faire, technological obsolescence, and the need for change in the U.S. agricultural system. In this last regard, Tugwell basically wanted farmers to act responsibly by adjusting production to market demands."[109] Essentially his ideas meshed with the practical concerns of Roosevelt to improve conditions for upstate New York farmers when he was Governor and then as he had campaigned for the presidency in 1932. Tugwell wrote about the need for establishing "production schedules and prices while maintaining a sufficient labor supply." His major books expounding his key economic ideas for Depression reform were *Industry's Coming of Age* which appeared in 1927 and *The Industrial Discipline and the Governmental Arts* published in 1933. A longtime Democrat, Tugwell had briefly advised Al Smith's presidential bid in 1928 and now joined forces with the Moley camp to advise Roosevelt's campaign. Tugwell "advised the candidate on a number of issues, especially the domestic allotment plan for controlling agricultural production." To the credit of Franklin Roosevelt, he could bind people of high intellect to himself and his politics with shrewd leadership and profound wisdom about human nature. FDR knew how to use power, both to attract intelligent advisers and to accommodate their views with his own through making smart decisions himself.

---

[109] Michael V. Namorato, "Rexford Guy Tugwell" in American National Biography. Edited by John A. Garraty and Mark C. Carnes, Vol. 21 (New York: Oxford University Press, 1999), pp. 923-925; Rexford Tugwell, Democratic Roosevelt, A Biography of Franklin D. Roosevelt (Garden City, NY: Doubleday, 1957); Rexford Tugwell, The Brains Trust (New York: Viking Press, 1968); Rexford Tugwell, In Search of Roosevelt (Cambridge, Mass: Harvard University Press, 1972); Elliot Rosen, Hoover, Roosevelt and the Brains Trust (New York: Columbia University Press, 1977).

FDR opened doors on a bi-partisan basis to accommodate his agenda. He could not be everywhere at once, but shrewdly distilled tremendous amounts of information gathered by his aides to serve his political needs. He was the professional's professional when it came to tapping the right mind for information and he made informed decisions that way, earning him wide respect. FDR was smart enough himself to know the facts when addressing any public issue. Most of his advisers worked without compensation, happy to have their ideas on FDR's political agenda for reform. They believed that together they could reform the nation, and FDR was a master of forwarding this consensus style of politics.

Adolf Augustus Berle (1895-1971), law professor at Columbia was from Brighton, Massachusetts. His father had been a Congregational minister active in the Social Gospel movement during the progressive period. Berle was highly intelligent and graduated from Harvard at age eighteen and received his law degree there by age twenty-one.[110] Berle worked in the law firm in Boston of Louis D. Brandeis, and following World War I worked as an intelligence officer at the Paris Peace conference in 1919. He returned to provide legal services for the Henry Street Settlement House directed by Lillian D. Wald. Here he further gained concern for the poor and disadvantaged and grew to understand the problems of Manhattan's Lower East Side just as Franklin and Eleanor Roosevelt had done when Eleanor had worked at the Rivington Street Settlement House in the same area. By 1933 Berle had started his own corporate law firm on Wall Street and was invited to teach at the Harvard Business School. Reflecting his strong scholarly interests, Berle wrote academic articles on finance for the *Nation, New Republic* and *Survey,* and his reputation grew widely in the field of corporate finance. In 1927 he studied at Columbia and the next year published *Studies in the Law of Corporate Finance* as a result of his academic study. He became a convert of William O. Douglas and the legal realism school of corporate law attempting to humanize the business world. Berle combined his academic research efforts with Gardiner C. Means and together they published *The Modern Corporation and Private Property* in a 1932 study of America's major corporations and their power over the government. Like FDR, Berle believed that government should enter into America's economy to protect consumers, workers, and stockholders. Government should be more than an umpire on the sidelines; *it should enter the economy directly* to supervise corporations to restore prosperity. FDR did not

---

[110] Jordon A. Schwarz, "Adolf Augustus Berle" in American National Biography. Edited by John A. Garraty and Mark C. Carnes, Vol. 2 (New York: Oxford University Press, 1999), pp. 657-659; Richard Kirkendall, "A.A. Berle, Jr.: Student of the Corporation, 1917-1932," Business History Review 35 (Spring 1961): 43-58; Otis L. Graham, Jr., Toward a Planned Society (New York: Oxford University Press, 1976).

believe that direct intervention in the economy to provide federal honest work to the unemployed constituted a 'dole'. Berle was asked by Governor FDR to advise him on corporations and business law and he assisted in shaping FDR's San Francisco Commonwealth speech that had put forth the economic planning ideals later accomplished by the New Deal.

These three professors were lauded as the 'Brains Trust' initially by Louis Howe and this label was picked up and published in the *New York Times*. FDR directed their ambitions to introduce more federal management of the U.S. economy to right the ship of state and allow recovery from the Depression. All of them saw the Democratic Party as the vehicle to secure control of political power to forward their economic agenda and promote necessary progressive social reforms. They envisioned "the necessity for business-government cooperation; legislation of the social minima, such as unemployment reserves and old-age insurance; massive spending for public works; regulation of securities issuance; the separation of commercial from investment banking; federal oversight of private utilities; restoration of pre-depression price and wage levels; and federal capital investment in regional power development as a yardstick for the fair pricing of private electric power."[111] Further, as a top speech-writer during the 1932 presidential campaign, Moley "drafted statements on the tariff, budget balance, industrial controls, and acreage allotments" effectively utilized by FDR. As a gifted speaker, FDR crafted his own final version of speeches, but relied heavily for essential facts from his loyal followers, the 'Brains Trust'. FDR surrounded himself with these excellent minds, allowing them freedom to draft political documents for him that he would then tailor himself in his own style. They acted as his research arms and legs and allowed him time to continue his important business for the state of New York as Governor. "They were young and intense world changers, smelling the heady aroma of power for the first time, plucked from the classroom and given a golden opportunity to implement their ideas."[112] Roosevelt's speeches now included references to the 'forgotten man', the farmer who was about to loose his farm, the laborer without work, the young without opportunity, and called for a 'concert of interests'. At the Chicago convention in the interest of Democratic political harmony the deal with Garner as his vice presidential candidate was struck and FDR received his party's nomination on the fourth ballot. William Randolph Hearst and William McAdoo had convinced the Garner forces to make the switch to Roosevelt, and when

---

[111] Rosen, "Raymond Moley," American National Biography, Vol. 15, pp. 665-667.
[112] Morgan, FDR: A Biography, p. 346; Cabell Phillips, From the Crash to the Blitz: 1929-1939 (New York: Macmillan, 1969); Richard E. Neustadt, Presidential Power (New York: New American Library, 1960).

California cast its forty-four delegate votes for FDR, Texas delegates followed to push FDR over the top.

The New York Governorship had proved to be a tremendous launching pad to succeed to the U.S. Presidency. FDR began the campaign for the presidency in an unusual way. Upsetting all precedents, Roosevelt flew to Chicago to accept the Democratic nomination in person, saying: "I have started out on the tasks that lie ahead by breaking the absurd tradition that the candidate should remain in professed ignorance of what has happened for weeks until he is formally notified of that event many weeks later . . . you have nominated me and I know it and I am here to thank you for that honor . . . Let it be symbolic that in doing so I broke traditions. I pledge you, I pledge myself . . . to a new deal for the American people."[113] The next day a cartoonist plucked from Roosevelt's speech "new deal" and henceforth the phrase was to be the hallmark for the FDR program. Hoover was re-nominated by the Republican Party. In the election Roosevelt amassed 22.8 million votes to Hoover's 15.8 million, and the electoral college vote was 472 to 59. Large Democratic majorities had been elected to both houses of Congress. By the day of the inauguration, March 4, 1933, the banking system of the United States had collapsed and weary outgoing President Hoover remarked: "We are at the end of our string. There is nothing more we can do." While the sunny optimism of Roosevelt had confided to the nation during the campaign, "the country needs, bold, persistent experimentation. It is common sense to take a method and try it. If it fails, admit it frankly and try another. But above all try something."[114] In retrospect, it is clear that many of the policies later enacted by the New Deal were brought up in the campaign. In his acceptance speech at the party convention Roosevelt had advocated a reforestation program which would employ the nation's youth, an obvious anticipation of the Civilian Conservation Corps. In Portland, Oregon, he had supported public power development and government regulation of utilities. In Columbus, Ohio, he promised regulation of financial dealings on Wall Street. Many historians have said that the New Deal was not foretold in the campaign, but while this was true concerning specifics, the key ideas were there as the game plan. Roosevelt in office was like a quarterback who called subsequent plays or policies forth based on the outcome of a preceding play. FDR had been the campaigner who had turned the perfect phrase as he had delivered his 'four horsemen' speech against 'Destruction, Delay, Deceit, and Despair' in October in Baltimore, a magnificent speech that had captured the hearts of his countrymen and boosted him into the presidency.

---

[113] Morgan, FDR: A Biography, p. 355; Roy Jenkins, Franklin Delano Roosevelt (New York: Times Books, Henry Holt and Company, 2003), p. 61.

[114] Morgan, p. 355-356.

Roosevelt's personal charisma and shrewd combination of practical politics and instinct for the common touch had surprised many. Before his policies were placed into action he was considered by some to be an intellectual lightweight as pundit Walter Lippmann wrote of him, "a pleasant man who, without any important qualifications, would very much like to be president."[115] But FDR's nerve and buoyant confidence were genuine, and accordingly Lippman eventually supported him in the 1932 election saying: "The nation which had lost confidence in everything and everybody has regained confidence in everything and everybody and regained confidence in the government and in itself." It was Roosevelt's style that was implicitly trusted. The November 1932 election had been almost a foregone conclusion that FDR would win after Hoover's disastrous treatment of the veterans. FDR had also been aided during his campaign by the resignation in September of corrupt New York City Mayor Jimmy Walker, whom he had been investigating. Lippmann commented: "My own judgement has been greatly modified by the manner in which he conducted the Walker hearings....I shall cheerfully vote for Governor Roosevelt." FDR was now seen as acting tough on crime, as well as being generous to the disadvantaged. Many had praised his "capaciousness of spirit," and ability to experiment to find solutions.[116] Franklin Delano Roosevelt had won the 1932 presidential election carrying forty-two of the forty-eight states. In his First Inaugural Address he galvanized Americans into action as he reassured the country on Saturday, March 4, 1933:

"I am certain that my fellow Americans expect that on my induction into the Presidency I will address them with a candor and a decision which the present situation of our Nation impels. This is pre-eminently the time to speak the truth, the whole truth, frankly and boldly. Nor need we shrink from honestly facing conditions in our country today. This great Nation will endure as it has endured, will revive and will prosper. So, first of all, let me assert my firm belief that the only thing we have to fear is fear itself, nameless, unreasoning, unjustified terror which paralyzes needed efforts to convert retreat into advance. In every dark hour of our national life a leadership of frankness and vigor has met with that understanding and support of the people themselves which is essential to victory. I am convinced that you will again give that support to leadership in these critical days.

---

[115] Graff, The Presidents, A Reference History, p. 427; Roy Jenkins, Franklin Delano Roosevelt (New York: Times Books Henry Holt and Company, 2003), p. 64.

[116] Morgan, p. 366; Lloyd J. Graybar, "John Nance Garner," in American National Biography. Edited by John A. Garraty and Mark C. Carnes, Vol. 8 (New York: Oxford University Press, 1999), pp. 733-735; Marquis James, Mr. Garner of Texas (New York: Bobbs-Merrill Company, 1939); Seth Koven and Sonya Michel, Mothers of a New World: Maternalist Politics and the Origins of Welfare States (New York: Routledge, 1993); Jenkins, Franklin Delano Roosevelt, p. 64.

In such a spirit on my part and on yours we face our common difficulties. They concern, thank God, only material things. Values have shrunken to fantastic levels; taxes have risen; our ability to pay has fallen; government of all kinds is faced by serious curtailment of income; the means of exchange are frozen in the currents of trade; the withered leaves of industrial enterprise lie on every side; farmers find no markets for their produce; the savings of many years in thousands of families are gone. More important, a host of unemployed citizens face the grim problem of existence, and an equally great number toil with little return. Only a foolish optimist can deny the dark realities of the moment.

Yet our distress comes from no failure of substance. We are stricken by no plague of locusts. Compared with the perils which our forefathers conquered because they believed and were not afraid, we have still much to be thankful for. Nature still offers her bounty and human efforts have multiplied it. Plenty is at our doorstep, but a generous use of it languishes in the very sight of the supply. Primarily this is because the rulers of the exchange of mankind's goods have failed, through their own stubbornness and their own incompetence, have admitted their failure, and abdicated. Practices of the unscrupulous money-changers stand indicted in the court of public opinion, rejected by the hearts and minds of men. True they have tried, but their efforts have been cast in the pattern of an outworn tradition. Faced by failure of credit they have proposed only the lending of more money. Stripped of the lure of profit by which to induce our people to follow their false leadership, they have resorted to exhortations, pleading tearfully for restored confidence. They know only the rules of a generation of self-seekers. They have no vision, and when there is no vision the people perish. The money-changers have fled from their high seats in the temple of our civilization. We may now restore that temple to the ancient truths. The measure of the restoration lies in the extent to which we apply social values more noble than mere monetary profit.

Happiness lies not in the mere possession of money; it lies in the joy of achievement, in the thrill of creative effort. The joy and moral stimulation of work no longer must be forgotten in the mad chase of evanescent profits. These dark days will be worth all they cost us if they teach us that our true destiny is not to be ministered unto but to minister to ourselves and to our fellow men.

Recognition of the falsity of material wealth as the standard of success goes hand in hand with the abandonment of the false belief that public office and high political position are to be valued only by the standards of pride of place and personal profit; and there must be an end to a conduct in banking and in business which too often has given to a sacred trust the likeness of callous and selfish wrongdoing. Small wonder that confidence languishes, for it thrives only on honesty, on honor, on the sacredness of obligations, on faithful protection, on unselfish performance; without them it cannot live.

Restoration calls, however, not for changes in ethics alone. This Nation asks for action and action now.

Our greatest primary task is to put people to work. This is no unsolvable problem if we face it wisely and courageously. It can be accomplished in part by direct recruiting by the Government itself, treating the task as we would treat the emergency of a war, but at the same time, through this employment, accomplishing greatly needed projects to stimulate and reorganize the use of our natural resources.

Hand in hand with this we must frankly recognize the overbalance of population in our industrial centers and, by engaging on a national scale in a redistribution, endeavor to provide a better use of the land for those best fitted for the land. The task can be helped by definite efforts to raise the values of agricultural products and with this the power to purchase the output of our cities. It can be helped by preventing realistically the tragedy of the growing loss through foreclosure of our small homes and our farms. It can be helped by insistence that the Federal, state, and local governments act forthwith on the demand that their cost be drastically reduced. It can be helped by the unifying of relief activities which today are often scattered, uneconomical, and unequal. It can be helped by national planning for and supervision of all forms of transportation and of communications and other utilities which have a definitely public character. There are many ways in which it can be helped, but it can never be helped merely by talking about it. We must act and act quickly.

Finally, in our progress toward a resumption of work we require two safeguards against a return of the evils of the old order; there must be a strict supervision of all banking and credits and investments; there must be an end to speculation with other people's money, and there must be provision for an adequate but sound currency.

There are the lines of attack. I shall presently urge upon a new Congress in special session detailed measures for their fulfillment, and I shall seek the immediate assistance of the several States.

Through this program of action we address ourselves to putting our own national house in order and making income balance outgo. Our international trade relations, though vastly important, are in point of time and necessity secondary to the establishment of a sound national economy. I favor as a practical policy the putting of first things first. I shall spare no effort to restore world trade by international economic readjustment, but the emergency at home cannot wait on that accomplishment. The basic thought that guides these specific means of national recovery is not narrowly nationalistic. It is the insistence, as a first consideration, upon the interdependence of the various elements in all parts of the United States, a recognition of the old and permanently important manifestation of the American spirit of the pioneer. It is the way to recovery. It is the immediate way. It is the strongest assurance that the recovery will endure.

In the field of world policy I would dedicate this Nation to the policy of the good neighbor, the neighbor who resolutely respects himself and, because he does so, respects the rights of others, the neighbor who respects his obligations and respects the sanctity of his agreements in and with a world of neighbors.

If I read the temper of our people correctly, we now realize as we have never realized before our interdependence on each other; that we can not merely take but we must give as well; that if we are to go forward, we must move as a trained and loyal army willing to sacrifice for the good of a common discipline, because without such discipline no progress is made, no leadership becomes effective. We are, I know, ready and willing to submit our lives and property to such discipline, because it makes possible a leadership which aims at a larger good. This I propose to offer, pledging that the larger purposes will bind upon us all as a sacred obligation with a unity of duty hitherto evoked only in time of armed strife.

With this pledge taken, I assume unhesitatingly the leadership of this great army of our people dedicated to a disciplined attack upon our common problems.

Action in this image and to this end is feasible under the form of government which we have inherited from our ancestors. Our Constitution is so simple and practical that it is possible always to meet extraordinary needs by changes in emphasis and arrangement without loss of essential form. That is why our constitutional system has proved itself the most superbly enduring political mechanism the modern world has produced. It has met every stress of vast expansion of territory, of foreign wars, of bitter internal strife, of world relations.

It is to be hoped that the normal balance of executive and legislative authority may be wholly adequate to meet the unprecedented task before us. But it may be that an unprecedented demand and need for undelayed action may call for temporary departure from that normal balance of public procedure.

I am prepared under my constitutional duty to recommend the measures that a stricken nation in the midst of a stricken world may require. These measures, or such other measures as the Congress may build out of its experience and wisdom, I shall seek, within my constitutional authority, to bring to speedy adoption.

But in the event that the Congress shall fail to take one of these two courses, and in the event that the national emergency is still critical, I shall not evade the clear course of duty that will then confront me. I shall ask the Congress for the one remaining instrument to meet the crisis--broad Executive power to wage a war against the emergency, as great as the power that would be given to me if we were in fact invaded by a foreign foe.

For the trust reposed in me I will return the courage and the devotion that befit the time. I can do no less.

We face the arduous days that lie before us in the warm courage of the national unity; with the clear consciousness of seeking old and precious moral values; with the clean satisfaction that comes from the stern performance of duty by old and young alike. We aim at the assurance of a rounded and permanent national life.

We do not distrust the future of essential democracy. The people of the United States have not failed. In their need they have registered a mandate that they want direct, vigorous action. They have asked for discipline and direction under leadership. They have made me the present instrument of their wishes. In the spirit of the gift I take it. In this dedication of a Nation we humbly ask the blessing of God. May He protect each and every one of us. May He guide me in the days to come."[117]

In magnificent ringing phrases FDR had reminded Americans that "the only thing we have to fear is fear itself," seeking to reassure them and outlined what he intended to do to solve the Depression. "Our true destiny is not be ministered unto but to minister to ourselves and to our fellow men," he had inspired. "This Nation asks for action, and action now.... I assume unhesitatingly the leadership of this great army of our people," he boldly asserted. So confident in his own leadership was he that he had concluded with a stern promise: "In the event that Congress shall fail...I shall not evade the clear course of duty that will then confront me. I shall ask the Congress for the one remaining instrument to meet the crisis, broad Executive power to wage a war against the emergency." FDR was a man of action and Americans looked to him for support, understanding, and guidance. They were confident he would find workable solutions as he promised. On March 5 Roosevelt declared a nationwide bank holiday and placed an embargo on gold. The president summoned Congress into session on March 9 and the first action of the legislators confirmed these fiscal measures by outlawing the hoarding of gold and giving the president broad powers over the Federal Reserve system. Arthur Krock wrote in the *New York Times*, March 12, 1933: "Never was there such a change in the transfer of a government. The President is the boss, the dynamo, the works."

The New Deal and its architect, President Roosevelt, were blessed with able administrators who had come up through the political avenues of the old Progressives. FDR's Vice President was John Nance Garner who had been born in Red River County, Texas. He had studied for the law, receiving degrees from John Marshall College of Law and from Baylor University. He entered politics as a congressman in the Texas legislature in 1898 and earned a reputation for progressive reform especially in regulating insurance companies and railroads. He entered the U.S. Congress in 1903 where he had specialized in tariff legislation, crafting the Underwood-Simmons Tariff law and certain provisions dealing with

---

[117] Franklin D. Roosevelt Library, Hyde Park, New York; Samuel I. Rosenman, The Public Papers and Addresses of Franklin D. Roosevelt, 13 vols. (New York: Random House, 1938-1950).

the income tax and inheritance tax laws passed during the administration of Woodrow Wilson. As Democratic whip he had lobbied hard for the graduated income tax and the Federal Reserve System. He, like FDR, was a friend to the farmers and had secured legislation to improve marketing and credit opportunities. Garner had also supported the National Defense Act 1916 and lobbied in Congress for the passage of Wilson's wartime preparedness programs. He was the senior member of the House Ways and Means Committee in 1923 and though he differed with the three Republican presidents after Wilson he remained on good terms to influence tariff and tax policies and was a master of compromise. By 1931 'Cactus Jack' Garner was Speaker of the House when the Democrats regained control and had been nominated as FDR's vice-presidential candidate in the campaign of 1932. Following victory, Garner would serve two terms as vice-president from 1932-1940. Garner was an early supporter of FDR's New Deal policies but would become increasingly disenchanted with deficit spending. However, he served FDR well especially in his role as president of the Senate and shepherded early New Deal bills through with a reputation for fairness. FDR often consulted with Garner about legislative procedures and tactics and placed him again on the ticket for re-election in 1936. Shortly thereafter Garner became less than enchanted with Roosevelt's court-packing scheme of 1937 and especially frowned on aims to purge the Congress of conservative Democrats in opposition to FDR's policies in 1938. Garner made his own bid for the presidency, challenging FDR for the nomination in 1940, but the Texas delegation would not oppose the third term for Roosevelt. Garner returned to private life following that election in which FDR bested the Republican challenger Wendell Willkie (1892-1944).

FDR selected as his Secretary of State Cordell Hull. His selection had been to bind the south to his presidency through Hull, a southerner born in Byrdstown, Tennessee. Hull had distinguished himself as a lawyer, circuit judge, and congressman. Like Roosevelt, Hull championed the rights of the farmers and sought solutions through reciprocal trade agreements to sell farm commodities. Hull, like FDR, had eagerly supported Woodrow Wilson and in many respects they both modeled their careers after the Democratic progressive president. Hull had served as chairman of the Democratic National Committee from 1920 to 1922 but returned to the U.S. House of Representatives in 1922 to help ameliorate the Republican policies of Harding. He worked with FDR on shaping the Democratic Party during the 1920s and had early on supported FDR's bid for the presidency

---

Volume 2 "The Year of Crisis" 1933 contains the March 4, 1933 Inaugural Address of FDR, pp. 11-17.

in 1932. Hull was appointed Secretary of State in January 1933 and his first overseas diplomatic assignment was to attend the London Economic Conference.[118] In England Hull had attempted to secure a reduction of international trade tariffs but his endeavors were thwarted. His second mission was to Montevido, Urguuay for the Seventh International Conference of American States. Hull secured the Reciprocal Trade Agreements Act by 1934 that allowed FDR to negotiate trade agreements that did not need congressional approval. This aided economic recovery immeasurably through a balancing of foreign trade and would remain a mainstay of American foreign policy. The ideal behind these acts was to make friends through trade. Hull also attempted to use trade to solve international problems as in East Asia he demanded access to China's markets and moved to hinder Japanese economic thrusts into the Chinese Mainland. Hull temporized the backlash following the Japanese attack on the *USS Panay* gunboat in the Yangtze River that resulted in two American deaths and fifty badly injured. Above all else he wished to stop a major war from breaking out anywhere in the world during these economic turbulent times. His diplomacy reflected his peacekeeping nature. He tried to be diplomatic in addressing the significant issue of granting visas to European Jews seeking American asylum when threatened by the Nazis. Cordell Hull was at his best when traveling to Pan-American conferences like the Inter-American Conference for the Maintenance of Peace that met in Buenos Aires, Argentina in 1936, and planning for hemispheric cooperation. Another vital conference was held in Peru in 1938 that produced the Declaration of Lima encouraging hemispheric solidarity and condemning foreign aggression and war. Sumner Welles became undersecretary of state in 1936 and was a close confidant to FDR, as was Hull as the international movements toward World War II accelerated.

Secretary of the Treasury was Henry Morgenthau, Jr., who had served Governor FDR in New York earlier as chairman of the Agricultural Advisory Committee in 1928 and Commissioner of Conservation in 1930. He had been carefully selected by FDR who knew him as a longtime friend and gentleman farmer from Dutchess County. Morgenthau had been born in New York City and his father Henry Morgenthau, Sr. had served the Democratic National Committee

---

[118] Irwin F. Gellman, "Cordell Hull" in American National Biography. Edited by John A. Garraty and Mark C. Carnes, Vol. 11 (New York: Oxford University Press, 1999), pp. 445-450; Harold Boaz Hinton, Cordell Hull: A Biography (New York: Doubleday, Doran and Company, 1942); Irwin F. Gellman, Good Neighbor Diplomacy: United States Policies in Latin America, 1933-1945 (Baltimore, MD: Johns Hopkins University Press, 1979); Irwin F. Gellman, Secret Affairs: Franklin Roosevelt, Cordell Hull and Sumner Wells (Baltimore, MD: Johns Hopkins University Press, 1995).

as finance chairman in 1912 the year Woodrow Wilson had been elected.[119] His parents actively used their wealth earned through shrewd real estate investments in New York City to promote progressive social causes like fire safety in tenements in the Bronx and in Harlem and had contributed to the Henry Street Settlement directed by Lillian Wald. Henry Morgenthau, Jr. continued the philanthropy of his parents and volunteered at the Henry Streetment on Manhatan's Lower East Side. His German-Jewish background and growing up in New York City as a youth allowed him to identify with the urban poor and attempt to mitigate their urban plight. After attending Cornell University, he purchased dairy farm property in Dutchess County where he made his home and befriended the Roosevelts, his neighbors. His wife supported Eleanor's progressive causes. Morgenthau took over publication of the *American Agriculturalist* in 1922 and, with FDR, promoted solutions to upstate New York farmers' problems in soil conservation, prices for crops, and reclamation of poor land. FDR and Morgenthau had shared many common interests, especially in their endeavors to build up the Democratic Party in upstate New York through aid to the region's farmers. While in New York politics Morgenthau had worked closely with Harry Hopkins on New York's reforestation project that was a forerunner to the New Deal's Civilian Conservation Corps. After the 1932 election FDR had first tapped Henry Morgenthau to head the Federal Farm Board. But in November 1933 Morgenthau was appointed first acting Secretary of the Treasury to take the place of William Woodin and then when it was clear that Woodin could not return because of illness, he took over as full Secretary early in 1934. Morgenthau oversaw management of the U.S. economy and the federal budget at the time when FDR was promoting programs to deficit spend to support New Deal programs. He agreed with Keynesian economics and FDR's ideas of priming the pump but believed that somewhere down the line the federal budget could be balanced following full economic recovery. He enjoyed working with FDR, who was ten years his senior, and utilized his business network to propagate the virtues of the New Deal policies. During the economic recession of 1937-1938 Morgenthau disagreed with the chairman of the Federal Reserve Marriner S. Eccles over the handling of the U.S. economy, as by then he wished to halt deficit spending and recommended balancing the budget as an ingredient for full recovery from the Depression. FDR, however, continued deficit spending policies and Morgenthau had to continue to support his chief. Eventually Morgenthau would also be asked to find money to conduct World War II and in 1939 he was

---

[119] Dean L. May, "Henry Morgenthau, Jr.," in American National Biography. Edited by John A. Garraty and Mark C. Carnes, Vol. 15 (New York: Oxford University Press, 1999), pp. 863-865.

asked by FDR to establish a procurement service in the Treasury department allowing Britain and France to purchase weapons from the U.S after Germany invaded Poland. America would become the great arsenal for democracy long before the Japanese attack on Pearl Harbor and Henry Morgenthau authorized all measures requested by FDR to aid the Allies and to plan for the defense of the U.S.

Secretary of the Interior was Harold Ickes, who brought with him into the New Deal his penchant for progressive reform. Born in Pennsylvania but raised in Chicago, Ickes had grown up in the reforming atmosphere of Jane Addams' Hull House, the Northwestern University Settlement House and its reforming leader Raymond Robins and his wife Margaret who had established with Addams the National Women's Trade Union League. Like Addams, he had started his early political reforms as a Republican, serving as TR's Illinois organizer during his Bull Moose campaign. But Ickes had become disenchanted with the party during the 1920s and by the 1930s supported the Democrats as leaders of reform.[120] During the 1932 presidential campaign FDR had asked Ickes to organize a Western Independent Republican Committee for Roosevelt that was successful. Following FDR's triumph at the polls, Ickes was tapped to become Secretary of the Interior and served for nearly thirteen years. He was a man of great accomplishment "whose dedication to liberal principles helped shape the character and quality of life in the depression and World War II years." "The inherited responsibilities of his agency included the supervision of more than 30,000 employees scattered over forty states and territories; the management of the National Park System, nearly 300 million acres of un-appropriated public lands, and all the grass, timber, oil, natural gas, hydropower, coal, and other mineral resources they contained; the government of Hawaii, Alaska, Puerto Rico, the Virgin Islands and other U.S. possessions (with the addition of the Philippines after 1934); and the administration of a plethora of agencies, institutions, and sub-bureaucracies, chief among them the Bureau of Reclamation, the Office of Education, the Geological Survey, and the...Bureau of Indian Affairs...." Among his first duties after January 1933 was to organize with Frances Perkins (Labor), Henry A. Wallace (Agriculture) and George Dern (War) the Civilian

---

[120] T.H. Watkins, "Harold LeClair Ickes," in American National Biography. Edited by John A. Garraty and Mark C. Carnes, Vol. 11 (New York: Oxford University Press, 1999), pp. 626-628; Linda Lear, Harold L. Ickes: The Aggressive Progressive, 1874-1933 (New York: Garland Press, 1981); T.H. Watkins, Righteous Pilgrim: The Life and Times of Harold L. Ickes, 1874-1952 (New York: Henry Holt and Company, 1990); Graham J. White and John Maze, Harold Ickes of the New Deal: His Private Life and Public Career (Cambridge, Mass: Harvard University Press, 1985); Roy Jenkins, Franklin Delano Roosevelt (New York: Times Books Henry Holt and Company, 2003), pp.68-74.

Conservation Corps. He was then made director of the Public Works Administration (PWA) and oversaw the construction of dams, bridges, tunnels, highways, irrigation projects, and social service agencies like hospitals and schools. "There were 19,000 projects in all, including 583 municipal water systems, 622 sewerage systems, 263 hospitals, 522 schools, 368 street and highway projects, as well as such well known items as Boulder (later Hoover) Dam on the Colorado River and many of the facilities of the Tennessee Valley Authority (TVA)." Loyal to his former mentors in conservation like Gifford Pinchot, Ickes encouraged passage of the Grazing Service in 1934 to withdraw barren lands from use to control erosion and the Soil Erosion Service [renamed the Soil Conservation Service] to control erosion on private lands. These acts aided states suffering from dust bowls and arid conditions. In his capacity as administrator over the National Park Service, Harold Ickes oversaw completion of several parks established earlier—The Everglades, Great Smoky Mountains, and the Shenandoah Valley parks and additionally established new ones—Jackson Hole National Monument in Wyoming, Kings Canyon National Park in California, and the Olympic National Park in Washington. Ickes after 1939 administered the National Wildlife Refuge System throughout America through the U.S. Biological Survey. He also expanded his oversight to the Bureau of Fisheries. These were organizations near and dear to Ickes and both he and FDR had supported the policies of TR to establish national parks and administer them wisely for younger generations to enjoy and to further conservation. During World War II Ickes had the daunting task of providing enough fuel for both home consumption and for military use. In 1941 he was made head of the Petroleum Administration for National Defense [later re-named Petroleum Administration for War]. He started gas rationing and oversaw construction of oil pipelines from Texas. Ickes was such an efficient administrator that U.S. forces were supplied with the oil, gasoline, and aviation fuel that they needed which was a remarkable achievement given the fact that Ickes also supervised all the other agencies within the Department of the Interior. FDR had found his 'go-to man' early on and kept adding responsibilities, so well did Ickes handle each new task. Ickes even found time to campaign ardently for FDR's re-election in 1936, 1940, and 1944. He also opened doors for Black Americans as he appointed William Hastie an African American, as a federal judge and introduced Marian Anderson at the Lincoln Memorial before her famous concert held there in 1939. Harold Ickes ran the Interior Department without a hint of scandal, for which he was dubbed 'Honest Harold' and without a hint of racism as he integrated his administration early in the New Deal.

Secretary of Agriculture was Henry A. Wallace from Iowa. His grandfather had founded a newspaper for the farming community in the mid-west called *Wallaces' Farmer* and Henry had become its editor in 1924.[121] Wallace became a Democrat during the election of 1928 and worked for FDR's election in 1932. Wallace was asked to become Secretary of Agriculture in 1933 and served until he won election as FDR's Vice-President in 1940 replacing John Nance Garner who had not sought re-election. Wallace carried the mid-west, a section important to FDR in seeking his third term. As an accomplished former editor and writer, Henry Wallace wrote several books supportive of New Deal policies including *America Must Choose* in 1935, *The American Choice* in 1940, and *Sixty Million Jobs* in 1945.

FDR's Secretary of Labor was Frances Perkins, who had been nominated by Jane Addams of Hull House, Grace Abbott of the Children's Bureau and Molly Dewson a leader in the Democratic Party. She served as Secretary of Labor from 1933 to 1945 and was the first woman to hold a federal Cabinet position. She was later appointed by President Truman to serve on the Civil Service Commission. Frances Perkins influenced the creation of the CCC and the drafting of the NIRA and significantly influenced the formulation of the Social Security Act and the Fair Labor Standards Act.[122] In 1934 she persuaded FDR to have the U.S. join the International Labor Organization. Perkins also had drafted many of FDR's speeches to American workers and labor organizations. In 1946 she published a tribute to her boss FDR in *The Roosevelt I Knew*, and praised his sense of social responsibility and caring for the greatness of America.

George Dern was chosen Secretary of War. He was a former Governor of Utah, a non-Mormon and a Democrat who served well until as World War II threatened he was replaced by Republican Henry L. Stimson in June 1940. Claude Swanson, former chairman of the Senate Committee on Naval Affairs, was tapped to be FDR's Secretary of the Navy. He was a comfortable team player who Roosevelt had worked with when he was assistant secretary of the navy under Wilson. Yet by June 1940 another internationalist Republican Frank Knox would be asked to lead the Navy Department as Nazism and Fascism threatened Europe. Survival dictated *bi-partisan politics* and FDR was the master at this craft. FDR was comfortable with both peace loving Democrats and hawkish Republicans when they served a just cause. He was an excellent judge of character. FDR was

---

[121] Richard S. Kirkendall, "Henry Agard Wallace" in American National Biography. Edited by John A. Garraty and Mark C. Carnes, Vol. 22 (New York: Oxford University Press, 1999), pp. 531-534.

[122] Susan Estabrook Kennedy, "Frances Perkins" in American National Biography. Edited by John A. Garraty and Mark C. Carnes, Vol. 17 (New York: Oxford University Press, 1999), pp. 339-341.

seen as the respected leader and beacon of hope both at home and abroad in a deteriorating world.

Secretary of Commerce was Daniel C. Roper who had served Wilson as assistant postmaster general. James Farley, former chairman of the Democratic National Committee and FDR's campaign manager was appointed postmaster general and served during the first two FDR administrations. Formerly an ally of Al Smith's, Farley had switched his allegiance to FDR during the campaign for the Governorship of New York in 1928 that Roosevelt had won. Farley had directed the 1930 re-election bid for FDR when he had won a resounding landslide triumph.[123] Interested primarily in keeping control of the Democratic Party to win future elections for FDR such as the successful 1932 presidential bid, Farley used his post as postmaster general to dole out patronage positions to key supporters of the New Deal. He maintained and continued to build a political machine that functioned to carry forth the president's mandates. During his first days as postmaster he canceled the Hoover administration's air-mail contracts as too expensive. The mail was to be conveyed by the Army Air Corps, but after a short while a number of mishaps caused this plan to be scrapped and FDR renewed the earlier postal contracts. The re-election of FDR in 1936 would also be managed by Farley. But soon thereafter Farley's personal hubris began to break his connection to President Roosevelt as Farley did not support the idea of a third term for FDR. Instead he harbored ambitions himself to replace Roosevelt and resigned his post in August 1940. Farley sought to control New York's Democratic Party as a base to launch his own political forays but he had lost control by 1944 and was never able to secure nomination for the governorship of New York that he craved.

For Attorney General, FDR selected Homer S. Cummings of Connecticut who had been a well-respected prosecuting attorney and a loyal member of the Democratic Party. Each member of FDR's team could be counted upon to bring valuable expertise into the Roosevelt administration, and he was the master of building a bi-partisan coalition to solve the country's problems. Both houses of the legislature held strong Democratic majorities that would quickly pass New Deal legislation. Henry Rainey from Illinois was selected Speaker of the House and cooperated fully with the president-elect who pointed the way to economic recovery, securing passage of FDR's bills.

Following FDR's inauguration, Louis Howe and his family moved into the White House to act as President Roosevelt's personal secretary. He often

---

[123] Elliot A. Rosen, "James Aloysius Farley," in American National Biography. Edited by John A. Garraty and Mark C. Carnes, Vol. 7 (New York: Oxford University Press, 1999), pp. 716-717.

controlled access to the president and remained a master of political technique. Harold Ickes described Howe's role. "Howe was the only one who dared to talk to him [FDR] frankly and fearlessly." "He could not only tell him what he believed to be the truth, but he could hang on like a pup to the root until he got results."[124] President Roosevelt found places for his former advisers and supporters in his administration and expected the best from them and usually received what he wanted. He was a shrewd judge of men and his personality and compassion allowed a wide toleration for the combative give and take of policy decision making. Yet with the force of his personality, FDR usually prevailed. "...And it was at once paradoxical and typical of many such contests throughout the world that the champion of the sansculottes should have been the most upper-class president since George Washington." [125] Soon the New Deal was placed in action by these strong personalities who followed their champion President Franklin Delano Roosevelt.

---

[124] Arthur M. Schlesinger, Jr., The Coming of the New Deal (Boston: Houghton Mifflin, 2003 originally published in 1958), p. 515; Richard Hofstadter, The American Political Tradition and the Men Who Made It (New York: Alfred A. Knopf, 1949); Eliot Janeway, The Struggle for Survival (New Haven: Yale University Press, 1950); William D. Hassett, Off the Record with F.D.R. (New Brunswick, NJ: Rutgers University Press, 1958); Joseph P. Lash, Dealers and Dreamers, A New Look at the New Deal (New York: Doubleday, 1988); William E. Leuchtenberg, The FDR Years: On Roosevelt and His Legacy (New York: Columbia University Press, 1995); Lawrence W. Levine, ed., The People and the President: America's Extraordinary Conversation with FDR (New York: Beacon Press, 2002).

[125] Jenkins, Franklin Delano Roosevelt, p. 92.

Chapter 4

FDR LAUNCHES THE NEW DEAL REFORMS

The first bill passed by the 73rd Congress that met from March 9 through July 16, 1933, known as the 'Hundred Days' Congress, was the Emergency Banking Relief Act that empowered the president to reopen solvent banks and to regulate foreign exchange and banking transactions.[126] The president soothed the public's crisis of confidence over the stability of the banking structure in the first of his Fireside Chats as he explained "that it is safer to keep your money in a re-opened bank than it is under the mattress." Protecting public confidence further was the Glass-Stegall Banking Act of May 17, 1933 that gave the Federal Reserve System broad powers over regulating interest rates and established the Federal Deposit Insurance Corporation which initially insured all bank deposits up to $5,000 [now $100,000]. To stabilize the value of the American dollar, all private holdings of gold were to be turned over to the Treasury in exchange for paper currency, and America was taken off the gold standard on April 19, 1933. The financial crisis in America was further shorn up by the Truth in Securities Act of March 29 later supplemented by the Securities and Exchange Act that established controls over the issue of stocks and established the Securities and Exchange Commission.

After addressing the nation's financial soundness, the next pressing problem was unemployment. In providing for both relief and recovery, the president understood Keynesian economics and the need to 'prime the pump' of the

---

[126] Nathan Miller, F.D.R., An Intimate History (Garden City, NY: Doubleday and Company, 1983), pp. 310-311; Elmus Wicker, "Roosevelt's 1933 Monetary Experiment," Journal of American History 57 (1970): 864-879; David M. Kennedy, Freedom From Fear: The American People in Depression and War, 1929-1945 (New York: Oxford University Press, 2001); Samuel I. Rosenman, Public Papers and Addresses of Franklin D. Roosevelt (New York: Random House, 1938-1950), Vol 2 pp. 17, 49, 54, 59, 61.

economy by creating jobs to regenerate purchasing power.[127] The Civilian Conservation Corps was one of the earliest and most popular of the alphabetical agencies and was created on March 21, 1933.[128] The CCC, established during the first Hundred Days of the New Deal, was jointly supervised by the U. S. Army and the Forest Service and provided employment for about three million young men. To fight massive unemployment, these youth were engaged in reforestation, fire fighting, flood control, and swamp drainage, and were paid $30 a month [$25 of it went automatically home their families]. Directed by Robert Fechner, the CCC was run through the Department of Labor and enrolled men between eighteen and twenty-five who were on public relief to work for six months. Each youth could re-new their work contracts with the CCC up to two years. The CCC planted more than 200 million young trees and reflected the ideal of conserving both natural and human resources. Giving dignity to the formerly unemployed, it made men out of thousands of boys who grew to know the value of a hard-earned dollar and took pride in doing so. They were transported to their job sites by the War Department and lived and worked in camps of 200 men each on jobs selected by the Departments of the Interior and Agriculture. The program, that enrolled three million men, lasted until June 1942 when extra manpower was needed for the war effort.

The first measure to assist adult employment, introduced March 21 in the Hundred Days' Congress, was the Federal Emergency Relief Act that created the Federal Emergency Relief Administration.[129] It was passed on May 12, 1933. Led by Harry Hopkins who had worked with FDR in New York as head of that city's

---

[127] Anthony J. Badger, The New Deal, The Depression Years, 1933-1940 (Chicago: Ivan R. Dee, 2002); William J. Barber, Designs Within Disorder: Franklin D. Roosevelt, the Economists, and the Shaping of American Economic Policy, 1933-1945 (Cambridge, England: Cambridge University Press, 1996); Arthur M. Schlesinger, The New Deal in Action, 1933-1938 (New York: Macmillan, 1939); R.F. Harrod, The Life of John Maynard Keynes (New York: Avon Books, 1971).

[128] John A. Salmond, The Civilian Conservation Corps, 1933-1942: A New Deal Case Study (Durham, NC: Duke University Press, 1967); Arthur M. Schlesinger, The American as Reformer (Cambridge, Mass: Harvard University Press, 1950); Samuel I. Rosenman, Working with Roosevelt (New York: Harper and Row, 1952); T.H. Watkins, The Hungry Years: A Narrative History of the Great Depression in America (New York: Owl Books, 2000); Rexford Tugwell, Roosevelt's Revolution: The First Year, A Personal Perspective (New York: Macmillan, 1977); Philip Abbott, The Exemplary Presidency: Franklin D. Roosevelt and the American Political Tradition (Amherst, Mass: University of Massachusetts Press, 1990); Raymond Moley, The First New Deal (New York: Harcourt Brace and World, 1966).

[129] Searle F. Charles, Minister of Relief: Harry Hopkins and the Depression (Syracuse, NY: Syracuse University Press, 1963); Conrad Black, Franklin Delano Roosevelt: Champion of Freedom (New York: Public Affairs and London: Weidenfeld and Nicolson, 2003); James MacGregor Burns, The Three Roosevelts: Patrician Leaders Who Transformed America (New York: Grove Press, 2002).

Temporary Emergency Relief Administration to provide jobs for New Yorkers, the states received $3 billion for direct dole payments or preferably for wages on work projects. Hopkins and FDR expanded the program that had worked so well in New York to the national level with similar success. Hopkins, under FERA, rapidly distributed money to the unemployed, saving the country from further downward free-fall. Hopkins also convinced FDR that additional measures should be undertaken immediately. The Civil Works Administration was established in 1934 as a branch of the FERA and authorized make-work projects such as leaf-raking, sometimes derisively called 'boon-doggles', but it did provide work relief for the able bodied who wanted the dignity of a job. The CWA employed rapidly expanded payrolls hiring four million workers for the winter of 1933-34 and did valuable projects such as building airports and improving post offices. Hopkins and FDR saw real process being made through work relief and they remained convinced that government providing these measures was essential to the very survival of capitalism. The CWA ended in the spring of 1934 but Hopkins successfully lobbied for a newer and larger program to take its place. The Works Progress Administration of 1935 vastly expanded the works projects as $11 billion was authorized for work on public buildings, bridges and hard-surfaced roads and for cultural projects which employed writers, musicians, and artists. FDR, Hopkins and Ickes worked together to bring about the immeasurable success of the WPA in funding work relief. The dignity of the working man was elevated and with it the belief in regulated capitalism. Hopkins' efforts and program designs were lauded by FDR, Eleanor Roosevelt, and Louis Howe, and he was mentioned as a possible successor to the president.[130] Ill-health forced Hopkins to resign from the administration after FDR's re-election in 1940, but his effectiveness as a party man and a trusted adviser to FDR in the realm of work relief cannot be over estimated.

In May 1933 the Agricultural Adjustment Act was passed by Congress with the goal of raising the farmers' income by raising the prices for his commodities by restricting production.[131] This act had been introduced on March 16 in the early part of the Hundred Days Congress to restore farm incomes and lower surpluses.

---

[130] George T. McJimsey, Harry Hopkins: Ally of the Poor and Defender of Democracy (Cambridge, Mass: Harvard University Press, 1987); George T. McJimsey, "Harry Lloyd Hopkins," in American National Biography. Edited by John A. Garraty and Mark C. Carnes, Vol. 11 (New York: Oxford University Press, 1999), pp. 172-174; June Hopkins, Harry Hopkins: Sudden Hero, Brash Reformer (New York: St. Martin's Press, 1999).

[131] Edwin Nourse, Joseph Davis, and John D. Black, Three Years of the Agricultural Adjustment Administration, (New York: Da Capo Press reprint edition, originally published in 1937); Arthur M. Schlesinger, The American As Reformer (Cambridge, Mass: Harvard University Press, 1950); Rexford Tugwell, F.D.R. Architect of An Era (New York: Macmillan, 1967).

The AAA concept was based on the domestic allotment plan which worked to take land out of production and reimburse the farmer from a tax placed on the processing of agricultural products like cotton, wheat, hogs, milk and tobacco. The scale of payments to the farmers was intended to raise the farmers' income level to that which the farmer had received in the base period 1909-1914. In addition, the government established quotas limiting production and the marketing of crops to restrict supply. Special agreements were made with the dairy farmers and hog producers to control distribution, markets and prices. The act was a resounding success, raising the farmers' income by one-third from 1932 to 1935 and greatly reducing staple production. The Farm Credit Administration, administered by Henry Morgenthau, Jr., was organized by executive order on March 27, 1933 to assist farmers secure loans to forestall foreclosures on their farms.

By 1935 farmers' had achieved parity of income with the general economy through the raising of farm prices, and the commodity surpluses that had depressed prices vanished. But the plight of sharecroppers and tenant farmers hurt by benefits given under this act to large commercial farmers raised constitutional questions.[132] The Act was declared unconstitutional in 1936 by the U.S. Supreme Court through the decision in the Hoosac Mills case that determined it to be illegal to levy a tax on one group of people, the producers, for the benefit of another group, the farmers, rather than the general welfare. But the Roosevelt administration found another way to support the farmers through passage of the Second Agricultural Adjustment Act in 1938. This Act gave farmers support through subsidies and price controls and federal legislation related to soil conservation. Hence the New Deal benefits extended to farmers were maintained and American agriculture saved. Following World War II agricultural benefits were continued through the Agricultural Department.

Another group that needed attention were small homeowners. The Home Owners' Loan Corporation was introduced in the Hundred Days Congress through the Home Owners' Loan Act of April 13, 1933 and was designated to refinance private homes at lower interest rates to pay mortgages to stop foreclosures. A vital part of the U.S. transportation system was also saved through the Emergency Railroad Transportation Act, introduced into the Hundred Days Congress on May 4, 1933 and passed on June 16. This act consolidated railway lines, established government regulation, and streamlined railroad operations to economize.[133]

---

[132] David E. Conrad, The Forgotten Farmers: The Story of Sharecroppers in the New Deal (Westport, Conn: Greenwood Press, 1965).
[133] Miller, F.D.R., An Intimate History, p. 316.

In June 1933 Congress enacted the National Industrial Recovery Act which established the National Recovery Administration to regulate wages, working hours and indirectly prices. Robert F. Wagner, Senator from New York and FDR's old friend from the days of the Triangle Shirtwaist Fire Investigating Commission of 1911, helped to draft this piece of legislation and squire its passage through Congress.[134] This act was aimed at aiding industry, labor and the unemployed. Codes of fair competition were to be worked out between labor and industry under which the hours of labor would be reduced so that employment could be spread to more people and a minimum wage established. Labor was encouraged to organize and bargain through agents of their own choosing and the 'yellow dog' or anti-union contract was prohibited. Posters emerged supporting this expanded idea of the trade association that bore the famous blue eagle and the slogan 'We Do Our Part'.

Section 7a of the NIRA bill stipulated that the codes guarantee minimum wages, maximum hours, and the right to collective bargaining for unions. These guarantees solicited labor's support for the new industrial codes in a working partnership with businesses. Workers were rallied with the slogan, 'The President Wants You to Join a Union'. While the government could not coerce industrialists to sign the codes, it could shame them into compliance by withholding the insignia of approval, the blue eagle. The Justice department was empowered to prosecute violators of the codes. Roosevelt called the NIRA 'the most important and far-reaching legislation ever passed by the American Congress'. The industrial codes brought stability to industrial sectors and illustrated the new role for government to intervene directly into the economy for rebalance. Several criticisms however arose over the NRA and the codes, the first being that it favored big business by exempting code signers from antitrust prosecution, and the second that adherence to the codes was dependent upon good will rather than legal constraint and good will was often not enough to ensure compliance. In relation to the former progressives, the NRA reflected the New Nationalism of Theodore Roosevelt more than it adhered to the ideals of the New Freedom of Woodrow Wilson. The NRA was modeled upon the World War I War Industries Board to harmonize production and end destructive competition. Under the direction of Hugh Johnson (1882-1942), the NRA had the support of over 500 industries, and the codes were hammered out by both labor and management.[135] In

---

[134] Ellis W. Hawley, The New Deal and the Problem of Monopoly (Princeton, NJ: Princeton University Press, 1966); Roy Jenkins, Franklin Delano Roosevelt (New York: Times Books, 2003), pp. 79-83, 88.

[135] William J. Barber, Designs Within Disorder: Franklin D. Roosevelt, the Economists, and the Shaping of American Economic Policy, 1933-1945 (Cambridge, England: Cambridge

all, the codes covered 2-1/2 million firms and 22 million workers, and factory production doubled between March and July 1933. Five hundred and forty-one codes were approved by President Roosevelt approving fair industrial practices and guaranteeing workers' rights. When the President had approved these codes of fair practice they became federal law. But some industrialists such as Henry Ford refused to sign, and some small operators discovered they could not financially honor the codes and resorted to evasion. Where codes could not be hammered out, the federal government stepped in to write them. The NRA codes were deemed patriotic and businesses working under codes proudly displayed the Blue Eagle agency symbol. Hugh Johnson, charged with administering the new codes of fair-trade, had been a Brigadier General during World War I and had acted decisively in the war's mobilization. In 1918 he had served on the War Industries Board as the Army's representative. He had headed the Purchase and Supply Branch and established the networks through which military procurement had taken place. In 1927 he had worked as Bernard Baruch's economic adviser and as a result of his record of earlier success in coordinating the intertwining of the military and industrial sectors to meet wartime common goals was tapped by Roosevelt in 1933 to administer the industrial codes.

But the NIRA was operating in peacetime and after early successes of the New Deal policies were felt, the impetus to agree on industrial codes seemed less acute. By mid-1934 the administrative breakdown of the NRA was derisively branded the 'National Run Around'. The failure of the NRA to compel cooperation from many special interests pointed to the necessity for stronger governmental enforcement policies. Many argued that the codes encouraged 'corporatism' and did not protect consumers and small businesses. Collapse of the NRA was perhaps imminent when the act establishing it was declared unconstitutional in the *Schechter Poultry Corp. v. United States* case of 1935. Unanimously the Supreme Court upheld the Schechter corporation, pointing out that since they were not involved in interstate commerce, the NRA code of fair practice could not regulate their business through the commerce clause. Moreover, in passing the NRA, the Congress had delegated legislative powers to the executive, which was also unconstitutional since it violated the ideal of separation of powers. But the NRA did lay the foundation for additional creative reforms

---

University Press, 1996); Ellis W. Hawley, "Hugh Samuel Johnson," in American National Biography. Edited by John A. Garraty and Mark C. Carnes, Vol. 12 (New York: Oxford University Press, 1999), pp. 82-83; Bernard Bellush, The Failure of the NRA (New York: W.W. Norton and Company, 1976); John Kennedy Ohl, Hugh S. Johnson and the New Deal (Dekalb: Northern Illinois University Press, 1985); John Kennedy Ohl, "General Hugh S. Johnson and the War Industries Board," Military Review 55 (May 1975): 35-48.

spawned by the federal government in the future, all the while protecting the foundations of capitalism at a time when other countries were experimenting with socialism, communism, Fascism or Nazism to correct the dislocations of the international Depression. And Wagner was especially proud of the Act's Section 7(a) that protected workers' rights and guaranteed collective bargaining. Wagner personified, as did FDR, the old progressive politician during the New Deal. They shared the ideal that government had the duty to mitigate the hardships caused by industrialization and poverty. Their ideals from the days of the Social Gospel rang true during the New Deal.

The same National Industrial Recovery Act that had created the NRA had also created the Public Works Administration in June 1933 and it had the same dual purpose of aiding industrial recovery and providing for unemployment relief. The PWA was headed by the secretary of the Interior Harold Ickes, proud of being an ex-Bull Mooser and ardent Progressive.[136] This program was committed both to relief and long range recovery and reform. Some 34,000 projects were completed under the PWA and some $4 billion spent on public buildings, highways, and parkways. One of the spectacular achievements of this program was the Grand Coulee Dam on the Columbia River.

The act creating the Tennessee Valley Authority introduced April 10, 1933 was passed by the Hundred Days Congress in May 1933, after the AAA but before the NIRA, and proved to be a broad experiment in social planning.[137] Since the Tennessee River, a branch of the Ohio, flowed through seven states, Tennessee, Kentucky, Virginia, North Carolina, Georgia, Alabama, and Mississippi, national control of the project was deemed essential. This had been a region of rural poverty where flooding and malaria were natural disasters. The project was inspired by FDR largely to develop a hydroelectric project which would produce public electricity, thus providing the federal government with a yardstick for judging the rates charged by private power companies and to put people to work. The president would be the most progressive in that area he knew best, the production of public electricity. In this endeavor FDR had the

---

[136] Linda Lear, Harold L. Ickes: The Aggressive Progressive, 1874-1933 (New York: Garland Press, 1981); Frances Perkins, The Roosevelt I Knew (New York: Viking Press, 1946); T.H. Watkins, Righteous Pilgrim: The Life and Times of Harold L. Ickes, 1874-1952 (New York: Henry Holt and Company, 1990); T.H. Watkins, "Harold LeClair Ickes," in American National Biography. Edited by John A. Garraty and Mark C. Carnes, Vol. 11 (New York: Oxford University Press, 1999), pp. 626-628; Harold Ickes, Back To Work: The Story of the PWA (New York: Da Capo Press, 1973 originally published in 1935); Graham J. White and John Maze, Harold Ickes of the New Deal: His Private Life and Public Career (Cambridge, Mass: Harvard University Press, 1985).

[137] Jenkins, Franklin Delano Roosevelt, pp. 76-78, 109, 156.

enthusiastic support of Republican senator George W. Norris of Nebraska who aided the president's proposal in Congress. The government owned valuable properties at Muscle Shoals where it had erected the Wilson Dam and power plant to produce nitrates for munitions during the World War I. The Tennessee Valley basin provided the New Dealers with an ideal area as the river drained 40,000 square miles which were badly eroded and which contained 2.5 million of the poorest people in the nation. By building dams on the Tennessee River the government both could provide employment and reform the private power monopoly. The Tennessee Valley Authority was governed by a board of three directors appointed by the president. It was a corporation protected by the power of government, but possessed with the initiative and business sense of a private enterprise. The TVA established nine dams on the Tennessee River and twenty dams on the tributaries and provided for the production of cheap electrical power, abundant cheap nitrates, restoration of eroded soil, reforestation, improved navigation and flood control. Additional smaller schemes were designed relating to fisheries, park and recreational facilities, and the elimination of malaria.

Prohibition was also ended and was justified as a means to raise much needed revenue from the taxation of alcoholic beverages for the federal government. Ending prohibition was further justified as a mechanism to control crime and gangsterism that had been spawned in the 1920s due to high demand for illegal alcohol. The theme song of FDR's first term was 'Happy Days are Here Again' which reflected America's relief that the noble experiment had ended. To further economize federal salaries were cut, the veterans did not receive their bonus, and a general attitude of thrift permeated the nation. Greedy businessmen were officially frowned upon while the government turned its attentions to humanitarian projects.

In June 1933 the World Monetary and Economic Conference, commonly known as the London Economic Conference because of the meeting site, was convened with delegates from sixty-six nations. It was called by the League of Nations established after World War I. FDR had sent Cordell Hull to represent the United States at the meeting designed to stabilize world currencies, reduce international tariffs, and agree on market mechanisms to restore prosperity from the depths of the Depression.[138] Many countries had gone off the gold standard and reparation payments stemming from the Treaty of Versailles were in default. Solutions were sought. FDR was taking America off the gold standard just at the

---

[138] Irwin F. Gellman, "Cordell Hull," in American National Biography. Edited by John A. Garraty and Mark C. Carnes, Vol. 11 (New York: Oxford University Press, 1999), pp. 445-450; Irwin F. Gellman, Secret Affairs: Franklin Roosevelt, Cordell Hull, and Sumner Wells (Baltimore, MD: Johns Hopkins University Press, 1995).

time of this London meeting and advocated a position of self-sufficiency to deal with the effects of the Depression believing problems should be solved first on a national level. He did not wish to be saddled with international agreements to return to the gold standard but he did favor tariff reductions world wide to stimulate trade and encourage business investment. The conference broke up in July without major decisions and was splintered by factions that supported either a return to the gold standard [European nations largely], or going to a sterling standard [Britain and the Commonwealth countries], or those who favored independent national policies [U.S. and Latin American nations]. But the conference did open lines of international discussion and harmonize friendships valuable later during World War II among the Allies.

No movement as significant as the New Deal could exist without having its ideals and ideologies, even its sentimentalities. Its indignation was directed toward the forgotten man and callousness and waste. Far less attention was focused against monopoly than during the earlier Progressive movement. The New Deal was much more inspired by engineering, technology, administration, economy, and by morals and uplift. The remarkable feature of the New Deal was that it took place constitutionally, without any illegal move, simply by stretching the extremely pliable fabric of American institutions. British socialist and professor of Political Science at the London School of Economics, Harold Laski, offered his view of the New Deal. "President Roosevelt is the first statesman in a great capitalist society who has sought deliberately and systematically to use the power of the state to subordinate the primary assumptions of that society to certain vital social purposes. He is the first statesman deliberately to experiment on a wholesale scale with the limitation of the profit-making motive. He is the first statesman who, of his own volition, and without coercion, either direct or indirect, has placed into the hands of organized labor a weapon which, if it be used successfully, is bound to result in a vital readjustment of the relative bargaining power of Capital and Labor."[139] Laski published *Democracy in Crisis* in 1933 and believed that FDR's policies were on track to correct the international downturn. He accepted a visiting post in America at Yale from 1931-1933 so that he might study the American situation more closely, wondering if democracy in the crisis of the Depression could be maintained. Laski continued his appraisal of FDR. "He is also the first statesman who, the taxing power apart, has sought to use the political authority of the state to compel, over the whole area of economic effort, a significant readjustment of the national income. No unbiased spectator of

---

[139] Barbara Bennett Peterson, America In British Eyes (Honolulu: Hawaii Chapter Fulbright Association, 1988), pp. 242-243.

the adventure involved can withhold his admiration for the courage such an effort has implied. Success or failure, it bears upon its face the hallmarks of great leadership. Improvised in haste, devised under the grim pressure of crisis, imposed in an atmosphere of panic and bewilderment, it stands out as remarkable, even significant, contrast to the economic policy of any other capitalist government in the world." In the eyes of foreign observers the New Deal was for the most part a remarkable success. The people of the United States had experienced a severe shock. The depression had been traumatic to their expectations, their values, and their confidence in themselves and their future. But the American leadership had tried something that was innovative and courageous, and in the words of Laski, had been more remarkable in its achievements than any other capitalistic country in the world.

However, domestic critics arose on both the left and right to challenge the Roosevelt goals, as the revolutionary spirit burgeons not when conditions are at their worst, but as they began to improve. The criticism of Roosevelt appeared not when things hit bottom but by 1934 when things were recovering as many progressives and most radicals had come to question many of the New Deal policies. Of all his political rivals none gave Roosevelt such deep concern as Louisiana's flamboyant Senator Huey Pierce Long.[140] In January 1934, Long, who had advocated re-distributions of wealth for many years, founded a national political organization with the slogan 'Share Our Wealth'. Although his program went through various versions he proposed in essence to liquidate all personal fortunes above $5 million and to establish a tax of 100% on incomes over $1 million per year. The money confiscated would be used to provide every family with a 'homestead' including a house, car and other necessities, and provide an annual family income of $2,000-$3,000. Additionally, old-age pensions, educational benefits and veterans pensions would be built into the scheme. Long advocated limiting the hours for labor in order to make more jobs and a balanced farm program. Share Our Wealth had an immense attraction, and by February 1935, Long supporters claimed more than 27,000 clubs. Contemptuous of Roosevelt and the well-educated urban New Deal reformers, Long used the barb of ridicule against them as he had against the southern planter-class culture and planter pretensions. The 'Kingfish' as he was called, hoped to win national power by pretending that Roosevelt's policies and claims to moral leadership shielded a national ruling class that held a monopoly of wealth and access to culture. Long's

---

[140] Arthur M. Schlesinger, Crisis of the Old Order: The Age of Roosevelt, 1919-1933 (New York: History Book Club, 2002); Arthur M. Schlesinger, Jr., The Politics of Upheaval, 1935-1936 (Boston: Houghton Mifflin, 2003); Miller, F.D.R., An Intimate History, pp. 267-269, 273, 281-288, 292-296, 364-365, 385.

supporters were located mostly in the rural South and scattered throughout the prairie states. His appeal seemed strong, and prior to the election of 1936 a third party seemed eminent, but Long was assassinated in Baton Rouge in September 1935. There would be no threat to divide the Democratic Party in the election of 1936, as the Republicans had divided their party in 1912.

Less powerful than Long but widely influential was Father Charles E. Coughlin, priest of the parish of Royal Oak, Michigan.[141] He proved to be such a popular speaker that by the fall of 1930 his talks were carried by CBS over a national network. Like Long, Coughlin had supported Roosevelt and then broke with him. Coughlin appealed to an audience bewildered by the Depression and hungry for some explanation. Coughlin told his 40 million listeners that the real evil-doers were the bankers; international complications were the work of the banker's conspiracy. Roosevelt had not inflated the currency and therefore purchasing power fast enough in his view, so Father Coughlin made government purchase of silver his rallying cry: 'Forward to Christ all ye people. God wills it! This religious crusade against the pagan God gold'. He organized a National Union for Social Justice, attracting people from every faith, and received over a million letters affirming his policies every year. He attacked bankers, New Deal planners, the farm program and the alleged sympathy of the administration for communism. He called for monetary inflation and for nationalization of banking. Vitriolic, anti-Semitic, and ambitious, his policies resembled fascism more than any leftist philosophy.

Of the challengers Roosevelt confronted, the most benign was Francis Townsend, a successful country doctor who had migrated to Long Beach, California and taken a position as a public health official.[142] A change of administration had cost him his job and Townsend came up with a plan that he believed would get the country on the road to recovery and incidentally provide security for the aged. In January 1934, Townsend set up Old Age Revolving Pensions Limited which advocated paying a pension of $200 per month to every citizen over sixty on the condition that he or she retire from gainful employment and spend the sum within one month. This pension would be financed by a 2% tax on business transactions and would build a revolving fund. Townsend argued that his plan would end mass joblessness because older people would be compelled to give up their jobs to younger unemployed citizens and because the rapid spending

---

[141] Miller, F.D.R., An Intimate History, pp. 292, 365-366, 386-388, 440; Jenkins, Franklin Delano Roosevelt, pp. 86-87.

[142] Miller, F.D.R., An Intimate History, pp. 366-374; Dexter Perkins, The New Age of Franklin Roosevelt (Chicago: University of Chicago Press, 1957); William E. Leuchtenberg, Franklin D. Roosevelt and the New Deal (New York: Harper and Row, 1963).

of pension checks would generate demand for more goods and services, stimulating production and creating more jobs.

The current of radicalism ran strongly in the 1934 elections and nowhere stronger than in California where well-known novelist Upton Sinclair launched his End Poverty in California campaign.[143] Instead of relief, the unemployed should be given a chance to produce for their own needs. EPIC called for the state to buy or lease lands on which the jobless could grow their own food. The state would also rent idle factories in which unemployed workers could turn out staples like clothing and furniture. The workers within this cooperative would be paid in script that could be used to buy goods within the 'production-use' system. Sinclair's EPIC program was his platform in the 1934 election for Governor of California and he won the Democratic primary. He was defeated however by the incumbent Frank Merriam who criticized Sinclair's position for 'concealing the communistic wolf in the dried skin of the Democratic donkey'.

Despite the radical discontent of individuals such as Huey Long, Father Coughlin, Francis Townsend, and Upton Sinclair, Roosevelt remained immensely popular and his popularity cut across all classes and ethnic groups. Roosevelt was vindicated in the elections of 1934 when the Democrats gained 13 seats in the House. FDR's charisma shown everywhere as people clamored to be associated with the president. With the exception of Huey Long, the extremists had little understanding of basic economics and practical affairs. Economists for example, had pointed out that with 10 million persons eligible for the Townsend pensions, the cost would have amounted to $24 billion a year, or half the national income. Collectively the extremists represented only a mild threat to Roosevelt and during 1934 and 1935 new bold New Deal programs were undertaken to quiet dissent.

In 1934 measures patterned after the Hundred Days Congress' emergency measures continued and were part of the so-called Second New Deal. The Federal Housing Authority was established in the spring, aimed at stimulating the building industry by granting small loans to householders for both new construction and home improvement.[144] So successful was the FHA that it was one of the few agencies to outlast the terms of the New Deal presidency. In 1937 Congress authorized the United States Housing Authority which was designed to lend money to states or communities for the construction of low-cost housing. Under

---

[143] William A. Bloodworth, Jr., Upton Sinclair (Boston: Twayne, 1977); Jon A. Yoder, Upton Sinclair (New York: Ungar, 1975); Alan Brinkley, Voices of Protest: Huey Long, Father Coughlin, and the Great Depression (New York: Vintage Books, 1983); Alan Brinkley, Culture and Politics in the Great Depression (Waco,TX: Markham Press, 1999).

[144] Joseph David Coppock, Government Agencies of Consumer Installment Credit (New York: National Bureau of Economic Research, 1940); Ray Smythe, Memo to F.D.R. (Washington, D.C.: Columbia Publishers, 1935).

its auspices 50,000 low-income units were constructed and slum clearance projects began. The quality of life was also improved by the Rural Electrification Administration, established in 1935.[145] Prior to its inception, only one farm in ten had power-line electrical service, and these were usually close to towns or cities. The REA offered low-interest loans to farmers' cooperatives, enabling them to build their own power lines and generate their own electricity. The spread of electricity transformed the countryside. Its success had been predicated upon the 1935 passage of the Public Utility Holding Company Act that eliminated monopolistic practices in the utilities industry. This act allowed the Federal Power Commission "to regulate the interstate transmission of electrical power, and the Federal Trade Commission to perform a similar function for natural gas."[146]

One of the most far reaching and lasting bills passed by the New Deal was the Social Security Act of 1935 providing for unemployment insurance and old age pensions.[147] The whole unemployment problem in the depression had pointed to the inadequacies of state, local, and private charities to cope with prolonged mass economic distress. Mounting unemployment had promoted emergency federal programs like the WPA and PWA and had spurred a search for ordered ways of providing safeguards against destitution and dependency in the future. In 1934, Roosevelt appointed a committee on Economic Security whose recommendations were forwarded to Congress and Congress shaped them into the Social Security bill. The measure offered three forms of aid. The first, pensions for people over sixty-five, was to be financed through a tax on wages [paid by employees] and a tax on payrolls [paid by employers] in commerce and industry. The second form of aid was unemployment compensation to be directed by states and to be financed by taxes on employers, who were to receive generous federal rebates providing they did not lay off workers. The third form of aid was federal money given to categories of individuals such as the blind, dependent and disabled who could not qualify for work under one of the work- projects agencies. Like the unemployment compensation measures, the categorical assistance involved state and federal coordination through matching funds. The Social Security Act was criticized for not covering agricultural and domestic workers and those who were self-employed, but in 1939 the law was amended to provide benefits for certain dependents and survivors of workers protected by the system. In future years,

---

[145] Sir William John McKell, Electricity Coordination in Great Britain and Rural Electrification in the United States of America (Sydney: T.H. Tennant, government printer, 1945); Joseph Peter Schaenzer, Rural Electrification (Milwaukee: Bruce Publishing Company, 5th rev. ed., 1955).

[146] Henry F. Graff, ed., The Presidents, A Reference History (New York: Charles Scribner's Sons, 1996), p. 432.

[147] Jenkins, Franklin Delano Roosevelt, pp. 88-96.

further categories of workers were added. The Social Security Act represented perhaps better than any other measure that the federal government was assuming responsibility for society's welfare and in doing so had adopted concepts and programs which had been developed in the populous, industrialized nations of Europe previously. The Depression had merely underscored the idea, long held by some progressives, that the country had needed such a plan that "offered a modicum of protection from the historic scourge of unemployment and guaranteed a minimum level of comfort for workers in their old age."[148] The Banking Act of 1935 strengthened the Federal Reserve Board and its supervision over the flow of money in the U.S. economy. The Public Utility Holding Company Act allowed the government to break up huge electrical power trusts and to regulate the rates and prices for power was also a part of the so-called Second New Deal and equally liberal in its policies. The Revenue Act of 1935 increased the surtaxes on high incomes, corporate profits and raised gift and inheritance taxes to raise federal revenues to help pay for the New Deal social programs. FDR believed that great accumulations of wealth could not be justified while others starved and sought to re-distribute benefits to the needy. The president strove to use consensus and bi-partisanship to accomplish his goals.

Another of the far-reaching accomplishments of the New Deal was the passage in July 1935, of the National Labor Relations Act, commonly known as the Wagner Act as it was sponsored in Congress by Senator Robert F. Wagner of New York.[149] This landmark legislation restored the labor guarantees that had been wiped out when the Schechter case determined the National Industrial Recovery Act to be unconstitutional. The NLR Act was upheld as constitutional in 1937. It recognized the right of workers to bargain collectively and prohibited employers from interfering with unionizing activities. The act established the National Labor Relations Board, which was authorized to supervise plant elections and designate successful unions as official bargaining agents, and to ensure that management 'bargained in good faith'. The NLRB could investigate unfair practices and issue 'cease and desist' orders when violations of the Wagner Act came to light. Reacting to New Deal support for collective bargaining, the labor movement grew stronger and launched massive organizational drives. The Act recognized that workers should have the right to participate in decision making about their workplaces and thus an element of democracy was encouraged within industry in regards to wages, hours, and workplace conditions. It protected

---

[148] Graff, ed., The Presidents, A Reference History, p.432. For FDR's Radio Address to the nation on the need for Social Security see Samuel I. Rosenman, Public Papers and Addresses of Franklin D. Roosevelt (New York: Macmillan, 1941) Vol 7 pp. 477-487.

[149] Jenkins, Franklin Delano Roosevelt, pp. 88, 96.

"the exercise by workers of full freedom of association, self-organization, and designation of representatives of their choosing, for the purpose of negotiating terms and conditions of their employment or other mutual aid or protection." Supported by government and public opinion, union membership increased from 3 million in 1933 to 4.7 million in 1936, and then to 8.2 million in 1939. America's largest industries were unionized, especially in the automobile, iron and steel, and electrical industries that employed thousands of workers. Union membership and recognition had become a worker's right and disallowed management from interfering with unions' rights to organize. In 1935 at the convention of the AF of L the delegates split on the question of craft v. industrial unions for the mass production industries. And after the traditional craft-oriented position of the federation won out, the minority leaders established the Committee [after 1938 Congress] for Industrial Organization with John L. Lewis as its chairman.[150] The CIO carried out efforts to unionize the mass production industries and established unions for steel, electrical, rubber, automobile, and textile workers. The CIO pioneered the sit-down strike whereby the workers remained in the plants rather than vacating them to strikebreakers. This device was effectively used to organize the United Automobile Workers Union and to receive recognition from General Motors and Chrysler Corporation by 1937. U.S. Steel became unionized in March 1937 and recognized the 40-hour week. Organized laborers recognized their debt to the Roosevelt administration and the CIO contributed heavily to his re-election campaign of 1936. The AF of L and the CIO re-merged in 1955.

One of the truly inspirational creations of the New Deal was the Federal Theater Project, established in August 1935, to employ out-of-work actors. Acting companies were organized wherever public relief rolls showed a concentration of needy theater professionals and they produced socially useful productions. This significant project offered public presentations to thousands of Americans who had never attended plays, children's theater, musicals, circus, puppet shows, vaudeville, dance, or classical productions before. The project raised America's spirit as regional festivals and outdoor dramas were organized. Sinclair Lewis' play *It Can't Happen Here* was a big draw and opened simultaneously in over twenty cities. Playwrights as well as actors were subsidized as culture was spread throughout America, reaching over 25 million people until 1939 when the project ended.

One of the issues that reminded FDR of just how dependent he was on the camaraderie of the Congress for the success of the New Deal was the issue of U.S.

---

[150] Robert H. Zieger, The CIO, 1935-1955 (Chapel Hill: University of North Carolina Press, 1995).

involvement in the World Court of International Justice. FDR wished the U.S. to adhere to this body but thirty-six senators voted down the proposal to join the World Court in January 1935. This was an illustration to FDR how strong the isolationist sentiment was in Congress and posed as a cautionary warning to temporize his international bent to safeguard domestic programs.

When presidential political aide Louis Howe died in 1936 in Washington, D.C. FDR arranged for a state funeral. It was held in the East Room of the White House as an indication of the respect he felt for his long-time political friend who had helped him reach his goal of the American presidency. Friends like Howe were a rare commodity in the world of politics, as by 1936 many former friends of the New Deal had become critics and the extremists attacked from both left and right.

During the second presidential campaign Roosevelt had illustrated his position with a parable. 'In the summer of 1932 a nice old gentleman wearing a silk hat fell off the end of a pier. A friend ran down the pier, dived overboard and pulled him out, but the silk hat floated off with the tide. After the old gentleman had been revived, he was effusive in his thanks. He praised his friend for saving his life. Today, three years later the old gentleman is berating his friend because the silk hat was lost'. Because Roosevelt had adopted the ideas of British economist John Maynard Keynes, who argued that the world depression could be solved if government would deliberately unbalance their budgets by increasing expenditures in order to stimulate consumption and investment, many conservative businessmen viewed him as financially irresponsible. 'America is in peril' the 1936 Republican platform declared under their nominee Governor Alfred M. Landon of Kansas. Landon was a wealthy oil-man whose chief claim to fame was that he had balanced the budget in his state in an era when unbalanced budgets were most common. Homespun and sincere, Landon was 'the Kansas Coolidge', but next to 'the Champ' FDR with his charm and political astuteness he stood little chance.[151] The Republicans won only two states, Maine and Vermont, and the Democrats won more than two-thirds of the seats in Congress. Landon did not even carry his home state of Kansas. Al Smith remarked after the election 'that no one wanted to shoot Santa Claus'. The 20th amendment moved the Inaugural Address to January instead of March and Roosevelt delivered one of the most stirring and memorable speeches in history as the Second Inaugural Address of Franklin D. Roosevelt was delivered on Wednesday, January 20, 1937.

---

[151] Miller, F.D.R., An Intimate History, pp. 381-390.

"When four years ago we met to inaugurate a President, the Republic, single-minded in anxiety, stood in spirit here. We dedicated ourselves to the fulfillment of a vision--to speed the time when there would be for all the people that security and peace essential to the pursuit of happiness. We of the Republic pledged ourselves to drive from the temple of our ancient faith those who had profaned it; to end by action, tireless and unafraid, the stagnation and despair of that day. We did those first things first.

Our covenant with ourselves did not stop there. Instinctively we recognized a deeper need, the need to find through government the instrument of our united purpose to solve for the individual the ever-rising problems of a complex civilization. Repeated attempts at their solution without the aid of government had left us baffled and bewildered. For, without that aid, we had been unable to create those moral controls over the services of science which are necessary to make science a useful servant instead of a ruthless master of mankind. To do this we knew that we must find practical controls over blind economic forces and blindly selfish men.

We of the Republic sensed the truth that democratic government has innate capacity to protect its people against disasters once considered inevitable, to solve problems once considered unsolvable. We would not admit that we could not find a way to master economic epidemics just as, after centuries of fatalistic suffering, we had found a way to master epidemics of disease. We refused to leave the problems of our common welfare to be solved by the winds of chance and the hurricanes of disaster.

In this we Americans were discovering no wholly new truth; we were writing a new chapter in our book of self-government.

This year marks the one hundred and fiftieth anniversary of the Constitutional Convention which made us a nation. At that Convention our forefathers found the way out of the chaos which followed the Revolutionary War; they created a strong government with powers of united action sufficient then and now to solve problems utterly beyond individual or local solution. A century and a half ago they established the Federal Government in order to promote the general welfare and secure the blessings of liberty to the American people. Today we invoke those same powers of government to achieve the same objectives.

Four years of new experience have not belied our historic instinct. They hold out the clear hope that government within communities, government within the separate States, and government of the United States can do the things the times require, without yielding its democracy. Our tasks in the last four years did not force democracy to take a holiday.

Nearly all of us recognize that as intricacies of human relationships increase, so power to govern them also must increase, power to stop evil; power to do good. The essential democracy of our Nation and the safety of our people depend not upon the absence of power, but upon lodging it with those whom the people can change or continue at stated intervals through an honest and free system of elections. The Constitution of 1787 did not make our democracy impotent.

In fact, in these last four years, we have made the exercise of all power more democratic; for we have begun to bring private autocratic powers into their proper subordination to the public's government. The legend that they were invincible, above and beyond the processes of a democracy, has been shattered. They have been challenged and beaten.

Our progress out of the depression is obvious. But that is not all that you and I mean by the new order of things. Our pledge was not merely to do a patchwork job with secondhand materials. By using the new materials of social justice we have undertaken to erect on the old foundations a more enduring structure for the better use of future generations.

In that purpose we have been helped by achievements of mind and spirit. Old truths have been relearned; untruths have been unlearned. We have always known that heedless self-interest was bad morals; we know now that it is bad economics. Out of the collapse of a prosperity whose builders boasted their practicality has come the conviction that in the long run economic morality pays. We are beginning to wipe out the line that divides the practical from the ideal; and in so doing we are fashioning an instrument of unimagined power for the establishment of a morally better world.

This new understanding undermines the old admiration of worldly success as such. We are beginning to abandon our tolerance of the abuse of power by those who betray for profit the elementary decencies of life. In this process evil things formerly accepted will not be so easily condoned. Hard-headedness will not so easily excuse hard-heartedness. We are moving toward an era of good feeling. But we realize that there can be no era of good feeling save among men of good will.

For these reasons I am justified in believing that the greatest change we have witnessed has been the change in the moral climate of America.

Among men of good will, science and democracy together offer an ever-richer life and ever-larger satisfaction to the individual. With this change in our moral climate and our rediscovered ability to improve our economic order, we have set our feet upon the road of enduring progress.

Shall we pause now and turn our back upon the road that lies ahead? Shall we call this the promised land? Or, shall we continue on our way? For 'each age is a dream that is dying, or one that is coming to birth.' Many voices are heard as we face a great decision. Comfort says, 'Tarry a while.' Opportunism says, 'This is a good spot.' Timidity asks, 'How difficult is the road ahead?'

True, we have come far from the days of stagnation and despair. Vitality has been preserved. Courage and confidence have been restored. Mental and moral horizons have been extended.

But our present gains were won under the pressure of more than ordinary circumstances. Advance became imperative under the goad of fear and suffering. The times were on the side of progress.

To hold to progress today, however, is more difficult. Dulled conscience, irresponsibility, and ruthless self-interest already reappear. Such symptoms of prosperity may become portents of disaster! Prosperity already tests the persistence of our progressive purpose.

Let us ask again: Have we reached the goal of our vision of that fourth day of March 1933? Have we found our happy valley?

I see a great nation, upon a great continent, blessed with a great wealth of natural resources. Its hundred and thirty million people are at peace among themselves; they are making their country a good neighbor among the nations. I see a United States which can demonstrate that, under democratic methods of government, national wealth can be translated into a spreading volume of human comforts hitherto unknown, and the lowest standard of living can be raised far above the level of mere subsistence.

But here is the challenge to our democracy: In this nation I see tens of millions of its citizens, a substantial part of its whole population, who at this very moment are denied the greater part of what the very lowest standards of today call the necessities of life.

I see millions of families trying to live on incomes so meager that the pall of family disaster hangs over them day by day.

I see millions whose daily lives in city and on farm continue under conditions labeled indecent by a so-called polite society half a century ago.

I see millions denied education, recreation, and the opportunity to better their lot and the lot of their children.

I see millions lacking the means to buy the products of farm and factory and by their poverty denying work and productiveness to many other millions.

I see one-third of a nation ill-housed, ill-clad, ill-nourished.

It is not in despair that I paint you that picture. I paint it for you in hope because the Nation, seeing and understanding the injustice in it, proposes to paint it out. We are determined to make every American citizen the subject of his country's interest and concern; and we will never regard any faithful law-abiding group within our borders as superfluous. The test of our progress is not whether we add more to the abundance of those who have much; it is whether we provide enough for those who have too little.

If I know aught of the spirit and purpose of our Nation, we will not listen to Comfort, Opportunism, and Timidity. We will carry on.

Overwhelmingly, we of the Republic are men and women of good will; men and women who have more than warm hearts of dedication; men and women who have cool heads and willing hands of practical purpose as well. They will insist that every agency of popular government use effective instruments to carry out their will.

Government is competent when all who compose it work as trustees for the whole people. It can make constant progress when it keeps abreast of all the facts. It can obtain justified support and legitimate criticism when the people receive true information of all that government does.

If I know aught of the will of our people, they will demand that these conditions of effective government shall be created and maintained. They will demand a nation uncorrupted by cancers of injustice and, therefore, strong among the nations in its example of the will to peace.

Today we reconsecrate our country to long-cherished ideals in a suddenly changed civilization. In every land there are always at work forces that drive men apart and forces that draw men together. In our personal ambitions we are individualists. But in our seeking for economic and political progress as a nation, we all go up, or else we all go down, as one people.

To maintain a democracy of effort requires a vast amount of patience in dealing with differing methods, a vast amount of humility. But out of the confusion of many voices rises an understanding of dominant public need. Then political leadership can voice common ideals, and aid in their realization.

In taking again the oath of office as President of the United States, I assume the solemn obligation of leading the American people forward along the road over which they have chosen to advance.

While this duty rests upon me I shall do my utmost to speak their purpose and to do their will, seeking Divine guidance to help us each and every one to give light to them that sit in darkness and to guide our feet into the way of peace."[152]

Roosevelt interpreted his landslide victory as a mandate for further reform in the old Progressive tradition of bi-partisanship and social morality. A third of the nation he stated was 'ill-housed, ill-clad, ill nourished' but the decisions of the Supreme Court had struck down some key elements of liberal reform and the decision in *Schechter Poultry Corp. v. United States* had been a unanimous one.[153] The Supreme Court had also declared unconstitutional the federal Guffey-Snyder Act that had established minimum wages in the coal industry as well as a New York state minimum wage statute. Apparently the Court seemed unable to determine which level of government should have this authority and seemed inconsistent in constitutional philosophy. Roosevelt feared that the major measures passed under the Second New Deal might be in jeopardy and the Court seemed to be blocking progress. Roosevelt conceived of a plan to make the Court fall into line with the New Deal. Drafted as the Judiciary Re-Organization Bill,

---

[152] Franklin D. Roosevelt Library, Hyde Park, New York; Samuel I. Rosenman, Public Papers and Addresses of Franklin D. Roosevelt, 13 Vols. (New York: Macmillan, 1941) Vol 6, pp. 1-6.
[153] Jenkins, Franklin Delano Roosevelt, pp. 82.

the scheme was to allow the appointment of an additional justice for every justice on the Court above the age of seventy, up to a maximum of six new potential appointees.[154] Roosevelt stressed overcrowded court dockets as the reason for the change. Conservatives attacked the bill as slippery, devious, and authoritarian. The Court itself issued a public statement that the hearing of its cases was up-to-date. FDR was criticized for attempting to upset the checks and balances established in the U.S. Constitution. The public held the Court as a sacred cow and prayers were heard 'God Bless the Supreme Court'. The composition [and their ages] of the nine-member court was four conservatives [Willis Van Devanter (78), James C. McReynolds (75), George Sutherland (75), and Pierce Butler (71) and three liberals Louis D. Brandeis (81), Harlan Fiske Stone (65), and Benjamin N. Cardozo (67).] Two justices who occasionally took the liberal side were Chief Justice Charles Evans Hughes and Justice Owen Roberts. Alarmed by the threat to the Court, the later two justices switched to support New Deal policies and their efforts were heralded as saving the composition of the high court as 'a switch in time saves nine'. Minor administrative reforms of the judiciary were enacted but the size and structure of the Court remained unchanged as the president's Court-reform bill went down to defeat in Congress. However, the Supreme Court upheld the Wagner Act and the Social Security Act as constitutional. In May 1937 justice Van Devanter retired and Roosevelt replaced him with Hugo Black of Alabama, an ardent New Dealer. Eventually FDR would appoint seven Supreme Court justices by 1941 as others retired including Stanley Reed, Felix Frankfurter, William O. Douglas, Frank Murphy, James Brynes, and Robert Jackson. But while this court fight temporarily hurt the prestige and leadership of Roosevelt, it did not diminish the successful New Deal policies. But when Roosevelt called a special session of Congress late in 1937 urging the passage of 'must' legislation, not a single bill passed and Congress grew increasingly quarrelsome and independent of his leadership. FDR might have enlisted the assistance of Congress in advance of introducing his court-packing bill and in the future, chastened, he was more careful to cultivate Congressional support—the old executive-legislative alliance that had worked so well in the first Hundred Days of the First New Deal.

---

[154] Jenkins, Franklin Delano Roosevelt, pp. 93-103; William E. Leuchtenberg, The Supreme Court Reborn: The Constitutional Revolution in the Age of Roosevelt (New York: Oxford University Press, 1996); Rosenman, Public Papers and Addresses of Franklin D. Roosevelt (New York: Macmillan, 1941) Vol 6 "The President Presents a Plan for the Reorganization of the Judicial Branch of Government" Feb. 5, 1937 pp. 51-66.

During the twilight of the New Deal the Second Agricultural Adjustment Act had been passed in 1938.[155] Farmers were to receive payments from the federal government if they followed soil conservation practices and planted only those allotted acreages calculated to meet normal demands and maintain prices. Growers of wheat, corn, rice, and tobacco were to receive parity payments with the base period 1919-1929 for tobacco and 1909-1914 for other crops. A last significant New Deal act was the Hatch Act of 1939 that prohibited federal administrators and officials from unlawful political campaigning and soliciting, and forbade the use of government funds for campaign purposes. The Hatch Act was expanded in 1940 to limit the amount of money that could be spent on any election. FDR advanced the cause of working women and children by securing passage of the Fair Labor Standards Act in June 1938 that abolished child labor. This act had finally embraced the cause of former progressive reformers as Florence Kelley, Robert Hunter, and Lillian Wald that had founded the New York Child Labor Committee to end this evil.[156] Now federal legislation had replaced haphazard state laws that had attempted to control child labor but had failed due to loopholes or lax enforcement. Woodrow Wilson's administration had earlier addressed this issue nationally and passed the Keating-Owen Child Labor Act in 1916, but it had been struck down by the Supreme Court in the *Hammer v. Dagenhart* case. FDR had stepped into this important void to accomplish yet another goal so dear to his old progressive friends and protected children from being exploited in industry.

The New Deal was fundamentally both a political and a social revolution. This was particularly true in the case of blacks and women. In some situations Afro-Americans were the victims of economic and political neglect but Roosevelt was sympathetic to black problems. He appointed many blacks to senior administrative positions and they mounted programs to assist their fellows. The blacks that Roosevelt appointed to administrative positions came to symbolize new opportunities for their race and overall the New Deal did more for blacks than any administration since Reconstruction.[157] "Black voters, long loyal to the party of Lincoln, switched their allegiance massively to the party of Roosevelt, who had avoided civil rights initiatives but had provided black Americans with unemployment relief and access to newly created agencies like the National

---

[155] Dean L. May, From New Deal to New Economics: The American Liberal Response to the Recession of 1937 (New York: Garland Publishers, 1981).

[156] Walter I. Trattner, Crusade for the Children: The National Child Labor Committee and Child Labor Reform in America (Chicago: Quadrangle Books, 1970).

[157] Harvard Sitkoff, A New Deal for Blacks (New York: Oxford University Press, 1981); Nancy J. Weiss, Farewell to the Party of Lincoln: Black Politics in the Age of FDR (Princeton, NJ: Princeton University Press, 1983).

Youth Administration."[158] FDR also attracted to the Democratic coalition immigrants and ethnic communities in large urban cities. "Roosevelt had thus forged a political coalition that would sustain the Democrats in power for nearly a generation. He had successfully wedded to the traditional southern and agricultural elements in his party the newly potent urban working class, including a variety of ethnic and racial minorities, and large sections of the middle class, grateful for the preservation of their threatened way of life."[159]

The experience of women in the depression was not drastically different from that of women during the 1920s in regards to the traditional focus on home and husband. However, like the situation for blacks, some new forces emerged and some women were elevated to leadership positions. The federal government came to concern itself with the plight of the working-woman, women's groups began to rally around the Equal Rights Amendment, and labor unions began to make a genuine commitment to the organization of women especially in the textile industry.[160] Women were often tapped for leadership positions within the growing social-welfare bureaucracy. The most active women's organizations remained the Woman's Party, the League of Women Voters, and the Consumer's League. The Business and Professional Women continued to work for equal employment for women in the professions, although the number of women professionals proportionally declined in the depression decade. The League of Women Voters successfully lobbied for the defeat of many state bills that proposed prohibiting the employment of married women and protested federal legislation which would disallow the employment of both husband and wife in the federal civil service. Women were actively speaking out to improve education, supporting the merit system within the civil service, and serving on panels to draft the National Recovery Administration's codes of fair practice. The League of Women Voters stated: 'We of the League are very much for the rights of women'. Eleanor Roosevelt supported women in leadership roles and served as an ombudsman and publicist for New Deal programs through radio broadcasts, newspaper columns, books, speeches, and as the president's wife. She was one of the instigators of the Federal Theater Project, the first extensive subsidy to the arts, and was a lobbyist for those groups like blacks, poor, and women, whose interests were overlooked. President Roosevelt's record in relating to women is excellent as he appointed a sizable number of women to important government offices including the first women as ministers to foreign countries. Ruth Bryan Owen, daughter of William

---

[158] Graff, ed., The Presidents, A Reference History, p. 432.
[159] Ibid.
[160] Joseph P. Lash, Eleanor and Franklin (New York: W. W. Norton and Company, 1971), pp. 280-291, 595, 602, 607.

Jennings Bryan served as minister to Denmark and Florence Jaffrey Harriman served as minister to Norway. The president elevated Florence Allen from the Ohio Supreme Court to the Circuit Court of Appeals. Frances Perkins, Secretary of Labor, was Roosevelt's most important female appointee and had come up through the ranks of settlement work and the Consumer's League. Rose Schneiderman of the Women's Trade Union League was FDR's appointee to the Labor Advisory Board of the NRA. Mary Dewson, former social worker and official of the Consumers' League was appointed head of the women's division of the Democratic party and under her leadership equal representation for women on the platform committee at the Democratic National Convention was achieved. Several acts enacted under the New Deal had special provisions for women such as the Social Security Act of 1935 that provided federal funding for state programs for both maternal and pediatric care as well as for state and local aid-to-dependent children programs.

The New Deal, of all its achievements, provided a recovery of faith and hope. Americans still had the capacity to reassert a measure of control over their social and economic destiny. In doing so, Americans were countering the prevailing ideologies of the day that fell back on socialism or authoritarianism. Americans had carved out something new, a mixed eclectic philosophy with wide, broad views of social possibility. America would be a stronger nation if everyone shared in its advantages and benefits. Roosevelt had spread his tent wide enough for all citizens to join in. He had committed his administration to deficit-spending to promote the general welfare and build a stronger America by making it better for everyone. The New Deal, with all its trials, mistakes, contradictions, successes, sentimentalities, and errors did not allow Americans to slip into despair. Intelligently the New Deal affirmed a faith in rational and intelligent experiment and humane social planning. By June 1938 through his re-fashioned executive-legislative alliance he secured a $3.75 billion budget.

One of the truly new themes in foreign policy during the first years of the Roosevelt New Deal was the theme of the Good Neighbor Policy with Latin America, introduced in FDR's First Inaugural Address.[161] TR's old theme of 'Speak Softly and Carry a Big Stick' had given way under FDR's carefully crafted philosophy of the good neighbor for all nations within the Western hemisphere—North and South Americas. Certainly there was the motivation to find new markets for American goods through trade and to tap new resources in the hemisphere, but there was also increasingly the strategic view of providing for

---

[161] Irwin F. Gellman, Good Neighbor Diplomacy: United States Policies in Latin America, 1933-1945 (Baltimore, MD: Johns Hopkins University Press, 1979); Harold Boaz Hinton, Cordell Hull: A Biography (New York: Doubleday, Doran and Company, 1942).

a common defense as war clouds threatened to spread over Europe. The philosophy of the Good Neighbor was again enunciated by FDR at the Pan American conferences held in Montevideo, Uruguay in 1933 and in Buenos Aires, Argentina in 1936. FDR pledged to respect the international and domestic integrity of the Latin American nations and adopted a policy of non-intervention as Hull had voted to support a resolution stating "no state has the right to intervene in the internal or external affairs of another."[162] America gave additional rights to Cuba, Panama, Haiti, Nicaragua and the Dominican Republic, former protectorate regions, and in March 1934 Congress voted to grant independence to the Philippines within ten years. Reciprocal trade agreements replaced interventionist military policies and encouraged endorsement of 'hemispheric solidarity' against Fascism and Nazism in Europe. Cultural understanding replaced decades of antagonism; trade cooperation stimulated economic recovery. The Roosevelt policy of the Good Neighbor was severely tested, however in 1938 when Mexico nationalized its oil industry, taking control of former U.S. investments. President Roosevelt applied patience and forbearance, refusing to militarily intervene, and eventually negotiated a financial settlement for the U.S. properties expropriated. The Good Neighbor policy worked ultimately to defend America through a united hemisphere as following the Japanese attack on Pearl Harbor, eighteen Latin American states either declared war against America's enemies or ended diplomatic relations with the Axis powers. Argentina and Chile remained neutral, but the entire hemisphere was largely cohesive in its support for the American and Allied cause and supplied the U.S. with wartime resources and friendly ports.

In 1937 Robert F. Wagner, with FDR's approval, spearheaded through Congress the U.S. Housing Act that provided federal subsidies for housing for low-income families. Wagner continued as 'the Chief Performer on the Hill' for FDR. And as war loomed across Europe, Wagner was alert to the need for the U.S. to press for the admission of Jewish refugees into Palestine and was supportive of the future Jewish state of Israel.

The re-election campaign of FDR in 1940 was unprecedented because of the president's desire for a third term.[163] He was challenged by the Republican nominee Wendell Willkie from Indiana. Willkie was a corporation lawyer who had worked for the Firestone company in Akron, Ohio, then became a partner in a law firm in New York that represented the Commonwealth and Southern

---

[162] Graff, ed., The Presidents, A Reference History, p. 435.
[163] Miller, F.D.R., An Intimate History, pp. 456-458.

Corporation engaged in administering public utilities.[164] He was also a liberal in regards to civil rights and had pressed for civil liberties for blacks especially in the south and campaigned against the Ku Klux Klan. FDR had based part of his career on regulating monopolistic holding companies like the Commonwealth and Southern Corporation so it was natural that the two men held opposing viewpoints. FDR's plans for the development of the Tennessee Valley Authority had further rankled Willkie and the Republicans who feared more government intrusion into the public utilities sector and advocated more laissez-faire methods defending private big business. Willkie was supported by the editor of *Fortune* magazine easterner Russell Davenport even though he carefully campaigned as a mid-westerner appealing also to the farming sectors. Ickes labeled Willkie the 'barefoot Wall Street lawyer' and FDR knew he was in for a tough contest. But FDR's incumbency, command of the radio air waves, and political machine overcame Willkie's down-home charisma, winning with 449 electoral votes to Willkie's 82, even though Willkie had captured 45% of the popular vote. Willkie was gracious in defeat and later aided Roosevelt's Lend-Lease program with public support and open declarations for preparedness as World War II opened in Europe. FDR had wanted to remain as president to combat Nazism to which he had a "deeply principled objection," "as a threat both to civilized values and to the medium-term security of the United States." In 1941 Willkie went to Britain, talked with Churchill, and spoke of America's loyalty to their cause of defeating Nazism. This trip was so successful that in 1942, with considerable daring in wartime, Willkie toured the world. He "logged 31,000 miles in forty-nine days as he visited with heads of state in North Africa, the Mideast, the Soviet Union, and China, including Charles de Gaulle, Joseph Stalin, Chiang Kai-shek, and Chou En-lai (Zhou Enlai)."[165] His book *One World* was published in 1943, arguing for mutual cultural respect and understanding among nations, a theme also favored by FDR in his plans for the United Nations. Willkie continued his activism supporting blacks during the war until his early death from a heart attack in 1944. To his credit FDR embraced many of the ideals held by Willkie, his popular

---

[164] James H. Madison, "Wendell Lewis Willkie," in American National Biography. Edited by John A. Garraty and Mark C. Carnes, Vol. 23 (New York: Oxford University Press, 1999), pp. 540-541; James H. Madison, ed., Wendell Willkie: Hoosier Internationalist (Bloomington: Indiana University Press, 1992); Warren Moscow, Roosevelt and Willkie (Englewood Cliffs, NJ: Prentice-Hall, 1968); Steve Neal, Dark Horse: A Biography of Wendell Willkie (Lawrence, KS: University Press of Kansas, 1989); Herbert S. Parmet and Marie B. Hecht, Never Again: A President Runs for a Third Term (New York: Macmillan, 1968).

[165] James H. Madison, "Wendell Lewis Willkie," in American National Biography, Vol. 23, pp. 540-541; Wendell Willkie, One World (New York: The Limited Editions Club, 1944); Wendell Willkie, This is Wendell Willkie (New York: Dodd, Mead, 1940); Jenkins, Franklin Delano Roosevelt, p. 110.

adversary. President Roosevelt was ever gracious in his victories, wisely attempting to bind those he defeated to his cause.

One of the most harmful indictments against the New Deal was that it did not really solve the Depression. Even in good times in early 1937 some 7.5 million Americans [out of a work force of 54 million] remained unemployed and the per capita national income did not reach 1929 levels until 1940. The Depression in America was swept away after the outbreak of World War II in Europe when orders for armaments bolstered the economy. The problems of unemployment and unbalanced production disappeared into the fringes of the economy. Roosevelt had been attacked from both Left and Right but had sustained the high moral ground promising to aid every American not just a privileged few. The Left pointed to Roosevelt's caution and conservative nature. They were critical that he had not moved to nationalize banking, sponsored laws against lynching, or done more for slum clearance and public housing, federal aid to education, civil rights, and health insurance. The Left believed Roosevelt was pro-business in his failure to break up monopolies. The Right on the other hand found Roosevelt too liberal, accusing him of conversing with communists, calling him Rooseveltski, and the extremists believe he wanted to make over America in the Marxist image. Moderates of a more rational bent accused Roosevelt of having no consistent philosophy, that the New Deal was fabricated in a sense of improvisation and ad hoc. Roosevelt seemed to vacillate between attempting to stimulate the economy by deficit spending and believing the budget should be balanced, between bolstering the business rich and helping the underprivileged, between attempting to solve America's economic problems through economic nationalism and engaging in broad-based economic internationalism. But perhaps that was part of the Roosevelt magic to walk a tightrope between various interest groups clamoring for assistance. Other critics pointed to the increase in the federal bureaucracy with the various alphabetical agencies making it more difficult to monitor government activities. While others criticized the growing power of the presidency largely due to Roosevelt's charisma as much as the drastic problems which confronted the nation in the first New Deal. Roosevelt's expansion of presidential powers seemed to threaten the balance between the executive, legislative, and judicial branches. Other foes pointed to the waste, incompetence, confusion, contradiction, and cross-purposes of the New Deal. And most of all critics lambasted the precedent of the dole and the establishment of the welfare state.

But there were many more friends than enemies of the New Deal. Americans everywhere applauded its efforts for combating the depression on a number of fronts that did provide relief, recovery, and reform. Shrewdly the president kept the nation informed through his Fireside Chats which established respect and confidence in his programs.[166] Capitalism was sustained in the face of crisis as the banks reopened, farm prices normalized, and debtors received relief. Fear was dispelled and the American people, America's greatest resource, were saved from further erosion of confidence in the system. Democracy was preserved as well at a time when democracies were eclipsed in Europe by both Fascism and Nazism. The New Deal was committed to the idea that the federal government should accept responsibility for the national welfare and this ideal has been accepted by both political parties since the landmark legislation of the 1930s. The New Deal introduced changes that Americans now simply take for granted and accept as positive measures: regulation of the stock exchange, agricultural price supports and acreage allotments to establish parity income for farmers, old age pensions, and relief for the needy. The New Deal in its encouragement of unions allowed workers to obtain a large share of the profits of industry. In changing the relationship between government and business Roosevelt had unwittingly geared the nation for war. The New Deal was the beginning of political modernization and the broad social experiments undertaken such as the TVA and the provision for Social Security were widely cheered.

The American nation had renounced laissez faire without embracing socialism. Government assumed the authority to underwrite the economic and social health of the nation. Built in stabilizers such as minimum wages, unemployment compensation, farm price supports, and society security helped to ensure that future depressions would not be as severe. Roosevelt however understood very well how to preserve American freedoms as he had avoided alike 'the revolution of radicalism and the revolution of conservatism'. This was the great triumph of the New Deal in addition to the renunciation of dark fatalism and the restoration of that bright sunny air of confidence. 'Happy Days' were indeed here again as the popular song had cheered the ending of Prohibition and the repeal of the Volstead Act as well as the stabilizing of the U.S. economy.

Many prominent figures of the FDR campaigns achieved prominence and, capitalizing upon the achievements of the New Deal, went on to achieve new goals after leaving President Roosevelt's administration. Members of the Brains Trust remained influential. Raymond Moley had received appointment to the State Department following FDR's 1932 election. Moley had advised FDR to remain uncommitted to international monetary designs at the London Economic Conference in 1933 "believing that recovery required insulation from

---

[166] Betty H. Winfield, FDR and the News Media (New York: Columbia University Press, 1994).

international economic pressures that would vitiate the New Deal program."[167] Moley served FDR as assistant secretary of state from the time of FDR's inauguration and worked with other New Dealers to craft the new legislation that became part of the Hundred Days programs initiated from FDR's Oval Office and passed by Congress. Moley assisted FDR in his goal to take America off the gold standard by taking the president's case for doing so to the U.S. Treasury department and to London bankers. Following the London Economic Conference where Moley and his superior Cordell Hull exchanged disagreements over currency devaluation and tariff reduction, Moley was moved by FDR to the Justice Department. He stayed briefly in Justice but resigned shortly thereafter to publish *Today* magazine that later merged with *Newsweek*. These magazines helped shape public opinion in support of New Deal policies and educated Americans on how government policies and programs worked. But eventually Moley and Roosevelt came to disagree over how the government should handle corporate businesses and FDR slowly saw Moley as a captive of conservative interests. Their disagreements ruptured in 1940 when Moley supported the campaign of Wendell Willkie against FDR's bid for a third term. They had grown apart and diverged on political goals for the New Deal. Moley increasingly felt that the New Deal government had grown too big. He later advised Republican candidates for office and by 1964 published *The Republican Opportunity* which was critical of what he viewed as bloated federal bureaucracy with the Great Society. FDR had been ever genial to his wayward former protégé who had joined the opposition. Moley looked back fondly to his years in government service in two books, *After Seven Years* published in 1939 and *The First New Deal* that appeared in 1966. Many of the Moley papers ended up at the Hoover Institute at Stanford University because of his friendship in later years with Herbert Hoover. But Moley had served FDR's goals especially during the 1932 election campaign and shortly after in the crafting of early New Deal legislation. Moley's falling out with Cordell Hull at the World Monetary and Economic Conference in London had proved his early undoing in the first four years of FDR's presidency, and he ceased being an effective participant in Democratic policies.

Adolf Berle had returned to Columbia University after the 1932 election of FDR but accepted temporary advisory assignments to aid the president during the Banking Crisis and the railroad emergency of 1933. In foreign policy, Berle made a trip with Sumner Welles for the president to the Caribbean to stabilize the government in Havana, Cuba. In New York during the early New Deal, Berle became the financial adviser to Mayor Fiorello La Guardia and was appointed

---

[167] Elliot A. Rosen, "Raymond Moley," in American National Biography, Vol. 15, pp. 665-667.

chamberlain of the city from 1934-1938. FDR graciously rewarded Berle's hard advisory work with funds from the federal Reconstruction Finance Corporation and the Public Works Administration. With these funds Berle was able to stabilize New York City's finances between 1934-35 and pull it back from the edge of bankruptcy. FDR continued to consult with Berle throughout the New Deal on economic issues. Berle was one of the founders of the Liberal Party in New York. After having solved economic problems in New York, Berle took a position offered by Roosevelt in 1938 in the State Department as an assistant secretary of state where he organized Pan-American economic conferences committed to fending off threats from fascism and communism. Berle effectively ran the State Department's intelligence world-wide network during World War II and later served as ambassador to Brazil. He returned to the States to work with the CIA formulating anti-Communist policies for Western Europe and Latin America. He kept a diary that was largely published by his wife, Beatrice Bishop Berle, and Travis Jacobs as *Navigating the Rapids, 1918-1971: From the Papers of Adolf A. Berle* that appeared in 1973. He was a New Dealer who bridged into the postwar world in a similar leadership position. In 1951 he chaired the Twentieth Century Fund, an organization that functioned as a political think tank aiming to solve postwar problems. During the administration of President John F. Kennedy, Berle headed the administration's Latin America task force and assisted in the design for the Alliance for Progress.[168] Thus New Deal liberalism infused the 1960s and perpetuated progressive reforms through individuals like Berle who remained influential in government politics.

Rexford Tugwell had joined FDR's New Deal administration first as assistant secretary of agriculture from 1933-1934, then as under secretary of agriculture from 1934 to 1935. He was made director of the Resettlement Administration from 1935 to 1936. Tugwell resigned from the administration in December 1936. Tugwell had worked on preparations for the London Economic Conference held in 1933 and was instrumental in drafting the first Agricultural Adjustment Act and implementing the domestic allotment program. He worked well with Secretary of Agriculture Henry Wallace and agreed with him on acreage allotments to restrict production and raise farm prices. But Tugwell had a falling out with George Peek, who administered the Agricultural Adjustment Administration, as Peek favored marketing agreements rather than cutting farm production. Tugwell and his liberal friends in U.S. Department of Agriculture wanted to protect small farmers against large land-owners and they disagreed with Peek's successor Chester Davis over

---

[168] Jordon A. Schwarz, "Adolf Augustus Berle," in American National Biography. Edited by John A. Garraty and Mark C. Carnes, Vol. 2 (New York: Oxford University Press, 1999), pp. 657-659.

the treatment of sharecroppers. At this juncture, Tugwell was moved by FDR to the Resettlement Administration as Henry Wallace sided with Davis. Through his work with the RA, Tugwell was able to advance many of his ideas concerning land use and to take less productive land out of production and resettle poor farmers on better farmland. Tugwell also incorporated ideas from urban planners and encouraged their ideas to create greenbelts around industrial cities for health and beauty. "In addition to his AAA role, Tugwell was influential in other areas. He was actively involved in the USDA reorganization, budget cutting, bureau revitalization, conservation work, relief measures, and formulation of Puerto Rican sugar quotas. Outside the USDA, he played a part in formulating and reviewing the National Recovery Administration and suggested specific programs to replace the NRA when the Supreme Court declared it unconstitutional."[169] Tugwell courted congressional representatives and senators and espoused the New Deal aims and programs on behalf of FDR. He lobbied for the Copeland Bill "designed to strengthen existing pure food and drug laws." He had resigned in 1936 under charges that he was too liberal and sympathetic towards the Soviet Union. He became the vice president of American Molasses Company in 1937, then was appointed by New York Mayor Fiorello LaGuardia as chairman of the city's Planning Commission. He served for three years designing zoning laws, creating master plans for New York City's growth and encouraging low-income housing. FDR called Tugwell back to federal service in 1941, naming Tugwell Governor of Puerto Rico and he also served as Chancellor of the University of Puerto Rico. Under his tutelage, the Puerto Ricans were guided through World War II and planned for the election of their own Governor by 1946. Tugwell returned to university life and lectured at various institutions including Harvard and the London School of Economics on economic planning. He had been a loyal New Dealer who forwarded many of FDR's key programs .

Former Vice-President from 1932 to 1940 John Nance Garner had believed firmly in secure property rights and in a sound U.S. currency. He had chafed at the vast public works projects that FDR utilized to 'prime the pump' of the depression economy. He challenged FDR on his 'court-packing scheme' and had decided to leave the vice-presidency by the election of 1940 to return to his ranch in Texas. He had performed his vice-presidential duties in an official capacity but found that basic disagreements prohibited him from staying on during the later two terms of the New Deal.

---

[169] Michael V. Namorato, "Rexford Guy Tugwell," in American National Biography. Edited by John A. Garraty and Mark C. Carnes, Vol. 21 (New York: Oxford University Press, 1999), pp. 923-925.

Henry Morgenthau, Jr. would remain as Secretary of Treasury after April 1945 as requested by President Harry Truman. He was intricately involved in funding nearly all of the war effort and was eager to see an end to he ordeal. He resigned, however, by July when he was not asked to attend the Potsdam conference that was to determine the fate of defeated Germany as he had wished to be there to represent U.S. financial interests. From his home in Dutchess County, he dispensed private funds to worthy charities. He served as chairman of the United Jewish Appeal 1947-1950 and of the Board of Governors of the American Financial and Development Corporation for Israel 1951-1954.

Former Secretary of Agriculture and Vice-President Henry A. Wallace was appointed Secretary of Commerce in 1945 but resigned by 1946 over foreign policy issues stemming from the aftermath of World War II. He became the editor of *The New Republic*. Like so many of the early New Dealers loyal to FDR, he had progressive and social gospel political roots. In 1948 Wallace ran for the presidency on the Progressive Party ticket attempting to solve many mid-westerners' farming issues. After defeat he returned to experimental farming and writing about new scientific agricultural techniques.

New Deal Secretary of the Interior Harold Ickes later worked for President Truman less than a year. He resigned from Truman's service and retired to a farm in Olney, Maryland, where he continued to write his diary of his time with the New Deal and FDR's administration. Part of his memoir was published in the *Saturday Evening Post* and he contributed liberal articles, usually on conservation and reclamation, for the *New York Post* and *The New Republic*. Ickes wrote one of the most amazing books to come out of the New Deal Era titled *Secret Diary*, edited by his second wife Jane Dahlman Ickes after his death.

Frances Perkins, after her tenure as New Deal Secretary of Labor that ended with her resignation July 1, 1945, was invited to lecture at the University of Illinois, in Salzburg, Austria, and at Cornell University on labor relations, a field she had helped pioneer. Perkins was appointed to the Civil Service Commission by President Truman in late 1945 and she continued there until 1953. From 1955 until shortly before her death, she taught as a visiting professor at Cornell in the School of Industrial and Labor Relations. As the first woman to hold a Cabinet position, Perkins, usually dressed in black dresses with a white bow and black hats, had carried her ideals for social reform from the settlement houses into the U.S. Presidency. She had achieved great ends in service to the man she greatly admired, FDR.

Harry Hopkins had resigned from the administration in 1940 after securing FDR's re-nomination and election but was kept on as a confidential aide. FDR sent Hopkins to London in 1941 to discuss America's Lend-Lease program to

Britain. Much goodwill was generated by Hopkins' endeavors in Britain in his meetings with Prime Minister Churchill and he hoped, as did the president, that Britain and the U.S. could agree on allied strategy. Harry Hopkins returned to Washington to organize Lend-Lease and to prepare for the Atlantic conference between FDR and Churchill. Following the Nazi invasion of the U.S.S.R. Hopkins was sent by FDR to Moscow to discuss with Marshal Joseph Stalin similar aid to the Russian armies, as now they faced a common enemy. After America had been drawn into the World War II, Hopkins headed the British-American Munitions Assignments Board and coordinated its efforts with the Army Chief of Staff Marshall. He worked closely with several kindred spirits on the task of coordinating U.S.-Britain supplies. Those within his immediate circle were W. Averell Harriman, America's Lend-Lease spokesman in Britain, Edward Stettinius head of Lend-Lease in the U.S., Oscar Cox within the U.S. Treasury supporting the program, Major General James H. Burns who headed the Army Ordnance Department, and Lewis W. Douglas head of the War Shipping Administration, all of whom collectively were known as 'the Hopkins Shop'.[170] Hopkins had a gift for winning the confidence of others through his hard work and stellar successes. Throughout the war Harry Hopkins was a lightning rod for Allied cooperation and displayed a keen intellect's hand in foreign policy decisions related to the invasion of North Africa and later the invasion of Normandy in France. He worked courageously and equally well with the British and the Soviets. During the war Averell Harriman became the U.S. ambassador to the Soviet Union and 'the Hopkins Shop' continued to shape policy and support good relations that culminated at the Yalta conference in February 1945. Hopkins wanted the allies to continue wartime friendships and was instrumental in securing foreign endorsements for the formation of the United Nations. Later Hopkins acted on behalf of President Truman to discuss postwar measures with Stalin. He resigned from government public service thereafter and was awarded the Distinguished Service Medal in late 1945.

Hugh Johnson, following his time with the National Recovery Administration, served briefly as head of the Works Progress Administration in New York City. A colorful figure, called 'Old Iron Pants' for his military directness while in civilian jobs, he began a syndicated column and became a radio commentator continuing to talk of the need for social reforms. He supported the New Deal as originally conceived, then began to criticize FDR over the mounting federal deficit. He had supported Wendell Willkie in 1940. Johnson

---

[170] George T. McJimsey, "Harry Lloyd Hopkins," in American National Biography. Edited by John A. Garraty and Mark C. Carnes, Vol. 11 (New York: Oxford University Press, 1999), pp. 172-174.

swung his support to the America First Committee as World War II threatened. But when he worked for FDR he had foreseen the merging of interests between businesses and industries and the federal government through national planning with his NRA work.

These were some of the colorful and responsible people around FDR who under the president's direction had made the New Deal work and saved the U.S. economy for capitalism and American civil liberties for freedom. The American system had worked under FDR's careful direction and leadership. He and those he chose to work with him were the right individuals, at the right place, at the right time to preserve America's spirit and hope. A renewed America was still the 'City Upon the Hill, a Beacon to the World'.

Figure 2. Franklin Delano Roosevelt campaigning for the Vice-President of the U. S. in the election of 1920. Reproduced from the Collection of the Library of Congress, LC-USZ62-113659

Chapter 5

FDR AND THE COMING OF WORLD WAR II

The 1920s and 1930s were times of isolationism in America. The senselessness and bloodiness of World War I had caused Americans to turn their back on the rest of the world in shouldering international responsibilities. Neither Harding nor Coolidge had taken an active role in foreign affairs, preferring to leave policy to their secretaries of state. Hoover, understanding the problems of foreign policy acutely, perhaps moved too cautiously to be effective. Americans wanted to steer clear of entanglements. In 1925 President Coolidge had explained that the American citizenry had had all the war, all the taxation, and all the military service that they had wanted and did not wish for more international sacrifice. The interest in disarmament at the Washington Naval Conferences in 1920-1921 had stemmed partly from the Republican desire to cut taxes and partly to stand away from any preparations for war and excessive military spending. Peace societies abounded such as the Women's International League for Peace and Freedom and the Carnegie Endowment for International Peace.

But isolationism did not deter the government from seeking to advance American economic interests abroad in Latin America and in China with the Open Door. To encourage self-determination of peoples in the Western Hemisphere, the Clark memorandum of 1930 advanced by Hoover's undersecretary of state J. Reuben Clark had denounced America's right to intervene in the internal affairs of Latin American countries. Under Franklin Rosevelt the Good Neighbor policy was developed attempting to dispel the image of 'the Colossus of the North' or 'rich Uncle Sam' and to extend the hand of a friendly trading partner. Cordell Hull, as secretary of state under FDR, had continued the theme of the Good Neighbor, supporting a resolution at the Montevideo Pan-American Conference of 1933 that no state had the right to intervene in the internal or external affairs of another.[171] American military forces stationed in Nicaragua were withdrawn in 1934 and thereafter the U.S. renounced the right to intervene in Cuban affairs.

But the futility and danger of isolationism were later exposed when Americans could not ignore nor remain aloof from swirling international events which moved the world closer to war. Some historians have said that World War II began on the windswept plains of Manchuria, in the war between Japan and China.[172] Between 1931 and 1933 the Japanese had occupied Manchuria, renaming it Manchukuo. China appealed to the League of Nations which authorized an investigative body, the Lytton commission [named after British statesman Lord Edward Robert Bulwer Lytton], that simply branded Japan as an aggressor state and the League officially refused to involve itself in China. So too, the United States refused China's appeal for intervention; thus in one sweep the Nine Power pact and the Kellogg-Briand pact were broken, being viewed in these circumstances as solely moral instruments without powers of coercion to prevent aggression. The United States issued the Hoover-Stimson Doctrine that stated idealistically that the United States would not recognize any territory taken by force. Japan's response to these developments was to withdraw from the League of Nations in 1933.

In 1937 Japanese forces crossed the Marco Polo Bridge on the boundary between Manchukuo and northern China, initiating a long protracted war that became one of the theaters of World War II.[173] The American State department now cast a wary eye on the events in the region and Congress passed a joint arms embargo against Japan. "Peace loving nations must take a concerted effort in opposition to those who violate treaties and who are creating a state of international anarchy," said President Roosevelt. The best response to lawlessness and anarchy was to quarantine it. This emboldened speech was temporized during the events following the sinking on December 12, 1937 of the *Panay*, an American gunboat on the Yangtze River. No issue of war was made and the

---

[171] Irwin F. Gellman, Good Neighbor Diplomacy: United States Policies in Latin America, 1933-1945 (Baltimore, MD: Johns Hopkins University Press, 1979); Harold Hinton Boaz, Cordell Hull: A Biography (New York: Doubleday, Doran and Company, 1942); Julius Pratt, Cordell Hull, 1933-1944 (New York: Cooper Square Publishers, 1964); Frederick B. Pike, FDR's Good Neighbor Policy: Sixty Years of Generally Gentle Chaos (Austin: University of Texas Press, 1995); Robert H. Holden, Latin America and the United States: A Documentary History (New York: Oxford University Press, 2000).

[172] Robert Dalleck, The Roosevelt Diplomacy and World War II (New York: Holt, Rinehart and Winston, 1970); Forrest Davis, How War Came, From Fall of France to Pearl Harbor (New York: Simon and Schuster, 1942).

[173] Laurence Lafore, The End of Glory: An Interpretation of the Origins of World War II (Philadelphia: J.B. Lippincott Co., 1970); Pierre Renouvin, World War II and Its Origins:

United States accepted Japanese apologies and an offer of an indemnity. Japan claimed their aviators had struck the gunboat in error but "visibility was excellent and an American flag was painted on the deck."[174] This mollification was partly due to the deeply entrenched isolationist sentiment in America. Roosevelt implied that personally he might have pressed for concessions but "its a terrible thing," he said, "to look over your shoulder when you are trying to lead and to find no one there."

Isolationistic sentiments had promoted an investigation of the munitions makers who had opposed the joint arms embargo against Japan. The Senate investigative commission of Gerald P. Nye of North Dakota found that the profits of corporate interests such as DuPont, had risen sharply during World War I as DuPont's earnings from the sale of munitions soared from five million in 1914 to eighty-two million in 1916. Thus these 'merchants of death' had held an interest in involving America in war, judged the committee. Walter Millis, in *The Road to War, 1914-1917* published in 1935, suggested that British propaganda, the heavy purchases of American supplies by the Allies, and Wilson's differing reaction to violation of neutral rights by Germany and Britain had drawn the U.S. into a war it could have avoided. These investigations and writings allowed isolationism to continue to triumph in the U.S. These sentiments also formed the backdrop for the Neutrality act of 1935 that forbid the sale of munitions to all belligerents whenever the president should proclaim that a state of war existed.[175] This was followed by two other acts in response to Italy's invasion of Ethiopia in 1935 and the Civil War in Spain in 1936, the Neutrality act of February 1936, forbidding loans to all belligerents, and the 1937 act which forbid Americans to travel on belligerent ships.[176] This neutrality legislation was designed to prohibit the kind of foreign and domestic entanglements that had drawn the U.S. into World War I. Americans did not have the right in the mid-Thirties as they had prior to World

---

International Relations, 1929-1945 translated from French by Remy Inglis Hall (New York: Harper and Row, 1968).

[174] Robert Dalleck, Franklin D. Roosevelt and American Foreign Policy, 1932-1945 (New York: Oxford University Press, 1979 republished 1995); Frank Freidel, America In the Twentieth Century (New York: Alfred A. Knopf, 1965), p. 373.

[175] Gordon A. Craig and Felix Gilbert, eds., The Diplomats, 1918-1939 (Princeton: Princeton University Press, 1994, originally published 1953); Keith Eubank, The Origins of World War II (New York: Crowell, 1969); Conrad Black, Franklin Delano Roosevelt: Champion of Freedom (New York: Public Affairs and London: Weidenfeld and Nicolson, 2003).

[176] George W. Baer, The Coming of the Italian-Ethiopian War (Cambridge, Mass: Harvard University Press, 1967); James Dugan and Laurence Lafore, Days of Emperor and Clown: The Italo-Ethiopian War, 1935-1936 (Garden City, NY: Doubleday, 1973); Esmonde Manning Robertson, Mussolini As Empire-builder: Europe and Africa, 1932-1936 (London and New York: Macmillan, 1977); John Strawson, The Italian Campaign (New York: Carroll and Graf Publishers, 1988).

War I, to travel on passenger liners belonging to belligerent nations, thus prohibiting events like the sinking of the *Lusitania* that had gone down with numerous U.S. citizens. Americans could not sell arms and munitions abroad and U.S. ships were banned from entering war zones for their own protection. FDR carefully enforced this neutrality legislation because isolationist voters were essential to carry forward his domestic legislation for New Deal reforms.

Beyond the activities of the Japanese in Manchuria were the developments within Fascist Italy and Nazi Germany that were increasingly disturbing to American leadership. In October 1922 King Victor Emmanuel of Italy had asked Benito Mussolini to form a Cabinet after the March on Rome. Mussolini was born in 1883 near Forli in north central Italy. His father was a blacksmith and his mother had taught school for four years. Largely self-educated, Mussolini was for a short time a village school master, then became interested in socialism, becoming the editor of *Avanti* the official socialist newspaper. Because he was an interventionist in World War I he was expelled from the socialist party which advocated pacifism and he became the editor of his own newspaper *Il Popolo D'Italia*. In 1915 he organized a rudimentary political party he called the Fasci D'azione revoluzionaria and he always considered this event to be the founding of the Fascist party in Italy. He fought in World War I, attaining the rank of corporal and early on had identified his fascists with anti-communism. In this role Mussolini as leader of the fascist Black Shirts or guardians of the party's discipline had been asked to form a conservative government. At the core of fascism was Mussolini's idea that the government should be entrusted to 'those who can rise above their individual natures to realize the aspirations of a collective society'. The doctrine of popular sovereignty was repudiated in the name of state sovereignty. Fascism required that the state be organized along corporate lines to make Italy an *autarky* or a nation independent from foreign countries economically. Mussolini and his Black Shirts advocated nationalism and super-patriotism and in the summer of 1922 when 3,000 of Mussolini's retinue had stormed Rome they had done so to 'slay the Red Dragon of Communism'. Mussolini had been made Il Duce or Premier and ruled through the Italian Cabinet responsible to himself alone and through the policy making Fascist Grand Council. The fascists nourished the idea that Italy had not received her just due from the treaties ending World War I.

Mussolini's ambition to connect Eritrea with Italian Somaliland on the Indian Ocean was successfully accomplished by his seizure of Ethiopia in 1935. But the United States was disturbed by this aggressive seizure and levied a moral embargo against the export of oil to Italy, and issued the Neutrality Acts of August 1935, February 1936 and May 1937. In October 1935 the League of Nations branded

Italy as an aggressor nation and Mussolini took Italy out of the League and joined Germany in the Rome-Berlin Axis and the Anti-Comintern [Anti-Communist International] Pact that effectively declared war on international communism. FDR aligned America with other members of the League of Nations in placing sanctions on Italy after the Ethiopian Crisis and through the enforcement of the Neutrality law of 1935 that prohibited arms shipments to the belligerents. "Similarly, Roosevelt artfully invoked the Neutrality Act during the Spanish Civil War, reinforcing the Anglo-French Nonintervention Committee's effort...to contain the conflict within Spanish borders."[177] Thus FDR found ingenious ways to attempt to stop aggression through legal means while being constrained by the Neutrality legislation.

The activities of Adolf Hitler likewise raised fears in America. Hitler had been born in Braunau in Austria in 1889 and in *Mein Kampf* he spoke of its significance. "Today it seems to me providential that fate should have chosen Braunau am Inn as my birthplace. For this little town lies on the boundary between two German states which we of the younger generation at least have made it our life-work to reunite by every means at our disposal....This little city on the border seems to me the symbol of a great mission."[178] Thus, Hitler foretold the *Anchluss* or the move to unify Germany and Austria in 1938. At the end of World War I, Hitler had joined the German Worker's party that became the nucleus of the NAZI party or the National Socialist German Worker's Party so named after 1920. He organized the Sturmabteilung (S.A.) or the Brown Shirts to protect Nazi rallies and designed the Nazi emblem-the red flag with the white disc and the black swastika. In *Mein Kampf* he explained: "In *red* we see the social idea of the movement, in *white* the nationalistic idea, in the *swastika* the mission of the struggle for the victory of the Aryan man."[179] In 1923 in Munich Hitler had been involved in a plot known as the Beer Hall Putsch that had attempted to topple the government of the democratic Weimar Republic. He was arrested and charged with treason. At his trial he had said: "I alone bear the responsibility. I am not a criminal, there is no such thing as treason against the traitors of 1918" who had

---

[177] Henry F. Graff, ed., The Presidents, A Reference History (New York: Charles Scribner's Sons, 1996), p. 436.

[178] Adolf Hitler, Mein Kampf (Boston: American edition, Houghton Mifflin, 1943), p. 3 quoted in William L. Shirer, The Rise and Fall of the Third Reich, A History of Nazism Germany (New York: Simon and Schuster, 1960), p. 6; Gordon A. Craig, Germans (New York: Putnam, 1982); Gordon A. Craig, Germany, 1866-1945 (Oxford: Clarendon Press, 1978).

[179] Hitler, Mein Kampf, pp. 496-497 quoted in Shirer, Rise and Fall of the Third Reich, p. 44; Esmond Manning Robertson, ed., Origins of the Second World War: Historical Interpretations (London: Macmillan, 1971).

signed the harsh Treaty of Versailles.[180] Thus, arose the 'stab in the back thesis', or the idea that the German signers of the treaty of Versailles had acted as traitors who had bound Germany in chains. Hitler and the Nazi Party, he promised, would liberate Germany from her bonds by systematically dismantling the Versailles treaty through actions such as the remilitarization of the Rhineland in 1936. Because of the rising strength of the Nazi Party at the polls, Hitler had been asked to become Chancellor of Germany in 1933 in the government of President Paul von Hindenberg.[181] Like Mussolini and the Fascists, Hitler and the Nazis came to power legally and proceeded to abolish any semblance of a democracy in favor of a military dictatorship. These events were troubling to FDR who recognized that any semblance of Weimar Republican democracy was being crushed by the beat of the Nazi anvil.

By the spring of 1938 FDR was worrying over the survival of the democracies of Western Europe, given the threatening speeches of Hitler and the German treatment of the Jews. During the summer Roosevelt went on a tour of the Galapagos Islands and returned with a marine collection "fully as important as the animal collection Theodore Roosevelt sent back from Africa." Waldo L. Schmitt, a scientist at the Smithsonian who received this collection, "named some species after Roosevelt as sponsor of the expedition, and some as discoverer. Among them were a fish, five species of mollusks, and *Rooseveltia frankliniana*-- a new kind of royal palm in Cocos Island, *Thalamita roosevelti*—a crablike creature, *Octopus roosevelti*—a hiterto undescribed species, and *Merriamium roosevelti*—a species of sponge."[182] This trip had given FDR time to reflect on the strategic importance of western hemispheric security and the possible uses of off-shore islands in both the Pacific and Atlantic to aid that security. The president had returned from his voyage to receive news of Hitler's further ambitions "to smash Czechoslovakia by military action in the near future," as the German Chancellor sought *Lebensraum* or living space for Germans and to dismantle the Treaty of Versailles. Within Germany there were few reasonable men willing to challenge Hitler's expansionist decisions, but one, chief of the German general staff, General Ludwig Beck, had protested, warning that the United States was

---

[180] Ibid.
[181] Shirer, Rise and Fall of the Third Reich, pp. 182-187.
[182] Frank Freidel, Franklin D. Roosevelt: A Rendezvous With Destiny, (Boston: Little, Brown and Company, 1990), p. 298-299; Basil H. Liddell-Hart, Other Side of the Hill: Germany's Generals, Their Rise and Fall, With Their Own Account of Military Events, 1939-1945 (London: Cassell, 1948); Karl-Dietrich Bracher, Manfred Funke, and Hans-Adolf Jacobsen, Deutschland, 1933-1945: Neue Studien zur Nationalsozialistischen Herrschaft (Bonn: Bundeszentrale fur Politische Bildung, 1993).

firmly committed to supplying Britain and France in case of war in Europe. But Beck found himself at odds with Hitler's plans and resigned in August 1938.

Hitler desired to annex the Sudetenland of Czechoslovakia that contained many German speaking peoples and Europe was in a frenzy throughout the summer of 1938. Neville Chamberlain was en route to discuss the situation with Hitler. FDR wrote a memo to American ambassador to Italy William Phillips in Rome saying "Chamberlain's visit to Hitler today may bring things to a head or may result in temporary postponement of what looks to me like an inevitable conflict within the next five years. Perhaps when it comes the United States will be in a position to pick up the pieces of European civilization and help them to save what remains of the wreck—not a cheerful prospect....You are right in saying that we are an unemotional people over here in the sense that we do not easily lose our heads, but if we get the idea that the future of our form of government is threatened by a coalition of European dictators, we might wade in with everything we have to give."[183] As Europe teetered on the brink of war and seemed to be going through a death-watch as Hitler maneuvered Chamberlain over the Sudetenland, Roosevelt sent a direct appeal throughout Europe for peace. FDR spoke in his circular appeal of September 26, 1938 about the Kellogg-Briand Pact that had outlawed war and pledged nations to preserving the peace through diplomacy. He immediately heard from Benes of Czechoslovakia, Chamberlain of Britain and Daladier of France, all of whom supported his peace appeal. Hitler replied that "it does not rest with the German government, but with the Czechoslovakian Government alone, to decide, whether it wants peace or war."[184] Mussolini, following FDR's appeal, urged Hitler to continue to negotiate. Chamberlain was invited to meet Hitler in Munich where a settlement was reached and in October gave his justification before the British Parliament:

> "Before I come to describe the Agreement which was signed at Munich in the small hours of Friday morning last, I would like to remind the House of two things which I think it very essential not to forget when those terms are being considered. The first is this: We did not go there to decide whether the predominantly German areas in the Sudetenland should be passed over to the German Reich. That had been decided already. Czechoslovakia had accepted the

---

[183] Frank Freidel, Franklin D. Roosevelt: A Rendezvous With Destiny, p. 299; John W. Wheeler-Bennett, Munich: Prologue to Tragedy (London: Macmillan, 1966); Keith Eubank, Munich (Westport, Conn: Greenwood Press, 1984); Martin Gilbert and Richard Gott, The Appeasers (Boston: Houghton Mifflin, 1963).

[184] FDR's Circular Appeal for peace of September 26, 1938 quoted in Samuel I. Rosenman, Public Papers and Addresses of Franklin D. Roosevelt, 13 Vols. (New York: Russell and Russell, 1938-1950), 1938 volume, pp. 531-535.

Anglo-French proposals. What we had to consider was the method, the conditions and the time of the transfer of the territory. The second point to remember is that time was one of the essential factors. All the elements were present on the spot for the outbreak of a conflict which might have precipitated the catastrophe. We had populations inflamed to a high degree; we had extremists on both sides ready to work up and provoke incidents; we had considerable quantities of arms which were by no means confined to regularly organised forces. Therefore, it was essential that we should quickly reach a conclusion, so that this painful and difficult operation of transfer might be carried out at the earliest possible moment and concluded as soon as was consistent, with orderly procedure, in order that we might avoid the possibility of something that might have rendered all our attempts at peaceful solution useless. . . . To those who dislike an ultimatum, but who were anxious for a reasonable and orderly procedure, every one of [the] modifications [of the Godesberg Memorandum by the Munich Agreement] is a step in the right direction. It is no longer an ultimatum, but is a method which is carried out largely under the supervision of an international body.

Before giving a verdict upon this arrangement, we should do well to avoid describing it as a personal or a national triumph for anyone. The real triumph is that it has shown that representatives of four great Powers can find it possible to agree on a way of carrying out a difficult and delicate operation by discussion instead of by force of arms, and thereby they have averted a catastrophe which would have ended civilisation as we have known it. The relief that our escape from this great peril of war has, I think, everywhere been mingled in this country with a profound feeling of sympathy. I have nothing to be ashamed of. Let those who have, hang their heads. We must feel profound sympathy for a small and gallant nation in the hour of their national grief and loss....I say in the name of this House and of the people of this country that Czechoslovakia has earned our admiration and respect for her restraint, for her dignity, for her magnificent discipline in face of such a trial as few nations have ever been called upon to meet.

The army, whose courage no man has ever questioned, has obeyed the order of their president, as they would equally have obeyed him if he had told them to march into the trenches. It is my hope and my belief, that under the new system of guarantees, the new Czechoslovakia will find a greater security than she has ever enjoyed in the past. . . . I pass from that subject, and I would like to say a few words in respect of the various other participants, besides ourselves, in the Munich Agreement. After everything that has been said about the German Chancellor today and in the past, I do feel that the House ought to recognise the difficulty for a man in that position to take back such emphatic declarations as he had already made amidst the enthusiastic cheers of his supporters, and to recognise that in consenting, even though it were only at the last moment, to discuss with the representatives of other Powers those things which he had declared he had already decided once for all, was a real and a substantial contribution on his part. With regard to Signor Mussolini, . . . I think that Europe and the world have reason to be grateful to the head of the Italian government for his work in contributing to a peaceful solution.

In my view the strongest force of all, one which grew and took fresh shapes and forms every day war, the force not of any one individual, but was that unmistakable sense of unanimity among the peoples of the world that war must somehow be averted. The peoples of the British Empire were at one with those of Germany, of France and of Italy, and their anxiety, their intense desire for peace, pervaded the whole atmosphere of the conference, and I believe that that, and not threats, made possible the concessions that were made. I know the House will want to hear what I am sure it does not doubt, that throughout these discussions the Dominions, the Governments of the Dominions, have been kept in the closest touch with the march of events by telegraph and by personal contact, and I would like to say how greatly I was encouraged on each of the journeys I made to Germany by the knowledge that I went with the good wishes of the Governments of the Dominions. They shared all our anxieties and all our hopes. They rejoiced with us that peace was preserved, and with us they look forward to further efforts to consolidate what has been done.

Ever since I assumed my present office my main purpose has been to work for the pacification of Europe, for the removal of those suspicions and those animosities which have so long poisoned the air. The path which leads to appeasement is long and bristles with obstacles. The question of Czechoslovakia is the latest and perhaps the most dangerous. Now that we have got past it, I feel that it may be possible to make further progress along the road to sanity."[185]

The Munich agreement averted war in 1938 but proved to be a "sellout" to the Germans that only bought time for the Allies to continue to prepare for the war that some viewed as inevitable given German ambitions and world designs. After the Sudetenland of Czechoslovakia had been given to Germany at Munich, Hitler confidentially winked to Mussolini "that they must fight France and Great Britain in their lifetime."[186] Yet FDR had not been fooled. He secretly let Britain and France know that they could buy weapons to bolster their countries' defenses against Hitler. President Roosevelt knew that the leaders of both Britain and France had backed down from Hitler's threats and compromised at Munich because the numbers of their airplanes could in no way match that of Germany's. They simply needed more time to build their military defenses. King George VI of Britain wrote to FDR expressing his thanks for intervening to solve Europe's problems with his appeal for peaceful negotiations during the Sudeten crisis of

---

[185] Great Britain, Parliamentary Debates, Commons, Vol. 339 (October 3, 1938).
[186] Freidel, Franklin D. Roosevelt: A Rendezvous With Destiny, p. 302.

September 1938. "I must say how greatly I welcomed your interventions....I have little doubt that they contributed largely to the preservation of peace."[187] FDR moved the U.S. toward building large numbers of airplanes for both its own defense and to supply the European democracies. When a nation held military superiority then fruitful negotiation was made much easier. FDR promised himself that there should be no more Munich agreements. Appeasement of bullies would not work. The moral of Munich was clear to FDR. "Had we this summer 5,000 planes and the capacity to immediately produce 10,000 per year," he said, to measure up to Germany's 6,500, "even though I might have to ask Congress for authority to sell or lend them to countries in Europe, Hitler would not have dared to take the stand he did."[188]

Earlier America's anti-involvement isolationistic sentiment had continued through the 1936 Civil War in Spain when the Spanish Falangists [similar to Fascists] under General Francisco Franco had revolted against the Loyalists or the Constitutionalists who remained loyal to a liberal republican constitution. Hitler and Mussolini sided with strongman Franco, while Britain, France and Russia had favored the Loyalists. During the events of this Spanish Civil War, Roosevelt suggested that U.S. Neutrality Acts be extended to civil insurrections as well as to international wars. The president had stated in 1936: "We shun political commitments which might entangle us in foreign wars; we avoid connection with the activities of the League of Nations.... We are not isolationists except in so far as we seek to isolate ourselves completely from war." FDR concluded: "I hate war."[189] Eventually Franco, aided by the Fascists and Nazis, ended the Spanish republican government and established a military dictatorship. America attempted to stand behind the third Neutrality Act of 1937 just at the same time that Japan was posed to cross the Marco Polo Bridge and attack China directly in Asia and as Germany pushed to take all of Czechoslovakia and annex Austria. The Sudetenland sellout with the Munich agreement of 1938 had only bought time, but Hitler continued on a course to expand German power and prestige to eliminate the bitterness of earlier defeat in World War I. Revenge, he pledged his German countrymen, would be his.

President Roosevelt came gradually to the realization after Munich that resisting aggression was more important than keeping out of war. He became

---

[187] Donald B. Schewe, ed., Franklin D. Roosevelt and Foreign Affairs, January 1937-August 1939 (New York: Garland, 1979) 1938: document 1333.
[188] Schewe, ed., Franklin D. Roosevelt and Foreign Affairs, 1938: documents 1288, 1306, 1306a; Keith Feiling, The Life of Neville Chamberlain (London: Macmillan, 1946); Neville Thompson, Anti- Appeasers: Conservative Opposition to Appeasement in the 30s (Oxford: Clarendon Press, 1971).
[189] Freidel, Franklin D. Roosevelt: A Rendezvous With Destiny, p. 371.

increasingly alarmed over the German treatment of the Jews saying he could scarcely believe that such things could occur, when told of vicious anti-Semitism, the takeover of many Jewish businesses and the burning of synagogues. Many Jews sought refuge abroad but Congress was slow to alter the immigration statutes to allow more to come into the country. But in March 1939 when all of Czechoslovakia was taken by Germany Roosevelt could no longer tolerate such overt aggression saying: "Acts of aggression against sister nations...automatically undermine all of us," and called "for methods short of war" to maintain democracy and freedom. When Hitler had threatened to take the Danzig Corridor which separated East Prussia from the rest of Germany to allow Poland access to the sea, Roosevelt sent a diplomatic note calling for peace. "Roosevelt hoped to preserve the United States from the scourge of war, but he also hoped, from at least 1935 on, to bring the power of his country to bear against the prairie fire of armed aggression that was licking its way around the globe."[190] FDR desired to act more decisively and boldly early on. But "three forces constrained him: the lack of political will in his potential allies, Premier Edouard Daladier of France and Prime Minister Neville Chamberlain of Great Britain, cowering in the face of Hitler's bullying; the isolationist mood in America, codified into formal statutes purposely designed to tie the president's hands; and his own uncertainty, both about the means to be employed abroad and about the political risks of frontally challenging the isolationists at home." Unfortunately the 'green light' for World War II was switched on by the Hitler-Stalin Non-Aggression Pact signed in August 1939 in which they agreed not to fight one another and secretly to divide Poland after the planned German invasion.

Thus, the opening of the war in Europe began with the German invasion of Poland on September 1, 1939. Upon hearing of Germany's thrust into eastern Europe, FDR said another great war had "come at last", "God help us all."[191] Why did Hitler gamble, knowing that Britain and France would possibly declare war after this act rather than extend further appeasement? Hitler believed that Germany held certain advantages such as military power built up since 1933, and recognized how his nation had been defeated in World War I by getting bogged down in the trenches. Hitler's answer was the *Blitzkrieg* or lightning warfare that offered the essentials of speed and movement. The military thinking at the time in France that proved erroneous was to place confidence in their well-fortified bastion, the famed Maginot Line. Hitler also realized through the 'peace in our time negotiations' with Britain and France over the annexation of parts of

---

[190] Graff, ed., The Presidents, A Reference History, p. 436.
[191] Graff, ed., The Presidents, A Reference History, p. 436; Walter Ansel, Hitler Confronts England (Durham, NC: Duke University Press, 1960).

Czechoslovakia that he enjoyed disunity among his enemies and he was able to play off their mutual rivalries and controversies. Strategically, Hitler calculated, Germany enjoyed the 'heartland' or the central axis position of Western Europe and could rotate outwards to conquer in both directions to make Germany the industrialized heart of Europe. This stimulated Hitler's dream to create a New Order in Europe. After the invasion of Poland, Hitler and Stalin deceitfully divided the country, the Russians arguing that they were protecting oppressed Ukrainian minorities.[192] During the remainder of the winter of 1939-1940 the so-called 'Phony War' or in German 'the *Sitzkrieg*' developed, but Stalin used the smoke screen of this chaos to move into and dominate Lithuania, Latvia and Estonia. Russia also became embroiled in a war with Finland and as a result Russia was expelled from the League of Nations, an unprecedented action. France and Britain wanted to send troops across Norway and Denmark to aid Finland but the two countries proclaimed neutrality. The successes of the campaigns in Eastern Europe accomplished Hitler's initial purpose of freeing the bulk of his forces for the campaign in the West and his hoped for conquest of Britain and France.

On April 9, 1940 Hitler opened his Western offensive with an attack on Norway and Sweden, essential to ensure Swedish ores and access to the Baltic and the Atlantic. Then the Germans overran Denmark, Belgium, Luxembourg and the Netherlands. Although there was rough equality in man power between the opposing forces, the Germans completely out-classed the allies in their use of parachutists, tanks, and planes in closely coordinated teams to open gaps that the infantry could exploit. The Dutch army capitulated in five days and Belgium in eighteen. By May 20 the Germans had reached the English Channel after cutting off the main body of French troops from the British and trapping nearly 340,000 British Expeditionary forces at Dunkirk. Heroically, between May 27 and June 4 British and French troops were evacuated to England by sea from the channel port of Dunkirk, as the Royal Air Force gave protective air cover. France's armies then broke in half, and final surrender came after the battles of the Somme. On June 14, 1940 the Germans entered Paris. The French government was evacuated to Tours and later Bordeaux. Marshall Petain signed an armistice with Germany that allowed the German occupation of the northern two-thirds of France while the southern portion was administered from Vichy by Petain. The French POWs were

---

[192] E.M. Robertson, Hitler's Pre-War Policy and Military Plans, 1933-1939 (New York: Citadel Press, 1967); Norman Rich, Hitler's War Aims (New York: W.W. Norton and Company, 1973); Gerhard L. Weinberg, The Foreign Policy of Hitler's Germany: Diplomatic Revolution in Europe, 1933-1936 (Chicago: University of Chicago Press, 1970).

to remain in Germany and the French navy was disarmed and left in French ports.[193]

Now standing alone, Britain hoped the English Channel would make a very good anti-tank obstacle. In response to these events of 1940, FDR's foreign policies changed decisively. After Hitler's blitz through Poland, Denmark, Norway, the Netherlands, Belgium and France and the beginning of the Battle of Britain, FDR began to gear up the U.S. for a possible attack. Only Britain remained between Nazism and the U.S. Mainland across the Atlantic. Only Hawaii remained between militarism in Japan and the U.S. Mainland across the Pacific. In Britain the government of Neville Chamberlain had been forced to resign because of these early German successes and the failure of appeasement policies. The government of Prime Minister Winston Churchill came to power on May 10, 1940 offering 'blood, toil, sweat and tears' to combat Nazism. Isolated and crippled after the fall of France, the British rallied to what Churchill called 'Britain's Finest Hour' and implored America for aid to resist the Germans.[194] Churchill expressed a single-minded policy: 'to wage war by sea, land, and air and with all our might and the strength that God gave us. We have but one aim-Victory'. American foreign policy almost from the beginning was pro-ally as after the German invasion of Poland Congress had adopted the policy of 'cash and carry'. American ships were not to enter the war zone but belligerents were allowed to purchase arms within the United States and carry them in their own vessels. Since Britain controlled the seas, the opportunity to pay cash and carry away U.S. military supplies gave her an advantage, but Hitler and the Nazis dominated Europe, proclaiming they would bring a quick end to the war after an invasion of Britain. FDR desired to ensure that Britain would win the fight against Hitler, extending all possible aid to Churchill's government that was permitted under U.S. laws and negotiated through presidential executive agreements.

---

[193] Gordon Wright, The Ordeal of Total War, 1939-1945 (New York: Harper and Row, 1968); Basil H. Liddell-Hart, eds., The History of the Second World War (New York: Exeter Books, 1980); Hans Adolf Jacobsen and J. Rohwer, eds., Decisive Battles of World War II: The German View translated from German by Edward Fitzgerald (New York: Putnam, 1965); Peter Calvocoressi and Guy Wint, Total War: The Causes and Courses of the Second World War (London: Allen Lane, Penguin Press, 1972); Don W. Alexander, "Repercussions of the Breda Variant," French Historical Studies, Vol. 8, No. 3 (Spring 1974); William L. Shirer, The Collapse of the Third Republic: An Inquiry into the Fall of France, 1940 (New York: Simon and Schuster, 1969); Guy Chapman, Why France Collapsed (London: Cassell, 1968); Andre Beaufre, 1940, The Fall of France translated from French by Desmond Flower (New York: Alfred A. Knopf, 1968).

[194] Derek Wood and Derek Dempster, The Narrow Margin: The Battle of Britain and the Rise of Air Power 1930-1940 (London: Arrow Books, 1967); Winston S. Churchill, Never Give In! The Best of Winston Churchill's Speeches (Selected and edited by his grandson Winston S. Churchill) (New York: Hyperion, 2003).

Following Hitler's aggressions in May and June of 1940, FDR improvised "a new government within a government" to "put the nation on a defense footing."[195] The president decided to become a candidate for an unprecedented third term because America needed him during the world crisis of war. "Roosevelt, with a national consensus supporting him, devised organizations to stimulate and direct the production of the supplies for hemispheric defense and overseas aid." Using executive orders based on World War I legislation, FDR designed defense machinery firmly under his presidential control. Through executive order he had created the Executive Office of the President that included an Office of Emergency Management and on May 21, 1940 he activated this office to prepare for America's defense. A Council of National Defense and an advisory committee to advise the president was inaugurated. He took pains to make his preparations bi-partisan, appointing former Republican candidate for vice president Frank Knox as Secretary of the Navy and Republican Henry L. Stimson, who had served in both the Taft and Hoover cabinets, as Secretary of War. Now FDR had a cadre of supporters for preparedness—Knox, Stimson, Morgenthau, Ickes, General Marshall and Admiral Stark.

FDR was outmaneuvering the Republicans before their party's convention in his bid for a third term against challenger Wendell Willkie. No other Democratic candidate besides FDR appeared to have the political assets to win, and 'circumstances of politics' as well as Nazi assaults dictated the re-nomination of Franklin D. Roosevelt. At the Democratic convention in Chicago, delegates were stampeded for FDR with shouts of 'Illinois wants Roosevelt....New York wants Roosevelt....America Wants Roosevelt....the world wants Roosevelt' and a move was made to nominate FDR unanimously. Henry A. Wallace was nominated as the vice-presidential candidate to attract votes from the mid-west. At the opposing Republican convention in Philadelphia Wendell Willkie of Indiana was nominated. Harold Ickes called him 'the barefoot boy from Wall Street', as Willkie had sprung into politics from the presidency of the Commonwealth and Southern Corporation, a large utilities firms, but still retained his boyish demeanor. Willkie and Roosevelt were close on the issues. Willkie did not oppose the future 'destroyer-for-bases' deal that would be confirmed by Congress during the campaign and favored both aid to Britain and conscription. But Willkie did charge that Roosevelt was moving the United States toward war as he said: 'If you elect him you may expect war in April 1941'. FDR campaigned on his defense policies that seemed to be working and his experienced leadership. During the

---

[195] Freidel, Franklin D. Roosevelt: A Rendezvous With Destiny, pp. 341-344; David Reynolds, From Munich to Pearl Harbor: Roosevelt's America and the Origins of the Second World War (Chicago: Ivan R. Dee, 2001).

summer of 1940 FDR had convinced Congress to appropriate several billions of dollars to build a projected fifty thousand airplanes a year. Courageously in an election year, in September 1940 FDR requested that a Selective Service Act be passed by Congress. FDR proclaimed that preparedness was paramount because America could not survive as "a lone island in a world dominated by force...handcuffed, hungry, and fed through the bars from day to day by the contemptuous unpitying masters of other continents."[196]

The president had responded to European events by other forms of preparedness including the appointment of a top-secret atomic energy program and the freezing of the American assets of the European conquered nations to keep them out of German hands. In his State of the Union message, President Roosevelt had begun by asking Congress for $1.8 billion to finance the greatest peacetime military buildup in United States history. A Roper poll had indicated in May 1940 that 67.5% of Americans favored giving active aid to Britain, endorsing FDR's policies. Italy had entered the war on the side of Germany as France fell to the Germans in June 1940 and President Roosevelt fearfully chided Mussolini, saying 'the hand that held the dagger has struck it into the back of its neighbor'. FDR used this circumstance to ask Congress for another $4.8 billion to build armaments and weapons. The U.S. moved towards closer cooperation with the British. He promised not to send Americans to fight in any foreign wars during the campaign, but he continued to fear that the U.S. might be attacked and drawn into the global fray. FDR wisely took precautions with the U.S. occupation of Greenland and Iceland to provide an early warning system and provide for hemispheric defense. Secretly his foreign officers met with Britons and Canadians to plan for mutual defense and strategic contingencies.

Churchill wrote to FDR stating with candor the dire straits of the British forces. "To prevail," wrote Churchill, "even to survive, he must have American war materiel and above all, American money."[197] America would ultimately provide Britain with $50 billion in military aid while the Battle of Britain allowed America additional time to prepare for military involvement. "Roosevelt's overall course was to build the American armed forces as rapidly as possible, strengthen hemispheric defenses in both Latin America and Canada, stall Japanese expansion, defer a showdown in the Pacific, give all aid possible to Britain, and

---

[196] Graff, ed., The Presidents, A Reference History, p. 437.
[197] Graff, ed., The Presidents, A Reference History, p. 437; Alan S. Milward, War, Economy, and Society, 1939-1945 (Berkeley: University of California Press, 1977).

resist Hitler."[198] FDR concluded an agreement with Canada's Prime Minister Mackenzie King to establish a Permanent Board of Joint Defense that included arrangements to use British Empire bases from Halifax to Trinidad.[199] He provided for hemispheric solidarity through a Pan-American conference held in Havana, Cuba in the summer of 1940 that issued the Act of Havana providing authorization for the U.S. to repel Nazis advances to control possessions of fallen European powers in Latin America. Agreements were made with key Latin American countries to buy strategic materials.

Germany was at the height of its military power in the summer of 1940, however, the German army was not equipped or trained to cross the English Channel. The British Chief of Staff admitted Britain lacked the army manpower to offensively drive out the Germans should Hitler's forces succeed in making a large landing with their vehicles. Operation Sea Lion had been the code name given to Hitler's preparations for crossing the Channel to invade Britain. But Hitler never developed enough amphibious landing craft nor extensively trained his personnel to make such a crossing, believing that his *Luftwaffe* could outclass the Royal Air Force and that Germany would win the Battle of Britain, the air joust during the summer and winter of 1940-1941. During the critical early months of August and September 1940, the RAF had destroyed 1244 German planes while 721 RAF fighters were downed. The bombings of London and the industrial centers continued through the winter of 1940-1941. But by the spring of 1941 the RAF had won the Battle of Britain.[200] And as a result, the Germans were forced to turn around and plan to invade Russia to find additional supplies of oil to refine into aviation gasoline to finish their plans to invade Britain, so well protected by its heroic air force.

Although Hitler could not cross the Channel in 1940, his submarines had wrecked havoc with the Royal Navy. Britain had only about 100 destroyers; far more were needed to convoy and protect shipping so the United States was approached about purchasing additional ships. But to sell the needed destroyers to Britain, Americans felt would have violated both the neutrality acts and international law. Furthermore, going through Congress to secure new legislation

---

[198] Freidel, Franklin D. Roosevelt, A Rendezvous With Destiny, p. 349. John Morton Blum, V Was For Victory: Politics and American Culture During World War II (New York: Harcourt Brace Jovanovich, 1976);

[199] J.W. Pickersgill, The Mackenzie King Record 4 Vols. (Toronto: University of Toronto Press, 1960), Vol. I, pp. 131-139.

[200] David Reynolds, Creation of the Anglo-American Alliance, 1937-1941 (Chapel Hill: University of North Carolina Press, 1982); Winston S. Churchill, Great Contemporaries (New York: Putnam, 1937); David Reynolds, In Command of History: Winston Churchill and the Second World War (New York: Random House, 2005).

would further inflame the isolationists' passions. Roosevelt in a shrewd move arranged to *trade* the fifty American destroyers for British naval bases in the Atlantic and the Caribbean—Newfoundland, Bermuda, the Bahamas, Jamaica, St. Lucia, Antigua, Trinidad, and British Guiana. Britain was bolstered by this destroyers-for-bases deal of August 1940 and America received this string of island bastions that were immediately used to set defenses. These crucial American efforts to assist the British were popularly supported in America, especially after Japan had signed a mutual assistance pact with Germany and Italy and affirmed adherence to the Rome-Berlin-Tokyo agreement that fused the Axis. The traded destroyers were refitted and placed in operation by the British in the spring of 1941. Churchill was pleased by what he confidentially termed FDR's 'decidedly un-neutral act' and America's show of support.[201] Churchill and Roosevelt had formed a partnership that would defend the west from Nazi aggression. By the time of FDR's re-election, his sons, to show ardent patriotism, had received commissions in America's armed services. Yet during his bid for re-election FDR promised voters: "We will not participate in foreign wars and we will not send our army, naval or air forces to fight in foreign lands outside of the Americas except in case of attack."[202] American voters returned FDR to the White House for a third term because they trusted his domestic and foreign policies. Masterfully, FDR had concluded his re-election campaign on November 2, 1940 with the ringing phrase in his 'I see an America' speech in Cleveland, Ohio: "It is the destiny of this American generation to point the road to the future for all the world to see....I see an America where factory workers are not discarded after they reach their prime, where there is no endless chain of poverty from generation to generation....I see an America whose...land and nature's wealth...are protected as the rightful heritage of all the people. I see an America where small business really has a chance to flourish and grow. I see an America of great cultural and educational opportunity for all its people....An America where those who have reached the evening of life shall live out their lives in peace and security....I see an America devoted to our freedom—unified by tolerance and by religious

---

[201] David Reynolds, Creation of the Anglo-American Alliance, 1937-1941, pp. 120-127; Forrest Davis, How War Came, From Fall of France to Pearl Harbor (New York: Simon and Schuster, 1942); James MacGregor Burns, Roosevelt: Soldier of Freedom, 1940-1945 (New York: Harvest/HBJ reprint edition 2002, originally published in 1970); David Cannadine, ed., Blood, Toil, Tears, and Sweat: Winston Churchill's Famous Speeches (London: Cassell, 1989); Warren F. Kimball, ed., Churchill and Roosevelt: The Complete Correspondence (Princeton: Princeton University Press, 1984); Martin Gilbert, ed., The Churchill War Papers (New York: W.W. Norton, 1995).

[202] Samuel I. Rosenman, Public Papers and Addresses of Franklin D. Roosevelt, Vol 9, pp. 485-495; Volume 8 pp. 552-554 explains restrictions on U.S. submarines in territorial waters; Neutrality proclamation of November 5, 1939, Volume 8, pp. 464-473.

faith....[203] FDR was returned with 449 electoral votes to Willkie's 82. During his presidential bid, he had also courted the black vote as FDR promised "we shall continue to strive for complete legislative safeguards against discrimination in government service and benefits, and in national defense forces."[204]

In his Third Inaugural Address Franklin D. Roosevelt spoke once again of America's challenges during a time of European war. Addressing the nation on Monday, January 20, 1941 he said:

> "On each national day of Inauguration since 1789, the people have renewed their sense of dedication to the United States.
> In Washington's day the task of the people was to create and weld together a nation.
> In Lincoln's day the task of the people was to preserve that Nation from disruption from within.
> In this day the task of the people is to save that Nation and its institutions from disruption from without.
> To us there has come a time, in the midst of swift happenings, to pause for a moment and take stock to recall what our place in history has been, and to rediscover what we are and what we may be. If we do not, we risk the real peril of inaction.
> Lives of Nations are determined not by the count of years, but by the lifetime of the human spirit. The life of a man is three-score years and ten: a little more, a little less. The life of a nation is the fullness of the measure of its will to live.
> There are men who doubt this. There are men who believe that democracy, as a form of Government and a frame of life, is limited or measured by a kind of mystical and artificial fate that, for some unexplained reason, tyranny and slavery have become the surging wave of the future and that freedom is an ebbing tide.
> But we Americans know that this is not true.
> Eight years ago, when the life of this Republic seemed frozen by a fatalistic terror, we proved that this is not true. We were in the midst of shock, but we acted. We acted quickly, boldly, decisively.
> These later years have been living years, fruitful years, for the people of this democracy. For they have brought to us greater security and, I hope, a better understanding that life's ideals are to be measured in other than material things.
> Most vital to our present and our future is this experience of a democracy which successfully survived crisis at home; put away many evil things; built new structures on enduring lines; and, through it all, maintained the fact of its democracy.

---

[203] Freidel, Franklin D. Roosevelt: A Rendezvous With Destiny, p. 356.

For action has been taken within the three-way framework of the Constitution of the United States. The coordinate branches of the Government continue freely to function. The Bill of Rights remains inviolate. The freedom of elections is wholly maintained. Prophets of the downfall of American democracy have seen their dire predictions come to naught.

No, democracy is not dying.

We know it because we have seen it revive and grow. We know it cannot die because it is built on the unhampered initiative of individual men and women joined together in a common enterprise, an enterprise undertaken and carried through by the free expression of a free majority.

We know it because democracy alone, of all forms of government, enlists the full force of men's enlightened will.

We know it because democracy alone has constructed an unlimited civilization, capable of infinite progress in the improvement of human life.

We know it because, if we look below the surface, we sense it still spreading on every continent, for it is the most humane, the most advanced, and in the end the most unconquerable of all forms of human society.

A Nation, like a person, has a body, a body that must be fed and clothed and housed, invigorated and rested, in a manner that measures up to the standards of our time. A Nation, like a person, has a mind, a mind that must be kept informed and alert, that must know itself, that understands the hopes and the needs of its neighbors, all the other Nations that live within the narrowing circle of the world.

A nation, like a person, has something deeper, something more permanent, something larger than the sum of all its parts. It is that something which matters most to its future which calls forth the most sacred guarding of its present.

It is a thing for which we find it difficult, even impossible, to hit upon a single, simple word.

And yet we all understand what it is, *the spirit, the faith of America*. It is the product of centuries. It was born in the multitudes of those who came from many lands, some of high degree, but mostly plain people, who sought here, early and late, to find freedom more freely.

The democratic aspiration is no mere recent phase in human history. It is human history. It permeated the ancient life of early peoples. It blazed anew in the Middle Ages. It was written in Magna Charta.

In the Americas its impact has been irresistible. America has been the New World in all tongues, to all peoples, not because this continent was a new found land, but because all those who came here believed they could create upon this continent a new life, a life that should be new in freedom.

---

[204] Nancy J. Weiss, Farewell to the Party of Lincoln: Black Politics in the Age of FDR (Princeton: Princeton University Press, 1983), pp. 272-282.

Its vitality was written into our own Mayflower Compact, into the Declaration of Independence, into the Constitution of the United States, into the Gettysburg Address.

Those who first came here to carry out the longings of their spirit, and the millions who followed, and the stock that sprang from them, all have moved forward constantly and consistently toward an ideal which in itself has gained stature and clarity with each generation.

The hopes of the Republic cannot forever tolerate either undeserved poverty or self-serving wealth.

We know that we still have far to go; that we must more greatly build the security and the opportunity and the knowledge of every citizen, in the measure justified by the resources and the capacity of the land.

But it is not enough to achieve these purposes alone. It is not enough to clothe and feed the body of this Nation, and instruct and inform its mind. *For there is also the spirit.* And of the three, the greatest is the spirit.

Without the body and the mind, as all men know, the Nation could not live.

But if the spirit of America were killed, even though the Nation's body and mind, constricted in an alien world, lived on, the America we know would have perished.

That spirit, that faith, speaks to us in our daily lives in ways often unnoticed, because they seem so obvious. It speaks to us here in the Capital of the Nation. It speaks to us through the processes of governing in the sovereignties of forty-eight States. It speaks to us in our counties, in our cities, in our towns, and in our villages. It speaks to us from the other Nations of the hemisphere and from those across the seas, the enslaved, as well as the free. Sometimes we fail to hear or heed these voices of freedom because to us the privilege of our freedom is such an old, old story.

The destiny of America was proclaimed in words of prophecy spoken by our first President in his first inaugural in 1789, words almost directed, it would seem, to this year of 1941: 'The preservation of the sacred fire of liberty and the destiny of the republican model of government are justly considered ... deeply, ... finally, staked on the experiment intrusted to the hands of the American people'. If you and I in this later day lose that sacred fire, if we let it be smothered with doubt and fear, then we shall reject the destiny which Washington strove so valiantly and so triumphantly to establish. The preservation of the spirit and faith of the Nation does, and will, furnish the highest justification for every sacrifice that we may make in the cause of national defense.

In the face of great perils never before encountered, our strong purpose is to protect and to perpetuate the integrity of democracy.

For this we muster the spirit of America, and the faith of America.

We do not retreat. We are not content to stand still. As Americans, we go forward, in the service of our country, by the will of God."[205]

FDR was still the master politician who rallied Americans to great causes and offered great solutions. By preserving America's spirit, he would protect American democracy as chief executive and defend the U.S. against foreign aggressors. Democracy and freedom would win out over Nazism and Fascism because Americans held to their faith and displayed the higher moral ground. Their faith in democracy disallowed them from giving in to tyranny and oppression, for themselves or for others victimized by Hitler.

After FDR's re-election, Lend-Lease aid was extended to Britain, China, and after June 1941 to the Soviet Union, as Americans began to see that these countries were 'fighting our fight' against Nazi aggression. The Lend-lease bill passed Congress as House Resolution 1776 in March 1941.[206] U.S. merchant marine ships participated in supply convoys to Britain and the armed forces practiced maneuvers and drills. Sea and air patrols were extended to Greenland in April and Iceland in July 1941 to ensure safe conduct of the supplies. Slowly, too, U.S. Neutrality legislation was removed that prohibited more overt aid to the Allies after the 1940 election. Secret negotiations among British and American military planners in early 1941 established the cardinal principle that in the event of war with both Germany and Japan, the United States and Britain would give priority to defeating Germany first across the Atlantic. Yet a number of Americans refused to be convinced of the threat of war to America. Among the groups that reacted against America's military preparedness was the America First Committee. Charles Lindbergh was the group's spokesman and spoke naively of the absence of any threat from Hitler, blaming the Roosevelt administration, the British and the Jewish lobby for moving the U.S. towards war. Yet the threat of a German invasion was real should Britain fall and the majority of Americans opposed this group of American Firsters and urged preparedness and defense in agreement with FDR.

Every night, CBS correspondent Edward R. Murrow had broadcast live from London telling of the firebombing of the city and of how the British were reaching the end of their financial tether. Between September 1939 and November 1940 the British government had spent $4.5 billion for armaments in the United States

---

[205] Franklin D. Roosevelt Library, Hyde Park, New York; Samuel I. Rosenman, Public Papers and Addresses of Franklin D. Roosevelt (New York: Harper & Brothers, 1949), Volume 10, pp. 3-7.
[206] Winston S. Churchill, The Second World War, 6 Vols. (London: Cassell and Boston: Houghton Mifflin 1948-1954); William Hardy McNeill, America, Britain, and Russia: Their Cooperation and Conflict, 1941-1946 (New York: Johnson Reprint Co., 1970); Herbert Feis, Churchill, Roosevelt, and Stalin: The War They Waged and the Peace They Sought (Princeton, NJ: Princeton University Press, 1957).

alone and held less than $2 billion in reserve. Therefore, shortly after re-election in 1940, President Roosevelt had called for the Lend-Lease Plan with a homily: "Suppose my neighbor's house catches fire, and I have a length of garden hose," intoned Roosevelt. "If he can take my garden hose and connect it up with his hydrant, I may help him to put out the fire. Now what do I do? I don't say to him before that operation 'Neighbor, my garden hose cost me $15.00; you have got to pay me $15 for it'. What is the transaction that goes on? I don't want $15 I want my garden hose back after the fire is over....In other words, if you lend certain munitions and get the munitions back at the end of the war,…you are all right."[207] Roosevelt, in this example hoped to eliminate the dollar sign, the exchange of money, in supplying Britain who was fighting our fight. To sanction Lend-Lease, FDR had delivered his 'arsenal of democracy' radio address to the nation on December 29, 1940 as a means to educate Americans about this plan that would go into effect in March 1941 and was stirring in his remarks:

> "This is not a fireside chat on war. *It is a talk on national security* because the nub of the whole purpose of your President is to keep you now, and your children later, and your grandchildren much later, out of a last-ditch war for the preservation of American independence, and all of the things that American independence means to you and to me and to ours.
>
> Tonight, in the presence of a world crisis, my mind goes back eight years ago to a night in the midst of a domestic crisis. It was a time when the wheels of American industry were grinding to a full stop, when the whole banking system of our country had ceased to function.
>
> I well remember that while I sat in my study in the White House, preparing to talk with the people of the United States, I had before my eyes the picture of all those Americans with whom I was talking. I saw the workmen in the mills, the mines, the factories; the girl behind the counter; the small shopkeeper; the farmer doing his spring plowing; the widows and the old men wondering about their life's savings.
>
> I tried to convey to the great mass of American people what the banking crisis meant to them in their daily lives.
>
> Tonight, I want to do the same thing, with the same people, in this new crisis which faces America.
>
> We met the issue of 1933 with courage and realism.
>
> We face this new crisis, this new threat to the security of our Nation, with the same courage and realism.
>
> Never before since Jamestown and Plymouth Rock has our American civilization been in such danger as now. For, on September 27, 1940, by an

---

[207] Freidel, Franklin D. Roosevelt, A Rendezvous With Destiny, p. 360; John Strawson, Churchill and Hitler: In Victory and Defeat (New York: Fromm International Publishing Co., 1998).

agreement signed in Berlin, three powerful nations, two in Europe and one in Asia [Germany, Italy and Japan], joined themselves together in the threat that if the United States interfered with or blocked the expansion program of these three nations, a program aimed at world control, they would unite in ultimate action against the United States.

The Nazi masters of Germany have made it clear that they intend not only to dominate all life and thought in their own country, but also to enslave the whole of Europe, and then to use the resources of Europe to dominate the rest of the world. It was only three weeks ago their leader stated this: 'There are two worlds that stand opposed to each other.' And then in defiant reply to his opponents, he said this: 'Others are correct when they say: 'With this world we cannot ever reconcile ourselves.' . . . I can beat any other power in the world.' So said the leader of the Nazis.

In other words, the Axis not merely admits but *proclaims* that there can be no ultimate peace between their philosophy of government and our philosophy of government.

In view of the nature of this undeniable threat, it can be asserted, properly and categorically, that the United States has no right or reason to encourage talk of peace until the day shall come when there is a clear intention on the part of the aggressor nations to abandon all thought of dominating or conquering the world.

At this moment, the forces of the states that are leagued against all peoples who live in freedom are being held away from our shores. The Germans and Italians are being blocked on the other side of the Atlantic by the British, and by the Greeks, and by thousands of soldiers and sailors who were able to escape from subjugated countries. In Asia, the Japanese are being engaged by the Chinese nation in another great defense.

In the Pacific is our fleet.

Some of our people like to believe that wars in Europe and in Asia are of no concern to us. But it is a matter of most vital concern to us that European and Asiatic war-makers should not gain control of the oceans which lead to this hemisphere.

One hundred and seventeen years ago the Monroe Doctrine was conceived by our Government as a measure of defense in the face of a threat against this hemisphere by an alliance in continental Europe. Thereafter, we stood on guard in the Atlantic, with the British as neighbors. There was no treaty. There was no 'unwritten agreement'.

And yet, there was the feeling, proven correct by history, that we as neighbors could settle any disputes in peaceful fashion. The fact is that during the whole of this time the Western Hemisphere has remained free from aggression from Europe or from Asia.

Does anyone seriously believe that we need to fear attack anywhere in the Americas while a free Britain remains our most powerful naval neighbor in the

Atlantic? Does any one seriously believe, on the other hand, that we could rest easy if the Axis powers were our neighbors there?

If Great Britain goes down, the Axis powers will control the continents of Europe, Asia, Africa, Australasia, and the high seas, and they will be in a position to bring enormous military and naval resources against this hemisphere. It is no exaggeration to say that all of us in the Americas would be living at the point of a gun, a gun loaded with explosive bullets, economic as well as military.

We should enter upon a new and terrible era in which the whole world, our hemisphere included, would be run by threats of brute force. To survive in such a world, we would have to convert ourselves permanently into a militaristic power on the basis of war economy.

Some of us like to believe that even if Great Britain falls, we are still safe, because of the broad expanse of the Atlantic and of the Pacific.

But the width of these oceans is not what it was in the days of clipper ships. At one point between Africa and Brazil the distance is less than from Washington to Denver, Colorado-five hours for the latest type of bomber. And at the North end of the Pacific Ocean, America and Asia almost touch each other.

Even today we have planes which could fly from the British Isles to New England and back without refueling. And remember that the range of the modern bomber is ever being increased.

During the past week many people in all parts of the Nation have told me what they wanted me to say tonight. Almost all of them expressed a courageous desire to hear the plain truth about the gravity of the situation. One telegram, however, expressed the attitude of the small minority who want to see no evil and hear no evil, even though they know in their hearts that evil exists. That telegram begged me not to tell again of the ease with which our American cities could be bombed by any hostile power which had gained bases in this Western Hemisphere. The gist of that telegram was: 'Please, Mr. President, don't frighten us by telling us the facts.'

Frankly and definitely there is danger ahead, danger against which we must prepare. But we well know that we cannot escape danger, or the fear of danger, by crawling into bed and pulling the covers over our heads.

Some nations of Europe were bound by solemn non-intervention pacts with Germany. Other nations were assured by Germany that they need *never* fear invasion. Non-intervention pact or not, the fact remains that they *were* attacked, overrun, and thrown into the modern form of slavery at an hour's notice or even without any notice at all. As an exiled leader of one of these nations said to me the other day: 'The notice was a minus quantity. It was given to my government two hours after German troops had poured into my country in a hundred places'.

The fate of these nations tells us what it means to live at the point of a Nazi gun.

The Nazis have justified such actions by various pious frauds. One of these frauds is the claim that they are occupying a nation for the purpose of 'restoring order'. Another is that they are occupying or controlling a nation on the excuse that they are 'protecting it' against the aggression of somebody else.

For example, Germany has said that she was occupying Belgium to save the Belgians from the British. Would she then hesitate to say to any South American country, 'We are occupying you to protect you from aggression by the United States'?

Belgium today is being used as an invasion base against Britain, now fighting for its life. Any South American country, in Nazi hands, would always constitute a jumping-off place for German attack on any one of the other Republics of this hemisphere.

Analyze for yourselves the future of two other places even nearer to Germany if the Nazis won. Could Ireland hold out? Would Irish freedom be permitted as an amazing pet exception in an unfree world? Or the Islands of the Azores which still fly the flag of Portugal after five centuries? You and I think of Hawaii as an outpost of defense in the Pacific. And yet, the Azores are closer to our shores in the Atlantic than Hawaii is on the other side.

There are those who say that the Axis powers would never have any desire to attack the Western Hemisphere. That is the same dangerous form of wishful thinking which has destroyed the powers of resistance of so many conquered peoples. The plain facts are that the Nazis have proclaimed, time and again, that all other races are their inferiors and therefore subject to their orders. And most important of all, the vast resources and wealth of this hemisphere constitute the most tempting loot in all the round world.

Let us no longer blind ourselves to the undeniable fact that the evil forces which have crushed and undermined and corrupted so many others are already within our own gates. Your Government knows much about them and every day is ferreting them out.

Their secret emissaries are active in our own and neighboring countries. They seek to stir up suspicion and dissension to cause internal strife. They try to turn capital against labor, and vice versa. They try to reawaken long slumbering racial and religious enmities which should have no place in this country. They are active in every group that promotes intolerance. They exploit for their own ends our natural abhorrence of war. These trouble-breeders have but one purpose. It is to divide our people into hostile groups and to destroy our unity and shatter our will to defend ourselves.

There are also American citizens, many of them in high places, who, unwittingly in most cases, are aiding and abetting the work of these agents. I do not charge these American citizens with being foreign agents. But I do charge them with doing exactly the kind of work that the dictators want done in the United States.

These people not only believe that we can save our own skins by shutting our eyes to the fate of other nations. Some of them go much further than that. They say that we can and should become the friends and even the partners of the

Axis powers. Some of them even suggest that we should imitate the methods of the dictatorships. Americans never can and never will do that.

The experience of the past two years has proven beyond doubt that no nation can appease the Nazis. No man can tame a tiger into a kitten by stroking it. There can be no appeasement with ruthlessness. There can be no reasoning with an incendiary bomb. We know now that a nation can have peace with the Nazis only at the price of total surrender.

Even the people of Italy have been forced to become accomplices of the Nazis; but at this moment they do not know how soon they will be embraced to death by their allies.

The American appeasers ignore the warning to be found in the fate of Austria, Czechoslovakia, Poland, Norway, Belgium, the Netherlands, Denmark, and France. They tell you that the Axis powers are going to win anyway; that all this bloodshed in the world could be saved; that the United States might just as well throw its influence into the scale of a dictated peace, and get the best out of it that we can.

They call it a 'negotiated peace'. Nonsense! Is it a negotiated peace if a gang of outlaws surrounds your community and on threat of extermination makes you pay tribute to save your own skins?

Such a dictated peace would be no peace at all. It would be only another armistice, leading to the most gigantic armament race and the most devastating trade wars in history. And in these contests the Americas would offer the only real resistance to the Axis powers.

With all their vaunted efficiency and parade of pious purpose in his war, there are still in their background the concentration camp and the servants of God in chains."

FDR was explaining in this 'arsenal of democracy' speech to Americans as well as to victims of Nazism why the U.S. was responding to Axis aggressions by aiding Britain. 'No man can tame a tiger by stroking it' FDR had warned the appeasers in justification of his standing up to Hitler. 'There can be no appeasement with ruthlessness' he had proclaimed, chiding those who would compromise. Many of President Roosevelt's speeches were broadcast by the Free French forces led by Charles DeGaulle based in London across the Channel to occupied France and behind enemy lines in occupied countries. FDR was justifying resistance to Hitler's tyranny everywhere because the designs of dictators—the concentration camps and enslavement of clergymen, plus the establishment of dictatorships were diametrically opposed to democracy and freedom. There was no room for negotiated peace; Britain's war must be won with the U.S. working as their arsenal. FDR continued:

"The history of recent years proves that shootings and chains and concentration camps are not simply the transient tools but the very altars of modern dictatorships. They may talk of a 'new order' in the world, but what they have in mind is but a revival of the oldest and the worst tyranny. In that there is no liberty, no religion, no hope.

The proposed 'new order' is the very opposite of a United States of Europe or a United States of Asia. It is not a Government based upon the consent of the governed. It is not a union of ordinary, self-respecting men and women to protect themselves and their freedom and their dignity from oppression. It is an unholy alliance of power and self to dominate and enslave the human race.

The British people and their allies today are conducting an active war against this unholy alliance. Our own future security is greatly dependent on the outcome of that fight. Our ability to 'keep out of war' is going to be affected by that outcome.

Thinking in terms of today and tomorrow, I make the direct statement to the American people that there is far less chance of the United States getting into war, if we do all we can now to support the nations defending themselves against attack by the Axis than if we acquiesce in their defeat, submit tamely to an Axis victory, and wait our turn to be the object of attack in another war later on.

If we are to be completely honest with ourselves, we must admit there is risk in any course we may take. But I deeply believe that the great majority of our people agree that the course that I advocate involves the least risk now and the greatest hope for world peace in the future.

The people of Europe who are defending themselves do not ask us to do their fighting. *They ask us for the implements of war, the planes, the tanks, the guns, the freighters, which will enable them to fight for their liberty and for our security.* Emphatically we must get these weapons to them in sufficient volume and quickly enough, so that we and our children will be saved the agony and suffering of war which others have had to endure.

Let not defeatists tell us that it is too late. It will never be earlier. Tomorrow will be later than today.

Certain facts are self-evident.

In a military sense Great Britain and the British Empire are today the spearhead of resistance to world conquest. They are putting up a fight which will live forever in the story of human gallantry.

There is no demand for sending an American Expeditionary Force outside our own borders. There is no intention by any member of your Government to send such a force. You can, therefore, nail any talk about sending armies to Europe as deliberate untruth.

Our national policy is not directed toward war. Its sole purpose is to keep war away from our country and our people.

Democracy's fight against world conquest is being greatly aided, and must be more greatly aided, by the rearmament of the United States and by sending every ounce and every ton of munitions and supplies that we can possibly spare to help the defenders who are in the front lines. It is no more unneutral for us to do that than it is for Sweden, Russia, and other nations near Germany to send steel and ore and oil and other war materials into Germany every day in the week.

We are planning our own defense with the utmost urgency; and in its vast scale we must integrate the war needs of Britain and the other free nations resisting aggression.

This is not a matter of sentiment or of controversial personal opinion. It is a matter of realistic, practical military policy, based on the advice of our military experts who are in close touch with existing warfare. These military and naval experts and the members of the Congress and the Administration have a single-minded purpose *the defense of the United States.*

This Nation is making a great effort to produce everything that is necessary in this emergency, and with all possible speed. This great effort requires great sacrifice.

I would ask no one to defend a democracy which in turn would not defend everyone in the Nation against want and privation. The strength of this Nation shall not be diluted by the failure of the Government to protect the economic well-being of its citizens.

If our capacity to produce is limited by machines, it must ever be remembered that these machines are operated by the skill and the stamina of the workers. As the Government is determined to protect the rights of workers, so the Nation has a right to expect that the men who man the machines will discharge their full responsibilities to the urgent needs of defense.

The worker possesses the same human dignity and is entitled to the same security of position as the engineer or manager or owner. For the workers provide the human power that turns out the destroyers, the airplanes, and the tanks.

The Nation expects our defense industries to continue operation without interruption by strikes or lock-outs. It expects and insists that management and workers will reconcile their differences by voluntary or legal means, to continue to produce the supplies that are so sorely needed.

And on the economic side of our great defense program, we are, as you know, bending every effort to maintain stability of prices and with that the stability of the cost of living.

Nine days ago I announced the setting up of a more effective organization to direct our gigantic efforts to increase the production of munitions. The appropriation of vast sums of money and a well-coordinated executive direction of our defense efforts are not in themselves enough. Guns, planes, ships and many other things have to be built in the factories and arsenals of America. They have to be produced by workers and managers and engineers with the aid of machines, which in turn have to be built by hundreds of thousands of workers throughout the land.

In this great work there has been splendid cooperation between the Government and industry and labor, and I am very thankful.

American industrial genius, unmatched throughout the world in the solution of production problems, has been called upon to bring its resources and its talents into action. Manufacturers of watches, of farm implements, linotypes, cash registers, automobiles, sewing machines, lawn mowers, and locomotives are now making fuses, bomb-packing crates, telescope mounts, shells, pistols, and tanks.

But all our present efforts are not enough. We must have more ships, more guns, more planes, more of everything. This can only be accomplished if we discard the notion of 'business as usual'. This job cannot be done merely by superimposing on the existing productive facilities the added requirements for defense.

Our defense efforts must not be blocked by those who fear the future consequences of surplus plant capacity. The possible consequence of failure of our defense efforts now are much more to be feared.

After the present needs of our defense are past, a proper handling of the country's peacetime needs will require all of the new productive capacity if not more.

No pessimistic policy about the future of America shall delay the immediate expansion of those industries essential to defense. We need them.

I want to make it clear that it is the purpose of the Nation to build now with all possible speed every machine, every arsenal, and every factory that we need to manufacture our defense material. We have the men the skill- the wealth- and above all, the will.

I am confident that if and when production of consumer or luxury goods in certain industries requires the use of machines and raw materials that are essential for defense purposes, then such production must yield, and will gladly yield, to our primary and compelling purpose.

I appeal to the owners of plants, to the managers, to the workers, to our own Government employees, to put every ounce of effort into producing these munitions swiftly and without stint. With this appeal I give you the pledge that all of us who are officers of your Government will devote ourselves to the same whole-hearted extent to the great task which lies ahead.

As planes and ships and guns and shells are produced, your Government, with its defense experts, can then determine how best to use them to defend this hemisphere. The decision as to how much shall be sent abroad and how much shall remain at home must be made on the basis of our over-all military necessities.

We must be the great arsenal of democracy. For us this is an emergency as serious as war itself. We must apply ourselves to our task with the same resolution, the same sense of urgency, the same spirit of patriotism and sacrifice, as we would show were we at war.

We have furnished the British great material support and we will furnish far more in the future.

There will be no 'bottlenecks' in our determination to aid Great Britain. No dictator, no combination of dictators, will weaken that determination by threats of how they will construe that determination.

The British have received invaluable military support from the heroic Greek army, and from the forces of all the governments in exile. Their strength is growing. It is the strength of men and women who value their freedom more highly than they value their lives.

I believe that the Axis powers are not going to win this war. I base that belief on the latest and best information.

We have no excuse for defeatism. We have every good reason for hope- hope for peace, hope for the defense of our civilization and for the building of a better civilization in the future.

I have the profound conviction that the American people are now determined to put forth a mightier effort than they have ever yet made to increase our production of all the implements of defense, to meet the threat to our democratic faith.

As President of the United States I call for that national effort. I call for it in the name of this Nation which we love and honor and which we are privileged and proud to serve. I call upon our people with absolute confidence that our common cause will greatly succeed."[208]

Thus FDR's proposal for Lend-Lease enabled the U.S. to become the 'arsenal for democracy' to aid Britain who was defending America. The program of Lend-Lease authorized the president to sell, transfer, exchange, lend, lease, or otherwise dispose of war equipment and other commodities to the government of any country whose defense the president deemed vital to the defense of the United States. But with Lend-Lease FDR knew he was only buying time to prepare for a much greater challenge and wider war in the future that would engulf the U.S. either in the Atlantic or the Pacific or possibly both at the same time.[209] America, he understood needed to be ready, as he stoked the fires of spirit and faith.

---

[208] U.S. Department of State, Publication 1983, Peace and War: United States Foreign Policy, 1931-1941 (Washington, D.C.: U.S. Government Printing Office, 1943), pp. 598-607; Samuel I. Rosenman, Public Papers and Addresses of Franklin D. Roosevelt (New York: Macmillan, 1941) Vol 9, pp. 633-644.

[209] Barbara Bennett Peterson, "FDR's 'Quarterbacking' of U.S. Naval Policy in the Pacific 1933-1939," in three parts The Pacific Historian Vol. 16 No. 4 (Winter 1972): 44-53; Vol. 17 No. 1 (Spring 1973): 61-72; Vol. 18 No. 2 (Summer 1973): 60-73.

Figure 3. President Roosevelt on an inspection tour of a U. S. Naval Base during World War II. Reproduced from the Collection of the Library of Congress, LC-USZ62-59582

Chapter 6

U.S. LEADERSHIP IN WORLD WAR II

After passage of Lend-Lease, a convoy of boats began to carry the goods to Britain. By the end of 1941, and nine hundred and fifty-one tanks had been sent, food shipments reached one million tons, and the overall output of trucks, planes, guns and ammunition was stepped up at a comparable pace. To ensure that Lend-Lease goods arrived in Britain, Roosevelt concluded an executive agreement with the Danish government-in-exile to send American troops to Greenland, thereby extending American naval and air patrols. Roosevelt dispatched troops also to Iceland to prepare American defenses to repel any attack on the Western Hemisphere. By May 1941 the president spoke of strengthening our defenses to the extreme limit of our national capabilities, and explained the need for additional preparedness as being based on hardheaded concern for U.S. homeland security and to preserve the civilized world. Earlier during his third inaugural parade there had appeared "the beginnings of the new armed forces: tanks, armored cars, and trucks carrying pontoon bridges and anti-aircraft guns, shaking the pavement as they sped by....Roosevelt's leadership was carrying the nation slowly toward massive rearmament and aid to the British, but only as new factories and shipyards could come into production."[210]

These developments continued to polarize great public debate between isolationists and interventionists.[211] In 1940 the Committee to Defend America by aiding the Allies had been established under the leadership of William Allen White. In 1941 the Fight for Freedom Committee contended for American entry

---

[210] Frank Freidel, Franklin D. Roosevelt, A Rendezvous With Destiny (New York: Little, Brown and Company, 1990), p. 364.
[211] Barbara Bennett Peterson, "FDR's 'Quarterbacking' of U.S. Naval Policy in the Pacific 1933-1939," The Pacific Historian, Vol. 16 No. 4 (Winter 1972): 44-49.

into the war. On the other side, the America First Committee argued that a German victory in Europe would not menace American security. Socialists like Norman Thomas and Progressives like Burton K. Wheeler were bitterly critical of President Roosevelt for moving the country toward preparedness for war. Each group cut across economic, political and social lines and each harnessed their own newspaper and radio campaigns. The isolationist viewpoint was reflected in the writings of Anne Morrow Lindbergh in her book *The Wave of the Future* in which she explained her husband Charles Lindbergh's views "that Americans must adjust themselves to an inevitable new order in Europe" dominated by Hitler. FDR had responded to these views saying "there are men who believe that...tyranny and slavery have become the surging wave of the future—that freedom is an ebbing tide. But we Americans know that this is not true."[212] There was a difference of opinion in America on what was patriotic—to remain pacifistic or to prepare for possible involvement in a war against Hitler. FDR's keen foresight and instincts told him exactly what to do. FDR had firmly believed in 1940 "the best immediate defense of the United States is the success of Great Britain in defending itself, and...it is equally important from a selfish point of view of American defense that we should do everything to help." Churchill concurred, saying to FDR "give us the tools and we will finish the job."[213]

In his annual message to Congress on January 6, 1941 FDR had put forth American goals in foreign policy with his famed Four Freedoms:

> "In the future days which we seek to make secure, we look forward to a world founded upon four essential human freedoms. The first is freedom of speech and expression—everywhere in the world. The second is freedom of every person to worship God in his own way—everywhere in the world. The third is freedom from want—which, translated into world terms means economic understandings which will secure to every nation a healthy peacetime life for its inhabitants—everywhere in the world. The fourth is freedom from fear—which, translated into world terms, means a world-wide reduction of armaments to such a point and in such a thorough fashion that no nation will be in a position to commit an act of physical aggression against any neighbor—anywhere in the world. That is no vision of a distant millennium. It is a definite basis for a kind of world attainable in our own time and generation."[214]

---

[212] Freidel, Franklin D. Roosevelt, A Rendezvous With Destiny, p 364.
[213] Joseph P. Lash, Roosevelt and Churchill, 1939-1941, The Partnership That Saved the West (Franklin Center, PA: Franklin Library, 1976, p. 284; Robert Dalleck, Franklin D. Roosevelt and American Foreign Policy, 1932-1945 (New York: Oxford University Press, 1979 republished 1995), pp. 259-260; Freidel, Franklin D. Roosevelt, A Rendezvous With Destiny, p. 361.
[214] Freidel, Franklin D. Roosevelt, Rendezvous With Destiny, p. 360-361.

Harry Hopkins, who had gone to London to negotiate the terms of Lend-Lease, became FDR's able administrator of this program and Averell Harriman continued in London as liaison officer and defense expediter. Britain was 'fighting our fight in Europe' so that the U.S. could "avoid the contest until we can be adequately prepared."[215] FDR speculated as early as January 1941 that the U.S. could indeed be attacked by either Germany or Japan and debated military strategies with his secretaries of state, war, and navy. He directed "that our military course must be very conservative until our strength had been developed."[216] But he knew that only if the U.S. were attacked could America enter the war with a united front. Meanwhile General Franco in Spain refused to enter the war or allow the Germans to attack British-held Gibraltar because he believed that the allies would win if the U.S. entered the war. FDR had worked to ensure Franco's neutrality and also appealed to Petain in Vichy France that he should side with the allies rather than collaborate with the Nazis. FDR sent Robert Murphy, counselor of the American embassy to Vichy, to pressure the French to resist German encroachments into French North Africa so that the allies might make a landing there in the future. Meanwhile in the spring of 1941 the Germans occupied Yugoslavia and Greece and threatened Crete.[217] Now British held Egypt was in jeopardy as General Erwin Rommel and his Afrika Korps approached across Libya. FDR determined to continue aid to Britain while the island nation defended her North African interests like the Suez Canal.

Meanwhile as Americans debated, the war in Europe widened in unexpected ways. Surprisingly, while Hitler and Stalin had signed their previous Non-Aggression pact and shared the spoils of Poland, they could not agree to ultimately share the world or what its ruling philosophy should be, Nazism or Communism.[218] The ultimate betrayal came when the two could no longer agree to possibly divide the world, a fortunate circumstance for history of the free world. When Hitler declared war on Russia in June 1941 he unleashed the largest

---

[215] Ibid.
[216] Ibid., p. 365
[217] John Strawson, Hitler's Battles for Europe (New York: Scribner, 1971); Walter Ansel, Hitler and the Middle Sea (Durham, NC: Duke University Press, 1972); John Erickson and David Dilks, eds., Barbarossa: The Axis and the Allies (Edinburgh: Edinburgh University Press, 1994); Alan Clark, The Fall of Crete (New York: Morrow, 1962 republished London: Cassell, 2001).
[218] Alan S. Milward, The German Economy at War (London: University of London, Athlone Press,1965); Albert Speer, Inside the Third Reich: Memoirs (New York: Collier Books, 1970 republished 1981) translated by Richard and Clara Winston; Trumbull Higgins, Winston Churchill and the Second Front, 1940-1943 (New York: Oxford University Press, 1957 republished in 1974); Alan S. Milward, Fascist Economy in Norway (Oxford: Clarendon Press, 1972); Alan S. Milward, The New Order and the French Economy (Oxford: Clarendon Press,

military struggle in the history of mankind. Nine million men were to eventually fight along a 1,000-mile border from the Baltic to the Black Sea. Despairing of his failure to effect an early defeat of Britain, Hitler had decided to eliminate the potential threat of Russia from his rear by a single blow and to capture much needed oil supplies in the Russian Crimea. The philosophy of this campaign was to be very different. It pitted German against Slav, Nazism against Communism, as Hitler explained: "The war against Russia will be such that it cannot be conducted in a knightly fashion. This struggle is one of ideologies and racial differences and will have to be conducted with unprecedented, unmerciful and unrelenting harshness. All officers will have to rid themselves of obsolete ideologies....I insist absolutely that my orders be executed without contradiction. The commissars are the bearers of ideologies directly opposed to National Socialism. Therefore the commissars will be liquidated. German soldiers guilty of breaking international law will be excused. Russia has not participated in the Hague Convention and therefore has no rights under it."[219]

The Russian front, once it was open, was to remain the main theater of war until the D-Day invasion of the allies on the Normandy beaches in 1944.[220] For almost two and one-half years, Russia bore the brunt of the war. Hitler, in attacking Russia, believed that the Soviets were unprepared and that German forces could quickly and easily capture Moscow and Leningrad. But his armies were unable to capture either city and this was a major turning point in the war. The Battle of Stalingrad in 1942 was vitally important, as had Hitler been successful in capturing Stalingrad he might have captured the tremendous oil reserves of the Caucasus. Had he done this his lines of communications and supply would not have been so sorely stretched along the 3,000-mile route into

---

1970); Henri Michel, The Shadow War: The European Resistance, 1939-1945 (New York: Harper and Row, 1972) translated from French by Richard Barry.

[219] Adolf Hitler planning the invasion of Russia or the Barbarossa campaign in June 1941 giving orders to the chiefs of the three German armed services and key Army field commanders in March 1941 quoted [as recorded by Halder affidavit Nov. 22, 1945 at Nuremberg, NCA, VIII, pp. 645-46] in William L. Shirer, The Rise and Fall of the Third Reich (New York: Simon and Schuster, 1960), p. 830.

[220] Alexander Dallin, German Rule in Russia, 1941-1945: A Study of Occupation Policies (London: Macmillan and New York: St. Martin's Press, 1957); Alan Clark, Barbarossa: The Russian-German Conflict, 1941-1945 (Harmondsworth: Penguin, 1965); Basil H. Liddell-Hart, ed., The Red Army (New York: Harcourt Brace, 1956); Trumbull Higgins, Hitler and Russia: The Third Reich in a Two-front War, 1937-1943 (New York: Macmillan, 1966); Seweryn Bialer, ed., Stalin and His Generals: Soviet Military Memoirs of World War II (New York: Pegasus, 1969); John Erickson, Main Front: Soviet Leaders Look Back on World War II (London and Washington, D.C.: Brassey's Defence Publishers, 1987); Bob Carruthers and John Erickson, Russian Front, 1941-1945 (London: Cassell, 1999); John Erickson, Road to Berlin (London: Cassell, 2003); Percy Ernst Schramm, Hitler: The Man and the Military Leader (Chicago: Academy of Chicago Publishers, 1999) translated by Donald S. Detwiler.

Russia. Roosevelt and Churchill agreed to help Stalin repel the Germans.[221] Roosevelt sent Harry Hopkins to Moscow in July 1941 and his optimistic report on Russian strength encouraged Roosevelt to begin to send supplies and equipment to Stalin in stiffening resistance to Hitler's forces. FDR understood immediately that Hitler had made a great mistake opening a war on two fronts. It was the old mistake of Napoleon. An invasion of Russia would prove as disastrous for Hitler as it had for Napoleon when he was forced to retreat from Moscow. FDR believed now that Nazism would ultimately be defeated. Both Churchill and FDR promised massive aid to Stalin who was now 'fighting their fight'. But there was the ideological difference between capitalism and communism. As Walter Lippmann stated Americans and Russians were "separated by an ideological gulf and joined by the bridge of national interest."[222] Yet FDR issued a statement aligning himself with Churchill and promised aid to the Soviets as "any defense against Hitlerism" would benefit the U.S. and it security.[223] FDR understood that this Russian diversion meant extra time for both Britain and America. Hitler's 'mistake' "will mean the liberation of Europe from Nazi domination—and at the same time I do not think we need to worry about any possibility of Russian domination" of the world.[224] Additional Lend-Lease aid was extended to the Soviets through the efforts of Harry Hopkins who met personally with Stalin in Moscow in July 1941. Stalin expressed confidence that the Soviet Union could resist Germany saying "Give us anti-aircraft guns and aluminum and we can fight for three or four years."[225] The Soviet forces inflicted heavy loses upon the Nazis and FDR and Churchill praised 'good old Uncle Joe' as their ally. Later Hopkins was replaced by Harriman as Lend-Lease mediator, and ultimately the Soviets would receive goods valued at $10 billion from the U.S. through Lend-Lease.

FDR debated through the winter of 1941 the wisdom of using U.S. military ships to protect convoys of needed supplies to Britain through the hostile war zones. He was hesitant to begin convoying as "obviously, when a nation convoys

---

[221] Albert Seaton, The Russo-German War, 1941-1945 (New York: Praeger, 1971 republished Novato, CA: Presidio, 1990); Albert Seaton, Battle for Moscow, 1941-1945 (New York: Stein and Day, 1971); Albert Seaton, Stalin as Warlord (London: Batsford, 1976); John Erickson, Road to Stalingrad (London: Cassell, 2003).
[222] Freidel, Franklin D. Roosevelt, A Rendezvous With Destiny, p. 373.
[223] Forrest Davis and Ernest K. Lindley, How War Came (New York: Simon and Schuster, 1942), pp. 243-245; William L. Langer and S. Everett Gleason, Undeclared War, 1940-1941 (Gloucester, Mass: P. Smith, 1968 originally published in 1953), pp. 538-539.
[224] Elliott Roosevelt, ed., F.D.R., His Personal Letters (New York: Duell, Sloan, and Pearce, 1947-1950), Vol. 2, p. 1175.
[225] Robert E. Sherwood, Roosevelt and Hopkins, An Intimate History (New York: Harper and Row, 1950 originally published in 1948), pp. 319-328.

ships…through a hostile zone…there is apt to be some shooting…and shooting comes awfully close to war….It might almost *compel* shooting to start."[226] The Japanese had been emboldened in the Pacific by the German invasion of the Russian front, and a Japanese thrust now into Southeast Asia seemed probable. But due to the German submarine menace FDR had already moved some of the U.S. naval forces out of Pearl Harbor for the Atlantic.[227] The U.S. would continue to patrol the western region of the Atlantic to the twenty-sixth parallel as a means to counter Nazi wolf packs of submarines. FDR would protect commerce and convoys but stopped short of inciting war with Germany. "I am not willing to fire the first shot," he declared.[228]

In August 1941 Roosevelt and Churchill met on a warship off the coast of Newfoundland to agree to the Atlantic Charter which listed common principles and war aims. It was agreed the United States and Britain sought no territorial aggrandizement, desired to see no territorial changes without self-determination of peoples, and affirmed the right of all peoples to chose the form of government under which they would live. They planned to assure all states equal access to trade and raw materials, proposed economic collaboration among all nations, guaranteed freedom of the seas in peacetime, freedom from fear and want, and recommended after the fall of Germany the disarmament of all aggressor nations. The Atlantic Charter read in its entirety:

> "The President of the United States of America and the Prime Minister Mr. Churchill, representing His Majesty's Government in the United Kingdom, being met together, deem it right to make known certain common principles in the national policies of their respective countries on which they base their hopes for a better future for the world.
>
> FIRST, their countries seek no aggrandizement, territorial or other;
>
> SECOND, they desire to see no territorial changes that do not accord with the freely expressed wishes of the peoples concerned;
>
> THIRD, they respect the right of all peoples to choose the form of government under which they will live; and they wish to see sovereign rights and self-government restored to those who have been forcibly deprived of them;

---

[226] Press conference Vol.17, pp. 86-87, Press Conference Transcripts, 25 Vols. Franklin D. Roosevelt Library, Hyde Park; Langer and Gleason, Undeclared War, 1940-1941, (1953), pp. 243, 266-267.

[227] Barbara Bennett Peterson, "FDR's 'Quarterbacking' of U.S. Naval Policy in the Pacific 1933-1945," The Pacific Historian in three parts (Winter 1972):44-53; (Spring 1973):61-72; (Summer 1973):60-71.

[228] Patrick Abbazia, Mr. Roosevelt's Navy: The Private War of the U.S. Atlantic Fleet, 1939-1942 (Annapolis, MD: Naval Institute Press, 1975), pp. 155-156.

FOURTH, they will endeavor, with due respect for their existing obligations, to further the enjoyment by all States, great or small, victor or vanquished, of access, on equal terms, to the trade and to the raw materials of the world which are needed for their economic prosperity;

FIFTH, they desire to bring about the fullest collaboration between all nations in the economic field with the object of securing, for all, improved labor standards, economic adjustment and social security;

SIXTH, after the final destruction of the Nazi tyranny, they hope to see established a peace which will afford to all nations the means of dwelling in safety within their own boundaries, and which will afford assurance that all the men in all the lands may live out their lives in freedom from fear and want;

SEVENTH, such a peace should enable all men to traverse the high seas and oceans without hindrance;

EIGHTH, they believe that all of the nations of the world, for realistic as well as spiritual reasons, must come to the abandonment of the use of force. Since no future peace can be maintained if land, sea or air armaments continue to be employed by nations which threaten, or may threaten, aggression outside of their frontiers, they believe, pending the establishment of a wider and permanent system of general security, that the disarmament of such nations is essential. They will likewise aid and encourage all other practicable measures which will lighten for peace-loving peoples the crushing burden of armaments." [229]

Franklin D. Roosevelt
Winston S. Churchill

The charter represented a psychological alliance with Britain, and shortly after the meeting the United States moved closer to a shooting war with Germany. Throughout the summer of 1941 American destroyers were escorting convoys of Lend-Lease supplies as far as Iceland where the British Navy conveyed them to England. This type of aid short of war brought America ever closer to belligerency and after the destroyer *Greer* was fired on by a German submarine off the coast of Iceland, President Roosevelt instructed the Navy to shoot on sight any Axis ships in the neutrality zone. In a special Fireside Chat of September 11, 1941 FDR proclaimed America's duty to protect the freedom of the seas and to stand-up to the Nazi threats as he broadcast from the White House:

"My Fellow Americans:
The Navy Department of the United States has reported to me that on the morning of September 4th the United States destroyer *Greer*, proceeding in full daylight towards Iceland, had reached a point southeast of Greenland. She was

---

[229] Franklin D. Roosevelt Library, Hyde Park, New York; Samuel I. Rosenman, Public Papers and Addresses of Franklin D. Roosevelt (New York: Harper & Brothers, 1950) Vol 10, pp. 314-315.

carrying American mail to Iceland. She was flying the American flag. Her identity as an American ship was unmistakable.

She was then and there attacked by a submarine. Germany admits that it was a German submarine. The submarine deliberately fired a torpedo at the *Greer*, followed later by another torpedo attack. In spite of what Hitler's propaganda bureau has invented, and in spite of what any American obstructionist organization may prefer to believe, I tell you the blunt fact that the German submarine fired first upon this American destroyer without warning, and with deliberate design to sink her.

Our destroyer, at the time, was in waters which the Government of the United States had declared to be waters of self-defense, surrounding outposts of American protection in the Atlantic.

In the North of the Atlantic, outposts have been established by us in Iceland, in Greenland, in Labrador and in Newfoundland. Through these waters there pass many ships of many flags. They bear food and other supplies to civilians; and they bear material of war, for which the people of the United States are spending billions of dollars, and which, by Congressional action, they have declared to be essential for the defense of our own land.

The United States destroyer, when attacked, was proceeding on a legitimate mission.

If the destroyer was visible to the submarine when the torpedo was fired, then the attack was a deliberate attempt by the Nazis to sink a clearly identified American warship. On the other hand, if the submarine was beneath the surface of the sea and, with the aid of its listening devices, fired in the direction of the sound of the American destroyer without even taking the trouble to learn its identity, as the official German communique would indicate, then the attack was even more outrageous. For it indicates a policy of indiscriminate violence against any vessel sailing the seas, belligerent or non-belligerent.

This was piracy, piracy legally and morally. It was not the first nor the last act of piracy which the Nazi Government has committed against the American flag in this war. For attack has followed attack.

A few months ago an American flag merchant ship, the *Robin Moor*, was sunk by a Nazi submarine in the middle of the South Atlantic, under circumstances violating long-established international law and violating every principle of humanity. The passengers and the crew were forced into open boats hundreds of miles from land, in direct violation of international agreements signed by nearly all nations including the Government of Germany. No apology, no allegation of mistake, no offer of reparations has come from the Nazi Government.

In July 1941, nearly two months ago an American battleship in North American waters was followed by a submarine which for a long time sought to maneuver itself into a position of attack upon the battleship. The periscope of the submarine was clearly seen. No British or American submarines were within hundreds of miles of this spot at the time, so the nationality of the submarine is clear.

Five days ago a United States Navy ship on patrol picked up three survivors of an American-owned ship operating under the flag of our sister Republic of Panama, the *S. S. Sessa*. On August 17th, she had been first torpedoed without warning, and then shelled, near Greenland, while carrying civilian supplies to Iceland. It is feared that the other members of her crew have been drowned. In view of the established presence of German submarines in this vicinity, there can be no reasonable doubt as to the identity of the flag of the attacker.

Five days ago, another United States merchant ship, the *Steel Seafarer*, was sunk by a German aircraft in the Red Sea two hundred and twenty miles south of Suez. She was bound for an Egyptian port.

So four of the vessels sunk or attacked flew the American flag and were clearly identifiable. Two of these ships were warships of the American Navy. In the fifth case, the vessel sunk clearly carried the flag of our sister Republic of Panama.

In the face of all this, we Americans are keeping our feet on the ground. Our type of democratic civilization has outgrown the thought of feeling compelled to fight some other nation by reason of any single piratical attack on one of our ships. We are not becoming hysterical or losing our sense of proportion. Therefore, what I am thinking and saying tonight does not relate to any isolated episode.

Instead, we Americans are taking a long-range point of view in regard to certain fundamentals, a point of view in regard to a series of events on land and on sea which must be considered as a whole, as a part of a world pattern.

It would be unworthy of a great nation to exaggerate an isolated incident, or to become inflamed by some one act of violence. But it would be inexcusable folly to minimize such incidents in the face of evidence which makes it clear that the incident is not isolated, but is part of a general plan."

FDR might have declared war against Germany following any one of these piratical sinkings but he wanted the entire country, including the isolationists behind him when he did so because he did not want to jeopardize support for domestic New Deal programs.

"The important truth is," FDR continued, "that these acts of international lawlessness are a manifestation of a design, a design that has been made clear to the American people for a long time. It is the Nazi design to abolish the freedom of the seas, and to acquire absolute control and domination of these seas for themselves.

For with control of the seas in their own hands, the way can obviously become clear for their next step, domination of the United States and domination of the Western Hemisphere by force of arms. Under Nazi control of the seas, no merchant ship of the United States or of any other American Republic would be free to carry on any peaceful commerce, except by the condescending grace of this foreign and tyrannical power. The Atlantic Ocean which has been, and which should always be, a free and friendly highway for us would then become a deadly menace to the commerce of the United States, to the coasts of the United States, and even to the inland cities of the United States.

The Hitler Government, in defiance of the laws of the sea, and in defiance of the recognized rights of all other nations, has presumed to declare, on paper, that great areas of the seas, even including a vast expanse lying in the Western Hemisphere, are to be closed, and that no ships may enter them for any purpose, except at peril of being sunk. Actually they are sinking ships at will and without warning in widely separated areas both within and far outside of these far-flung pretended zones.

This Nazi attempt to seize control of the oceans is but a counterpart of the Nazi plots now being carried on throughout the Western Hemisphere, all designed toward the same end. For Hitler's advance guards, not only his avowed agents but also his dupes among us, have sought to make ready for him footholds, and bridgeheads in the New World, to be used as soon as he has gained control of the oceans.

His intrigues, his plots, his machinations, his sabotage in this New World are all known to the Government of the United States. Conspiracy has followed conspiracy.

For example, last year a plot to seize the Government of Uruguay was smashed by the prompt action of that country, which was supported in full by her American neighbors. A like plot was then hatching in Argentina and that government has carefully and wisely blocked it at every point. More recently, an endeavor was made to subvert the government of Bolivia. And within the past few weeks the discovery was made of secret air-landing fields in Colombia, within easy range of the Panama Canal. I could multiply instance upon instance.

To be ultimately successful in world mastery, Hitler knows that he must get control of the seas. He must first destroy the bridge of ships which we are building across the Atlantic and over which we shall continue to roll the implements of war to help destroy him, to destroy all his works in the end. He must wipe out our patrol on sea and in the air if he is to do it. He must silence the British Navy.

I think it must be explained over and over again to people who like to think of the United States Navy as an invincible protection, that this can be true only if the British Navy survives. And that, my friends, is simple arithmetic.

For if the world outside of the Americas falls under Axis domination, the shipbuilding facilities which the Axis powers would then possess in all of Europe, in the British Isles and in the Far East would be much greater than all the shipbuilding facilities and potentialities of all of the Americas, not only greater, but two or three times greater, enough to win. Even if the United States threw all its resources into such a situation, seeking to double and even redouble the size of our Navy, the Axis powers, in control of the rest of the world, would have the manpower and the physical resources to out build us several times over.

It is time for all Americans, Americans of all the Americas to stop being deluded by the romantic notion that the Americas can go on living happily and peacefully in a Nazi-dominated world.

Generation after generation, America has battled for the general policy of the freedom of the seas. And that policy is a very simple one, but a basic, a fundamental one. It means that no nation has the right to make the broad oceans of the world at great distances from the actual theater of land war, unsafe for the commerce of others.

That has been our policy, proved time and again, in all of our history.

Our policy has applied from the earliest days of the Republic, and still applies, not merely to the Atlantic but to the Pacific and to all other oceans as well.

Unrestricted submarine warfare in 1941 constitutes a defiance, an act of aggression, against that historic American policy. It is now clear that Hitler has begun his campaign to control the seas by ruthless force and by wiping out every vestige of international law, every vestige of humanity.

His intention has been made clear. The American people can have no further illusions about it.

No tender whisperings of appeasers that Hitler is not interested in the Western Hemisphere, no soporific lullabies that a wide ocean protects us from him can long have any effect on the hard-headed, far-sighted and realistic American people.

Because of these episodes, because of the movements and operations of German warships, and because of the clear, repeated proof that the present government of Germany has no respect for treaties or for international law, that it has no decent attitude toward neutral nations or human life, we Americans are now face to face not with abstract theories but with cruel, relentless facts.

This attack on the *Greer* was no localized military operation in the North Atlantic. This was no mere episode in a struggle between two nations. *This was one determined step towards creating a permanent world system based on force, on terror and on murder.*

And I am sure that even now the Nazis are waiting, waiting to see whether the United States will by silence give them the green light to go ahead on this path of destruction.

The Nazi danger to our Western world has long ceased to be a mere possibility. The danger is here now not only from a military enemy but from an enemy of all law, all liberty, all morality, all religion.

There has now come a time when you and I must see the cold inexorable necessity of saying to these inhuman, unrestrained seekers of world conquest and permanent world domination by the sword: 'You seek to throw our children and our children's children into your form of terrorism and slavery. You have now attacked our own safety. You shall go no further'.

Normal practices of diplomacy, note writing, are of no possible use in dealing with international outlaws who sink our ships and kill our citizens.

One peaceful nation after another has met disaster because each refused to look the Nazi danger squarely in the eye until it had actually had them by the throat. The United States will not make that fatal mistake."

FDR carefully laid out his presidential plan to protect America's freedom of the seas and to defend America.

"No act of violence," he boldly stated, "no act of intimidation will keep us from maintaining intact two bulwarks of American defense: First, our line of supply of material to the enemies of Hitler; and second, the freedom of our shipping on the high seas.

No matter what it takes, no matter what it costs, we will keep open the line of legitimate commerce in these defensive waters of ours. We have sought no shooting war with Hitler. We do not seek it now. But neither do we want peace so much, that we are willing to pay for it by permitting him to attack our naval and merchant ships while they are on legitimate business.

I assume that the German leaders are not deeply concerned, tonight or any other time, by what we Americans or the American Government say or publish about them. We cannot bring about the downfall of Nazism by the use of long-range invective.

But when you see a rattlesnake poised to strike, you do not wait until he has struck before you crush him.

These Nazi submarines and raiders are the rattlesnakes of the Atlantic. They are a menace to the free pathways of the high seas. They are a challenge to our own sovereignty. They hammer at our most precious rights when they attack ships of the American flag, symbols of our independence, our freedom, our very life.

It is clear to all Americans that the time has come when the Americas themselves must now be defended. A continuation of attacks in our own waters or in waters that could be used for further and greater attacks on us, will inevitably weaken our American ability to repel Hitlerism.

Do not let us be hair-splitters. Let us not ask ourselves whether the Americas should begin to defend themselves after the first attack, or the fifth attack, or the tenth attack, or the twentieth attack.

The time for active defense is now.

Do not let us split hairs. Let us not say : 'We will only defend ourselves if the torpedo succeeds in getting home, or if the crew and the passengers are drowned'.

This is the time for prevention of attack.

If submarines or raiders attack in distant waters, they can attack equally well within sight of our own shores. Their very presence in any waters which America deems vital to its defense constitutes an attack.

In the waters which we deem necessary for our defense, American naval vessels and American planes will no longer wait until Axis submarines lurking under the water, or Axis raiders on the surface of the sea, strike their deadly blow first.

Upon our naval and air patrol, now operating in large number over a vast expanse of the Atlantic Ocean, falls the duty of maintaining the American policy of freedom of the seas now. That means, very simply, very clearly, that our patrolling vessels and planes will protect all merchant ships, not only American ships but ships of any flag, engaged in commerce in our defensive waters. They will protect them from submarines; they will protect them from surface raiders.

This situation is not new. The second President of the United States, John Adams, ordered the United States Navy to clean out European privateers and European ships of war which were infesting the Caribbean and South American waters, destroying American commerce.

The third President of the United States, Thomas Jefferson, ordered the United States Navy to end the attacks being made upon American and other ships by the corsairs of the nations of North Africa.

My obligation as President is historic; it is clear. Yes, it is inescapable.

It is no act of war on our part when we decide to protect the seas that are vital to American defense. The aggression is not ours. Ours is solely defense.

But let this warning be clear. From now on, if German or Italian vessels of war enter the waters, the protection of which is necessary for American defense they do so at their own peril.

The orders which I have given as Commander-in-Chief of the United States Army and Navy are to carry out that policy at once. The sole responsibility rests upon Germany. There will be no shooting unless Germany continues to seek it.

That is my obvious duty in this crisis. That is the clear right of this sovereign nation. This is the only step possible, if we would keep tight the wall of defense which we are pledged to maintain around this Western Hemisphere.

I have no illusions about the gravity of this step. I have not taken it hurriedly or lightly. It is the result of months and months of constant thought and anxiety and prayer. In the protection of your nation and mine it cannot be avoided. The American people have faced other grave crises in their history with American courage, with American resolution. They will do no less today.

They know the actualities of the attacks upon us. They know the necessities of a bold defense against these attacks. They know that the times call for clear heads and fearless hearts.

And with that inner strength that comes to a free people conscious of their duty, conscious of the righteousness of what they do, they will, with Divine help and guidance, stand their ground against this latest assault upon their democracy, their sovereignty, and their freedom."[230]

FDR faced his adversaries squarely. At the same time he was speaking of the need to stand up to Hitler and Nazi aggression on the high seas Roosevelt spoke of the need to strike at America's enemies financially. In the summer of 1941 FDR had frozen the assets of Germany, Italy and all nations under their domination. All German diplomatic personnel were ordered to leave the United States. The American destroyer the *Kearny* was also attacked with German torpedoes in the following weeks and U.S. vessels were placed on high alert. After the Germans sank the American vessel *Reuben James* on October 30, 1941, Congress revised the Neutrality Act to allow American merchant vessels to proceed to British ports with Lend-Lease goods and these merchant ships were armed. The *Reuben James* had been sunk by the Germans, killing the over one hundred American sailors on board. If Pearl Harbor had not drawn the United States into the war in the Pacific, almost certainly the attacks by the Germans on American shipping would have drawn in America in the Atlantic. FDR foresaw this better than anyone and had taken giant measures for preparedness. The U.S. sent troops to Iceland and Admiral Stark noted "I realize that this is practically an act of war."[231]

Japan saw in this European crisis an opportunity to establish a New Order in Asia with itself at the industrialized center of the Pacific. There were many similarities between the rise of totalitarianism in both Germany and Japan that had made them join the Rome-Berlin-Tokyo Axis. Both governments had moved away from parliamentary government, both promoted a narrow-minded nationalism and terrorism to promote dictatorship, both abolished the freedoms of speech and press and religion, persecuting liberals when they attempted to speak out against the government, and finally, both were expansionist states aggressively seeking new land areas. In spite of these similarities, there were basic differences too between Germany and Japan. In Japan victory at the polls was not a pre-requisite for power, while in Germany the Nazi party gained a plurality of the vote and had been legally elected. In Japan the government was considerably less modern and the social structure more firm. Finally there was a vast spiritual difference between Germany and Japan as the Nazis used race to sanction aggression such as with the invasion of Russia. Japan had allied with Italy and

---

[230] Franklin D. Roosevelt Library, Hyde Park, New York; Samuel I. Roseman, Public Papers and Addresses of Franklin D. Roosevelt (New York: Harper & Brothers, 1950) Vol 10, pp. 384-392.
[231] Sherwood, Roosevelt and Hopkins, p. 290; Thomas A. Bailey and Paul B. Ryan, Hitler vs. Roosevelt, The Undeclared Naval War (New York: Free Press, 1979), pp. 168-173.

Germany because these were the only two countries in western Europe that were not critical of her expansion in China. Yet Japan's concerns were Asian and not European. From 1937 on Japan desired to achieve victory in the war with China and all policy decisions were made with that aim. Her major problems were the growing antagonism of the United States over the Japanese involvement in China and Southeast Asia and the strength of the United States Navy in the Pacific. For a period after Japan's 1937 direct invasion into northern China, FDR had refused to recognize the belligerency of the powers involved because he wished to continue to aid China with weapons to resist the Japanese. The situation in China was labeled "an incident" for a time so that FDR would not be fettered by the neutrality legislation. Thus China's ability to secure U.S. supplies was preserved. But slowly Japan grew more confident and directly challenged the U.S. By late 1941 the U.S. insisted that Japan withdraw from Indo-China and Mainland China, directly opposing Japan's war aims in Asia. This was a pre-condition to restoring economic relations between the U.S. and Japan. The Japanese were adamant about pursuing the war in China proper but were watching their oil gauge drop. They badly needed aviation gasoline to conquer China. Japan felt new sources of oil could be found in Southeast Asia, especially Indonesia. When Russia was invaded by Germany in June 1941, Japan believed her long awaited opportunities had come in Asia. Seizing this unprecedented opportunity, Japan had invaded Indo-China in July 1941 and in September Japan had joined Germany and Italy in the Tripartite Pact. With Britain and France involved in the war against Hitler's Germany in Europe, only the U.S. seemed to be blocking Japan's way in Asia.[232]

The United States as well as Britain and France reacted to Japan's occupation of Indo-China by placing a total embargo on all exports to Japan and freezing the assets of Japan within their countries. The U.S. stopped all trade with Japan, especially in oil and aviation gasoline. The Japanese war machine required twelve thousand tons of oil a day to feed her war theaters. Japan viewed the oil embargo as a threatening move on the part of the U.S. Militarists in Japan designed a plan to attack oil-rich countries of Southeast Asia held by the Dutch and British, and to prohibit U.S. retaliation by an air strike on the United States Pacific fleet stationed at Pearl Harbor, Hawaii. Behind the scenes, American representatives took part in staff discussions with British and Dutch officials to consider plans for the defense of the western Pacific in case a Japanese attack forced the United States into war. Japan had been dependent on the United States for 90% of its scrap metal, 91% of its copper, and 66% of its oil. The American embargo effectively cut Japanese

---

[232] Barbara Bennett Peterson, "FDR's 'Quarterbacking' of U.S. Naval Policy in the Pacific 1933-1945, The Pacific Historian.

importation of oil and gas to 10% of the pre-war level, so that she faced a crisis of dwindling stockpiles. To counter these American measures Japanese Prime Minister Fumimaro Konoye, a moderate, in August 1941 proposed a meeting with Roosevelt. Japan, he promised, would withdraw from Indo-China as soon as the 'China incident' was settled. Japan he promised would not expand into the Dutch East Indies or declare war on the Soviet Union unless attacked, and would not feel bound by the Tripartite Pact to declare war on the United States if America became involved in a war with Germany. But Secretary of State Cordell Hull encouraged Roosevelt to reject these potential agreements, refusing to abandon the United States' commitment to the Open Door and the independence of China. Diplomacy broke down between Cordell Hull and Japanese diplomats over these critical issues and positions. The U.S. military personnel and the president were also aware of the secret Japanese plans to attack farther south in Asia after mid-November 1941 because they had cracked the Japanese military code. There would be no Pacific armistice. Japan would continue her military course of widening the war in Asia. With this failure to reach a peace settlement, the government of Prince Konoye fell in Japan and General Tojo and the militarists came to power. Japan calculated that she had oil reserves for only two years, so the decision was made to carve out an area in Southeast Asia that would give her oil and economic self-sufficiency. Japan believed she could hold this newly conquered area until the United States grew tired of war. The plan was predicated upon knocking out the United States Pacific Fleet at Pearl Harbor and was based upon the assumption that Japan would face the United States on a one-to-one basis in the Pacific. Japan bet her land-based air power and shorter supply lines in Asia against America's productivity. By pursuing her policy to establish the New Order in Asia, Japan calculated that she would be operating along interior lines, much closer to her target areas. The American garrisons in the target areas, for example in the Philippines, were judged to be weak and surmountable. The oil of Southeast Asia was essential in Japan's view for a successful campaign over China. Russia was pinned down and Britain seemed on the verge of collapse. Tojo judged that America would never concentrate its forces against Japan while Germany remained undefeated. He calculated that if Japan could capture China and the islands of Oceania, Japan could make itself invincible against attack and maintain self-sufficiency that would be impregnable.

The strike at Pearl Harbor was planned by Admiral Yamamoto and carried out by Admiral Namura.[233] In Hawaii Admiral Husband E. Kimmel, in command of the U.S. Pacific fleet, and Major General Walter Short received notification

---

[233] Ibid.

from Washington that hostilities might begin at any time. They were instructed to protect their forces from sabotage so they had grouped the planes and ships making them vulnerable to air strikes. Fortunately the aircraft carriers *Lexington* and *Enterprise* had left Hawaii to fortify Wake and Guam. A strike force of Japanese aircraft carriers left the Kurile Islands on November 26 and made its way toward Hawaii. On the day before December 7, 1941 the Japanese code 'Climb Mount Niitake' was delivered, which meant proceed to the attack area on Oahu. Within minutes the Japanese air strike on Hawaii on December 7th killed over twenty-five hundred troops and civilians.

Following this attack on Pearl Harbor President Roosevelt delivered a stirring and memorable address on December 8th:

> "Yesterday December 7, 1941- a date which will live in infamy- the United States of America was suddenly and deliberately attacked by naval and air forces of the Empire of Japan.
>
> The United States was at peace with that Nation and, at the solicitation of Japan, was still in conversation with its Government and its Emperor looking toward the maintenance of peace in the Pacific. Indeed, one hour after Japanese air squadrons had commenced bombing in the American Island of Oahu, the Japanese Ambassador to the United States and his colleague delivered to our Secretary of State a formal reply to a recent American message. And while this reply stated that it seemed useless to continue the existing diplomatic negotiations, it contained no threat or hint of war or armed attack.
>
> It will be recorded that the distance of Hawaii from Japan makes it obvious that the attack was deliberately planned many days or even weeks ago. During the intervening time the Japanese Government has deliberately sought to deceive the United States by false statements and expressions of hope for continued peace.
>
> The attack yesterday on the Hawaiian Islands has caused severe damage to American naval and military forces. I regret to tell you that very many American lives have been lost. In addition American ships have been reported torpedoed on the high seas between San Francisco and Honolulu.
>
> Yesterday the Japanese Government also launched an attack against Malaya.
>
> Last night Japanese forces attacked Hong Kong.
>
> Last night Japanese forces attacked Guam.
>
> Last night Japanese forces attacked the Philippine Islands.
>
> Last night the Japanese attacked Wake Island.
>
> And this morning the Japanese attacked Midway Island.
>
> Japan has, therefore, undertaken a surprise offensive extending throughout the Pacific area. The facts of yesterday and today speak for themselves. The people of the United States have already formed their opinions and well understand the implications to the very life and safety of our Nation.

As Commander-in-Chief of the Army and Navy I have directed that all measures be taken for our defense.

But always will our whole Nation remember the character of the onslaught against us.

No matter how long it may take us to overcome this premeditated invasion, the American people in their righteous might will win through to absolute victory.

I believe I interpret the will of the Congress and of the people when I assert that we will not only defend ourselves to the uttermost but will make it very certain that this form of treachery shall never endanger us again.

Hostilities exist. There is no blinking at the fact that our people, our territory and our interests are in grave danger.

With confidence in our armed forces- with the unbounding determination of our people-we will gain the inevitable triumph- so help us God.

I ask that the Congress declare that since the unprovoked and dastardly attack by Japan on Sunday, December 7th, 1941, a state of war has existed between the United States and the Japanese Empire."[234]

Immediately following this presidential request the *Congressional Declaration of War on Japan* was adopted through the formality of a joint resolution declaring that a state of war existed between the Imperial Government of Japan and the U.S. Government and the people of the United States were making provisions to prosecute the same:

"Whereas the Imperial Government of Japan has committed unprovoked acts of war against the Government and the people of the United States of America: Therefore be it Resolved by the Senate and House of Representatives of the United States of America in Congress assembled, that the state of war between the United States and the Imperial Government of Japan which has thus been thrust upon the United States is hereby formally declared; and the President is hereby authorized and directed to employ the entire naval and military forces of the United States and the resources of the Government to carry on war against the Imperial Government of Japan; and, to bring the conflict to a successful termination, all of the resources of the country are hereby pledged by the Congress of the United States."[235]

Approved, December 8, 1941, 4:10 p.m. E.S.T.

---

[234] Samuel I. Rosenman, Public Papers and Addresses of Franklin D. Roosevelt (New York: Harper & Brothers, 1950), Vol 10, pp. 514-516 [Infamy Speech, Declarartion of War Request]; Press conference Dec 9, 1941 pp. 516-522.

FDR addressed the nation and the world through a world-wide radio hookup the next day on December 9, 1941 in a broadcast from the Oval Office. He further justified America's entry into World War II, outlining a plan for immediate action and sacrifice, and calling for a will to win the war and protect American democracy and liberty:

> "My Fellow Americans:
> The sudden criminal attacks perpetrated by the Japanese in the Pacific provide the climax of a decade of international immorality.
> Powerful and resourceful gangsters have banded together to make war upon the whole human race. Their challenge has now been flung at the United States of America. The Japanese have treacherously violated the long-standing peace between us. Many American soldiers and sailors have been killed by enemy action. American ships have been sunk; American airplanes have been destroyed.
> The Congress and the people of the United States have accepted that challenge.
> Together with other free peoples, we are now fighting to maintain our right to live among our world neighbors in freedom, in common decency, without fear of assault.
> I have prepared the full record of our past relations with Japan, and it will be submitted to the Congress. It begins with the visit of Commodore Perry to Japan eighty-eight years ago. It ends with the visit of two Japanese emissaries to the Secretary of State last Sunday, an hour after Japanese forces had loosed their bombs and machine guns against our flag, our forces and our citizens.
> I can say with utmost confidence that no Americans today or a thousand years hence, need feel anything but pride in our patience and in our efforts through all the years toward achieving a peace in the Pacific which would be fair and honorable to every nation, large or small. And no honest person, today or a thousand years hence, will be able to suppress a sense of indignation and horror at the treachery committed by the military dictators of Japan, under the very shadow of the flag of peace borne by their special envoys in our midst.
> The course that Japan has followed for the past ten years in Asia has paralleled the course of Hitler and Mussolini in Europe and in Africa. Today, it has become far more than a parallel. It is actual collaboration so well calculated that all the continents of the world, and all the oceans, are now considered by the Axis strategists as one gigantic battlefield.
> In 1931, ten years ago, Japan invaded Manchukuo without warning. In 1935, Italy invaded Ethiopia without warning. In 1938, Hitler occupied Austria without warning. In 1939, Hitler invaded Czechoslovakia without warning. Later in 1939, Hitler invaded Poland without warning. In 1940, Hitler invaded Norway,

---

[235] Ibid.

Denmark, the Netherlands, Belgium and Luxembourg without warning. In 1940, Italy attacked France and later Greece without warning. And this year, in 1941, the Axis powers attacked Yugoslavia and Greece and they dominated the Balkans without warning. In 1941, also, Hitler invaded Russia without warning. And now Japan has attacked Malaya and Thailand and the United States without warning. It is all of one pattern.

We are now in this war. We are all in it all the way. Every single man, woman and child is a partner in the most tremendous undertaking of our American history. We must share together the bad news and the good news, the defeats and the victories, the changing fortunes of war.

So far, the news has been all bad. We have suffered a serious setback in Hawaii. Our forces in the Philippines, which include the brave people of that Commonwealth, are taking punishment, but are defending themselves vigorously. The reports from Guam and Wake and Midway Islands are still confused, but we must be prepared for the announcement that all these three outposts have been seized.

The casualty lists of these first few days will undoubtedly be large. I deeply feel the anxiety of all of the families of the men in our armed forces and the relatives of people in cities which have been bombed. I can only give them my solemn promise that they will get news just as quickly as possible.

This Government will put its trust in the stamina of the American people, and will give the facts to the public just as soon as two conditions have been fulfilled: first, that the information has been definitely and officially confirmed; and, second, that the release of the information at the time it is received will not prove valuable to the enemy directly or indirectly.

Most earnestly I urge my countrymen to reject all rumors. These ugly little hints of complete disaster fly thick and fast in wartime. They have to be examined and appraised.

As an example, I can tell you frankly that until further surveys are made, I have not sufficient information to state the exact damage which has been done to our naval vessels at Pearl Harbor. Admittedly the damage is serious. But no one can say how serious, until we know how much of this damage can be repaired and how quickly the necessary repairs can be made.

I cite as another example a statement made on Sunday night that a Japanese carrier had been located and sunk off the Canal Zone. And when you hear statements that are attributed to what they call 'an authoritative source', you can be reasonably sure from now on that under these war circumstances the 'authoritative source' is not any person in authority.

Many rumors and reports which we now hear originate, of course, with enemy sources. For instance, today the Japanese are claiming that as a result of their one action against Hawaii they have gained naval supremacy in the Pacific. This is an old trick of propaganda which has been used innumerable times by the Nazis. The purposes of such fantastic claims are, of course, to spread fear and confusion among us, and to goad us into revealing military information which our enemies are desperately anxious to obtain.

Our Government will not be caught in this obvious trap and neither will the people of the United States.

It must be remembered by each and every one of us that our free and rapid communication these days must be greatly restricted in wartime. It is not possible to receive full and speedy and accurate reports from distant areas of combat. This is particularly true where naval operations are concerned. For in these days of the marvels of the radio it is often impossible for the commanders of various units to report their activities by radio at all, for the very simple reason that this information would become available to the enemy and would disclose their position and their plan of defense or attack.

Of necessity there will be delays in officially confirming or denying reports of operations, but we will not hide facts from the country if we know the facts and if the enemy will not be aided by their disclosure.

To all newspapers and radio stations all those who reach the eyes and ears of the American people, I say this: 'You have a most grave responsibility to the nation now and for the duration of this war.

If you feel that your Government is not disclosing enough of the truth, you have every right to say so. But in the absence of all the facts, as revealed by official sources, you have no right, in the ethics of patriotism, to deal out unconfirmed reports in such a way as to make people believe that they are gospel truth.

Every citizen, in every walk of life, shares this same responsibility. The lives of our soldiers and sailors, the whole future of this nation, depend upon the manner in which each and every one of us fulfills his obligation to our country'.

Now a word about the recent past and the future. A year and a half has elapsed since the fall of France, when the whole world first realized the mechanized might which the Axis nations had been building up for so many years. America has used that year and a half to great advantage. Knowing that the attack might reach us in all too short a time, we immediately began greatly to increase our industrial strength and our capacity to meet the demands of modern warfare. Precious months were gained by sending vast quantities of our war material to the nations of the world still able to resist Axis aggression. Our policy rested on the fundamental truth that the defense of any country resisting Hitler or Japan was in the long run the defense of our own country. That policy has been justified. It has given us time, invaluable time, to build our American assembly lines of production.

Assembly lines are now in operation. Others are being rushed to completion. A steady stream of tanks and planes, of guns and ships and shells and equipment, that is what these eighteen months have given us.

But it is all only a beginning of what still has to be done. We must be set to face a long war against crafty and powerful bandits. The attack at Pearl Harbor can be repeated at any one of many points, points in both oceans and along both our coastlines and against all the rest of the Hemisphere.

It will not only be a long war, it will be a hard war. That is the basis on which we now lay all our plans. That is the yardstick by which we measure what we shall need and demand; money, materials, doubled and quadrupled production, ever-increasing. The production must be not only for our own Army and Navy and air forces. It must reinforce the other armies and navies and air forces fighting the Nazis and the war lords of Japan throughout the Americas and throughout the world.

I have been working today on the subject of production. Your Government has decided on two broad policies.

The first is to speed up all existing production by working on a seven-day week basis in every war industry, including the production of essential raw materials.

The second policy, now being put into form, is to rush additions to the capacity of production by building more new plants, by adding to old plants, and by using the many smaller plants for war needs.

Over the hard road of the past months, we have at times met obstacles and difficulties, divisions and disputes, indifference and callousness. That is now all past and, I am sure, forgotten.

The fact is that the country now has an organization in Washington built around men and women who are recognized experts in their own fields. I think the country knows that the people who are actually responsible in each and every one of these many fields are pulling together with a teamwork that has never before been excelled.

On the road ahead there lies hard work, grueling work, day and night, every hour and every minute. I was about to add that ahead there lies sacrifice for all of us.

But it is not correct to use that word. The United States does not consider it a sacrifice to do all one can, to give one's best to our nation, when the nation is fighting for its existence and its future life. It is not a sacrifice for any man, old or young, to be in the Army or the Navy of the United States. Rather it is a privilege.

It is not a sacrifice for the industrialist or the wage earner, the farmer or the shopkeeper, the trainmen or the doctor, to pay more taxes, to buy more bonds, to forego extra profits, to work longer or harder at the task for which he is best fitted. Rather it is a privilege.

It is not a sacrifice to do without many things to which we are accustomed if the national defense calls for doing without it."

To sacrifice was to be patriotic and FDR pointed to need for rationing.

"A review this morning leads me to the conclusion that at present we shall not have to curtail the normal use of articles of food. There is enough food today for all of us and enough left over to send to those who are fighting on the same side with us.

But there will be a clear and definite shortage of metals for many kinds of civilian use for the very good reason that in our increased program we shall need for war purposes more than half of that portion of the principal metals which during the past year have gone into articles for civilian use. Yes, we shall have to give up many things entirely.

And I am sure that the people in every part of the nation are prepared in their individual living to win this war. I am sure that they will cheerfully help to pay a large part of its financial cost while it goes on. I am sure they will cheerfully give up those material things that they are asked to give up.

And I am sure that they will retain all those great spiritual things without which we cannot win through."

Americans were issued ration cards and grew Victory Gardens. FDR pointed to the lessons learned from the attack on Pearl Harbor and the need to persevere to win over cruelty, deceit, racial hatred, and immorality.

"I repeat that the United States can accept no result save victory, final and complete. Not only must the shame of Japanese treachery be wiped out, but the sources of international brutality, wherever they exist, must be absolutely and finally broken. In my Message to the Congress yesterday I said that we 'will make very certain that this form of treachery shall never endanger us again'. In order to achieve that certainty, we must begin the great task that is before us by abandoning once and for all the illusion that we can ever again isolate ourselves from the rest of humanity.

In these past few years and, most violently, in the past three days we have learned a terrible lesson.

It is our obligation to our dead. It is our sacred obligation to their children and to our children that we must never forget what we have learned.

And what we have learned is this: 'There is no such thing as security for any nation, or any individual, in a world ruled by the principles of gangsterism. There is no such thing as impregnable defense against powerful aggressors who sneak up in the dark and strike without warning.

We have learned that our ocean-girt hemisphere is not immune from severe attack. That we cannot measure our safety in terms of miles on any map any more.

We may acknowledge that our enemies have performed a brilliant feat of deception, perfectly timed and executed with great skill. It was a thoroughly dishonorable deed, but we must face the fact that modern warfare as conducted in the Nazi manner is a dirty business. We don't like it, we didn't want to get in it, but we are in it and we are going to fight it with everything we've got'.

I do not think any American has any doubt of our ability to administer proper punishment to the perpetrators of these crimes.

Your Government knows that for weeks Germany has been telling Japan that if Japan did not attack the United States, Japan would not share in dividing the spoils with Germany when peace came. She was promised by Germany that if she came in she would receive the complete and perpetual control of the whole of the Pacific area and that means not only the Far East, but also all of the Islands in the Pacific, and also a stranglehold on the west coast of North, Central and South America.

We know also that Germany and Japan are conducting their military and naval operations in accordance with a joint plan. That plan considers all peoples and nations which are not helping the Axis powers as common enemies of each and every one of the Axis powers.

That is their simple and obvious grand strategy. And that is why the American people must realize that it can be matched only with similar grand strategy. We must realize for example that Japanese successes against the United States in the Pacific are helpful to German operations in Libya. That any German success against the Caucasus is inevitably an assistance to Japan in her operations against the Dutch East Indies; that a German attack against Algiers or Morocco opens the way to a German attack against South America and the Canal.

On the other side of the picture, we must learn also to know that guerrilla warfare against the Germans in, let us say Serbia or Norway helps us. That a successful Russian offensive against the Germans helps us; and that British successes on land or sea in any part of the world strengthen our hands.

Remember always that Germany and Italy, regardless of any formal declaration of war, consider themselves at war with the United States at this moment just as much as they consider themselves at war with Britain or Russia. And Germany puts all the other Republics of the Americas into the same category of enemies. The people of our sister Republics of this Hemisphere can be honored by that fact.

The true goal we seek is far above and beyond the ugly field of battle. When we resort to force, as now we must, we are determined that this force shall be directed toward ultimate good as well as against immediate evil. We Americans are not destroyers, we are builders.

We are now in the midst of a war, not for conquest, not for vengeance, but for a world in which this nation, and all that this nation represents, will be safe for our children. We expect to eliminate the danger from Japan, but it would serve us ill if we accomplished that and found that the rest of the world was dominated by Hitler and Mussolini.

We are going to win the war and we are going to win the peace that follows. And in the difficult hours of this day, through dark days that may be yet to come, we will know that the vast majority of the members of the human race are on our side. Many of them are fighting with us. All of them are praying for us. But, in representing our cause, we represent theirs as well, our hope and their hope for liberty under God."[236]

The president had wisely advised to abandon any future notion of remaining in isolation from the world's problems. The United States had not been able to stay out of the war, and once in it, FDR promised Americans 'are going to win the war, and we are going to win the peace that follows'. Following the attack on Pearl Harbor, Germany and Italy immediately declared war on the United States, believing America would be pinned down in the Pacific by their ally Japan, and the American Congress responded with declarations of war upon them. The president's request for war and the *Congressional Declaration of War on Germany* read:

> December 11, 1941
> The President's Message
>
> "To the Congress of the United States:
> On the morning of Dec. 11 the Government of Germany, pursuing its course of world conquest, declared war against the United States. The long-known and the long-expected has thus taken place. The forces endeavoring to enslave the entire world now are moving toward this hemisphere. Never before has there been a greater challenge to life, liberty and civilization. Delay invites great danger. Rapid and united effort by all of the peoples of the world who are determined to remain free will insure a world victory of the forces of justice and of righteousness over the forces of savagery and of barbarism. Italy also has declared war against the United States.
> I therefore request the Congress to recognize a state of war between the United States and Germany, and between the United States and Italy."[237]
>
> Franklin D. Roosevelt
>
> The Congressional War Resolution
>
> "Declaring that a state of war exists between the Government of Germany and the government and the people of the United States and making provision to prosecute the same.

---

[236] Samuel I. Rosenman, Public Papers and Addresses of Franklin D. Roosevelt (New York: Harper & Brothers, 1950) Vol 10, pp. 522-531.
[237] Ibid pp.531-532.

Whereas the Government of Germany has formally declared war against the government and the people of the United States of America:

Therefore, be it Resolved by the Senate and House of Representatives of the United States of America in Congress assembled, that the state of war between the United States and the Government of Germany which has thus been thrust upon the United States is hereby formally declared; and the President is hereby authorized and directed to employ the entire naval and military forces of the government to carry on war against the Government of Germany; and to bring the conflict to a successful termination, all of the resources of the country are hereby pledged by the Congress of the United States."[238]

The U.S. also declared war on Italy; Britain declared war on Japan; and bravely thirty-five nations, called the United Nations by FDR, around the globe fought against the evil Axis with the United States. The Japanese attack on Pearl Harbor had 'ended isolationism for any realist' stated Senator Arthur Vandenberg and America geared up for a war to maintain its freedom. America went into full-scale production for war setting goals for 1942 of producing 60,000 planes, 45,000 tanks, 20,000 anti-aircraft guns and 8 million tons of food supplies to the Allies. To oversee the administration of the war effort the War Production Board was established. The federal government let $100 billion in war contracts and the proportion of the economy devoted to war production rose to 33%. Total federal spending during the war was over $320 billion.

In a radio broadcast world-wide FDR addressed the nation celebrating the 210th anniversary of George Washington's Birthday speaking on February 23, 1942 and reminded Americans of the need to be more than a 'summer soldier or sunshine patriot' just as Americans had done during Revolutionary times. Americans, said FDR most eloquently in his speeches, must be possessed of unusual *strength of character to survive:*

> "My Fellow Americans:
>
> Washington's Birthday is a most appropriate occasion for us to talk with each other about things as they are today and things as we know they shall be in the future.
>
> For eight years, General Washington and his Continental Army were faced continually with formidable odds and recurring defeats. Supplies and equipment were lacking. In a sense, every winter was a Valley Forge. Throughout the thirteen states there existed fifth columnists, and selfish men, jealous men, fearful men, who proclaimed that Washington's cause was hopeless, and that he should ask for a negotiated peace.

---

[238] Ibid.

Washington's conduct in those hard times has provided the model for all Americans ever since, *a model of moral stamina*. He held to his course, as it had been charted in the Declaration of Independence. He and the brave men who served with him knew that no man's life or fortune was secure without freedom and free institutions.

The present great struggle has taught us increasingly that freedom of person and security of property anywhere in the world depend upon the security of the rights and obligations of liberty and justice everywhere in the world.

This war is a new kind of war. It is different from all other wars of the past, not only in its methods and weapons but also in its geography. It is warfare in terms of every continent, every island, every sea, every air-lane in the world.

That is the reason why I have asked you to take out and spread before you a map of the whole earth, and to follow with me in the references which I shall make to the world-encircling battle lines of this war. Many questions will, I fear, remain unanswered tonight, but I know you will realize that I cannot cover everything in any one short report to the people.

The broad oceans which have been heralded in the past as our protection from attack have become endless battlefields on which we are constantly being challenged by our enemies.

We must all understand and face the hard fact that our job now is to fight at distances which extend all the way around the globe.

We fight at these vast distances because that is where our enemies are. Until our flow of supplies gives us clear superiority we must keep on striking our enemies wherever and whenever we can meet them, even if, for a while, we have to yield ground. Actually, though, we are taking a heavy toll of the enemy every day that goes by.

We must fight at these vast distances to protect our supply lines and our lines of communication with our allies protect these lines from the enemies who are bending every ounce of their strength, striving against time, to cut them. The object of the Nazis and the Japanese is to of course separate the United States, Britain, China and Russia, and to isolate them one from another, so that each will be surrounded and cut off from sources of supplies and reinforcements. It is the old familiar Axis policy of 'divide and conquer'.

There are those who still think, however, in terms of the days of sailing-ships. They advise us to pull our warships and our planes and our merchant ships into our own home waters and concentrate solely on last ditch defense. But let me illustrate what would happen if we followed such foolish advice.

Look at your map. Look at the vast area of China, with its millions of fighting men. Look at the vast area of Russia, with its powerful armies and proven military might. Look at the islands of Britain, Australia, New Zealand, the Dutch Indies, India, the Near East and the continent of Africa, with their resources of raw materials, and of peoples determined to resist Axis domination. Look too at North America, Central America and South America.

It is obvious what would happen if all of these great reservoirs of power were cut off from each other either by enemy action or by self-imposed isolation.

First, in such a case, we could no longer send aid of any kind to China, to the brave people who, for nearly five years, have withstood Japanese assault, destroyed hundreds of thousands of Japanese soldiers and vast quantities of Japanese war munitions. It is essential that we help China in her magnificent defense and in her inevitable counteroffensive, for that is one important element in the ultimate defeat of Japan.

Second, if we lost communication with the southwest Pacific, all of that area, including Australia and New Zealand and the Dutch Indies would fall under Japanese domination. Japan in such a case could release great numbers of ships and men to launch attacks on a large scale against the coasts of the Western Hemisphere, South America and Central America, and North America, including Alaska. At the same time, she could immediately extend her conquests in the other direction toward India, through the Indian Ocean, to Africa, to the Near East and try to join forces with Germany and Italy.

Third, if we were to stop sending munitions to the British and the Russians in the Mediterranean area, in the Persian Gulf and the Red Sea, we would be helping the Nazis to overrun Turkey, and Syria, and Iraq, and Persia (that is now called Iran), Egypt and the Suez Canal, the whole coast of North Africa itself and with that inevitably the whole coast of West Africa putting Germany within easy striking distance of South America fifteen hundred miles away.

Fourth, if by such a fatuous policy, we ceased to protect the North Atlantic supply line to Britain and to Russia, we would help to cripple the splendid counteroffensive by Russia against the Nazis, and we would help to deprive Britain of essential food supplies and munitions.

Those Americans who believed that we could live under the illusion of isolationism wanted the American eagle to imitate the tactics of the ostrich. Now, many of those same people, afraid that we may be sticking our necks out, want our national bird to be turned into a turtle. But we prefer to retain the eagle as it is, flying high and striking hard.

I know I speak for the mass of the American people when I say that we reject the turtle policy and will continue increasingly the policy of carrying the war to the enemy in distant lands and distant waters, as far away as possible from our own home grounds.

There are four main lines of communication now being traveled by our ships: the North Atlantic, the South Atlantic, the Indian Ocean, and the South Pacific. These routes are not one-way streets, for the ships that carry our troops and munitions out-bound bring back essential raw materials which we require for our own use.

The maintenance of these vital lines is a very tough job. It is a job which requires tremendous daring, tremendous resourcefulness, and, above all, tremendous production of planes and tanks and guns and also of the ships to carry them. And I speak again for the American people when I say that we can and will do that job.

The defense of the worldwide lines of communication demands, compels, relatively safe use by us of the sea and of the air along the various routes; and this, in turn, depends upon control by the United Nations of many strategic bases along those routes.

Control of the air involves the simultaneous use of two types of planes: first, the long-range heavy bomber; and, second, the light bombers, the dive bombers, the torpedo planes, the short-range pursuit planes, all of which are essential to cooperate with and protect the bases and the bombers themselves.

Heavy bombers can fly under their own power from here to the southwest Pacific, either way, but the smaller planes cannot. Therefore, these lighter planes have to be packed in crates and sent on board cargo ships. Look at your map again. And you will see that the route is long, and at many places perilous, either across the South Atlantic all the way around South Africa and the Cape of Good Hope or from California to the East Indies direct. A vessel can make a round trip by either route in about four months or only three round trips in a whole year.

In spite of the length, in spite of the difficulties of this transportation, I can tell you that in two and a half months we already have a large number of bombers and pursuit planes, manned by American pilots and crews, which are now in daily contact with the enemy in the Southwest Pacific. And thousands of American troops are today in that area engaged in operations not only in the air but on the ground as well.

In this battle area, Japan has had an obvious initial advantage. For she could fly even her short-range planes to the points of attack by using many stepping stones open to her bases in a multitude of Pacific islands and also bases on the China coast, Indo-China coast, and in Thailand and Malaya. Japanese troop transports could go south from Japan and from China through the narrow China Sea, which can be protected by Japanese planes throughout its whole length."

As a beacon of light in a dark world, President Roosevelt instructed Americans in the Allied strategies of the war to keep them safe and prepared.

"I ask you to look at your maps again, particularly at that portion of the Pacific Ocean lying west of Hawaii. Before this war even started, the Philippine Islands were already surrounded on three sides by Japanese power. On the west, the China side, the Japanese were in possession of the coast of China and the coast of Indo-China which had been yielded to them by the Vichy French. On the North are the islands of Japan themselves, reaching down almost to northern Luzon. On the east, are the Mandated Islands which Japan had occupied exclusively, and had fortified in absolute violation of her written word.

The islands that lie between Hawaii and the Philippines, these islands, hundreds of them, appear only as small dots on most maps, or do not appear at all. But they cover a large strategic area. Guam lies in the middle of them, a lone outpost which we have never fortified.

Under the Washington Treaty of 1921 we had solemnly agreed not to add to the fortification of the Philippines. We had no safe naval bases there, so we could not use the islands for extensive naval operations.

Immediately after this war started, the Japanese forces moved down on either side of the Philippines to numerous points south of them thereby completely encircling the Philippines from north, and south, and east and west.

It is that complete encirclement, with control of the air by Japanese land-based aircraft, which has prevented us from sending substantial reinforcements of men and material to the gallant defenders of the Philippines. For forty years it has always been our strategy, a strategy born of necessity, that in the event of a full-scale attack on the Islands by Japan, we should fight a delaying action, attempting to retire slowly into Bataan Peninsula and Corregidor.

We knew that the war as a whole would have to be fought and won by a process of attrition against Japan itself. We knew all along that, with our greater resources, we could ultimately out-build Japan and ultimately overwhelm her on sea, and on land and in the air. We knew that, to obtain our objective, many varieties of operations would be necessary in areas other than the Philippines.

Now nothing that has occurred in the past two months has caused us to revise this basic strategy of necessity except that the defense put up by General MacArthur has magnificently exceeded the previous estimates of endurance, and he and his men are gaining eternal glory therefore.

MacArthur's army of Filipinos and Americans, and the forces of the United Nations in China, in Burma and the Netherlands East Indies, are all together fulfilling the same essential task. They are making Japan pay an increasingly terrible price for her ambitious attempts to seize control of the whole Asiatic world. Every Japanese transport sunk off Java is one less transport that they can use to carry reinforcements to their army opposing General MacArthur in Luzon.

It has been said that Japanese gains in the Philippines were made possible only by the success of their surprise attack on Pearl Harbor. I tell you that this is not so.

Even if the attack had not been made, your map will show that it would have been a hopeless operation for us to send the Fleet to the Philippines through thousands of miles of ocean, while all those island bases were under the sole control of the Japanese. The consequences of the attack on Pearl Harbor, serious as they were, have been wildly exaggerated in other ways. And these exaggerations come originally from Axis propagandists; but they have been repeated, I regret to say, by Americans in and out of public life.

You and I have the utmost contempt for Americans who, since Pearl Harbor, have whispered or announced 'off the record' that there was no longer any Pacific Fleet, that the Fleet was all sunk or destroyed on December 7th, that more than a thousand of our planes were destroyed on the ground. They have suggested slyly that the Government has withheld the truth about casualties, that eleven or twelve thousand men were killed at Pearl Harbor instead of the figures as officially announced. They have even served the enemy propagandists by spreading the incredible story that ship-loads of bodies of our honored American dead were about to arrive in New York harbor to be put into a common grave.

Almost every Axis broadcast, Berlin, Rome, Tokyo, directly quotes Americans who, by speech or in the press, make damnable misstatements such as these.

The American people realize that in many cases details of military operations cannot be disclosed until we are absolutely certain that the announcement will not give to the enemy military information which he does not already possess.

Your Government has unmistakable confidence in your ability to hear the worst, without flinching or losing heart. You must, in turn, have complete confidence that your Government is keeping nothing from you except information that will help the enemy in his attempt to destroy us. In a democracy there is always a solemn pact of truth between government and the people, but there must also always be a full use of discretion, and that word 'discretion' applies to the critics of government as well.

This is war. The American people want to know, and will be told, the general trend of how the war is going. But they do not wish to help the enemy any more than our fighting forces do, and they will pay little attention to the rumor-mongers and the poison peddlers in our midst."

As a point of light FDR held his radio audience in rapt attention as Americans desired to really be part of the U.S. war effort. Everyone was asked to contribute as FDR continued:

"To pass from the realm of rumor and poison to the field of facts: the number of our officers and men killed in the attack on Pearl Harbor on December 7th was 2,340, and the number wounded was 940. Of all of the combatant ships based at Pearl Harbor, battleships, heavy cruisers, light cruisers, aircraft carriers, destroyers and submarines, only three are permanently put out of commission.

Very many of the ships of the Pacific Fleet were not even in Pearl Harbor. Some of those that were there were hit very slightly, and others that were damaged have either rejoined the Fleet by now or are still undergoing repairs. And when those repairs are completed, the ships will be more efficient fighting machines than they were before.

The report that we lost more than a thousand planes at Pearl Harbor is as baseless as the other weird rumors. The Japanese do not know just how many planes they destroyed that day, and I am not going to tell them. But I can say that to date, and including Pearl Harbor, we have destroyed considerably more Japanese planes than they have destroyed of ours.

We have most certainly suffered losses from Hitler's U-Boats in the Atlantic as well as from the Japanese in the Pacific and we shall suffer more of them before the turn of the tide. But, speaking for the United States of America, let me say once and for all to the people of the world: 'We Americans have been compelled to yield ground, but we will regain it. *We and the other United Nations are committed to the destruction of the militarism of Japan and Germany. We are daily increasing our strength. Soon, we and not our enemies, will have the offensive; we, not they, will win the final battles; and we, not they, will make the final peace'.*

Conquered nations in Europe know what the yoke of the Nazis is like. And the people of Korea and of Manchuria know in their flesh the harsh despotism of Japan. All of the people of Asia know that if there is to be an honorable and decent future for any of them or any of us, that future depends on victory by the United Nations over the forces of Axis enslavement.

If a just and durable peace is to be attained, or even if all of us are merely to save our own skins, there is one thought for us here at home to keep uppermost, the fulfillment of our special task of production, uninterrupted production. I stress that word 'uninterrupted'.

Germany, Italy and Japan are very close to their maximum output of planes, guns, tanks, and ships. The United Nations are not, especially the United States of America.

Our first job then is to build up production, uninterrupted production, so that the United Nations can maintain control of the seas and attain control of the air, not merely a slight superiority, but an overwhelming superiority.

On January 6th of this year, I set certain definite goals of production for airplanes, tanks, guns, and ships. The Axis propagandists called them fantastic. Tonight, nearly two months later, and after a careful survey of progress by Donald Nelson and others charged with responsibility for our production, I can tell you that those goals will be attained. In every part of the country, experts in production and the men and women at work in the plants are giving loyal service. With few exceptions, labor, capital, and farming realize that this is no time either to make undue profits or to gain special advantages, one over the other. We are calling for new plants and additions, additions to old plants.

We are calling for plant conversion to war needs. We are seeking more men and more women to run them. We are working longer hours. We are coming to realize that one extra plane or extra tank or extra gun or extra ship completed tomorrow may, in a few months, turn the tide on some distant battlefield; it may make the difference between life and death for some of our own fighting men. We know now that if we lose this war it will be generations or even centuries before our conception of democracy can live again. And we can lose this war only if we slow up our effort or if we waste our ammunition sniping at each other.

Here are three high purposes for every American:

We shall not stop work for a single day. If any dispute arises we shall keep on working while the dispute is solved by mediation, or conciliation or arbitration until the war is won.

We shall not demand special gains or special privileges or special advantages for any one group or occupation.

We shall give up conveniences and modify the routine of our lives if our country asks us to do so. We will do it cheerfully, remembering that the common enemy seeks to destroy every home and every freedom in every part of our land.

This generation of Americans has come to realize, with a present and personal realization, that there is something larger and more important than the life of any individual or of any individual group, something for which a man will sacrifice, and gladly sacrifice, not only his pleasures, not only his goods, not only his associations with those he loves, but his life itself. In time of crisis when the future is in the balance, we come to understand, with full recognition and devotion, what this nation is and what we owe to it."

America's greatest generation that had a rendezvous with destiny was being asked by their president to step forward and acknowledge their responsibilities.

"The Axis propagandists have tried in various evil ways to destroy our determination and our morale. Failing in that, they are now trying to destroy our confidence in our own allies. They say that the British are finished; that the Russians and the Chinese are about to quit. Patriotic and sensible Americans will reject these absurdities. And instead of listening to any of this crude propaganda, they will recall some of the things that Nazis and Japanese have said and are still saying about us.

Ever since this nation became the arsenal of democracy, ever since enactment of Lend-Lease, there has been one persistent theme through all Axis propaganda.

This theme has been that Americans are admittedly rich, that Americans have considerable industrial power, but that Americans are soft and decadent, that they cannot and will not unite and work and fight.

From Berlin, Rome and Tokyo we have been described as a nation of weaklings, 'playboys' who would hire British soldiers, or Russian soldiers, or Chinese soldiers to do our fighting for us. Let them repeat that now! Let them tell that to General MacArthur and his men. Let them tell that to the sailors who today are hitting hard in the far waters of the Pacific. Let them tell that to the boys in the Flying Fortresses. Let them tell that to the Marines! The United Nations constitute an association of independent peoples of equal dignity and equal importance.

The United Nations are dedicated to a common cause. We share equally and with equal zeal the anguish and the awful sacrifices of war. In the partnership of our common enterprise, we must share in a unified plan in which all of us must play our several parts, each of us being equally indispensable and dependent one on the other.

We have unified command and cooperation and comradeship.

We Americans will contribute unified production and unified acceptance of sacrifice and of effort. That means a national unity that can know no limitations of race or creed or selfish politics. The American people expect that much from themselves. And the American people will find ways and means of expressing their determination to their enemies, including the Japanese Admiral who has said that he will dictate the terms of peace here in the White House.

We of the United Nations are agreed on certain broad principles in the kind of peace we seek. The Atlantic Charter applies not only to the parts of the world that border the Atlantic but to the whole world; disarmament of aggressors, self-determination of nations and peoples, and the four freedoms – freedom of speech, freedom of religion, freedom from want, and freedom from fear.

The British and the Russian people have known the full fury of Nazi onslaught. There have been times when the fate of London and Moscow was in serious doubt. But there was never the slightest question that either the British or the Russians would yield. And today all the United Nations salute the superb Russian Army as it celebrates the twenty-fourth anniversary of its first assembly.

Though their homeland was overrun, the Dutch people are still fighting stubbornly and powerfully overseas.

The great Chinese people have suffered grievous losses; Chungking has been almost wiped out of existence, yet it remains the capital of an unbeatable China.

That is the conquering spirit which prevails throughout the United Nations in this war.

The task that we Americans now face will test us to the uttermost. Never before have we been called upon for such a prodigious effort. Never before have we had so little time in which to do so much.

'These are the times that try men's souls'. Tom Paine wrote those words on a drumhead, by the light of a campfire. That was when Washington's little army of ragged, rugged men was retreating across New Jersey, having tasted naught but defeat.

And General Washington ordered that these great words written by Tom Paine be read to the men of every regiment in the Continental Army, and this was the assurance given to the first American armed forces:

'The summer soldier and the sunshine patriot will, in this crisis, shrink from the service of their country; but he that stands it now, deserves the love and thanks of man and woman. Tyranny, like hell, is not easily conquered, yet we

have this consolation with us, that the harder the sacrifice, the more glorious the triumph'.
So spoke Americans in the year 1776.
So speak Americans today!"[239]

Overseas and at home Americans were called upon by FDR to self-strengthen and press on to overcome all challengers with moral courage. It was more than his apt phrases in his speeches that moved citizens to action; it was his heartfelt actions and pleas for *the moral rightness of the American cause* that swayed Americans to make great sacrifices. FDR was a beacon of light and everywhere people turned their uplifted faces towards him.

---

[239] Rosenman, Public Papers and Addresses of Franklin D. Roosevelt, Vol 11, pp. 105-116.

Chapter 7

HOME FRONT DURING WORLD WAR II

America was now at war following the Japanese attack on Pearl Harbor in December 1941, but in reality FDR had foreseen that the U.S. would have to prepare for involvement well over a year and seven months before.[240] But FDR's attention had been focused in Europe and on Britain's needs to form a bulwark against a Hitler attack on North America, and in no way was Roosevelt responsible for concealing any fore knowledge of an attack on Pearl Harbor by the Japanese. He was stunned as all Americans were on December 7th, and if he could have prevented loses to his beloved Pacific Navy he certainly would have done so. FDR did not need any excuse to enter the war, as the German sinkings of American ships in the Atlantic certainly were cause enough. For as the war in Western Europe had been gathering momentum in the Spring of 1940 when Hitler had opened his invasions into Scandinavia, the Low Countries and France, Americans had become apprehensive about the state of foreign countries suffering from the *Blitzkrig*. Watching events in Europe unfold, FDR had recognized that these overseas events had deeply touched Americans as he had spoken to the nation in a home front radio broadcast in May 1940 just as World War II in Europe had accelerated:

> "My Friends:
> At this moment of sadness throughout most of the world, I want to talk with you about a number of subjects that directly affect the future of the United States. We are shocked by the almost incredible eyewitness stories that come to us,

---

[240] Barbara Bennett Peterson, "FDR's 'Quarterbacking' of U.S. Naval Policy in the Pacific 1933-1945," The Pacific Historian Vol.16 No. 4 (Winter 1972):44-53; Vol. 17 No. 3 (Spring 1973):61-72; Vol. 17 No.2 (Summer 1973): 60-73

stories of what is happening at this moment to the civilian populations of Norway and Holland and Belgium and Luxembourg and France.

I think it is right on this Sabbath evening that I should say a word in behalf of women and children and old men who need help, immediate help in their present distress, help from us across the seas, help from us who are still free to give it.

Tonight over the once peaceful roads of Belgium and France millions are now moving, running from their homes to escape bombs and shells and fire and machine gunning, without shelter, and almost wholly without food. They stumble on, knowing not where the end of the road will be. I speak to you of these people because each one of you that is listening to me tonight has a way of helping them. The American Red Cross that represents each of us is rushing food and clothing and medical supplies to these destitute civilian millions. Please, I beg you, please give according to your means to your nearest Red Cross chapter. Give as generously as you can. I ask this in the name of our common humanity....

There are some among us who were persuaded by minority groups that we could maintain our physical safety by retiring within our continental boundaries, the Atlantic on the east, the Pacific on the west, Canada on the north and Mexico on the south. I illustrated the futility, the impossibility, of that idea in my Message to the Congress last week.... It is whispered by some that only by abandoning our freedom, our ideals, our way of life, can we build our defenses adequately, can we match the strength of the aggressors.

I did not share those illusions. I do not share these fears. Today we are more realistic. But let us not be calamity-howlers and discount our strength. Let us have done with both fears and illusions. On this Sabbath evening, in our homes in the midst of our American families, let us calmly consider what we have done and what we must do.

In the past two or three weeks all kinds of stories have been handed out to the American public about our lack of preparedness. It has even been charged that the money we have spent on our military and naval forces during the last few years has gone down the rat-hole. I think that it is a matter of fairness to the nation that you hear the facts.

We have spent large sums of money on the national defense. This money has been used to make our Army and Navy today the largest, the best equipped, and the best trained peacetime military establishment in the whole history of this country."

Hence just after Hitler had begun his onslaught into Western Europe, causing the fall of France following this FDR speech, Roosevelt had spoken to Americans about what he had done and what he planned to do further to make the U.S. safe.

"Let me tell you just a few of the many things accomplished during the past few years," he continued. "I do not propose, I cannot go into every detail. It is a known fact, however, that in 1933, when this Administration came into office, the United States Navy had fallen in standing among the navies of the world, in power of ships and in efficiency, to a relatively low ebb. The relative fighting power on the Navy had been greatly diminished by failure to replace ships and equipment, which had become out-of-date.

But between 1933 and this year, 1940, seven fiscal years, your Government will have spent a billion, four hundred eighty-seven million dollars more than it spent on the Navy during the seven years that preceded 1933.

What did we get for the money?- money, incidentally, not included in the new defense appropriations, only the money heretofore appropriated?

The fighting personnel of the Navy rose from 79,000 to 145,000. During this period 215 ships for the fighting fleet have been laid down or commissioned, practically seven times the number in the preceding seven-year period. Of these 215 ships we have commissioned 12 cruisers; 63 destroyers; 26 submarines; 3 aircraft carriers; 2 gunboats; 7 auxiliaries and many smaller craft. And among the many ships now being built and paid for as we build them are 8 new battleships.

Ship construction, of course, costs millions of dollars more in the United States than anywhere else in the world. But it is a fact that we cannot have adequate navy defense for all American waters without ships, ships that sail the surface of the ocean, ships that move under the surface and ships that move through the air. And, speaking of airplanes, airplanes that work with the Navy, in 1933 we had 1,127 of them, 1,127 useful aircraft, and today we have 2,892 on hand and on order. Of course, nearly all of the old planes of 1933 have been replaced by new planes because they became obsolete or worn out. The Navy is far stronger today than at any peacetime period in the whole long history of the nation. In hitting power and in efficiency, I would even make the assertion that it is stronger today than it was during the [First] World War.

The Army of the United States in 1933 consisted of 122,000 enlisted men. Now, in 1940, that number has been practically doubled. The Army of 1933 had been given few new implements of war since 1919, and had been compelled to draw on old reserve stocks left over from the World War.

The net result of all this was that our Army by l933 had very greatly declined in its ratio of strength with the armies of Europe and of the Far East. That was the situation I found.

But, since then, great changes have taken place. Between 1933 and 1940, these past seven fiscal years, your Government will have spent $1,292,000,000 more than it spent on the Army the previous seven years.

What did we get for this money? The personnel of the Army, as I have said, has been almost doubled. And by the end of this year every existing unit of the present regular Army will be equipped with its complete requirements of modern weapons. Existing units of the National Guard will also be largely equipped with similar items.

Here are some striking examples taken from a large number of them. Since 1933 we have actually purchased 5,640 airplanes, including the most modern type of long-range bombers and fast pursuit planes, though, of course, many of these which were delivered four and five and six and seven years ago have worn out through use and been scrapped. We must remember that these planes cost money, a lot of it. For example, one modern four-engine long-range bombing plane costs $350,000; one modern interceptor pursuit plane costs $133,000; one medium bomber costs $160,000.

To go on, in 1933 we had only 355 anti-aircraft guns. We now have more than 1,700 modern anti-craft guns of all types on hand or on order. And you ought to know that a three-inch anti-aircraft gun costs $40,000 without any of the fire control equipment that goes with it. In 1933 there were only 24 modern infantry mortars in the entire Army. We now have on hand and on order more than 1,600. In 1933 we had only 48 modern tanks and armored cars; today we have on hand and on order 1,700. Each one of our heavier tanks costs $46,000.

There are many other items in which our progress since 1933 has been rapid. And the great proportion of this advance consists of really modern equipment.

For instance, in 1933, on the personnel side we had 1,263 Army pilots. Today the Army alone has more than 3,200 of the best fighting flyers in the world, flyers who last year flew more than one million hours in combat training. And that figure does not include the hundreds of splendid pilots in the National Guard and in the organized reserves."

FDR held great anticipatory powers, was an excellent judge of Hitler's maniacal schemes, and drew the line in the sand asking Americans to defend liberty and democracy. He never equivocated, but understood the exact course of action needed as early as May 1940 and citizens instinctively responded to his profound and quick-witted leadership.

"Within the past year the productive capacity of the aviation industry to produce military planes has been tremendously increased. In the past year the capacity more than doubled, but that capacity is still inadequate. But the Government, working with industry is determined to increase that capacity to meet our needs. We intend to harness the efficient machinery of these manufacturers to the Government's program of being able to get 50,000 planes a year.

One additional word about aircraft about which we read so much. Recent wars, including the current war in Europe, have demonstrated beyond doubt that fighting efficiency depends on unity of command, unity of control.

In sea operations the airplane is just as much an integral part of the unity of operations as are the submarine, the destroyer and the battleship. And in land warfare the airplane is just as much a part of military operations as are the tank corps, the engineers, the artillery or the infantry itself. Therefore, the air forces should continue to be part of the Army and Navy.

In line with my request, the Congress, this week, is voting the largest appropriation ever asked by the Army or the Navy in peacetime, and the equipment and training provided for them will be in addition to the figures I have given you.

The world situation may so change that it will be necessary to reappraise our program at any time. And in such case I am confident that the Congress and the Chief Executive will work in harmony as a team, work in harmony as they are doing today.

I will not hesitate at any moment to ask for additional funds when they are required.

In this era of swift, mechanized warfare, we all have to remember that what is modern today and up-to-date, what is efficient and practical becomes obsolete and outworn tomorrow.

Even while the production line turns out airplanes, new airplanes are being designed on the drafting table.

Even as a cruiser slides down the launching ways, plans for improvement, plans for increased efficiency in the next model, are taking shape in the blueprints of designers. Every day's fighting in Europe, on land, on sea, and in the air, discloses constant changes in methods of warfare. We are constantly improving and redesigning, testing new weapons, learning the lessons of the immediate war, and seeking to produce in accordance with the latest that the brains in science can conceive.

We are calling upon the resources, the efficiency and the ingenuity of the American manufacturers of war material of all kinds, airplanes and tanks and guns and ships, and all the hundreds of products that go into this material. The Government of the United States itself manufactures few of the implements of war. Private industry will continue to be the source of most of this material, and private industry will have to be speeded up to produce it at the rate and efficiency called for by the needs of the times.

I know that private business cannot be expected to make all of the capital investment required for expansions of plants and factories and personnel which this program calls for at once. It would be unfair to expect industrial corporations or their investors to do this, when there is a chance that a change in international affairs may stop or curtail future orders a year or two hence.

Therefore, the Government of the United States stands ready to advance the necessary money to help provide for the enlargement of factories, the establishment of new plants, the employment of thousands of necessary workers, the development of new sources of supply for the hundreds of raw materials required, the development of quick mass transportation of supplies. And the details of all of this are now being worked out in Washington, day and night.

We are calling on men now engaged in private industry to help us in carrying out this program and you will hear more of this in detail in the next few days.

This does not mean that the men we call upon will be engaged in the actual production of this material. That will still have to be carried on in the plants and factories throughout the land. Private industry will have the responsibility of providing the best, speediest and most efficient mass production of which it is capable. The functions of the businessmen whose assistance we are calling upon will be to coordinate this program, to see to it that all of the plants continue to operate at maximum speed and efficiency.

Patriotic Americans of proven merit and of unquestioned ability in their special fields are coming to Washington to help the Government with their training, their experience and their capability.

It is our purpose not only to speed up production but to increase the total facilities of the nation in such a way that they can be further enlarged to meet emergencies of the future.

But as this program proceeds there are several things we must continue to watch and safeguard, things which are just as important to the sound defense of a nation as physical armament itself. While our Navy and our airplanes and our guns and our ships may be our first line of defense, it is still clear that way down at the bottom, underlying them all, giving them their strength, sustenance and power, are the spirit and morale of a free people.

For that reason, we must make sure, in all that we do, that there be no breakdown or cancellation of any of the great social gains which we have made in these past years. We have carried on an offensive on a broad front against social and economic inequalities and abuses which had made our society weak. That offensive should not now be broken down by the pincers movement of those who would use the present needs of physical military defense to destroy it.

There is nothing in our present emergency to justify making the workers of our nation toll for longer hours than now limited by statute. As more orders come in and as more work has to be done, tens of thousands of people, who are now unemployed, will, I believe, receive employment.

There is nothing in our present emergency to justify a lowering of the standards of employment. Minimum wages should not be reduced. It is my hope, indeed, that the new speed-up of production will cause many businesses which now pay below the minimum standards to bring their wages up.

There is nothing in our present emergency to justify a breaking down of old age pensions or of unemployment insurance. I would rather see the systems extended to other groups who do not now enjoy them. There is nothing in our present emergency to justify a retreat from any of our social objectives, from conservation of natural resources, assistance to agriculture, housing, and help to the underprivileged.

Conversely, however, I am sure that responsible leaders will not permit some specialized group, which represents a minority of the total employees of a plant or an industry, to break up the continuity of employment of the majority of the employees. Let us remember that the policy and the laws that provide for collective bargaining are still in force. And I can assure you that labor will be adequately represented in Washington in the carrying out of this program of defense.

And one more point on this: Our present emergency and a common sense of decency make it imperative that no new group of war millionaires shall come into being in this nation as a result of the struggles abroad. The American people will not relish the idea of any American citizen growing rich and fat in an emergency of blood and slaughter and human suffering.

And, last of all, this emergency demands that the consumers of America be protected so that our general cost of living can be maintained at a reasonable level. We ought to avoid the spiral processes of the World War, the rising spiral of costs of all kinds. The soundest policy is for every employer in the country to help give useful employment to the millions who are unemployed. By giving to those millions an increased purchasing power, the prosperity of the whole nation will rise to a much higher level.

Today's threat to our national security is not a matter of military weapons alone. We know of other methods, new methods of attack. The Trojan Horse. The Fifth Column that betrays a nation unprepared for treachery. Spies, saboteurs and traitors are the actors in this new strategy. With all of these we must and will deal vigorously. But there is an added technique for weakening a nation at its very roots, for disrupting the entire pattern of life of a people. And it is important that we understand it.

The method is simple. It is, first, discord, a dissemination of discord. A group, not too large, a group that may be sectional or racial or political, is encouraged to exploit its prejudices through false slogans and emotional appeals. The aim of those who deliberately egg on these groups is to create confusion of counsel, public indecision, political paralysis and eventually, a state of panic.

Sound national policies come to be viewed with a new and unreasoning skepticism, not through the wholesome debates of honest and free men, but through the clever schemes of foreign agents. As a result of these new techniques, armament programs may be dangerously delayed. Singleness of national purpose may be undermined. Men can lose confidence in each other, and therefore lose confidence in the efficacy of their own united action. Faith and courage can yield to doubt and fear. The unity of the state can be so sapped that its strength is destroyed.

All this is no idle dream. It has happened time after time, in nation after nation, here in the last two years. Fortunately, American men and women are not easy dupes. Campaigns of group hatred or class struggle have never made much headway among us, and are not making headway now. But new forces are being unleashed, deliberately planned propaganda to divide and weaken us in the face of danger as other nations have been weakened before.

These dividing forces I do not hesitate to call undiluted poison. They must not be allowed to spread in the New World as they have in the Old. Our morale, our mental defenses must be raised up as never before against those who would cast a smoke screen across our vision.

The development of our defense program makes it essential that each and every one of us, men and women, feel that we have some contribution to make toward the security of our nation.

At this time, when the world and the world includes our own American Hemisphere, when the world is threatened by forces of destruction, it is my resolve and yours to build up our armed defenses.

We shall build them to whatever heights the future may require. We shall rebuild them swiftly, as the methods of warfare swiftly change.

For more than three centuries we Americans have been building on this continent a free society, a society in which the promise of the human spirit may find fulfillment. Commingled here are the blood and genius of all the peoples of the world who have sought this promise.

We have built well. We are continuing our efforts to bring the blessings of a free society, of a free and productive economic system, to every family in the land. This is the promise of America.

It is this that we must continue to build, this that we must continue to defend. It is the task of our generation, yours and mine. But we build and defend not for our generation alone. We defend the foundations laid down by our fathers. We build a life for generations yet unborn. We defend and we build a way of life, not for America alone, but for all mankind. Ours is a high duty, a noble task.

Day and night I pray for the restoration of peace in this mad world of ours. It is not necessary that I, the President ask the American people to pray in behalf of such a cause, for I know you are praying with me.

I am certain that out of the hearts of every man, woman and child in this land, in every waking minute, a supplication goes up to Almighty God. That all of us beg that suffering and starving, that death and destruction may end, and that peace may return to the world. In common affection for all mankind, your prayers join with mine, that God will heal the wounds and the hearts of humanity."[241]

---

[241] Franklin D. Roosevelt Library, Hyde Park, New York; Samuel I. Rosenman, Public Papers and Addresses of Franklin D. Roosevelt (New York: Macmillan, 1941) Vol 9, pp. 230-240.

With this speech delivered long before the Pearl Harbor attack, FDR had warned Americans early on that *preparedness* was the key to survival as Europe convulsed into war. He had often recounted how the U.S. was rebuilding its military resources to establish a bulwark for defense. And that not to act quickly would be suicidal. He had kept citizens appraised of foreign threats to our way of life and had prepared them to shoulder the burdens of Lend-Lease and the responsibilities of being the world's 'arsenal of democracy'. This sure-footed and generous response would protect America. FDR was a realist who had called the reckless behavior of the Nazis and the Fascists to account, stating Hitler's design for a New Order in Europe was immoral. Certainly the war in China and the activities of the Japanese took a back seat to the problems and threats in Europe, yet preparedness in America's spirit to resist the Axis everywhere as well as production of war material was deemed essential.

A year after the war had opened in the spring of 1940 with Hitler's rush to occupy Scandinavia, the Low Countries and France, FDR had proclaimed a state of *national emergency* for the home front in the United States on May 27, 1941. Once again he had eagerly sought to bind the Western Hemisphere in common cause against foreign aggression and immorality as he stated:

> "My Fellow Americans of all the Americas, My Friends:
>
> I am speaking tonight from the White House in the presence of the Governing Board of the Pan-American Union, the Canadian Minister, and their families. The members of this Board are the Ambassadors and Ministers of the American Republics in Washington. It is appropriate that I do this for now, as never before, the unity of the American Republics is of supreme importance to each and every one of us and to the cause of freedom throughout the world. Our future, our future independence is bound up with the future independence of all of our sister Republics.
>
> The pressing problems that confront us are military and naval problems. We cannot afford to approach them from the point of view of wishful thinkers or sentimentalists. What we face is cold, hard fact.
>
> The first and fundamental fact is that what started as a European war has developed, as the Nazis always intended it should develop, into a world war for world domination. Adolf Hitler never considered the domination of Europe as an end in itself. European conquest was but a step toward ultimate goals in all the other continents. It is unmistakably apparent to all of us that, unless the advance of Hitlerism is forcibly checked now, the Western Hemisphere will be within range of the Nazi weapons of destruction.
>
> For our own defense we have accordingly undertaken certain obvious necessary measures:

First, we have joined in concluding a series of agreements with all the other American Republics. This further solidified our hemisphere against the common danger.

And then, a year ago, we launched, and are successfully carrying out, the largest armament production program we have ever undertaken.

We have added substantially to our splendid Navy, and we have mustered our manpower to build up a new Army which is already worthy of the highest traditions of our military service.

We instituted a policy of aid for the democracies, the nations which have fought for the continuation of human liberties.

This policy had its origin in the first month of the war, when I urged upon the Congress the repeal of the arms embargo provisions in the old Neutrality Law. And in that Message of September 1939, I said, 'I should like to be able to offer the hope that the shadow over the world might swiftly pass. I cannot. The facts compel my stating, with candor, that darker periods may lie ahead'.

In the subsequent months, the shadows did deepen and lengthen. And the night spread over Poland, Denmark, Norway, Holland, Belgium, Luxembourg and France.

In June 1940, Britain stood alone, faced by the same machine of terror which had overwhelmed her allies. Our Government rushed arms to meet her desperate needs. In September 1940, an agreement was completed with Great Britain for the trade of fifty destroyers for eight important off-shore bases.

And in March 1941, this year, the Congress passed the Lend-Lease Bill and an appropriation of seven billion dollars to implement it. This law realistically provided for material aid 'for the government of any country whose defense the President deems vital to the defense of the United States'.

Our whole program of aid for the democracies has been based on hard-headed concern for our own security and for the kind of safe and civilized world in which we wish to live. Every dollar of material that we send helps to keep the dictators away from our own hemisphere, and every day that they are held off gives us time to build more guns and tanks and planes and ships.

We have made no pretense about our own self-interest in this aid. Great Britain understands it and so does Nazi Germany.

And now, after a year, Britain still fights gallantly, on a far-flung battle line. We have doubled and redoubled our vast production, increasing, month by month our material supply of the tools of war for ourselves and for Britain and for China and eventually for all the democracies.

The supply of these tools will not fail. It will increase. With greatly augmented strength, the United States and the other American Republics now chart their course in the situation today.

Your Government knows what terms Hitler, if victorious, would impose. They are, indeed, the only terms on which he would accept a so-called 'negotiated' peace.

And, under those terms, Germany would literally parcel out the world, hoisting the swastika itself over vast territories and populations, and setting up puppet governments of its own choosing, wholly subject to the will and the policy of a conqueror. To the people of the Americas, a triumphant Hitler would say, as he said after the seizure of Austria, and as he said after Munich, and as he said after the seizure of Czechoslovakia: 'I am now completely satisfied. This is the last territorial readjustment I will seek'. And he would of course add, 'All we want is peace and friendship, and profitable trade relations with you in the New World'.

Were any of us in the Americas so incredibly simple and forgetful as to accept those honeyed words, what would then happen?

Those in the New World who were seeking profits would be urging that all that the dictatorships desired was 'peace'. They would oppose toil and taxes for more American armament. And meanwhile, the dictatorships would be forcing the enslaved peoples of their Old World conquests into a system they are even now organizing, to build, to build a naval and air force intended to gain and hold and be master of the Atlantic and the Pacific as well.

They would fasten an economic stranglehold upon our several nations. Quislings would be found to subvert the governments in our Republics; and the Nazis would back their fifth columns with invasion, if necessary.

No, I am not speculating about all this. I merely repeat what is already in the Nazi book of world conquest. They plan to treat the Latin American nations as they are now treating the Balkans. They plan then to strangle the United States of America and the Dominion of Canada."

Hence six months before the attack on Pearl Harbor on the American home front FDR had proclaimed this state of national emergency to prepare for possible war. All delusion or illusion that the U.S. could stay out of this World War II had really been erased by German attacks on American shipping on the high seas that were supposed to be neutral. For FDR, Hitler was the real villain in the theater of war for his evil designs would, if successful and achieved, alter America forever. Again FDR's speech and focus remained on Europe rather than the war in the Pacific even at a time when the U.S. attempted to send aid to the Nationalist-Communist forces in China, united after the Xian incident of 1936, fighting against the invading Japanese as he continued:

"The American laborer would have to compete with slave labor in the rest of the world. Minimum wages, maximum hours? Nonsense. Wages and hours would be fixed by Hitler. The dignity and power and standard of living of the American worker and farmer would be gone. Trade unions would become historic relics, and collective bargaining a joke.

Farm income? What happens to all farm surpluses without any foreign trade? The American farmer would get for his products exactly what Hitler wanted to give. The farmer would face obvious disaster and complete regimentation.

Tariff walls, Chinese walls of isolation, would be futile. Freedom to trade is essential to our economic life. We do not eat all the food we produce; and we do not burn all the oil we can pump; we do not use all the goods we can manufacture. It would not be an American wall to keep Nazi goods out; it would be a Nazi wall to keep us in.

The whole fabric of working life as we know it, business and manufacturing, mining and agriculture, all would be mangled and crippled under such a system. Yet to maintain even that crippled independence would require permanent conscription of our manpower. It would curtail the funds we could spend on education, on housing, on public works, on flood control, on health and, instead, we should be permanently pouring our resources into armaments; and, year in and year out, standing day and night watch against the destruction of our cities.

Yes, even our right of worship would be threatened. The Nazi world does not recognize any God except Hitler; for the Nazis are as ruthless as the Communists in the denial of God. What place has religion which preaches the dignity of the human being, of the majesty of the human soul, in a world where moral standards are measured by treachery and bribery and Fifth Columnists? Will our children, too, wander off, goose-stepping in search of new gods?

We do not accept, we will not permit this Nazi shape of things to come. It will never be forced upon us, if we act in this present crisis with the wisdom and the courage which have distinguished our country in all the crises of the past.

Today, the Nazis have taken military possession of the greater part of Europe. In Africa they have occupied Tripoli and Libya, and they are threatening Egypt, the Suez Canal, and the Near East. But their plans do not stop there, for the Indian Ocean is the gateway to the farther East. They also have the armed power at any moment to occupy Spain and Portugal, and that threat extends not only to French North Africa and the western end of the Mediterranean Sea. It extends also to the Atlantic fortress of Dakar, and to the island outposts of the New World, the Azores and Cape Verde Islands.

The Cape Verde Islands are only seven hours distance from Brazil by bomber or troop-carrying planes. They dominate shipping routes to and from the South Atlantic.

The war is approaching the brink of the Western Hemisphere itself. It is coming very close to home. Control or occupation by Nazi forces of any of the islands of the Atlantic would jeopardize the immediate safety of portions of North and South America and of the island possessions of the United States, and, therefore, of the ultimate safety of the continental United States itself.

Hitler's plan of world domination would be near its accomplishment today, were it not for two factors. One is the epic resistance of Britain, her colonies, and the great Dominions, fighting not only to maintain the existence of the Island of Britain but also to hold the Near East and Africa. The other is the magnificent defense of China, which will, I have reason to believe, increase in strength. And all of these, together, are preventing the Axis from winning control of the seas by ships and aircraft.

The Axis Powers can never achieve their objective of world domination unless they first obtain control of the seas. That is their supreme purpose today, and to achieve it, they must capture Great Britain.

They could then have the power to dictate to the Western Hemisphere. No spurious argument, no appeal to sentiment, no false pledges like those given by Hitler at Munich, can deceive the American people into believing that he and his Axis partners would not, with Britain defeated, close in relentlessly on this hemisphere of ours.

But if the Axis Powers fail to gain control of the seas, then they are certainly defeated. Their dreams of world domination will then go by the board; and the criminal leaders who started this war will suffer inevitable disaster.

Both they and their people know this and they and their people are afraid. That is why they are risking everything they have, conducting desperate attempts to break through to the command of the ocean. Once they are limited to a continuing land war, their cruel forces of occupation will be unable to keep their heel on the necks of the millions of innocent, oppressed peoples on the Continent of Europe; and in the end, their whole structure will break into little pieces. And let us remember, the wider the Nazi land effort, the greater is their ultimate danger.

We do not forget the silenced peoples. The masters of Germany, those, at least, who have not been assassinated or escaped to free soil, have marked these silenced peoples and their children's children for slavery. But those people, spiritually unconquered: Austrians, Czechs, Poles, Norwegians, Dutch, Belgians, Frenchmen, Greeks, Southern Slavs, yes, even those Italians and Germans who themselves have been enslaved will prove to be a powerful force in the final disruption of the Nazi system.

All freedom, meaning freedom to live, and not freedom to conquer and subjugate other peoples, depends on freedom of the seas. All of American history, North, Central and South American history, has been inevitably tied up with those words, *freedom of the seas.*

Since 1799, one hundred and forty-two years ago, when our infant Navy made the West Indies and the Caribbean and the Gulf of Mexico safe for American ships. Since 1804 and 1805, when we made all peaceful commerce safe from the depredations of the Barbary pirates. Since the War of 1812, which was fought for the preservation of sailors' rights; since 1867, when our sea power made it possible for the Mexicans to expel the French Army of Louis Napoleon, we have striven and fought in defense of freedom of the seas. Freedom of the seas for our own shipping, for the commerce of our sister Republics, for the right of all nations to use the highways of world trade, and for our own safety.

During the First World War we were able to escort merchant ships by the use of small cruisers and gunboats and destroyers; and that type, called a convoy, was effective against submarines. In this Second World War however, the problem is greater. It is different because the attack on the freedom of the seas is now fourfold. First the improved submarine. Second the much greater use of the heavily armed raiding cruiser or the hit-and-run battleship. Third the bombing airplane, which is capable of destroying merchant ships seven or eight hundred miles from its nearest base. And fourth the destruction of merchant ships in those ports of the world that are accessible to bombing attack.

The Battle of the Atlantic now extends from the icy waters of the North Pole to the frozen continent of the Antarctic. Throughout this huge area, there have been sinkings of merchant ships in alarming and increasing numbers by Nazi raiders or submarines. There have been sinkings even of ships carrying neutral flags. There have been sinkings in the South Atlantic, off West Africa and the Cape Verde Islands; between the Azores and the islands off the American coast; and between Greenland and Iceland. Great numbers of these sinkings have been actually within the waters of the Western Hemisphere itself.

The blunt truth of this seems to be this, and I reveal this with the full knowledge of the British Government. The present rate of Nazi sinkings of merchant ships is more than three times as high as the capacity of British shipyards to replace them; it is more than twice the combined British and American output of merchant ships today.

We can answer this peril by two simultaneous measures: first, by speeding up and increasing our own great shipbuilding program; and second, by helping to cut down the losses on the high seas.

Attacks on shipping off the very shores of land which we are determined to protect present an actual military danger to the Americas. And that danger has recently been heavily underlined by the presence in Western Hemisphere waters of a Nazi battleship of great striking power.

You remember that most of the supplies for Britain go by a northerly route, which comes close to Greenland and the nearby island of Iceland. Germany's heaviest attack is on that route. Nazi occupation of Iceland or bases in Greenland would bring the war close to our own continental shores. Because those places are stepping-stones to Labrador and Newfoundland, to Nova Scotia, yes, to the northern United States itself, including the great industrial centers or the north, the east and the middle west.

Equally, the Azores and the Cape Verde Islands, if occupied or controlled by Germany, would directly endanger the freedom of the Atlantic and our own American physical safety. Under German domination those islands would became bases for submarines, warships, and airplanes raiding the waters that lie immediately off our own coasts and attacking the shipping in the South Atlantic.

They would provide a springboard for actual attack against the integrity and the independence of Brazil and her neighboring Republics.

I have said on many occasions that the United States is mustering its men and its resources only for purposes of defense only to repel attack. I repeat that statement now. But we must be realistic when we use the word 'attack'; we have to relate it to the lightning speed of modern warfare.

Some people seem to think that we are not attacked until bombs actually drop in the streets of New York or San Francisco or New Orleans or Chicago. But they are simply shutting their eyes to the lesson that we must learn from the fate of every nation that the Nazis have conquered.

The attack on Czechoslovakia began with the conquest of Austria. The attack on Norway began with the occupation of Denmark. The attack on Greece began with occupation of Albania and Bulgaria. The attack on the Suez Canal began with the invasion of the Balkans and North Africa and the attack on the United States can begin with the domination of any base which menaces our security, north or south.

Nobody can foretell tonight just when the acts of the dictators will ripen into attack on this hemisphere and us. But we know enough by now to realize that it would be suicide to wait until they are in our front yard.

When your enemy comes at you in a tank or a bombing plane, if you hold your fire until you see the whites of his eyes, you will never know what hit you. Our Bunker Hill of tomorrow may be several thousand miles from Boston, Massachusetts.

Anyone with an Atlas, anyone with a reasonable knowledge of the sudden striking force of modern war, knows that it is stupid to wait until a probable enemy has gained a foothold from which to attack. Old-fashioned common sense calls for the use of a strategy that will prevent such an enemy from gaining a foothold in the first place.

We have, accordingly, extended our patrol in north and south Atlantic waters. We are steadily adding more and more ships and planes to that patrol. It is well known that the strength of the Atlantic Fleet has been greatly increased during the past year, and that it is constantly being built up.

These ships and planes warn of the presence of attacking raiders, on the sea, under the sea, and above the sea. The danger from these raiders is, of course, greatly lessened if their location is definitely known. We are thus being forewarned. We shall be on our guard against efforts to establish Nazi bases closer to our Hemisphere.

The deadly facts of war compel nations, for simple preservation, to make stern choices. It does not make sense, for instance, to say, 'I believe in the defense of all the Western Hemisphere', and in the next breath to say, 'I will not fight for that defense until the enemy has landed on our shores'. If we believe in the independence and the integrity of the Americas, we must be willing to fight, to fight to defend them just as much as we would fight for the safety of our own homes.

It is time for us to realize that the safety of American homes even in the center of this, our own country, has a very definite relationship to the continued safety of homes in Nova Scotia or Trinidad or Brazil."

Again long before the attack on December 7, 1941, FDR had urged a worldwide view upon Americans, inviting them to consult with him in his speeches maps of the globe so that they could examine the theaters of war that the U.S. might be drawn into and plan hemispheric defense. The U.S., FDR had promised, would never play the role of a turtle and withdraw into a shell, but would constantly move our lines of defense outward to Iceland and Greenland, Latin America, and Hawaii. In these speeches the axis of evil remained Germany due to Hitler's aggressions breaking the Treaty of Versailles, violating the rights of neutrals on the high seas, and partly because of the previous World War I with Germany that FDR had traveled to Europe to witness. Thus the beacon was aimed more often across the Atlantic and not across the Pacific, as he stated:

> "Our national policy today, therefore, is this: First, we shall actively resist wherever necessary, and with all our resources, every attempt by Hitler to extend his Nazi domination to the Western Hemisphere, or to threaten it. We shall actively resist his every attempt to gain control of the seas. We insist upon the vital importance of keeping Hitlerism away from any point in the world which could be used or would be used as a base of attack against the Americas.
>
> Secondly, from the point of view of strict naval and military necessity, we shall give every possible assistance to Britain and to all who, with Britain, are resisting Hitlerism or its equivalent with force of arms. Our patrols are helping now to insure delivery of the needed supplies to Britain. All additional measures necessary to deliver the goods will be taken. Any and all further methods or combination of methods, which can or should be utilized, are being devised by our military and naval technicians, who, with me, will work out and put into effect such new and additional safeguards as may be needed.
>
> I say that the delivery of needed supplies to Britain is imperative. I say that this can be done; it must be done; and it will be done.
>
> To the other American nations, twenty Republics and the Dominion of Canada, I say this: the United States does not merely propose these purposes, but is actively engaged today in carrying them out.
>
> I say to them further: you may disregard those few citizens of the United States who contend that we are disunited and cannot act.
>
> There are some timid ones among us who say that we must preserve peace at any price, lest we lose our liberties forever. To them I say this: never in the history of the world has a nation lost its democracy by a successful struggle to

defend its democracy. We must not be defeated by the fear of the very danger which we are preparing to resist. Our freedom has shown its ability to survive war, but our freedom would never survive surrender. 'The only thing we have to fear is fear itself'.

There is, of course, a small group of sincere, patriotic men and women whose real passion for peace has shut their eyes to the ugly realities of international banditry and to the need to resist it at all costs. I am sure they are embarrassed by the sinister support they are receiving from the enemies of democracy in our midst, the Bundists, the Fascists, and Communists, and every group devoted to bigotry and racial and religious intolerance. It is no mere coincidence that all the arguments put forward by these enemies of democracy, all their attempts to confuse and divide our people and to destroy public confidence in Government, all their defeatist foreboding that Britain and democracy are already beaten. All their selfish promises that we can 'do business with Hitler', all of these are but echoes or the words that have been poured out from the Axis bureaus of propaganda. Those same words have been used before in other countries, to scare them, to divide them, to soften them up. Invariably, those same words have formed the advance guard of physical attack.

Your Government has the right to expect of all citizens that they take part in the common work of our common defense, take loyal part from this moment forward.

I have recently set up the machinery for civilian defense. It will rapidly organize, locality by locality. It will depend on the organized effort of men and women everywhere. All will have opportunities and responsibilities to fulfill.

Defense today means more than merely fighting. It means morale, civilian as well as military; it means using every available resource; it means enlarging every useful plant. It means the use of a greater American common sense in discarding rumor and distorted statement. It means recognizing, for what they are, racketeers and fifth columnists, the incendiary bombs in this country of the moment.

All of us know that we have made very great social progress in recent years. We propose to maintain that progress and strengthen it. When the nation is threatened from without, however, as it is today, the actual production and transportation of the machinery of defense must not be interrupted by disputes between capital and capital, labor and labor, or capital and labor. The future of all free enterprise, of capital and labor alike, is at stake.

This is no time for capital to make, or be allowed to retain, excess profits. Articles of defense must have undisputed right of way in every industrial plant in the country.

A Nation-wide machinery for conciliation and mediation of industrial disputes has been set up. That machinery must be used promptly, and without stoppage of work. Collective bargaining will be retained, but the American people expect that impartial recommendations of our Government conciliation and mediation services will be followed both by capital and by labor."

FDR had really placed America on a war footing with this national emergency declaration of May 1941, believing a war against Germany was almost inevitable given Nazi sinkings of U.S. convoys. The U.S., he felt must fight to protect the freedom of the seas and the independence of all nations of the Western Hemisphere, anticipating the idea of 'an attack upon one is an attack upon all'.

"The overwhelming majority of our citizens," he wisely intoned, "expect their Government to see that the tools of defense are built. And for the very purpose of preserving the democratic safeguards of both labor and management, this Government is determined to use all of its power to express the will of its people, and to prevent interference with the production of materials essential to our nation's security.

Today the whole world is divided, divided between human slavery and human freedom, between pagan brutality and the Christian ideal.

We choose human freedom which is the Christian ideal. No one of us can waver for a moment in his courage or his faith. We will not accept a Hitler-dominated world. And we will not accept a world, like the post-war world of the 1920s, in which the seeds of Hitlerism can again be planted and allowed to grow.

We will accept only a world consecrated to freedom of speech and expression, freedom of every person to worship God in his own way, freedom from want, and freedom from terror. Is such a world impossible of attainment? Magna Charta, the Declaration of Independence, the Constitution of the United States, the Emancipation Proclamation and every other milestone in human progress, all were ideals which seemed impossible of attainment, and yet they were attained.

As a military force, we were weak when we established our independence, but we successfully stood off tyrants, powerful in their day, tyrants who are now lost in the dust of history.

Odds meant nothing to us then. Shall we now, with all our potential strength, hesitate to take every single measure necessary to maintain our American liberties? Our people and our Government will not hesitate to meet that challenge.

As the President of a united and determined people, I say solemnly: We reassert the ancient American doctrine of *freedom of the seas*. We reassert the solidarity of the twenty-one American Republics and the Dominion of Canada in the preservation of the independence of the hemisphere. We have pledged material support to the other democracies of the world, and we will fulfill that pledge. We in the Americas will decide for ourselves whether, and when, and where, our American interests are attacked or our security threatened. We are placing our armed forces in strategic military position. We will not hesitate to use our armed forces to repel attack.

We reassert our abiding faith in the vitality of our constitutional republic as a perpetual home of freedom, of tolerance, and of devotion to the word of God.

Therefore, with profound consciousness of my responsibilities to my countrymen and to my country's cause, I have tonight issued a proclamation that an *unlimited national emergency exists and requires the strengthening of our defense to the extreme limit of our national power and authority.* The nation will expect all individuals and all groups to play their full parts, without stint, and without selfishness, and without doubt that our democracy will triumphantly survive.

I repeat the words of the Signers of the Declaration of Independence, that little band of patriots, fighting long ago against overwhelming odds, but certain, as we are now, of ultimate victory. 'With a firm reliance on the protection of Divine Providence, we mutually pledge to each other our lives, our fortunes, and our sacred honor'."[242]

Thus long before the Japanese attacked, FDR had expressed eloquently that Americans should standup to Hitler to defeat tyranny. The U.S. must work with all nations of the Western Hemisphere to repeal Nazi threats to freedom and independence. The old American principle of freedom of the seas for neutral nations must be upheld and to do any less would be to embolden German aggressiveness to invade the Hemisphere. Canada and the Latin American countries should bind together, he had said, with the United States in common defense and never give in to appeasement. By proclaiming a state of national emergency in America eight months before the Pearl Harbor strike by the Japanese, FDR had made it apparent to Americans on the home front that it was only a matter of time before the U.S. might be drawn into the conflict. He was surprised that the attack came at Pearl Harbor in the Pacific rather than in the Atlantic, and was in no way responsible for withholding any intelligence that might have prevented the strike. As contrary to some recent conjecture, there is no credible evidence that FDR suppressed any forewarning. Rather, had he known, he would have acted quickly to save the Pacific fleet and sailors' lives; he did not need an excuse to enter the war, as he had cause with the German sinkings. Realizing this, he had been preparing Americans for some foreign strike, especially from the Germans, for months before the Pearl Harbor attack. The war in China between the Chinese and Japanese and the attendant struggles between the Nationalists and the Communists had been held as a secondary theater, almost

---

[242] Rosenman, Public Papers and Addresses of Franklin D. Roosevelt (New York: Harper & Brothers, 1950) Vol 10, pp. 181-195.

as a civil war in the region. Americans, he had said in this 'national emergency' proclamation of May 1941, should never fear preparing for war against Germany or for common defense. No bargains or short-term deals could be made with Hitler who challenged all that America stood for since the inception of the Republic. There was far more to fear from appeasement that would appear as weakness warned FDR, indeed Americans could lose their entire nation to the horrors of Nazism. But FDR's warnings against Hitler also rang true as warnings ultimately against the boldness of the Japanese who were still pretending to peacefully negotiate when they struck Hawaii. U.S. attitudes regarding Japan, and to some extent Americans' feelings for Italy [especially after its 'liberation' from the fascists by the Allies in the future], were colored by the fact that both Japan and Italy had been allied with the U.S. in World War I, and that Germany was the enemy in both World Wars.

When the attack came on December 7th, President Roosevelt had delivered his message to Congress asking its members to declare war against Japan and its Axis allies Germany and Italy with the knowledge that *the U.S. stood on the moral high ground* and was undertaking *a just cause*. Perhaps that is why, in his imagery explaining America's entry and conduct of the war, he invoked the life and military history of George Washington who had viewed the American Revolutionary War also as a *just cause*. Historians have also determined that World War II was a 'just war,' as A.J.P. Taylor, writing in *The Second World War* wrote, "future generations may dismiss the Second World War as 'just another war'. Those who experienced it know that it was a war justified in its aims and successful in accomplishing them. Despite all the killing and destruction that accompanied it, the Second World War was a good war," in the sense of being morally justified.[243] Many veterans would later remark that among the greatest accomplishments of their lives was "serving in the United States Army in the greatest conflict in the history of man."[244]

FDR was seen as the *leader* of the 'free world' and of U.S. fighting forces in all major theaters of the war. Under the Selective Service System of 1940, 18,633 men were drafted, followed by 923,842 in 1941, 3,033,361 in 1942, 3,323,970 in 1943, 1,591,942 in 1944, 945,862 in 1945, and 183,383 in 1946. Movie star Audie Murphy volunteered for service and later wrote of his experiences in *To Hell and Back:* "Thus, with a pocket full of holes, a head full of dreams, and an ignorance

---

[243] Killian Jordon, Our Finest Hour, The Triumphant Spirit of America's World War II Generation (New York: Time Inc., 2000), p. 6.
[244] Ibid., p. 7.

beyond my years, I boarded a bus for the induction center. Previously I had never been over a hundred miles from home."[245]

The stunning surprise blow to Pearl Harbor had galvanized domestic war efforts and governmental re-organization beginning with the formation of the Joint Chiefs of Staff in January 1942, a mere three weeks after the Japanese attack. Diplomatically President Roosevelt and Prime Minister Churchill had organized the Combined Chiefs of Staff (CCS) to coordinate strategy to fight global enemies. The U.S. domestic Joint Chiefs of Staff mirrored its British counterpart, the British Chiefs of Staff, and they held a meeting February 9 combining the heads of the services—army, navy and air forces—and the president's chief of staff chaired this military body.[246] Members of the Joint Chiefs of Staff also served FDR as advisers and met with their opposite numbers, the British Chiefs of Staff, to design overall plans to win the war in Europe, North Africa, and Asia. They coordinated their activities with the War Production Board and requisitioned supplies for the armed services. They authorized combining units of American and British forces and immediately sent U.S. airmen to join in Battle of Britain to repel German aircraft and to ward off the nightly bombing raids over London. [Inter-service cooperation in the U.S. was continued later after the war by the creation of the Department of Defense authorized through the National Security Act of 1947.] The Joint Chiefs of Staff continued to advise the president and the secretary of defense [and after 1986 the National Security Council as well] on all issues affecting the U.S. military and conduct of the war. [The U.S. Marine Corps commandant was included in the Joint Chiefs of Staff in 1978.] This organization, the JCS, was consulted daily by FDR and he was briefed fully on the status of armed forces in all major theaters. The JCS worked with General George C. Marshall, the Head of the War Plans Division of the Army general staff, and after April 1939, FDR's chief of staff. All military operations went through General Marshall for approval and FDR counted heavily upon his chief's wisdom in processing the war effort. Marshall had been elevated to the rank of General on September 1, 1939 following Hitler's invasion of Poland and he had set about to prepare the U.S. for possible conflict to stop Nazi aggression. Marshall was especially effective in working with Congress to secure passage of bills to supply U.S. armed forces and to re-arm.[247] Both FDR and

---

[245] Ibid., p. 19.
[246] Mark A. Stoler, Allies and Adversaries: The Joint Chiefs of Staff, The Grand Alliance, and U.S. Strategy in World War II (Chapel Hill, NC: University of North Carolina Press, 2000).
[247] Larry I. Bland, et al., The Papers of George Catlett Marshall (Baltimore, MD: Johns Hopkins University Press, 1981-1996) especially the Vols. The Papers of George Catlett Marshall: 'The Right Man for the Job', December 7, 1941-May 31, 1943 (1991) and The Papers of George

Marshall had worked strenuously to secure the passage of the Selective Service Act, America's first peacetime draft in 1940, and lobby for billion dollar defense budgets. These preparedness efforts were applauded after the Pearl Harbor attack as fear raced through the nation. Marshall had elevated the number of army troops from 175,000 to 1.4 million between 1939 and 1941 and had plans set in motion to raise troop levels to 8 million so the U.S. was prepared to a high degree when struck by the Japanese.

General Marshall coordinated his efforts with the British through the JCS and agreed that Europe should be the first and primary target with the goal of defeating Hitler. The U.S. would fight a holding action against the Japanese in the Pacific, a reflection of FDR's and Churchill's belief that Hitler and the German war machine were an even greater evil for the world and had to be stopped first.[248] Supplies and war materials were scarce and to Marshall's credit he allocated fairly to both the Lend-Lease programs for the Allies overseas and to the U.S.' own military combat forces now deployed. He was FDR's right-hand military man, an efficient organizer with a reputation for total honesty and integrity. He had reorganized the War Department following Pearl Harbor to streamline decision-making. Marshall became the key figure representing the U.S. on the Anglo-American Combined Chiefs of Staff and applied his principle of 'unity of command' over these forces. He would have preferred to open up a second front in Normandy to defeat the Germans earlier than 1944, but worked with the FDR-Churchill plan to invade North Africa first and then come up through the 'soft underbelly' of Europe through Italy. He was a team player who understood that FDR was the ultimate authority in making war decisions on a grand scale. He would make certain the plans worked to the best of his ability. FDR came to depend upon Marshall to such an extent that when the time came for the invasion of Normandy in 1944 he asked Marshall to stay in Washington, D.C. as his adviser. FDR sent Dwight D. Eisenhower who had led the successful invasion of North Africa to go to England and carryout the planned Normandy invasion. Marshall would continue to direct the overall strategy for all theaters of war in which the U.S. was involved and would become irreplaceable to FDR directing World War II strategy. Eisenhower was a Marshall protégé and accomplished the later task in Normandy brilliantly. Marshall would be elevated to a five-star General in 1944. Congress named him General of the Army, and *Time* named him Man of the Year for coordinating with FDR and Churchill the grand design for

---

Catlett Marshall: Aggressive and Determined Leadership, June 1, 1943-December 31, 1944 (1996).

[248] Roy Jenkins, Franklin Delano Roosevelt (New York: Times Books, Henry Holt and Company, 2003), p. 128.

military victory over the Nazis. Again FDR had chosen his trusted aides wisely, expecting and receiving their best in carrying out his mandates.

FDR was a human dynamo who worked on all fronts during the war. His face often seemed as if he had little sleep and in fact he did not as he was up at all hours of the day and night to receive important cables and communications from intelligence sources abroad. Indeed the president received intelligence from numerous agencies and needed to coordinate them. In this manner FDR kept ultimate control in his own hands as he was the real crucible in which all intelligence passed to him was refined. One of the war's most significant new organizations formed early in 1942 was the Office of Strategic Services (OSS).[249] FDR asked William "Wild Bill" Donovan, who he had appointed OSS head, to establish links with British intelligence. The OSS was under the supervision of the Joint Chiefs of Staff and was authorized to employee intelligence agents, gather secret strategic information, and pass it on through channels to the president. OSS was especially interested in breaking enemy codes and gaining knowledge of enemy battle plans that could be intercepted. This organization was the forerunner to the CIA and learned much from British intelligence.[250] But there were competing intelligence agencies such as the signals intelligence services of the army and navy, and all needed to pool their information to be effective. The OSS was a success during the war until 1945 when it was disbanded and many of its agents joined the newly formed CIA.

The Manhattan Project, established in June 1942, reflected another defensive course taken by FDR following Pearl Harbor and America's entry into World War II. It was undertaken to produce the ultimate weaponry—a nuclear arsenal.[251] This was the code name for the atomic research done with the goal of building an atomic bomb for military purposes. It was officially named the Army Corps of Engineers Manhattan Engineer District. Interest in developing such a weapon came as a result of Albert Einstein's letter written to FDR in August 1939 informing him of the possibilities of harnessing nuclear and atomic power.

---

[249] Joseph Persico, Roosevelt's Secret War: FDR and World War II Espionage (New York: Random House, 2002); Thomas F. Troy, Donovan and the CIA (Washington, D.C.: University Publications of America, 1981); Thomas F. Troy, Wild Bill and Intrepid: Donovan, Stephenson, and the Origin of the CIA (New Haven: Yale University Press, 1996); Evan Thomas, The Very Best Men: Four Who Dared: The Early Years of the CIA (New York: Simon and Schuster, 1996).

[250] Patrick K. O'Donnell, Operations, Spies, and Saboteurs: The Unknown Story of the Men and Women of World War II's OSS (New York: Free Press, 2004).

[251] Richard Rhodes, The Making of the Atomic Bomb (New York: Simon and Schuster, 1995); Stephanie Groueff, Manhattan Project: The Untold Story of the Making of the Atomic Bomb (New York: Little, Brown and Company, 1967); Leslie R. Groves, Now It Can Be Told: The Story of the Manhattan Project (New York: Da Capo Press, 1983).

Einstein's interest had developed after the work of Lise Meitner and Otto Frisch in explaining nuclear fission and he was encouraged to write to FDR to tell him of this new science by Leo Szilard, a Hungarian physicist who had emigrated to the U.S. to escape Hitler's persecution. FDR had formed the Office of Scientific Research and Development with Vannevar Bush at its head and was eager to have Einstein's ideas explored further in relation to atomic energy. Colonel Leslie Groves became the director of the Manhattan Project that had facilities throughout the U.S.—the Los Alamos, New Mexico site where the actual nuclear bombs were constructed, the Berkeley Radiation Laboratory, and supply sites at Oak Ridge, Tennessee, and Hanford, Washington. Enrico Fermi, working at the University of Chicago and with the Chicago Metallurgical Laboratory, pioneered research and development for the project by demonstrating an atomic nuclear fission chain reaction in December 1942.[252] Now possibilities lay open to develop a bomb and the race was on among scientists to find a means to accomplish this task that appeared so vital to America's security. Fermi was an Italian physicist educated at the University of Pisa who had taught at the University of Florence and the University of Rome before coming to the U.S. in 1939 to teach at Columbia University and to interest the government in his theoretical research. He had been awarded the Nobel Prize in physics in 1938. After Einstein's letter to FDR, President Roosevelt had intervened on Fermi's behalf and the scientist was awarded $6,000 for a start up lab in February 1940. At Columbia Fermi had attempted to set up a nuclear reactor or a 'uranium pile' to produce a fission reaction. In late 1941 Fermi's work was transferred to the University of Chicago where his experiments were successful. There had been a sustained and controlled release of nuclear energy in the Chicago Metallurgical Laboratory test. Fermi continued his work there, becoming a professor of physics at the University in 1946, working with neutrons, electrons, radioactive beta-rays and their properties. The leading scientist appointed by Colonel Groves to coordinate gathering experimental data and research operations of this 'big science' to use Fermi's ideas in creating an atomic bomb was J. Robert Oppenheimer and the secret site selected was at Los Alamos, New Mexico. Some of the biggest names in physics joined the Manhattan Project—Hans Bethe, Niels Bohr, Edward Teller, Richard Feynman, John von Neumann—and they all worked together amicably to reach their patriotic goal before the Nazis could beat them to the ultimate atomic weapon. It had to be developed in America, in a safe area where tests could be conducted, and with great haste. Finally a successful test was made at

---

[252] Dan Cooper, *Enrico Fermi and the Revolutions of Modern Physics* (New York: Oxford University Press, 1998).

Alamogordo, New Mexico July 16, 1945 and would be used against Japan less than a month later. The Manhattan Project was endorsed by FDR who, like Truman who followed him, believed an atomic bomb could shorten the war and save American lives. It was the weapon to ensure unconditional surrender of the enemy so important to FDR so as to eliminate the hated doctrines of Nazism and Fascism that had glorified war and engaged in genocide.

As the war clouds had gathered in Europe, FDR had secured the Reorganization Act of 1939 and issued Executive Order 8248 that established the Executive Office of the President (EOP). This re-organization had been suggested by the Brownlow Committee chaired by Louis Brownlow, a prominent political scientist, to increase the efficiency of the White House operations. The EOP began functioning in July 1939 and was composed of five sections—the White House Office (WHO), the Bureau of the Budget, the Office of Government Reports, the National Resources Planning Board, and the Liaison Office for Personnel Management. FDR was further empowered to add another division "in the event of a national emergency, or threat of a national emergency." The White House Office was to serve the U.S. President "in the performance of the many detailed activities incident to his immediate office."[253] This allowed FDR to pay his senior advisers who were so important to carry forth the defense effort. In 1939, as created, there were eight paid officials to aid the president—three secretaries to the president, four administrative assistants, and one executive clerk. FDR was able to appoint his inner-most trusted advisers to his EOP who acted to support the president's political agenda and expedite the administration of presidential duties and responsibilities, most notably to conduct the war effort after the attack on Pearl Harbor. At various times the WHO included a press secretary who arranged for FDR's radio addresses and Fireside Chats. "Other divisions of the WHO are concerned with presidential appointments and scheduling—including those of the First Lady, the management of national security and foreign matters, the development of economic, scientific, and technological policies, the recruitment of high officials, and the arranging of social functions."[254] Activities of the president's cabinet were coordinated through the Office of the Cabinet Secretary, and legal advice to FDR was provided by the person serving as White House Counsel. War activities were coordinated by the Military Office and hence daily FDR worked within a few doors of high level military officials who functioned with the single aim to win the war.

---

[253] Graff, Henry F., ed., The Presidents, A Reference History (New York: Charles Scribner's Sons, 1996), p. 743.
[254] Ibid., p. 744.

FDR was at his best when speaking to subordinates in his easy informal manner. Even in the most pressing of circumstances, he deliberately gave the air of being casual, well informed, and extremely competent. His cabinet was amazed at his mastery of details and his high intelligence in distilling charts, graphs, facts, and maps on which to base his judgments. It was really under President Franklin Delano Roosevelt that the position of U.S. President became the most important position in the world. FDR handled every responsibility with extreme care, knowing that a mistake in wartime could prove disastrous. Yet he always spread his smiling enthusiasm to instill confidence in others that he depended upon to carry out his orders. The consequences of his actions were never left to chance, as he planned his actions diligently to be certain of success. He had grown to magnificent heights and accomplished grand goals because of his wisdom, personality, and moral conscience to set the world to right. FDR *cared* about people just as he *cared* about the fate of the world. His youthful manner of joking had given way to a seriousness and intense devotion to task so requisite to his post as leader of the international free world. This was the role he felt born for—to lead America and the world towards further greatness with the aid of Providence. FDR never was overwhelmed nor shirked from duty. His effervescent confident air, tilt of his head, his powerful voice, and penetrating gaze all bespoke of the talents of a very great man—an American hero who had saved America during the Depression and who would win victory over the Nazis. He became the symbol and the savior of the generation of Americans that had a 'rendezvous with destiny'. People enjoyed his company and he loved having his friends and children around him. FDR played the entertainer to revive himself from worries. Yet the war effort would take a serious toll on FDR causing him to overwork, over-worry, and over-strain his physical and mental capacity. He attempted to conceal this fact, with his warm-hearted confident air. He did not want others to despair. Always while campaigning he rode in an open to car and stood to speak, gripping a special handrail extending across the back of the front seat. He deliberately appeared sunny and 'energetic', hiding his legs withered by polio, and after 1944 suffered from arteriosclerosis. Still he would fight on.

As men volunteered or were drafted for military service, women in America also stepped up to aid the military effort on the home front in every occupation. 'It's our fight too!' proclaimed posters encouraging young women to enter jobs in war industries. A popular song immortalized Rosie the Riveter [Lyric and music by Redd Evans and John Jacob Loeb]:[255]

---

[255] Jordon, Our Finest Hour, The Triumphant Spirit of America's World War II Generation, p. 24.

"While other girls attend their favorite cocktail bar
Sipping dry martinis, munching caviar,
There's a girl who's really putting them to shame.
Rosie is her name.
All the day long whether rain or shine,
She's part of the assembly line.
She's making history working for victory,
Rosie the riveter.
Keeps a sharp lookout for sabotage
Sitting up there on the fuselage.
That little frail can do more than a male can do,
Rosie the riveter.
Rosie's got a boyfriend, Charlie.
Charlie, he's a Marine
Rosie, is protecting Charlie
Working overtime on the riveting machine.
When they gave her a production "E"
She was as proud as a girl could be.
There's something true about,
Red, white and blue about
Rosie the riveter."

FDR asked all Americans on the home front for sacrifices in his Fireside Chat to the nation titled "The Price for Civilization Must Be Paid in Hard Work and Sorrow and Blood" of April 28, 1942:

"My Fellow Americans:
It is nearly five months since we were attacked at Pearl Harbor. For the two years prior to that attack this country had been gearing itself up to a high level of production of munitions. And yet our war efforts had done little to dislocate the normal lives of most of us.

Since then we have dispatched strong forces of our Army and Navy, several hundred thousand of them, to bases and battle fronts thousands of miles from home. We have stepped up our war production on a scale that is testing our industrial power, our engineering genius, and our economic structure to the utmost. We have had no illusions about the fact that this is a tough job- and a long one.

American warships are now in combat in the North and South Atlantic, in the Arctic, in the Mediterranean, in the Indian Ocean, and in the North and South Pacific. American troops have taken stations in South America, Greenland, Iceland, the British Isles, the Near East, the Middle East and the Far East, the continent of Australia, and many islands of the Pacific. American war planes, manned by Americans, are flying in actual combat over all the continents and all the oceans.

On the European front the most important development of the past year has been without question the crushing counter-offensive on the part of the great armies of Russia against the powerful German Army. These Russian forces have destroyed and are destroying more armed power of our enemies- troops, planes, tanks and guns- than all the other United Nations put together.

In the Mediterranean area, matters remain on the surface much as they were. But the situation there is receiving very careful attention.

Recently we received news of a change in government in what we used to know as the Republic of France- a name dear to the hearts of all lovers of liberty- a name and an institution which we hope will soon be restored to full dignity.

Throughout the Nazi occupation of France, we have hoped for the maintenance of a French Government which would strive to regain independence, to re-establish the principles of 'Liberty, Equality and Fraternity', and to restore the historic culture of France. Our policy has been consistent from the very beginning. However, we are now greatly concerned lest those who have recently come to power may seek to force the brave French people into submission to Nazi despotism.

The United Nations will take measures, if necessary, to prevent the use of French territory in any part of the world for military purposes by the Axis powers. The good people of France will readily understand that such action is essential for the United Nations to prevent assistance to the armies or navies or air forces of Germany, or Italy or Japan. The overwhelming majority of the French people understand that the fight of the United Nations is fundamentally their fight, that our victory means the restoration of a free and independent France- and the saving of France from the slavery which would be imposed upon her by her external enemies and by her internal traitors.

We know how the French people really feel. We know that a deep-seated determination to obstruct every step in the Axis plan extends from occupied France through Vichy France all the way to the people of their colonies in every ocean and on every continent.

Our planes are helping in the defense of French colonies today, and soon American Flying Fortresses will be fighting for the liberation of the darkened continent of Europe itself.

In all the occupied countries there are men and women, and even little children who have never stopped fighting, never stopped resisting, never stopped proving to the Nazis that their so-called 'New Order' will never be enforced upon free peoples.

In the German and Italian peoples themselves there is a growing conviction that the cause of Nazism and Fascism is hopeless- that their political and military leaders have led them along the bitter road which leads not to world conquest but to final defeat. They cannot fail to contrast the present frantic speeches of these leaders with their arrogant boasting of a year ago, and two years ago.

On the other side of the world, in the Far East, we have passed through a phase of serious losses.

We have inevitably lost control of a large portion of the Philippine Islands. But this whole nation pays tribute to the Filipino and American officers and men who held out so long on Bataan Peninsula, to those grim and gallant fighters who still hold Corregidor, where the flag flies, and to the forces that are still striking effectively at the enemy on Mindanao and other islands.

The Malayan Peninsula and Singapore are in the hands of the enemy; the Netherlands East Indies are almost entirely occupied, though resistance there continues. Many other islands are in the possession of the Japanese. But there is good reason to believe that their southward advance has been checked. Australia, New Zealand, and much other territory will be bases for offensive action, and we are determined that the territory that has been lost will be regained. The Japanese are pressing their northward advance against Burma with considerable power, driving toward India and China. They have been opposed with great bravery by small British and Chinese forces aided by American fliers.

The news in Burma tonight is not good. The Japanese may cut the Burma Road; but I want to say to the gallant people of China that no matter what advances the Japanese may make, ways will be found to deliver airplanes and munitions of war to the armies of Generalissimo Chiang Kai-shek."

FDR's fireside broadcasts were sent world-wide from the White House, enlisting support not only from his American listeners, but also from resistance movements and citizens in occupied countries, and certainly the Allies' military forces overseas. For an hour or so on selected evenings FDR could reach out and raise the wartime morale of combatants and non-combatants alike in common cause. Foreign leaders came to really know and understand FDR through these broadcasts and were inspired to continue the fight. For many FDR was now known as 'Dr. Win the War' rather than 'Dr. New Deal,' as a political cartoon had shown, whose plan would lead them to victory. The president did not forget the significance of the Asian theater where China was 'fighting America's fight' too against the Japanese.

"We remember," praised FDR, "that the Chinese people were the first to stand up and fight against the aggressors in this war; and in the future a still unconquerable China will play its proper role in maintaining peace and prosperity, not only in eastern Asia but in the whole world.

For every advance that the Japanese have made since they started their frenzied career of conquest, they have had to pay a very heavy toll in warships, in transports, in planes, and in men. They are feeling the effects of those losses.

It is even reported from Japan that somebody has dropped bombs on Tokyo, and on other principal centers of Japanese war industries. If this be true, it is the first time in history that Japan has suffered such indignities.

Although the treacherous attack on Pearl Harbor was the immediate cause of our entry into the war, that event found the American people spiritually prepared for war on a world-wide scale."

FDR now balanced his views both East and West, in the Pacific and in the Atlantic theaters. His beacon of light shone radiantly on a global scale. Everywhere people worldwide turned to him as the architect and the hope of victory. "We went into this war fighting," he continued. "We know what we are fighting for. We realize that the war has become what Hitler originally proclaimed it to be- a total war."

FDR intentionally linked the war efforts made on the home front to those making sacrifices on the battlefields. Together, Americans would do battle with one heart and one mind.

> "Not all of us," he reminded his listeners, "can have the privilege of fighting our enemies in distant parts of the world.
>
> Not all of us can have the privilege of working in a munitions factory or a shipyard, or on the farms or in oil fields or mines, producing the weapons or the raw materials that are needed by our armed forces.
>
> But there is one front and one battle where everyone in the United States- every man, woman, and child- is in action, and will be privileged to remain in action throughout this war. That front is right here at home, in our daily lives, and in our daily tasks. Here at home everyone will have the privilege of making whatever self-denial is necessary, not only to supply our fighting men, but to keep the economic structure of our country fortified and secure during the war and after the war.
>
> This will require, of course, the abandonment not only of luxuries but of many other creature comforts.
>
> Every loyal American is aware of his individual responsibility. Whenever I hear anyone saying 'The American people are complacent- they need to be aroused', I feel like asking him to come to Washington to read the mail that floods into the White House and into all departments of this Government. The one question that recurs through all these thousands of letters and messages is: 'What more can I do to help my country in winning this war?'
>
> To build the factories, to buy the materials, to pay the labor, to provide the transportation, to equip and feed and house the soldiers, sailors and marines, and to do all the thousands of things necessary in a war, all cost a lot of money, more money than has ever been spent by any Nation at any time in the long history of the world.

We are now spending, solely for war purposes, the sum of about $100,000,000 every day in the week. But, before this year is over, that almost unbelievable rate of expenditure will be doubled.

All of this money has to be spent- and spent quickly- if we are to produce within the time now available the enormous quantities of weapons of war which we need. But the spending of these tremendous sums presents grave danger of disaster to our national economy.

When your Government continues to spend these unprecedented sums for munitions month by month and year by year, that money goes into the pocketbooks and bank accounts of the people of the United States. At the same time raw materials and many manufactured goods are necessarily taken away from civilian use; and machinery and factories are being converted to war production.

You do not have to be a professor of mathematics or economics to see that if people with plenty of cash start bidding against each other for scarce goods, the price of those goods goes up.

Yesterday I submitted to the Congress of the United States a seven-point program of general principles which taken together could be called the national economic policy for attaining the great objective of keeping the cost of living down.

I repeat them now to you in substance: First. We must, through heavier taxes, keep personal and corporate profits at a low reasonable rate.

Second. We must fix ceilings on prices and rents.

Third. We must stabilize wages.

Fourth. We must stabilize farm prices.

Fifth. We must put more billions into War Bonds.

Sixth. We must ration all essential commodities which are scarce.

Seventh. We must discourage installment buying, and encourage paying off debts and mortgages.

I do not think it is necessary to repeat what I said yesterday to the Congress in discussing these general principles.

The important thing to remember is that each one of these points is dependent on the others if the whole program is to work.

Some people are already taking the position that every one of the seven points is correct except the one point which steps on their own individual toes. A few seem very willing to approve self-denial- on the part of their neighbors. The only effective course of action is a simultaneous attack on all of the factors which increase the cost of living, in one comprehensive, all-embracing program covering prices, and profits, and wages, and taxes and debts.

The blunt fact is that every single person in the United States is going to be affected by this program. Some of you will be affected more directly by one or two of these restrictive measures, but all of you will be affected indirectly by all of them.

Are you a business man, or do you own stock in a business corporation? Well, your profits are going to be cut down to a reasonably low level by taxation. Your income will be subject to higher taxes. Indeed in these days, when every available dollar should go to the war effort, I do not think that any American citizen should have a net income in excess of $25,000 per year after payment of taxes.

Are you a retailer or a wholesaler or a manufacturer or a farmer or a landlord? Ceilings are being placed on the prices at which you can sell your goods or rent your property.

Do you work for wages? You will have to forego higher wages for your particular job for the duration of the war.

All of us are used to spending money for things that we want, things, however, which are not absolutely essential. We will all have to forego that kind of spending. Because we must put every dime and every dollar we can possibly spare out of our earnings into war bonds and stamps. Because the demands of the war effort require the rationing of goods of which there is not enough to go around. Because the stopping of purchases of non-essentials will release thousands of workers who are needed in the war effort.

As I told the Congress yesterday, 'sacrifice' is not exactly the proper word with which to describe this program of self-denial. When, at the end of this great struggle we shall have saved our free way of life, we shall have made no 'sacrifice'.

The price for civilization must be paid in hard work and sorrow and blood. The price is not too high. If you doubt it, ask those millions who live today under the tyranny of Hitlerism. Ask the workers of France and Norway and the Netherlands, whipped to labor by the lash, whether the stabilization of wages is too great a 'sacrifice'.

Ask the farmers of Poland and Denmark, of Czechoslovakia and France, looted of their livestock, starving while their own crops are stolen from their land, ask them whether 'parity' prices are too great a 'sacrifice'.

Ask the businessmen of Europe, whose enterprises have been stolen from their owners, whether the limitation of profits and personal incomes is too great a 'sacrifice'.

Ask the women and children whom Hitler is starving whether the rationing of tires and gasoline and sugar is too great a 'sacrifice'.

We do not have to ask them. They have already given us their agonized answers.

This great war effort must be carried through to its victorious conclusion by the indomitable will and determination of the people as one great whole.

It must not be impeded by the faint of heart. It must not be impeded by those who put their own selfish interests above the interests of the nation.

It must not be impeded by those who pervert honest criticism into falsification of fact.

It must not be impeded by self-styled experts either in economics or military problems who know neither true figures nor geography itself.

It must not be impeded by a few bogus patriots who use the sacred freedom of the press to echo the sentiments of the propagandists in Tokyo and Berlin.

And, above all, it shall not be imperiled by the handful of noisy traitors- betrayers of America, betrayers of Christianity itself- would-be dictators who in their hearts and souls have yielded to Hitlerism and would have this Republic do likewise.

I shall use all of the executive power that I have to carry out the policy laid down. If it becomes necessary to ask for any additional legislation in order to attain our objective of preventing a spiral in the cost of living, I shall do so.

I know the American farmer, the American workman, and the American businessman. I know that they will gladly embrace this economy and equality of sacrifice- satisfied that it is necessary for the most vital and compelling motive in all their lives winning through to victory.

Never in the memory of man has there been a war in which the courage, the endurance and the loyalties of civilians played so vital a part.

Many thousands of civilians all over the world have been and are being killed or maimed by enemy action. Indeed, it was the fortitude of the common people of Britain under fire which enabled that island to stand and prevented Hitler from winning the war in 1940. The ruins of London and Coventry and other cities are today the proudest monuments to British heroism.

Our own American civilian population is now relatively safe from such disasters. And, to an ever increasing extent, our soldiers, sailors, and marines are fighting with great bravery and great skill on far distant fronts to make sure that we shall remain safe.

I should like to tell you one or two stories about the men we have in our armed forces:

There is, for example, Dr. Corydon M. Wassell. He was a missionary, well known for his good works in China. He is a simple, modest, retiring man, nearly sixty years old, but he entered the service of his country and was commissioned a Lieutenant Commander in the Navy.

Dr. Wassell was assigned to duty in Java caring for wounded officers and men of the cruisers *Houston* and *Marblehead* which had been in heavy action in the Java seas.

When the Japanese advanced across the island, it was decided to evacuate as many as possible of the wounded to Australia. But about twelve of the men were so badly wounded that they couldn't be moved. Dr. Wassell remained with them, knowing that he would be captured by the enemy. But he decided to make a last desperate attempt to get the men out of Java. He asked each of them if he wished to take the chance, and every one agreed.

He first had to get the twelve men to the sea coast- fifty miles away. To do this, he had to improvise stretchers for the hazardous journey. The men were suffering severely, but Dr. Wassell kept them alive by his skill, and inspired them by his own courage.

And as the official report said, Dr. Wassell was 'almost like a Christ-like shepherd devoted to his flock'.

On the seacoast, he embarked the men on a little Dutch ship. They were bombed, they were machine-gunned by waves of Japanese planes. Dr. Wassell took virtual command of the ship, and by great skill avoided destruction, hiding in little bays and little inlets.

A few days later, Dr. Wassell and his small flock of wounded men reached Australia safely.

And today Dr. Wassell wears the Navy Cross.

Another story concerns a ship rather than an individual man. You may remember the tragic sinking of the submarine, the *U.S.S. Squalus* off the New England coast in the summer of 1939. Some of the crew were lost, but others were saved by the speed and the efficiency of the surface rescue crews. The *Squalus* itself was tediously raised from the bottom of the sea.

She was repaired and put back into commission, and eventually she sailed again under a new name, the *U.S.S. Sailfish*. Today, she is a potent and effective unit of our submarine fleet in the Southwest Pacific.

The *Sailfish* has covered many thousands of miles in operations in those waters.

She has sunk a Japanese destroyer.

She has torpedoed a Japanese cruiser.

She has made torpedo hits- two of them- on a Japanese aircraft carrier.

Three of the enlisted men of our Navy who went down with the *Squalus* in 1939 and were rescued, are today serving on the same ship, the *U.S.S. Sailfish*, in this war.

It seems to me that it is heartening to know that the *Squalus*, once given up as lost, rose from the depths to fight for our country in time of peril.

One more story, that I heard only this morning:

This is a story of one of our Army Flying Fortresses operating in the western Pacific. The pilot of this plane is a modest young man, proud of his crew for one of the toughest fights a bomber has yet experienced.

The bomber departed from its base, as part of a flight of five bombers, to attack Japanese transports that were landing troops against us in the Philippines. When they had gone about halfway to their destination, one of the motors of this bomber went out of commission. The young pilot lost contact with the other bombers. The crew, however, got the motor working again and the plane proceeded on its mission alone.

By the time it arrived at its target the other four Flying Fortresses had already passed over, had dropped their bombs, and had stirred up the hornets' nest of Japanese 'Zero' planes. Eighteen of these 'Zero' fighters attacked our one Flying Fortress. Despite this mass attack, our plane proceeded on its mission, and dropped all of its bombs on six Japanese transports which were lined up along the docks.

As it turned back on its homeward journey, a running fight between the bomber and the eighteen Japanese pursuit planes continued 75 miles. Four pursuit planes of the [Japanese] attacked simultaneously at each side. Four were shot down with the side guns. During this fight, the bomber's radio operator was killed, the engineer's right hand was shot off, and one gunner was crippled, leaving only one man available to operate both side guns. Although wounded in one hand, this gunner alternately manned both side guns, bringing down three more Japanese 'Zero' planes. While this was going on, one engine on the American bomber was shot out, one gas tank was hit, the radio was shot off, and the oxygen system was entirely destroyed. Out of eleven control cables all but four were shot away. The rear-landing wheel was blown off entirely, and the two front wheels were both shot flat.

The fight continued until the remaining Japanese pursuit ships exhausted their ammunition and turned back. With two engines gone and the plane practically out of control, the American bomber returned to its base after dark and made an emergency landing. The mission had been accomplished.

The name of that pilot is Captain Hewitt T. Wheless, of the United States Army. He comes from a place called Menard, Texas- with a population 2,375. He has been awarded the Distinguished Service Cross. And I hope that he is listening.

These stories I have told you are not exceptional. They are typical examples of individual heroism and skill.

As we here at home contemplate our own duties, our own responsibilities, let us think and think hard of the example which is being set for us by our fighting men.

Our soldiers and sailors are members of well-disciplined units. But they are still and forever individuals- free individuals. They are farmers, and workers, businessmen, professional men, artists, clerks.

They are the United States of America.

That is why they fight.

We too are the United States of America.

That is why we must work and sacrifice.

It is for them. It is for us. It is for victory."[256]

FDR continued to rally Americans to the great cause and toured factories, military installations and training camps to see that the effort was rapidly and effectively carried forward. In an address on October 12, 1942 the president spoke of the strongest asset of the United States:

---

[256] Samuel I. Rosenman, Public Papers and Addresses of Franklin D. Roosevelt New York: Harper & Brothers, 1950) Vol 11, pp. 227-238.

"My Fellow Americans:

As you know, I have recently come back from a trip of inspection of camps and training stations and war factories.

The main thing that I observed on this trip is not exactly news. It is the plain fact that the American people are united as never before in their determination to do a job and to do it well.

This whole Nation of 130,000,000 free men, women, and children is becoming one great fighting force. Some of us are soldiers or sailors, some of us are civilians. Some of us are fighting the war in airplanes five miles above the continent of Europe or the islands of the Pacific, and some of us are fighting it in mines deep down in the earth of Pennsylvania or Montana. A few of us are decorated with medals for heroic achievement, but all of us can have that deep and permanent inner satisfaction that comes from doing the best we know how, each of us playing an honorable part in the great struggle to save our democratic civilization.

Whatever our individual circumstances or opportunities- we are all in it, and our spirit is good, and we Americans and our allies are going to win, and do not let anyone tell you anything different.

That is the main thing that I saw on my trip around the country, *unbeatable spirit.*"[257]

This was America's strongest weapon—the will to win.

In May 1943 when a coal workers' strike threatened to harm the U.S. war effort, FDR stepped in immediately to take drastic action. The national officers of the United Mine Workers had declined to abide by their wartime pledge not to strike and they had refused to cooperate with the fact-finding of the War Labor Board. FDR addressed the nation on May 2, 1943 to explain the situation and his remedial actions stating "the War Labor Board has been and is ready to give this case a fair and impartial hearing. I have given my assurance that if any adjustment of wages is made by the Board, it will be made retroactive to April First. But the national officers of the United Mine Workers refused to participate in the hearing, when asked to do so last Monday.

On Wednesday of this past week, while the Board was proceeding with the case, stoppages began to occur in some mines. On Thursday morning I telegraphed to the officers of the United Mine Workers asking that the miners continue mining coal on Saturday morning. However, a general strike throughout the industry became effective on Friday night.

The responsibility for the crisis that we now face rests squarely on these national officers of the United Mine Workers, and not on the Government of the United States." FDR would step in, acting decisively just as TR had done during the Anthracite Coal strike of his administration. "But the consequences of this

---

[257] Rosenman, Public Papers and Addresses of Franklin D. Roosevelt, Vol 11, pp. 416-426.

arbitrary action," during wartime warned FDR, now "threaten all of us everywhere.

At ten o'clock, yesterday morning, the Government took over the mines. I called upon the miners to return to work for their Government. The Government needs their services just as surely as it needs the services of our soldiers, and sailors, and marines, and the services of the millions who are turning out the munitions of war."[258]

FDR was a no nonsense president who took bold action when necessary to operate the mines. The president made it known that he expected coal miners to be back at work under the Stars and Stripes. *Striking was unpatriotic*, indeed it bordered on treason. FDR would not let the coal miners undermine their nation or its security and the rest of Americans agreed with his actions to nationalize the mines if necessary and operate them with federal troops. Americans had to stand shoulder to shoulder if they were to win the war. FDR used his powers as commander-in-chief to ensure coal production and therefore energy for the home front's production of war materials.

Hard work was a war requisite. By 1943 65% of U.S. aviation employees were women and of the 16 million women who were working during the years 1941-1945 a quarter of them worked in war industries. "Although the concept of the weaker sex sweating near blast furnaces is accepted in England and Russia, it has always been foreign to American tradition. Only the rising need for labor has forced this revolutionary adjustment."[259] Americans purchased war bonds and celebrities pitched them. Kate Smith, a popular singer, bought a $50,000 war bond herself after opening a booth to sell them to the public for the U.S. Treasury. Some gave their lives for the patriotic cause as actress Carole Lombard died on January 16, 1942 in a plane crash in the Sierra Nevada Mountains following an appearance in Indianapolis, Indiana were she had sold over $2 million worth of war bonds. Following her death, her husband Clark Gable enlisted in the Army Air Corps as a gunner, flying bomber missions from 1942-1944. Henry Fonda served as air combat intelligence officer in the Pacific, winning the Bronze Star. Everyone who could supported the war effort as loyal Americans. Other movie stars like Hedy Lamarr served food in G.I. Canteens and danced with servicemen in Los Angeles to raise morale. New Deal public works projects and the war effort came together with the Federal Art project. Many artists were paid to paint pictures of military officers to instill morale in camps, the favorite subject being General Douglas MacArthur. Over three thousand women worked in the New

---

[258] Rosenman, The Public Papers and Addresses of Franklin D. Roosevelt, Vol 12, pp. 192-193.
[259] Jordon, Our Finest Hour, The Triumphant Spirit of America's World War II Generation, p. 27.

York Stock Exchange for the first time to replace clerks drafted for the war.[260] Families planted Victory Gardens in their backyards to ensure their food supply and to patriotically conserve food for the U.S. troops. Children were taught to clean their plates. All available scrap metal was rounded up by the War Production Board to recycle into planes, guns and tanks. Women went without silk stockings to conserve this fabric for parachutes. Food stamps and gas cards regulated rations of scarce items. Dressmakers restricted themselves to two-inch hems to conserve cloth for uniforms. Love songs reinforced marriages and attachments in spite of the distances caused by the war. "As Time Goes By" written by Herman Hupfeld depicted fundamental feelings in wartime:[261]

"This day and age we're living in
Gives cause for apprehension,
With speed and new invention,
And things like third dimension,
Yet, we get a trifle weary,
With Mister Einstein's theory,
So we must get down to earth,
At times relax, relieve the tension.
No matter what the progress,
Or what may yet be proved,
The simple facts of life are such
They cannot be removed.

You must remember this,
A kiss is still a kiss, a sigh is just a sigh;
The fundamental things apply,
As time goes by.
And when two lovers woo,
They still say 'I love you',
On that you can rely;
No matter what the future brings,
As time goes by.

Moonlight and love songs
Never out of date,
Hearts full of passion,
Jealously and hate;
Woman needs man

---

[260] Ibid., p. 34.
[261] Ibid. p. 52.

And man must have his mate,
That no one can deny.
It's still the same old story,
A fight for love and glory,
A case of do or die!
The world will always welcome lovers,
As time goes by."

The need for money was a major wartime concern and FDR proved to be the greatest fund-raiser of all with his speeches asking the American public to support war loans. He spoke on September 8, 1943 in a radio broadcast of the need for further sacrifice and monetary contributions to the war effort in his appeal for a Third War Loan drive:

"Because the Nation's needs are greater than ever before," he appealed, "our sacrifices too must be greater than they have ever been before.

Nobody knows when total victory will come, but we do know that the harder we fight now, the more might and power we direct at the enemy now, the shorter the war will be and the smaller the sum total of sacrifice.

Success of the Third War Loan will be the symbol that America does not propose to rest on its arms, that we know the tough, bitter job ahead and will not stop until we have finished it.

Now it is your turn!

Every dollar that you invest in the Third War Loan is your personal message of defiance to our common enemies- to the ruthless savages of Germany and Japan- and it is your personal message of faith and good cheer to our allies and to all the men at the front. God bless them!"[262]

FDR worked night and day on the home front to oversee the conduct of the war as commander-in-chief, greatly extending the powers of the U.S. Presidency through his war powers, and instilling hope and confidence in his fellow Americans. Diligently overworking, he would later pay the ultimate price and make the ultimate sacrifice as so many other fellow patriots. Truly FDR was the world's champion of freedom and faith.

---

[262] Samuel I. Rosenman, Public Papers and Addresses of Franklin D. Roosevelt, Vol 12, pp. 377-381

Chapter 8

FDR LEADS U.S. TO VICTORY

FDR never became bogged down by the statistics and always used the common touch to keep Americans informed of the major events of World War II military action. In a Fireside Chat on the cost of living and the progress of the war of September 7, 1942 he had brought the meaning of the need for war sacrifices home to the listening public:

"My Friends:
I wish that all the American people could read all the citations for various medals recommended for our soldiers, sailors, and marines. I am picking out one of these citations which tells of the accomplishments of Lieutenant John James Powers, United States Navy, during three days of the battles with Japanese forces in the Coral Sea.
During the first two days, Lieutenant Powers, flying a dive-bomber in the face of blasting enemy anti-aircraft fire, demolished one large enemy gunboat, put another gunboat out of commission, severely damaged an aircraft tender and a 20,000 ton transport, and scored a direct hit on an aircraft carrier which burst into flames and sank soon after.
The official citation then describes the morning of the third day of battle. As the pilots of his squadron left the ready room to man their planes, Lieutenant Powers said to them, 'Remember, the folks back home are counting on us. I am going to get a hit if I have to lay it on their flight deck'.
He led his section down to the target from an altitude of 18,000 feet, through a wall of bursting anti-aircraft shells and swarms of enemy planes. He dived almost to the very deck of the enemy carrier, and did not release his bomb until he was sure of a direct hit. He was last seen attempting recovery from his dive at the extremely low altitude of 200 feet, amid a terrific barrage of shell and bomb

fragments, smoke, flame and debris from the stricken vessel. His own plane was destroyed by the explosion of his own bomb. But he had made good his promise to 'lay it on their flight deck'.

I have received a recommendation from the Secretary of the Navy that Lieutenant John James Powers of New York City, missing in action, be awarded the Medal of Honor. I hereby and now make this award.

You and I are 'the folks back home' for whose protection Lieutenant Powers fought and repeatedly risked his life. He said that we counted on him and his men. We did not count in vain. But have not those men a right to be counting on us? How are we playing our part 'back home' in winning this war?

The answer is that we are not doing enough.

Today I sent a message to the Congress, pointing out the overwhelming urgency of the serious domestic economic crisis with which we are threatened. Some call it 'inflation', which is a vague sort of term, and others call it a 'rise in the cost of living', which is much more easily understood by most families.

That phrase, 'the cost of living', means essentially what a dollar can buy.

From January 1, 1941, to May of this year, nearly a year and a half, the cost of living went up about 15 per cent. And at that point last May we undertook to freeze the cost of living. But we could not do a complete job of it, because the Congressional authority at the time exempted a large part of farm products used for food and for making clothing, although several weeks before, I had asked the Congress for legislation to stabilize all farm prices.

At that time I had told the Congress that there were seven elements in our national economy, all of which had to be controlled; and that if any one essential element remained exempt, the cost of living could not be held down.

On only two of these points- both of them vital however- did I call for Congressional action. These two vital points were: first, taxation; and second, the stabilization of all farm prices at parity.

'Parity' is a standard for the maintenance of good farm prices. It was established as our national policy way back in 1933. It means that the farmer and the city worker are on the same relative ratio with each other in purchasing power as they were during a period some thirty years before at a time then the farmer had a satisfactory purchasing power. One hundred percent of parity, therefore, has been accepted by farmers as the fair standard for the prices they receive.

Last January, however, the Congress passed a law forbidding ceilings on farm prices below 110 per cent of parity on some commodities. And on other commodities the ceiling was even higher, so that the average possible ceiling is now about 116 per cent of parity for agricultural products as a whole.

This act of favoritism for one particular group in the community increased the cost of food to everybody- not only to the workers in the city or in the munitions plants, and their families, but also to the families of the farmers themselves.

Since last May, ceilings have been set on nearly all commodities, rents, services, except the exempted farm products. Installment buying, for example, has been effectively controlled.

Wages in certain key industries have been stabilized on the basis of the present cost of living.

But it is obvious to all of us that if the cost of food continues to go up, as it is doing at present, the wage earner, particularly in the lower brackets, will have a right to an increase in his wages. I think that would be essential justice and a practical necessity.

Our experience with the control of other prices during the past few months has brought out one important fact- the rising cost of living can be controlled, providing that all elements making up the cost of living are controlled at the same time. I think that also is an essential justice and a practical necessity. We know that parity prices for farm products not now controlled will not put up the cost of living more than a very small amount; but we also know that if we must go up to an average of 116 per cent of parity for food and other farm products- which is necessary at present under the Emergency Price Control Act before we can control all farm prices- the cost of living will get well out of hand. We are face to face with this danger today. Let us meet it and remove it.

I realize that it may seem out of proportion to you to be over-stressing these economic problems at a time like this, when we are all deeply concerned about the news from far distant fields of battle. But I give you the solemn assurance that failure to solve this problem here at home- and to solve it now- will make more difficult the winning of this war.

If the vicious spiral of inflation ever gets under way, the whole economic system will stagger. Prices and wages will go up so rapidly that the entire production program will be endangered. The cost of the war, paid by taxpayers, will jump beyond all present calculations. It will mean an uncontrollable rise in prices and in wages, which can result in raising the overall cost of living as high as another 20 per cent soon. That would mean that the purchasing power of every dollar that you have in your pay envelope, or in the bank, or included in your insurance policy or your pension, would be reduced to about eighty cents' worth. I need not tell you that this would have a demoralizing effect on our people, soldiers and civilians alike.

Over-all stabilization of prices, and salaries, and wages and profits is necessary to the continued increasing production of planes and tanks and ships and guns.

In my Message to Congress today, I have said that this must be done quickly. If we wait for two or three or four or six months it may well be too late.

I have told the Congress that the Administration can not hold the actual cost of food and clothing down to the present level beyond October 1st. Therefore, I have asked the Congress to pass legislation under which the President would be specifically authorized to stabilize the cost of living, including the price of all farm commodities. The purpose should be to hold farm prices at parity, or at levels of a recent date, whichever is higher. The purpose should also be to keep wages at a point stabilized with today's cost of living. Both must be regulated at the same time; and neither one of them can or should be regulated without the other.

At the same time that farm prices are stabilized, I will stabilize wages.

That is plain justice- and plain common sense.

And so I have asked the Congress to take this action by the first of October. We must now act with the dispatch which the stern necessities of war require.

I have told the Congress that inaction on their part by that date will leave me with an inescapable responsibility to the people of this country to see to it that the war effort is no longer imperiled by the threat of economic chaos.

As I said in my Message to the Congress:

In the event that the Congress should fail to act, and act adequately, I shall accept the responsibility, and I will act.

The President has the powers, under the Constitution and under Congressional Acts, to take measures necessary to avert a disaster which would interfere with the winning of the war.

I have given the most careful and thoughtful consideration to meeting this issue without further reference to the Congress. I have determined, however, on this vital matter to consult with the Congress.

There may be those who will say that, if the situation is as grave as I have stated it to be, I should use my powers and act now. I can only say that I have approached this problem from every angle, and that I have decided that the course of conduct which I am following in this case is consistent with my sense of responsibility as President in time of war, and with my deep and unalterable devotion to the processes of democracy.

The responsibilities of the President in wartime to protect the Nation are very grave. This total war, with our fighting fronts all over the world, makes the use of the executive power far more essential than in any previous war.

If we were invaded, the people of this country would expect the President to use any and all means to repel the invader. The Revolution and the War Between the States were fought on our own soil, but today this war will be won or lost on other continents and in remote seas. I cannot tell what powers may have to be exercised in order to win this war.

The American people can be sure that I will use my powers with a full sense of responsibility to the Constitution and to my country. The American people can also be sure that I shall not hesitate to use every power vested in me to accomplish the defeat of our enemies in any part of the world where our own safety demands such defeat.

And when the war is won, the powers under which I act will automatically revert to the people of the United States to the people to whom those powers belong.

I think I know the American farmers. I know they are as wholehearted in their patriotism as any other group. They have suffered from the constant fluctuations of farm prices- occasionally too high, more often too low. Nobody knows better than farmers the disastrous effects of wartime inflationary booms, and postwar deflationary panics.

So I have also suggested today that the Congress make our agricultural economy more stable. I have recommended that in addition to putting ceilings on all farm products now, we also place a definite floor under those prices for a period beginning now, continuing through the war, and for as long as necessary after the war. In this way we will be able to avoid the collapse of farm prices that happened after the last war. The farmers must be assured of a fair minimum price during the readjustment period which will follow the great, excessive world food demands that now prevail.

We must have some floor under farm prices, as we must have under wages, if we are to avoid the dangers of a postwar inflation on the one hand, or the catastrophe of a crash in farm prices and wages on the other.

Today I have also advised the Congress of the importance of speeding up the passage of the tax bill. The Federal Treasury is losing millions of dollars each and every day because the bill has not yet been passed. Taxation is the only practical way of preventing the incomes and profits of individuals and corporations from getting too high.

I have told the Congress once more that all net individual incomes, after payment of all taxes, should be limited effectively by further taxation to a maximum net income of $25,000 a year. And it is equally important that corporate profits should not exceed a reasonable amount in any case.

The Nation must have more money to run the war. People must stop spending for luxuries. Our country needs a far greater share of our incomes.

For this is a global war, and it will cost this Nation nearly $100,000,000,000 in 1943.

In that global war there are now four main areas of combat; and I should like to speak briefly of them, not in the order of their importance, for all of them are vital and all of them are interrelated.

1. The Russian front. Here the Germans are still unable to gain the smashing victory which, almost a year ago, Hitler announced he had already achieved. Germany has been able to capture important Russian territory. Nevertheless, Hitler has been unable to destroy a single Russian Army; and this, you may be sure, has been, and still is, his main objective. Millions of German troops seem doomed to spend another cruel and bitter winter on the Russian front. Yes, the Russians are killing more Nazis, and destroying more airplanes and tanks than are being smashed on any other front. They are fighting not only bravely but brilliantly. In spite of any setbacks Russia will hold out, and with the help of her Allies will ultimately drive every Nazi from her soil.

2. The Pacific Ocean Area. This area must be grouped together as a whole every part of it, land and sea. We have stopped one major Japanese offensive; and we have inflicted heavy losses on their fleet. But they still possess great strength; they seek to keep the initiative; and they will undoubtedly strike hard again. We must not over-rate the importance of our successes in the Solomon Islands, though we may be proud of the skill with which these local operations were conducted. At the same time, we need not underrate the significance of our victory at Midway. There we stopped the major Japanese offensive.

3. In the Mediterranean and the Middle East area the British, together with the South Africans, Australians, New Zealanders, Indian troops and others of the United Nations, including ourselves, are fighting a desperate battle with the Germans and Italians. The Axis powers are fighting to gain control of that area, dominate the Mediterranean and the Indian Ocean, and gain contact with the Japanese Navy. The battle in the Middle East is now joined. We are well aware of our danger, but we are hopeful of the outcome.

4. The European area. Here the aim is an offensive against Germany. There are at least a dozen different points at which attacks can be launched. You, of course, do not expect me to give details of future plans, but you can rest assured that preparations are being made here and in Britain toward this purpose. The power of Germany must be broken on the battlefields of Europe.

Various people urge that we concentrate our forces on one or another of these four areas, although no one suggests that any one of the four areas should be abandoned. Certainly, it could not be seriously urged that we abandon aid to Russia, or that we surrender all of the Pacific to Japan, or the Mediterranean and Middle East to Germany, or give up an offensive against Germany. The American people may be sure that we shall neglect none of the four great theaters of war.

Certain vital military decisions have been made. In due time you will know what these decisions are and so will our enemies. I can say now that all of these decisions are directed toward taking the offensive.

Today, exactly nine months after Pearl Harbor, we have sent overseas three times more men than we transported to France in the first nine months of the first World War. We have done this in spite of greater danger and fewer ships. And every week sees a gain in the actual number of American men and weapons in the fighting areas. These reinforcements in men and munitions are continuing, and will continue to go forward.

This war will finally be won by the coordination of all the armies, navies and air forces of all of the United Nations operating in unison against our enemies.

This will require vast assemblies of weapons and men at all the vital points of attack. We and our allies have worked for years to achieve superiority in weapons. We have no doubts about the superiority of our men. We glory in the individual exploits of our soldiers, our sailors, our marines, our merchant seamen. Lieutenant John James Powers was one of these, and there are thousands of others in the forces of the United Nations.

Several thousand Americans have met death in battle. Other thousands will lose their lives. But many millions stand ready to step into their places to engage in a struggle to the very death. For they know that the enemy is determined to destroy us, our homes and our institutions that in this war it is kill or be killed.

Battles are not won by soldiers or sailors who think first of their own personal safety. And wars are not won by people who are concerned primarily with their own comfort, their own convenience, their own pocketbooks.

We Americans of today bear the gravest of responsibilities. And all of the United Nations share them.

All of us here at home are being tested for our fortitude, for our selfless devotion to our country and to our cause.

This is the toughest war of all time. We need not leave it to historians of the future to answer the question whether we are tough enough to meet this unprecedented challenge. We can give that answer now. The answer is yes."[263]

FDR was eloquent and succinct with the great ability to touch the human soul with his earnestness and purpose. And beyond using informational channels, conducting the war required monumental efforts from the president down through his staff. Former Supreme Court Justice James F. Byrnes headed first the Office of Economic Stabilization and after 1943 the Office of War Mobilization, and both organizations coordinated America's domestic war effort. Roosevelt appointed a National Defense Mediation Board to assist labor and management in avoiding work stoppages, and the 'Little Steel' case of July 1942 laid down the rule that wage increases should not normally exceed 15% of the rates of January 1941 or a normal cost of living increase. The Smith-Connally War Labor Disputes Act of June 1943 gave the president the power to take over any war plant threatened by a strike. The war created boom times and 40% of total war costs were met by taxation. From December 7, 1941 until May 8, 1945, World War II dominated American life as no struggle had ever before done with fighting in the Pacific, in North Africa, and in Europe.

Henry Morgenthau Jr., as Secretary of the Treasury, was charged with financing America's involvement in World War II. He had started by setting up

---

[263] Samuel I. Rosenman, The Public Papers and Addresses of Franklin D. Roosevelt (New York: Harper & Brothers, 1950) Vol 11 pp. 368-377.

funds to allow Britain and France to buy weapons as early as the fall of 1939 following the collapse of Poland under the heel of the Nazis. Being of Jewish ancestry, Morgenthau was acutely aware of Nazi atrocities against German and eastern European Jews and recommended to FDR that aid be given to refugees through the War Refugee Board, and he later supported the creation of Israel.[264] As World War II had erupted across Europe he had stabilized the American dollar world-wide amidst chaos and pressured FDR to stop selling scrap metal to the Japanese. Earlier, following the Japanese invasion of China directly in 1937, FDR and Morgenthau had worked to aid the Chinese war effort to defend their homeland, and encouraged the sale of planes to Chiang-Kai-shek. Morgenthau proposed additional military aid through the Flying Tigers, led by Brigadier General Claire L. Chennault, flying supplies into China 'over the hump' of the Himalayas from Burma and India. He oversaw the sale of war bonds and opposed the relocation camps for American Japanese.[265] FDR had signed Executive Order 9066 on February 19, 1942 that established internment camps and relocated over 100,000 Japanese immigrants, many American nationals, caught up by the wartime mentality of fear. Ironically, the most decorated military unit in World War II would be composed of Japanese Americans fighting in Italy and France from 1944 to 1945—the 442nd Regimental Combat Team fighting for freedom when many of their family members were incarcerated. Beyond his generous ethnic sympathies and Treasury responsibilities, Morgenthau would later lay the

---

[264] Ted Morgan, FDR, A Biography (New York: Simon and Schuster, 1985), pp. 715-716; John Morton Blum, From the Morgenthau Diaries, 3 Vols. (Boston: Houghton Mifflin, 1959-1967); John Morton Blum, Roosevelt and Morgenthau (Boston: Houghton Mifflin, 1970); Louis L. Snyder, National Socialist Germany: Twelve Years That Shook the World (Malabar, Fla: Krieger, 1984); Louis L. Snyder, German Nationalism: The Tragedy of a People; Extremism Contra Liberalism in Modern German History (Port Washington, NY: Kennikat Press, 1969); Louis L. Snyder, Hitler and Nazism (New York: F. Watts, 1961).

[265] Morgan, FDR, A Biography, pp. 625-630; James MacGregor Burns, Roosevelt: Soldier of Freedom, 1940-1945 (New York: Harvest/HBJ Book, 2002 published originally in 1970); The relocation camps were thought to be a defensive measure to defend the homeland against sabotage and disloyalty but the policy was not universally endorsed by members of the administration. Several Japanese farmers in the Coachella Valley of California had their farms protected and run by friends who later returned many Japanese farms following the end of the war. These Japanese were "appreciative of the concern and caring of their neighbors." Cited in "Coachella Valley During World War II," edited by Patricia Laflin for The Periscope, 2001, a publication of the Coachella Valley Historical Society, Indio, California. General Patton ran a tank and Desert Training Center near Indio, California at Camp Young during WW II that was established in the spring of 1942 and continued until 1994. The desert training that took place at this camp laid the foundation for the landings and tank maneuvers in North Africa during the war. Information is available through the La Quinta Historical Society in La Quinta, California or the Coachella Valley Historical Society.

pioneering foundations for the establishment of the International Monetary Fund and the World Bank at the Bretton Woods conference by 1944.

Following Japan's attack on Pearl Harbor and the crippling of the U.S. Pacific fleet, Japan had continued to move into Southeast Asia, seizing Thailand, Malaya, and Burma, the Dutch East Indies [Indonesia], the Philippines, Wake Island, and Guam. New Guinea was invaded and India and Australia in the Pacific Rim were threatened with invasion. U.S. naval forces had halted the Japanese advance at the Battle of the Coral Sea and the Battle of Midway during May to June 1942.[266] U.S. domestic armaments production went full tilt round the clock and out-produced the combined enemies' production by 1943. U.S. home production lines made 47,000 planes to the Axis 27,000, and 24,000 tanks and manufactured six times the arms.[267] American naval shipyards produced 8,000 warships and 87,000 landing ship tanks (LSTs) between the attack on Pearl Harbor and 1945. America out-built Japan in the creation of new naval vessels by 16 to 1. Much larger industrial resources lay with the Allies after Britain and Russia had held the line against German conquest of their nations in Europe. U.S. aid to Russia allowed the Soviet Union to outstrip Germany in the production of guns, planes, and tanks, and allowed Russian forces to bleed the *Wehrmacht* to death in 1943 and 1944 in eastern Europe, forcing them out of Russia.[268] Ultimately superior American technology and industrial capabilities won the war on land, at sea, and in the air. By mid-943, through increased construction of merchant ships and escort carriers, as well as intelligence breakthroughs, the Anglo-American struggle against Nazi subs turned in the Allies' favor. By war's end, some 29,000 German submarine crew members had been killed, almost three-fourths of those who had entered combat. American airmen, from the summer of 1942 to the end of the war, joined the British Royal Air Force in bombing raids over German occupied targets. By 1944 this air armada had disrupted Hitler's military machine and had worn down the German *Luftwaffe* to an extent that would permit the Allied military forces to land in Normandy successfully, establishing a large western front to relieve pressure on the Russians fighting in eastern Europe.

The stimulated domestic U.S. economy opened new opportunities for blacks but segregation and discrimination in labor unions and the armed forces remained.

---

[266] Morgan, FDR, A Biography, p. 641; Conrad Black, Franklin Delano Roosevelt, Champion of Freedom (New York: Public Affairs, 2003), pp. 738-741.

[267] Winston S. Churchill, The Second World War 6 Vols. (Boston: Houghton Mifflin, 1948-1953); Robert Dalleck, The Roosevelt Diplomacy and World War II (New York: Holt, Rinehart and Winston, 1970); Robert Dalleck, Franklin D. Roosevelt and American Foreign Policy 1932-1945 (New York: Oxford University Press, 1995); Milton Derber, The American Ideal of Industrial Democracy, 1865-1965 (Urbana: University of Illinois Press, 1970).

[268] Ibid.

'A Jim Crow army', should not be asked to 'fight for a free world' voiced activists. Denouncing segregation, A. Philip Randolph, civil rights leader and head of the Brotherhood of Sleeping Car Porters, organized a march on Washington in the spring 1941. He believed that the fate of American Blacks was tied up with democracy and urged an end to discrimination in war industries. Not only was it imperative to defeat Nazism and Hitler but to end racial prejudice in America and promote constitutionally guaranteed equality as a reality. In response to these pleas, in June 1941 FDR organized the Fair Employment Practices Committee and ordered all defense plants integrated.[269] FDR's actions moving the U.S. towards a fully integrated society converted many Blacks from Republicans, the Party of Lincoln, to Democrats and this political partnership continued throughout the rest of the 20th Century. The Congress on Racial Equality (CORE), using non-violent tactics, successfully employed sit-ins in the 1940s to desegregate several business establishments in the North and by 1945 used freedom rides to desegregate public transportation in the South. It should be said that FDR, with the urgings from Eleanor Roosevelt, strongly believed that the Constitutional guarantees of equality before the law should be an active driving force and made a reality in America.

Some advancement on the home front was apparent for women as well as more than six million women went to work for the first time during World War II. The proportion of women in the labor market increased from 25% in 1940 to 36% in 1945. They filled jobs vacated by men. They worked in armor plating factories with acetylene torches and with rivet guns in the aircraft industry.[270] Women entered government service at four times the rate of men. Women went into uniform and founded the non-combatant Navy Waves and the Women's Auxiliary Army Corps. Child-care centers for 100,000 children were founded by 1945. Women pressed for equal pay for equal work. The war represented a second emancipation for women. The movement into war industries had caused a quadrupling of female membership in the CIO. After the war women in large numbers returned to the home and the percentage of women in the labor force dropped from 36% in 1935 to 28% in 1947. Upon conclusion of the war, women typically would be demoted to lower paying jobs, but after 1953 the percentage of women in the labor force continued to increase. Women's incomes supplemented

---

[269] Lorraine Glennon, ed., The 20th Century, An Illustrated History of Our Lives and Times (New York: JG Press, 2000), p. 305; Nancy J. Weiss, Farewell to the Party of Lincoln: Black Politics in the Age of FDR (Princeton: Princeton University Press, 1983).
[270] Killian Jordon, Our Finest Hour, The Triumphant Spirit of America's World War II Generation (New York: Time Books, 2000), pp. 26-27.

their husband's and their earnings gave families access to the necessities and some of the comforts of a middle-class standard of living.

America had made the decision with Churchill's encouragement to beat Hitler in Europe before throwing its main force against Japan in the Far East. Dominating the ports of coastal Europe, Germany presented a direct threat to the Western Hemisphere. Because Hitler had invaded Russia, it was also assumed that the Allies would have a good opportunity to win in Europe given the fact that Hitler's forces and supplies were divided between fighting Russia and Britain. A decision was made by FDR, Churchill, and Joint Chief of Staff leader General Marshall that a massive thrust across the English Channel into France and Germany would achieve victory. As a prelude to this ultimate goal, the Allies attacked the soft underbelly of Europe coming up through North Africa and the Mediterranean.[271]

Americans had participated in the first major land-offensive invasion in North Africa in November 1942. U.S. forces had selected this battle site where they could be relatively confident of winning. Combined Anglo-American forces, led by General Dwight David Eisenhower, landed in North Africa and moved eastward to join forces with General Montgomery to fight against German Erwin Rommel's Afrika Korps.[272] Victory for the Allies was secured by May 1943 following success at the Battle of El Alamein, and Rommel was recalled to Germany where he became involved in a plot to remove Hitler from power. In January 1943 the Casablanca conference was held between leaders of the Allies to make plans for the Allied invasion of Sicily and then southern Italy. This southern front would occupy German attention while the Allies planned the even larger invasion of Normandy France. FDR announced that the Allies would demand unconditional surrender from the Axis powers. Following the successful Allied invasion of Sicily from North Africa, Italian officials scrambled to halt the advance by ousting Benito Mussolini from power and negotiating a peace. King

---

[271] Trumbull Higgins, Soft Underbelly, the Anglo-American Controversy Over the Italian Campaign, 1939-1945 (New York: Macmillan, 1968); Trumbull Higgins, Winston Churchill and the Second Front, 1940-1943 (New York: Oxford University Press, 1974); Raymond de Belot, The Struggle for the Mediterranean (New York: Greenwood Press, 1969) translated from French by James A. Field, Jr.; Lawrence J. Korb, The Joint Chiefs of Staff: The First Twenty-five Years (Bloomington: Indiana University Press, 1976).

[272] Herbert Feis, Churchill, Roosevelt, and Stalin: The War They Waged and the Peace They Sought (Princeton: Princeton University Press, 1957); Warren F. Kimball, Churchill and Roosevelt: The Complete Correspondence (Princeton, NJ: Princeton University Press, 1984); Eric Larrabee, Commander in Chief: Franklin Delano Roosevelt, His Lieutenants, and Their War (New York: Naval Institute Press, 2004); Louis L. Snyder, The War: A Concise History (New York: J. Messner, 1960); Chester Wilmot, The Struggle for Europe (Westport, Conn: Greenwood Press,

Victor Emmanuel III dismissed Mussolini after the Fascist Grand Council deserted him. A new Italian government was in the process of being formed in the summer of 1943 under Marshall Pietro Badoglio, who signed an armistice with the Allies.[273]

In a message of July 28, 1943 FDR delivered the war news of the successful Italian campaign, and raised morale on the home front by projecting peace plans. He reminded Americans too about the continuing patriotic need for sacrifice in rationing, buying war bonds, and producing food at home in victory gardens:

> "My Fellow Americans:
> Over a year and a half ago I said this to the Congress: 'The militarists of Berlin and Tokyo started this war. But the massed, angered forces of common humanity will finish it'.
>
> Today that prophecy is in the process of being fulfilled. The massed, angered forces of common humanity are on the march. They are going forward- on the Russian front, in the vast Pacific area, and into Europe- converging upon their ultimate objectives: Berlin and Tokyo.
>
> The first crack in the Axis has come. The criminal, corrupt Fascist regime in Italy is going to pieces.
>
> The pirate philosophy of the Fascists and the Nazis cannot stand adversity. The military superiority of the United Nations, on sea and land, and in the air, has been applied in the right place and at the right time.
>
> Hitler refused to send sufficient help to save Mussolini. In fact, Hitler's troops in Sicily stole the Italians' motor equipment, leaving Italian soldiers so stranded that they had no choice but to surrender. Once again the Germans betrayed their Italian allies, as they had done time and time again on the Russian front and in the long retreat from Egypt, through Libya and Tripoli, to the final surrender in Tunisia.
>
> And so Mussolini came to the reluctant conclusion that the 'jig was up'; he could see the shadow of the long arm of justice.
>
> But he and his Fascist gang will be brought to book, and punished for their crimes against humanity. No criminal will be allowed to escape by the expedient of 'resignation'.
>
> So our terms to Italy are still the same as our terms to Germany and Japan, 'unconditional surrender'.
>
> We will have no truck with Fascism in any way, in any shape or manner. We will permit no vestige of Fascism to remain.

1972); James MacGregor Burns, Roosevelt: The Lion and the Fox, 1882-1940 (New York: Harvest/HBJ Books, 2002 originally published 1956).

[273] Norman Kogan, Italy and the Allies (Westport, Conn: Greenwood Press, 1982); David M. Kennedy, Freedom From Fear: The American People in Depression and War, 1929-1945 (New York: Oxford University Press, 2001).

Eventually Italy will reconstitute herself. It will be the people of Italy who will do that, choosing their own government in accordance with the basic democratic principles of liberty and equality. In the meantime, the United Nations will not follow the pattern set by Mussolini and Hitler and the Japanese for the treatment of occupied countries- the pattern of pillage and starvation.

We are already helping the Italian people in Sicily. With their cordial cooperation, we are establishing and maintaining security and order- we are dissolving the organizations which have kept them under Fascist tyranny- we are providing them with the necessities of life until the time comes when they can fully provide for themselves.

Indeed, the people in Sicily today are rejoicing in the fact that for the first time in years they are permitted to enjoy the fruits of their own labor- they can eat what they themselves grow, instead of having it stolen from them by the Fascists and the Nazis.

In every country conquered by the Nazis and the Fascists, or the Japanese militarists, the people have been reduced to the status of slaves or chattels.

It is our determination to restore these conquered peoples to the dignity of human beings, masters of their own fate, entitled to freedom of speech, freedom of religion, freedom from want, and freedom from fear.

We have started to make good on that promise.

I am sorry if I step on the toes of those Americans who, playing party politics at home, call that kind of foreign policy 'crazy altruism' and 'starry-eyed dreaming'.

Meanwhile, the war in Sicily and Italy goes on. It must go on, and will go on, until the Italian people realize the futility of continuing to fight in a lost cause, a cause to which the people of Italy never gave their wholehearted approval and support.

It is a little over a year since we planned the North African campaign. It is six months since we planned the Sicilian campaign. I confess that I am of an impatient disposition, but I think that I understand and that most people understand the amount of time necessary to prepare for any major military or naval operation. We cannot just pick up the telephone and order a new campaign to start the next week.

For example, behind the invasion forces in North Africa, the invasion forces that went out of North Africa, were thousands of ships and planes guarding the long, perilous sea lanes, carrying the men, carrying the equipment and the supplies to the point of attack. And behind all these were the railroad lines and the highways here back home that carried the men and the munitions to the ports of embarkation- there were the factories and the mines and the farms here back home that turned out the materials- there were the training camps here back home where the men learned how to perform the strange and difficult and dangerous tasks which were to meet them on the beaches and in the deserts and in the mountains.

All this had to be repeated, first in North Africa and then in the attack on Sicily. Here in Sicily the factor of air attack was added- for we could use North Africa as the base for softening up the landing places and lines of defense in Sicily, and the lines of supply in Italy.

It is interesting for us to realize that every Flying Fortress that bombed harbor installations at Naples from its base in North Africa, required 1,110 gallons of gasoline for each single mission, and that this is the equal of about 375 'A' ration tickets- enough gas to drive your car five times across this continent. You will better understand your part in the war- and what gasoline rationing means- if you multiply this by the gasoline needs of thousands of planes and hundreds of thousands of jeeps, trucks and tanks now serving overseas.

I think that the personal convenience of the individual, or the individual family, back home here in the United States will appear somewhat less important when I tell you that the initial assault force on Sicily involved 3,000 ships which carried 160,000 men- Americans, British, Canadians and French- together with 14,000 vehicles, 600 tanks, and 1,800 guns. And this initial force was followed every day and every night by thousands of reinforcements.

The meticulous care with which the operation in Sicily was planned has paid dividends. Our casualties in men, in ships and materiel have been low- in fact, far below our estimate.

All of us are proud of the superb skill and courage of the officers and men who have conducted and are conducting those operations. The toughest resistance developed on the front of the British Eighth Army, which included the Canadians. But that is no new experience for that magnificent fighting force which has made the Germans pay a heavy price for each hour of delay in the final victory. The American Seventh Army, after a stormy landing on the exposed beaches of southern Sicily, swept with record speed across the island into the capital at Palermo. For many of our troops this was their first battle experience, but they have carried themselves like veterans.

And we must give credit for the coordination of the diverse forces in the field, and for the planning of the whole campaign, to the wise and skillful leadership of General Eisenhower. Admiral Cunningham, General Alexander, and Air Marshal Tedder have been towers of strength in handling the complex details of naval, ground, and air activities.

You have heard some people say that the British and the Americans can never get along well together- you have heard some people say that the Army and the Navy and the Air Forces can never get along well together- that real cooperation between them is impossible. Tunisia and Sicily have given the lie, once and for all, to these narrow-minded prejudices.

The dauntless fighting of the British people in this war has been expressed in the historic words and deeds of Winston Churchill- and the world knows how the American people feel about him.

Ahead of us are much bigger fights. We and our Allies will go into them as we went into Sicily together. And we shall carry on together.

Today our production of ships is almost unbelievable. This year we are producing over 19 million tons of merchant shipping and next year our production will be over 21 million tons. And in addition to our shipments across the Atlantic, we must realize that in this war we are operating in the Aleutians, in the distant parts of the Southwest Pacific, in India, and off the shores of South America.

For several months we have been losing fewer ships by sinking, and we have been destroying more and more U-boats. We hope this will continue. But we cannot be sure. We must not lower our guard for one single instant.

One tangible result of our great increase in merchant shipping, which I think will be good news to civilians at home- is that tonight we are able to terminate the rationing of coffee.

We also expect that within a short time we shall get greatly increased allowances of sugar.

Those few Americans who grouse and complain about the inconveniences of life here in the United States should learn some lessons from the civilian populations of our allies- Britain, China, and Russia- and of all the lands occupied by our common enemy.

The heaviest and most decisive fighting today is going on in Russia. I am glad that the British and we have been able to contribute somewhat to the great striking power of the Russian armies.

In 1941-1942 the Russians were able to retire without breaking, to move many of their war plants from western Russia far into the interior, to stand together with complete unanimity in the defense of their homeland.

The success of the Russian armies has shown that it is dangerous to make prophecies about them- a fact which has been forcibly brought home to that mystic master of strategic intuition, Herr Hitler.

The short-lived German offensive, launched early this month, was a desperate attempt to bolster the morale of the German people. The Russians were not fooled by this. They went ahead with their own plans for attack- plans which coordinate with the whole United Nations' offensive strategy.

The world has never seen greater devotion, determination, and self-sacrifice than have been displayed by the Russian people and their armies, under the leadership of Marshal Joseph Stalin.

With a Nation which in saving itself is thereby helping to save all the world from the Nazi menace, this country of ours should always be glad to be a good neighbor and a sincere friend in the world of the future.

In the Pacific, we are pushing the [Japanese] around from the Aleutians to New Guinea. There too we have taken the initiative and we are not going to let go of it.

It becomes clearer and clearer that the attrition, the whittling-down process against the Japanese is working. The [Japanese] have lost more planes and more ships than they have been able to replace.

The continuous and energetic prosecution of the war of attrition will drive the [Japanese] back from their overextended line running from Burma and Siam and the Straits Settlement through the Netherlands Indies to eastern New Guinea and the Solomons. We have good reason to believe that their shipping and their air power cannot support such outposts.

Our naval, and land, and air strength in the Pacific is constantly growing. If the Japanese are basing their future plans for the Pacific on a long period in which they will be permitted to consolidate and exploit their conquered resources, they had better start revising their plans now. I give that to them merely as a helpful suggestion.

We are delivering planes and vital war supplies for the heroic armies of Generalissimo Chiang Kai-shek, and we must do more at all costs.

Our air supply line from India to China across enemy territory continues despite attempted Japanese interference. We have seized the initiative from the Japanese in the air over Burma and now we enjoy superiority. We are bombing Japanese communications, supply dumps, and bases in China, in Indo-China, in Burma.

But we are still far from our main objectives in the war against Japan. Let us remember how far we were a year ago from any of our objectives in the European theatre. We are pushing forward to occupation of positions which in time will enable us to attack the Japanese Islands themselves from the north, from the south, from the east, and from the west.

You have heard it said that while we are succeeding greatly on the fighting front, we are failing miserably on the home front. I think this is another of those immaturities- a false slogan easy to state but untrue in the essential facts.

For the longer this war goes on the clearer it becomes that no one can draw a blue pencil down the middle of a page and call one side 'the fighting front' and the other side 'the home front'. For the two of them are inexorably tied together.

Every combat division, every naval task force, every squadron of fighting planes is dependent for its equipment and ammunition and fuel and food, as indeed it is for its manpower, on the American people in civilian clothes in the offices and in the factories and on the farms at home.

The same kind of careful planning that gained victory in North Africa and Sicily is required, if we are to make victory an enduring reality and do our share in building the kind of peaceful world that will justify the sacrifices made in this war.

The United Nations are substantially agreed on the general objectives for the post-war world. They are also agreed that this is not the time to engage in an international discussion of *all* the terms of peace and *all* the details of the future. Let us win the war first. We must not relax our pressure on the enemy by taking time out to define every boundary and settle every political controversy in every part of the world. The important thing, the all-important thing now, is to get on with the war and to win it.

While concentrating on military victory, we are not neglecting the planning of the things to come, the freedoms which we know will make for more decency and greater justice throughout the world.

Among many other things we are, today, laying plans for the return to civilian life of our gallant men and women in the armed services. They must not be demobilized into an environment of inflation and unemployment, to a place on a bread line, or on a corner selling apples. We must, this time, have plans ready- instead of waiting to do a hasty, inefficient, and ill-considered job at the last moment.

I have assured our men in the armed forces that the American people would not let them down when the war is won.

I hope that the Congress will help in carrying out this assurance, for obviously the executive branch of the Government cannot do it alone. May the Congress do its duty in this regard. The American people will insist on fulfilling this American obligation to the men and women in the armed forces who are winning this war for us.

Of course, the returning soldier and sailor and marine are a part of the problem of demobilizing the rest of the millions of Americans who have been living in a war economy since 1941. That larger objective of reconverting wartime America to a peacetime basis is one for which your government is laying plans to be submitted to the Congress for action.

But the members of the armed forces have been compelled to make greater economic sacrifice and every other kind of sacrifice than the rest of us, and they are entitled to definite action to help take care of their special problems.

The least to which they are entitled, it seems to me, is something like this:

First, mustering-out pay to every member of the armed forces and merchant marine when he or she is honorably discharged; mustering-out pay large enough in each case to cover a reasonable period of time between his discharge and the finding of a new job.

Secondly, in case no job is found after diligent search, then unemployment insurance if the individual registers with the United States Employment Service.

Third, an opportunity for members of the armed services to get further education or trade training at the cost of the government.

Fourth, allowance of credit to all members of the armed forces, under unemployment compensation and Federal old-age and survivors' insurance, for their period of service. For these purposes they ought to be treated as if they had continued their employment in private industry.

Fifth, improved and liberalized provisions for hospitalization, for rehabilitation, for medical care of disabled members of the armed forces and the merchant marine.

And finally, Sixth, sufficient pensions for disabled members of the armed forces.

Your Government is drawing up other serious, constructive plans for certain immediate forward moves. They concern food, manpower, and other domestic problems that tie in with our armed forces.

Within a few weeks I shall speak with you again in regard to definite actions to be taken by the executive branch of the Government, and with specific recommendations for new legislation by the Congress.

All our calculations for the future, however, must be based on clear understanding of the problems involved. And that can be gained only by straight thinking- not guess work, not political manipulation.

I confess that I myself am sometimes bewildered by conflicting statements that I see in the press. One day I read an 'authoritative' statement that we will win the war this year, 1943 and the next day comes another statement equally 'authoritative', that the war will still be going on in 1949.

Of course, both extremes, of optimism and pessimism, are wrong.

The length of the war will depend upon the uninterrupted continuance of all-out effort on the fighting fronts and here at home, and that effort is all one.

The American soldier doesn't like the necessity of waging war. And yet if he lays off for a single instant he may lose his own life and sacrifice the lives of his comrades.

By the same token a worker here at home may not like the driving, wartime conditions under which he has to work and live. And yet if he gets complacent or indifferent and slacks on his job, he too may sacrifice the lives of American soldiers and contribute to the loss of an important battle.

The next time anyone says to you that this war is 'in the bag', or says 'it's all over but the shouting', you should ask him these questions:

'Are you working full time on your job?

Are you growing all the food you can?

Are you buying your limit of war bonds?

Are you loyally and cheerfully cooperating with your Government in preventing inflation and profiteering, and in making rationing work with fairness to all?'

'Because if your answer is 'No', then the war is going to last a lot longer than you think'.

The plans we made for the knocking out of Mussolini and his gang have largely succeeded. But we still have to knock out Hitler and his gang, and Tojo and his gang. No one of us pretends that this will be an easy matter. We still have to defeat Hitler and Tojo on their own home grounds. But this will require a far greater concentration of our national energy and our ingenuity and our skill.

It is not too much to say that we must pour into this war the entire strength and intelligence and will power of the United States. We are a great Nation, a rich nation, but we are not so great or so rich that we can afford to waste our substance or the lives or our men by relaxing along the way.

We shall not settle for less than total victory. That is the determination of every American on the fighting fronts. That must be, and will be, the determination of every American here at home."[274]

While elated over Allied victories, FDR cautioned that there was still much fighting to do to win the war and achieve 'total victory'. Hitler, in retaliation for the Italians dropping out of the war, had moved into Italy and occupied the northern two-thirds of the country. Increasingly Hitler's forces were strung out and he had to station a tremendous number of troops in the conquered territories, 1.3 million in France, 612,000 in the Balkans, 486,000 in Denmark and Norway, and 412,000 in Italy. Hitler hoped to forestall an Allied landing along the coast of France, and the German occupation forces worked to establish Hitler's New Order in Europe. Hitler had written of this new order in *Mein Kampf* wherein he had visualized a Greater Germany including all of Central Europe surrounded by a number of associate or satellite nations.[275] The whole community would be integrated economically. Europe's industrial production would be concentrated in Germany and the countries surrounding the Reich would furnish raw materials and act as markets for industrial production. The plan was modified after Hitler failed to capture Soviet Russia following the Battle of Stalingrad.[276] The German plan then became a type of 'Fortress Europe' to defend Germany against Russia and her western allies converging on Europe's center.

Within German occupied Europe repression became a more blatant aim of Nazism and the concentration camps started before the war became not only places for Jews and revolutionaries but places to train SS troops in brutal tactics. They were to provide human guinea pigs for scientific experiments with SS doctors inoculating healthy patients with typhus and malaria virus to see the effects, and performing selective breeding experiments. Special extermination camps were equipped with huge gas chambers and crematoriums, the bodies being rendered into fat for use in soap and the gold from their teeth was collected and melted into bars. The camps were super efficient hells.[277] German atrocities made Allied leaders even more determined to win the war and wipeout Nazism forever .

---

[274] Samuel I. Rosenman, Public Papers and Addresses of Franklin D. Roosevelt (New York: Harper & Brothers, 1950) Vol 12, pp. 326-336.

[275] H. Stuart Hughes, Contemporary Europe: A History (Englewood Cliffs, NJ: Prentice-Hall, 1966), pp. 236-255; William L. Shirer, The Rise and Fall of the Third Reich (New York: Simon and Schuster, 1960 republished 1990); Alan Bullock, Hitler: A Study in Tyranny (Harmondsworth, England: Penguin Books, 1962).

[276] John Erickson, The Road to Stalingrad (London: Cassell, 2003

[277] H. Stuart Hughes, Contemporary Europe: A History, pp. 249-250; Eugen Kogon, The Theory and Practice of Hell: The German Concentration Camps and the System Behind Them (London: Secker and Warburg, 1950) translated by Heinz Norden; Eugen Kogon, Hermann Langbein, and

When Italy surrendered to the Allies on September 8, 1943 it took up the sword against its former ally Germany. American sentiments now shifted to the belief that the fascist government had been corrupt and our enemy, but the Italian people were our friends. On the eve of the Allied invasion of Normandy, Rome was finally liberated. FDR then journeyed to Cairo and Teheran to confer with his wartime Allies on strategy and returned to inform Americans of the situation in Europe and the Middle East in a Christmas Eve radio broadcast on December 24, 1943:

> My Friends:
> I have recently returned from extensive journeyings in the region of the Mediterranean and as far as the borders of Russia. I have conferred with the leaders of Britain and Russia and China on military matters of the present, especially on plans for stepping up our successful attack on our enemies as quickly as possible and from many different points of the compass.
> On this Christmas Eve there are over 10,000,000 men in the armed forces of the United States alone. One year ago 1,700,000 were serving overseas. Today, this figure has been more than doubled to 3,800,000 on duty overseas. By next July 1 that number overseas will rise to over 5,000,000 men and women.
> That this is truly a world war was demonstrated to me when arrangements were being made with our overseas broadcasting agencies for the time to speak today to our soldiers, sailors, and marines, and merchant seamen in every part of the world. In fixing the time for this broadcast, we took into consideration that at this moment here in the United States, and in the Caribbean and on the northeast coast of South America, it is afternoon. In Alaska and in Hawaii and the mid-Pacific, it is still morning. In Iceland, in Great Britain, in North Africa, in Italy and the Middle East, it is now evening.
> In the Southwest Pacific, in Australia, in China and Burma and India, it is already Christmas Day. So we can correctly say that at this moment, in those Far Eastern parts where Americans are fighting, today is tomorrow.
> But everywhere throughout the world, throughout this war that covers the world, there is a special spirit that has warmed our hearts since our earliest childhood- a spirit that brings us close to our homes, our families, our friends and neighbors- the Christmas spirit of 'peace on earth, good will toward men'. It is an unquenchable spirit.
> During the past years of international gangsterism and brutal aggression in Europe and in Asia, our Christmas celebrations have been darkened with apprehension for the future. We have said, 'Merry Christmas, Happy New Year', but we have known in our hearts that the clouds which have hung over our world have prevented us from saying it with full sincerity and conviction.

Adalbert Ruckerl, eds., Nazi Mass Murder: A Documentary History of the Use of Poison Gas (New Haven: Yale University Press, 1994) translated by Mary Scott and Caroline Lloyd-Morris.

And even this year, we still have much to face in the way of further suffering, and sacrifice, and personal tragedy. Our men, who have been through the fierce battles in the Solomons, the Gilberts, Tunisia and Italy know, from their own experience and knowledge of modern war, that many bigger and costlier battles are still to be fought.

But on Christmas Eve this year, I can say to you that at last we may look forward into the future with real, substantial confidence that, however great the cost, 'peace on earth, good will toward men' can be and will be realized and insured. This year I *can* say that. Last year I could not do more than express a hope. Today I express a certainty, though the cost may be high and the time may be long.

Within the past year, within the past few weeks, history has been made, and it is far better history for the whole human race than any that we have known, or even dared to hope for, in these tragic times through which we pass.

A great beginning was made in the Moscow conference last October by Mr. Molotov, Mr. Eden and our own Mr. Hull. There and then the way was paved for the later meetings.

At Cairo and Teheran we devoted ourselves not only to military matters; we devoted ourselves also to consideration of the future, to plans for the kind of world which alone can justify all the sacrifices of this war.

Of course, as you all know, Mr. Churchill and I have happily met many times before, and we know and understand each other very well. Indeed, Mr. Churchill has become known and beloved by many millions of Americans, and the heartfelt prayers of all of us have been with this great citizen of the world in his recent serious illness.

The Cairo and Teheran Conferences, however, gave me my first opportunity to meet the Generalissimo Chiang Kai-shek,[278] and Marshal Stalin, and to sit down at the table with these unconquerable men and talk with them face to face. We had planned to talk to each other across the table at Cairo and Teheran; but we soon found that we were all on the same side of the table. We came to the conferences with faith in each other. But we needed the personal contact. And now we have supplemented faith with definite knowledge.

It was well worth traveling thousands of miles over land and sea to bring about this personal meeting, and to gain the heartening assurance that we are absolutely agreed with one another on all the major objectives, and on the military means of obtaining them.

At Cairo, Prime Minister Churchill and I spent four days with the Generalissimo Chiang Kai-shek. It was the first time that we had an opportunity to go over the complex situation in the Far East with him personally. We were

---

[278] Xiaoyuan Liu, Partnership for Disorder: China, the United States, and Their Policies for the Postwar Disposition of the Japanese Empire, 1941-1945 (Cambridge, England: Cambridge

able not only to settle upon definite military strategy, but also to discuss certain long-range principles which we believe can assure peace in the Far East for many generations to come.

Those principles are as simple as they are fundamental. They involve the restoration of stolen property to its rightful owners, and the recognition of the rights of millions of people in the Far East to build up their own forms of self-government without molestation. Essential to all peace and security in the Pacific and in the rest of the world is the permanent elimination of the Empire of Japan as a potential force of aggression. Never again must our soldiers, sailors and marines be compelled to fight from island to island as they are fighting so gallantly and so successfully today.

Increasingly powerful forces are now hammering at the Japanese at many points over an enormous arc which curves down through the Pacific from the Aleutians to the Jungles of Burma. Our own Army and Navy, our Air Forces, the Australians and New Zealanders, the Dutch, and the British land, air, and sea forces are all forming a band of steel which is slowly but surely closing in on Japan.

On the mainland of Asia, under the Generalissimo's leadership, the Chinese ground and air forces augmented by American air forces are playing a vital part in starting the drive which will push the invaders into the sea.

Following out the military decisions at Cairo, General Marshall has just flown around the world and has had conferences with General MacArthur and Admiral Nimitz, conferences which will spell plenty of bad news for the [Japanese] in the not too far distant future.

I met in the Generalissimo a man of great vision, great courage, and a remarkably keen understanding of the problems of today and tomorrow. We discussed all the manifold military plans for striking at Japan with decisive force from many directions, and I believe I can say that he returned to Chungking with the positive assurance of total victory over our common enemy. Today we and the Republic of China are closer together than ever before in deep friendship and in unity of purpose.

After the Cairo conference, Mr. Churchill and I went by airplane to Teheran. There we met with Marshal Stalin. We talked with complete frankness on every conceivable subject connected with the winning of the war and the establishment of a durable peace after the war.

Within three days of intense and consistently amicable discussions, we agreed on every point concerned with the launching of a gigantic attack upon Germany.

The Russian army will continue its stern offensives on Germany's eastern front, the Allied armies in Italy and Africa will bring relentless pressure on

---

University Press, 2002); Robert Dalleck, Franklin D. Roosevelt and American Foreign Policy, 1932-1945 (New York: Oxford University Press, 1979).

Germany from the south, and now the encirclement will be complete as great American and British forces attack from other points of the compass.

The Commander selected to lead the combined attack from these other points is General Dwight D. Eisenhower. His performances in Africa, in Sicily, and in Italy have been brilliant. He knows by practical and successful experience the way to coordinate air, sea, and land power. All of these will be under his control. Lieutenant General Carl Spaatz will command the entire American strategic bombing force operating against Germany.

General Eisenhower gives up his command in the Mediterranean to a British officer whose name is being announced by Mr. Churchill. We now pledge that new Commander that our powerful ground, sea, and air forces in the vital Mediterranean area will stand by his side until every objective in that bitter theater is attained.

Both of these new Commanders will have American and British subordinate Commanders whose names will be announced in a few days.

During the last two days at Teheran, Marshal Stalin, Mr. Churchill and I looked ahead to the days and months and years that will follow Germany's defeat. We were united in determination that Germany must be stripped of her military might and be given no opportunity within the foreseeable future to regain that might.

The United Nations have no intention to enslave the German people. We wish them to have a normal chance to develop, in peace, as useful and respectable members of the European family. But we most certainly emphasize that word 'respectable' for we intend to rid them once and for all of Nazism and Prussian militarism and the fantastic and disastrous notion that they constitute the 'master race'.

We did discuss international relationships from the point of view of big, broad objectives, rather than details. But on the basis of what we did discuss, I can say even today that I do not think any insoluble differences will arise among Russia, Great Britain and the United States.

In these conferences we were concerned with basic principles, principles which involve the security and the welfare and the standard of living of human beings in countries large and small.

To use an American and somewhat ungrammatical colloquialism, I may say that I 'got along fine' with Marshal Stalin. He is a man who combines a tremendous, relentless determination with a stalwart good humor. I believe he is truly representative of the heart and soul of Russia; and I believe that we are going to get along very well with him and the Russian people, very well indeed.

Britain, Russia, China, and the United States and their allies represent more than three-quarters of the total population of the earth. As long as these four Nations with great military power stick together in determination to keep the peace there will be no possibility of an aggressor nation arising to start another world war.

But those four powers must be united with and cooperate with the freedom-loving peoples of Europe, and Asia, and Africa and the Americas. The rights of every Nation, large or small, must be respected and guarded as jealously as are the rights of every individual within our own Republic.

The doctrine that the strong shall dominate the weak is the doctrine of our enemies, and we reject it.

But, at the same time, we are agreed that if force is necessary to keep international peace, international force will be applied for as long as it may be necessary.

It has been our steady policy, and it is certainly a common sense policy, that the right of each Nation to freedom must be measured by the willingness of that Nation to fight for freedom. And today we salute our unseen allies in occupied countries, the underground resistance groups and the armies of liberation. They will provide potent forces against our enemies, when the day of the counter-invasion comes.

Through the development of science the world has become so much smaller that we have had to discard the geographical yardsticks of the past. For instance, through our early history the Atlantic and Pacific Oceans were believed to be walls of safety for the United States. Time and distance made it physically possible, for example, for us and for the other American Republics to obtain and maintain independence against infinitely stronger powers. Until recently very few people, even military experts, thought that the day would ever come when we might have to defend our Pacific coast against Japanese threats of invasion.

At the outbreak of the first World War relatively few people thought that our ships and shipping would be menaced by German submarines on the high seas or that the German militarists would ever attempt to dominate any Nation outside of central Europe.

After the Armistice in 1918, we thought and hoped that the militaristic philosophy of Germany had been crushed; and being full of the milk of human kindness we spent the next twenty years disarming, while the Germans whined so pathetically that the other Nations permitted them, and even helped them, to rearm.

For too many years we lived on pious hopes that aggressor and warlike Nations would learn and understand and carry out the doctrine of purely voluntary peace.

The well-intentioned but ill-fated experiments of former years did not work. It is my hope that we will not try them again. No, that is putting it too weakly, it is my intention to do all that I humanly can as President and Commander in Chief to see to it that these tragic mistakes shall not be made again.

There have always been cheerful idiots in this country who believed that there would be no more war for us if everybody in America would only return into their homes and lock their front doors behind them. Assuming that their motives were of the highest, events have shown how unwilling they were to face the facts.

The overwhelming majority of all the people in the world want peace. Most of them are fighting for the attainment of peace, not just a truce, not just an armistice, but peace that is as strongly enforced and as durable as mortal man can make it. If we are willing to fight for peace now, is it not good logic that we should use force if necessary, in the future, to keep the peace?

I believe, and I think I can say, that the other three great Nations who are fighting so magnificently to gain peace are in complete agreement that we must be prepared to keep the peace by force. If the people of Germany and Japan are made to realize thoroughly that the world is not going to let them break out again, it is possible, and, I hope, probable, that they will abandon the philosophy of aggression, the belief that they can gain the whole world even at the risk of losing their own souls.

I shall have more to say about the Cairo and Teheran Conferences when I make my report to the Congress in about two weeks' time. And, on that occasion, I shall also have a great deal to say about certain conditions here at home.

But today I wish to say that in all my travels, at home and abroad, it is the sight of our soldiers and sailors and their magnificent achievements which have given me the greatest inspiration and the greatest encouragement for the future.

To the members of our armed forces, to their wives, mothers and fathers, I want to affirm the great faith and confidence that we have in General Marshall and in Admiral King, who direct all of our armed might throughout the world. Upon them falls the responsibility of planning the strategy of determining where and when we shall fight. Both of these men have already gained high places in American history, places which will record in that history many evidences of their military genius that cannot be published today.

Some of our men overseas are now spending their third Christmas far from home. To them and to all others overseas or soon to go overseas, I can give assurance that it is the purpose of their Government to win this war and to bring them home at the earliest possible time.

We here in the United States had better be sure that when our soldiers and sailors do come home they will find an America in which they are given full opportunities for education, and rehabilitation, social security, and employment and business enterprise under the free American system, and that they will find a Government which, by their votes as American citizens, they have had a full share in electing.

The American people have had every reason to know that this is a tough and destructive war. On my trip abroad, I talked with many military men who had faced our enemies in the field. These hard headed realists testify to the strength and skill and resourcefulness of the enemy generals and men whom we must beat before final victory is won. The war is now reaching the stage where we shall all have to look forward to large casualty lists, dead, wounded and missing.

War entails just that. There is no easy road to victory. And the end is not yet in sight.

I have been back only for a week. It is fair that I should tell you my impression. I think I see a tendency in some of our people here to assume a quick ending of the war, that we have already gained the victory. And, perhaps as a result of this false reasoning, I think I discern an effort to resume or even encourage an outbreak of partisan thinking and talking. I hope I am wrong. For, surely, our first and most foremost tasks are all concerned with winning the war and winning a just peace that will last for generations.

The massive offensives which are in the making both in Europe and the Far East will require every ounce of energy and fortitude that we and our Allies can summon on the fighting fronts and in all the workshops at home. As I have said before, you cannot order up a great attack on a Monday and demand that it be delivered on Saturday.

Less than a month ago I flew in a big Army transport plane over the little town of Bethlehem, in Palestine.

Tonight, on Christmas Eve, all men and women everywhere who love Christmas are thinking of that ancient town and of the star of faith that shone there more than nineteen centuries ago.

American boys are fighting today in snow-covered mountains, in malarial jungles, on blazing deserts; they are fighting on the far stretches of the sea and above the clouds, and fighting for the thing for which they struggle. I think it is best symbolized by the message that came out of Bethlehem.

On behalf of the American people, your own people, I send this Christmas message to you, to you who are in our armed forces:

In our hearts are prayers for you and for all your comrades in arms who fight to rid the world of evil.

We ask God's blessing upon you, upon your fathers, mothers, and wives and children, all your loved ones at home.

We ask that the comfort of God's grace shall be granted to those who are sick and wounded, and to those who are prisoners of war in the hands of the enemy, waiting for the day when they will again be free.

And we ask that God receive and cherish those who have given their lives, and that He keep them in honor and in the grateful memory of their Countrymen forever.

God bless all of you who fight our battles on this Christmas Eve.

God bless us all. Keep us strong in our faith that we fight for a better day for human kind, here and everywhere."[279]

---

[279] Samuel I. Rosenman, Public Papers and Addresses of Franklin D. Roosevelt (New York: Harper & Brothers, 1950) Vol 12, pp. 553-563.

Thus FDR kept the American public informed as to the war successes with the fall of Italy, and how discussions and planning continued among the Allied leaders in their wartime conferences over how the invasion of France should be accomplished to open up yet another military front to defeat Germany. Operation Overlord, the code name for the Allied Normandy invasion, was designed by the Supreme Headquarters Allied Expeditionary Forces (SHAEF) led by General Eisenhower. He explained what Operation Overlord should entail: "It is imperative," he advocated, "that our Air Force would be at the chosen moment, overwhelming in strength." "That the air bombers would have to isolate the attack area from re-enforcement; that the U-boat could be so effectively countered that our convoys could count on a safe Atlantic crossing." "That our supporting naval vessels would batter down local defenses; that specialized landing craft could be available in such numbers as to make possible the pouring ashore of a great army through an initial breach."[280] Not until May of 1944 were all of Eisenhower's conditions met. Eisenhower's message from his SHAEF headquarters to his Allied troops before the Normandy invasion was also memorable:

"Soldiers, Sailors and Airmen of the Allied Expeditionary Force! You are about to embark upon the Great Crusade, toward which we have striven these many months. The eyes of the world are upon you. The hopes and prayers of liberty-loving people everywhere march with you. In company with our brave Allies and brothers-in-arms on other Fronts, you will bring about the destruction of the German war machine, the elimination of Nazi tyranny over the oppressed peoples of Europe, and security for ourselves in a free world. Your task will not be an easy one. Your enemy is well trained, well equipped and battle hardened. He will fight savagely. But this is the year 1944! Much has happened since the Nazi triumphs of 1940-41. The United Nations have inflicted upon the Germans great defeats, in open battle, man-to-man. Our air offensive has seriously reduced their strength in the air and their capacity to wage war on the ground. Our Home Fronts have given us an overwhelming superiority in weapons and munitions of war, and placed at our disposal great reserves of trained fighting men. The tide has turned! The free men of the world are marching together to Victory!

I have full confidence in your courage and devotion to duty and skill in Battle. We will accept nothing less than full Victory!

Good luck! And let us beseech the blessing of Almighty God upon this great and noble undertaking."[281]

---

[280] Theodore A. Wilson, D-Day 1944 (Lawrence, Kansas: Eisenhower Foundation published by the University of Kansas Press, 1994).
[281] Wilson, D-Day 1944; Gerhard L. Weinberg, A World At Arms: A Global History of World War II (Cambridge, England: Cambridge University Press, 1995).

SIGNED: Dwight D. Eisenhower

On June 6, 1944, D-Day, the invasion of the Normandy beachheads, occurred successfully with landings on Gold, Sword, and Juno beaches. An offensive was launched and in August France was re-captured. Within six weeks of the initial landings, over a million Allied forces were fighting in Brittany and Normandy. On August 25, Paris was liberated by the combined Free French and Allied forces and German forces completely withdrew. Belgium was liberated in September. General George Patton's Third Army broke through France toward Germany with massive tank units.[282] Earlier, before D-Day and following victories at Stalingrad in January 1943 and at Kursk by August 1943, Soviet armies had chased the Germans out of Russia and into Poland and East Prussia in pursuit. Hitler's situation became desperate. With these German defeats morale dropped and there was an attempt on Hitler's life on July 20, 1944 that provided evidence of resistance within the Reich. Had the assassination been successful Rommel would have been proclaimed chief of state and probably the war ended much earlier. After the failure of the plot and the investigation on October 14, 1944, Rommel was abducted from his home and forced to swallow poison.

While the war both in Europe and Asia was winding down, the American political scene domestically was growing a bit more conservative. Congressional refusal in the spring of 1943 to continue the National Resources Planning Board was a symbolic challenge to the whole idea of New Deal planning. And Roosevelt himself quipped that he realized that 'Dr. New Deal', had given way to 'Dr. Win-the-War', as public expectations had changed. Increasingly liberals listened to new voices such as Wendell Willkie whose book *One World* published in 1943 after his trip as a presidential emissary to Britain, the Soviet Union, the Middle East, and China seemed to sum up the best aspirations of American liberal internationalists. But during the presidential campaign of 1944, the Republicans turned to Thomas E. Dewey, governor of New York since 1942. Franklin Roosevelt accepted the nomination of the Democrats to maintain continuity in wartime even though his health was failing. He also chose to run because he felt he may have been the only Democratic candidate to be able to carry the election and he wanted to preserve the New Deal.[283] Senator Harry S. Truman of Missouri

---

[282] Weinberg, A World At Arms: A Global History of World War II; John Morton Blum, V Was for Victory: Politics and American Culture During World War II (New York: Harcourt Brace Jovanovich, 1976).

[283] Frank Freidel, Franklin D. Roosevelt, A Rendezvous With Destiny (Boston: Little, Brown and Company, 1990), pp. 516-517. See also FDR's Annual Message on the State of the Union in Samuel I. Rosenman, Public Papers and Addresses of Franklin D. Roosevelt, Vol 13, pp. 483-507.

was selected as his vice-presidential running mate on the ticket. The campaign was overshadowed by the war and FDR wanted to stand for re-election to win the war for the Allies. Roosevelt received 25.6 million popular votes to Dewey's 22 million and the candidates received 432 and 99 electoral votes respectively.

FDR won re-election to an unprecedented fourth term in November 1944 largely due to the urgencies of war and Americans' confidence in their leader. Roosevelt had capitalized upon the successes of the D-Day invasion the previous June and the subsequent Allied frontal assault on German forces throughout western Europe. America was well on its way to victory after the successful Normandy invasion and FDR had used this theme throughout the 1944 presidential campaign. In his Inaugural Address on Saturday, January 20, 1945 FDR reassured his citizens:

"Mr. Chief Justice, Mr. Vice President, My Friends:
You will understand and, I believe, agree with my wish that the form of this inauguration be simple and its words brief.

We Americans of today, together with our allies, are passing through a period of supreme test. It is a test of our courage, of our resolve, of our wisdom, of our essential democracy.

If we meet that test, successfully and honorably, we shall perform a service of historic importance which men and women and children will honor throughout all time.

As I stand here today, having taken the solemn oath of office in the presence of my fellow countrymen, in the presence of our God, I know that it is America's purpose that we shall not fail.

In the days and in the years that are to come, we shall work for a just and honorable peace, a durable peace, as today we work and fight for total victory in war.

We can and we will achieve such a peace.

We shall strive for perfection. We shall not achieve it immediately, but we still shall strive. We may make mistakes, but *they must never be mistakes which result from faintness of heart or abandonment of moral principle.*

I remember that my old schoolmaster, Dr. Peabody, said, in days that seemed to us then to be secure and untroubled, 'Things in life will not always run smoothly. Sometimes we will be rising toward the heights, then all will seem to reverse itself and start downward. The great fact to remember is that the trend of civilization itself is forever upward; that a line drawn through the middle of the peaks and the valleys of the centuries always has an upward trend'.

Our Constitution of 1787 was not a perfect instrument; it is not perfect yet. But it provided a firm base upon which all manner of men, of all races and colors and creeds, could build our solid structure of democracy.

> Today, in this year of war, 1945, we have learned lessons, at a fearful cost, and we shall profit by them.
>
> We have learned that we cannot live alone, at peace; that our own well-being is dependent on the well-being of other Nations far away. We have learned that we must live as men and not as ostriches, nor as dogs in the manger.
>
> We have learned to be citizens of the world, members of the human community.
>
> We have learned the simple truth, as Emerson said, that 'the only way to have a friend is to be one'.
>
> We can gain no lasting peace if we approach it with suspicion and mistrust or with fear. We can gain it only if we proceed with the understanding and the confidence and the courage which flow from conviction.
>
> The Almighty God has blessed our land in many ways. He has given our people stout hearts and strong arms with which to strike mighty blows for freedom and truth. He has given to our country a faith which has become the hope of all peoples in an anguished world.
>
> So we pray to Him now for the vision to see our way clearly, to see the way that leads to a better life for ourselves and for all our fellow men and to the achievement of His will to peace on earth."[284]

Due to the war, FDR had made his remarks brief and dispensed with any inaugural balls to economize. On December 16, 1944, only a few weeks before FDR's fourth inaugural address, Hitler had launched a last ditch attempt to hold back the advancing Allies from Normandy with a counterattack against the center of their military lines in the Ardennes Forest producing the Battle of the Bulge.[285] The Germans had hoped to break through to the Belgian port of Antwerp by splitting the Allied forces. The Germans had driven a swath or 'bulge' about 50 miles into Belgium. But the American forces held at Bastogne and Hitler's counter-offensive failed. The iron ring was pulling tighter around Germany with the British-French and American forces in the West closing in while Russian forces moved from the East. British and American allied forces had crossed the Rhine into Germany proper by March 1945. Allied bombers had pounded Berlin and German industrial sites into rubble by the spring of 1945, despite the loss of 21,000 bombers and 140,000 British and American air deaths. These high-flying bombing raids caused massive German civilian casualties with the firestorms generated with raids on Dresden and Hamburg. Germany's plans to utilize long-

---

[284] Samuel I. Rosenman, Public Papers and Addresses of Franklin D. Roosevelt (New York: Harper & Brothers, 1950) Vol 13, pp. 523-525.
[285] Snyder, The War: A Concise History, 1939-1945; Louis L. Snyder, Hitler's Third Reich: A Documentary History (Chicago: Nelson-Hall, 1981); H.R. (Hugh Redwald) Trevor-Roper, The Last Days of Hitler (New York: Collier Books, 1962).

range V-1 and V-2 rockets and planes propelled by jet engines had not been successful, but their threat had stimulated American minds to create weapons of even greater range and superior fire-power. American scientists through the Manhattan project would develop the atomic bomb.[286]

As victory over Germany seemed imminent the Yalta conference had been held in the Russian Crimea in February 1945 just after FDR's fourth inauguration. Midway through the war in January 1943 at Casablanca the Allies had agreed on unconditional surrender. And at Cairo in November 1943 they had reached an accord that all territory taken from China by Japan would be returned. At Yalta in February 1945 Roosevelt, Churchill, and Stalin, the Big Three, seeing the war was coming to a victorious end, agreed to divide Germany into four military zones so that Germany might be disarmed and demilitarized. The Allied powers agreed to help liberated Europeans solve their social and economic problems after the war by democratic means. And Stalin agreed to declare war against Japan three months after the defeat of Germany to aid the Allies in the Pacific theater that seemed like a major concession at the time.[287] And to complete the Yalta accords, the wartime military Allied alliance was turned into a permanent world organization, the United Nations.

As the Russians made their last assault on Berlin, Hitler committed suicide in an air raid bunker beneath the city after marrying his mistress Eva Braun. Prior to this act, he had dismissed Goering and Himmler from the Nazi party for trying to close down the war behind his back. May 8, 1945 was proclaimed Victory in Europe (V-E) Day and the Third Reich that was supposed to last a thousand years had died in twelve.[288] The Potsdam conference was held to divide Germany into the four military zones of occupation and to plan for the de-Nazification of Germany. All authority was to be placed in the hands of military provisional governments in the occupied sectors, and Germany's boundaries were fixed at her 1938 status.

Meanwhile events accelerated in Asia. Rainbow 5 had been the code name given to the overall Allied strategy for the Pacific after the attack on Pearl Harbor. This called for a defensive stand in the Pacific until a major victory could be won to launch a major counter-offensive. Initially Rainbow 5 accepted the loss of Guam, Wake, and the Philippines. Douglas MacArthur thought in 1941 that he could save the Philippines largely with the B-17 bomber, the Flying Fortress. But they lacked the range to attack Japanese cities and the accuracy to consistently hit

---

[286] Richard Rhodes, The Making of the Atomic Bomb (New York: Simon and Schuster, 1986).
[287] John L. Snell, ed., The Meaning of Yalta: Big Three Diplomacy and the New Balance of Power (Baton Rouge: Louisiana State University Press, 1956)
[288] Trevor-Roper, The Last Days of Hitler.

targets on the seas. On December 23, 1941 MacArthur had been forced to evacuate Manila and moved to the Bataan Peninsula and established his headquarters on Corregidor. By this defensive move, he had stalled the Japanese for four months but merely prolonged the inevitable that was the loss of the Philippines. President Roosevelt had then ordered MacArthur to leave Corregidor when it was evident that the American bastion was about to fall. MacArthur was smuggled to Mindinao and then Australia with his wife and son. The American forces on Corregidor surrendered on April 9, 1942 and experienced the Bataan death march from Marveles to San Fernando.[289] The Japanese then swept to a series of victories taking the Solomon Islands, New Guinea, Midway, the Aleutian chain, Wake, the Marshalls and the Gilberts. But the U.S. naval forces soon went on the offensive. The Battle of the Coral Sea was a turning point in the Pacific War. In an extra-ordinary battle between carrier-based aircraft, the Americans turned back the enemy. This was the first sea battle in which the ships fired no shots, indeed they did not come within sight of one another. The battle was won by using planes launched at sea. Shortly after the Battle of the Coral Sea, Admiral Yamamoto had decided to force the American fleet into a showdown by assaulting Midway Island, west of the main islands of Hawaii. But his aircraft carriers never reached their destination as on June 4 Americans bombed four large Japanese aircraft carriers destroying 300 planes. The United States force lost only the *Yorktown* and this American victory strengthened the American military strategy in the Pacific.[290] The American counter-offensive had been waged at Guadalcanal in the Solomon Islands as intelligence reports indicated that a Japanese air-strip was being constructed there, and the Americans swept in to victory and the Japanese abandoned the island in February 1943.

This had begun a long offensive thrust toward Tokyo by American forces. The path involved capturing Pacific islands and atolls fortified by Japanese airstrips and harbors from Micronesia to the Aleutians. Two strategies were used. One plan was advocated by the Army and General Douglas MacArthur who was to advance from the South Pacific through New Guinea to the Philippines and then on to Japan. The second strategy was advanced by the Navy and Admiral Chester Nimitz who advanced through the central pacific to Formosa and the China Coast and thence to Japan after capturing key islands in the Gilberts,

---

[289] Snyder, The War: A Concise History, 1939-1945.
[290] Conrad Black, Franklin Delano Roosevelt, Champion of Freedom (New York: Public Affairs, 2003), pp. 738-741, 762-763, 772-774, 976; Ted Morgan, FDR, A Biography (New York: Simon and Schuster, 1985), p. 641.

Marshalls, and Marianas.[291] Eventually both plans were adopted with parallel attack routes and both plans utilized leapfrogging or island hopping over Japanese fortified islands to achieve their objectives. Much of America's early strategy and diplomacy with Japan had been aimed at protecting the political integrity of China. But this design was undermined by the local civil war in China that had broken out between the Nationalists led by Chiang and the Communists led by Mao which had severely weakened the former united stance against Japan.

By February 1944 the Fifth fleet under Admiral Sprurance steamed toward and captured Truk, the so-called the Gibraltar of the Pacific, a great air base in the Carolinas. Next Saipan fell to the American offensive after a ghoulish *banzai* charge and after Japanese citizens hurled their children and themselves over the steep cliffs along the northern section of the island. Saipan would be a base from which the U.S. B-29 Superfort planes coming into production would be launched. The fall of Saipan marked the fall of Tojo as Japanese war leader. Guam and Tinian, where napalm was first used, became captured bases and strongholds for the Superforts after August 1944. MacArthur had promised to return when he had evacuated the Philippines, and MacArthur's returning forces captured Mindanao during a military campaign in November 1944. On October 20, 1944 he had arrived on the beach at Leyte saying 'people of the Philippines, I have returned'. A few days later at the Battle of Leyte Gulf, the war's single greatest naval battle, the American navy completed the destruction of Japanese sea power and reduced its air force to suicide kamikaze pilots with only a defensive strike force. MacArthur's forces liberated Luzon in the Philippines in February 1945 fulfilling his promises.[292] Japanese occupied Iwo Jima was captured in March and Okinawa surrendered in June 1945. Meanwhile, General Stilwell had been flying supplies 'Over the Hump', the Himalayas at 17,000 feet, to keep the Chinese forces led by Chiang-Kai-shek (Jiang Jieshi) reinforced to continue their war in China against the Japanese occupying forces. Soon the B-29s, the Superfortresses, took off in the Marianas and blasted Japanese cities including Tokyo which had experienced a huge firestorm during March 9-10, 1945.

Near the end of March 1945 FDR went to Warm Springs for rest and relaxation following his fourth inauguration January 20, 1945 and his arduous trip to Yalta in February 1945. On April 12, 1945 while at his cottage in Warm

---

[291] David Reynolds, In Command of History: Winston Churchill and the Second World War (New York: Random House, 2005); David Reynolds, Creation of the Anglo-American Alliance, 1937-1941 (Chapel Hill: University of North Carolina Press, 1982).

[292] Black, Franklin Delano Roosevelt, Champion of Freedom, p. 1046; Herbert Feis, China Tangle: The American Effort in China From Pearl Harbor to the Marshall Mission (Princeton: Princeton University Press, 1953).

Springs at his spa retreat Franklin D. Roosevelt was working on some letters that had just arrived in a pouch of official documents from Washington brought by William D. Hassett his appointments secretary. At the same time he chatted informally with a few relatives and visiting friends, and was having his portrait painted as he sat working at a small table. Just before lunch he put the finishing touches on his Jefferson Day speech to be delivered the next day and concluded it with "the only limit to our realization of tomorrow will be our doubts of today. Let us move forward with strong and active faith." Suddenly, the president experienced a staggering headache, saying "I have a terrific pain in the back of my head."[293] He had suffered a cerebral hemorrhage and would soon die after lapsing into a coma. He was carried by his valet and a waiter from the living room to an adjoining bedroom to rest. "The President's breathing was loud and became labored" and then stopped completely at 3:35 p.m. as Drs. Bruenn and Paullin consulted on his treatment. An attempt to recover the president was made by injecting adrenalin directly into FDR's heart but he did not respond. The President died in a bed at the cottage, perhaps a casualty of war stresses just as so many other soldiers had died in combat. Franklin Delano Roosevelt's name "headed the following day's official list of American war dead." At the White House, Eleanor received the news of her husband's death after she returned from making a speech to the Sulgrave Club in Washington, D.C. and then journeyed to Warm Springs to take charge of funeral arrangements. FDR's body was returned to Washington by train with thousands of mourners hailing his achievements along the way in a spirit akin to the death of Abraham Lincoln. His body lay in state at the Capitol and thousands came to pay their respects. FDR's sons, involved in various war fronts, could not immediately come home, but Jimmy soon traveled from the Philippines but not in time for the services. Franklin Jr. and John were in Okinawa and could not leave their war units. Son Elliott and his sister Anna attended their father's funeral procession in Washington with Eleanor. Following the nation's grateful tribute, FDR's body was conducted to Hyde Park where there was a family ceremony and internment in the Rose Garden completed by a gun salute from West Point cadets as the casket was lowered into the ground. Wishing to show their respect, at a pre-arranged moment, all Americans stopped whatever they were doing and observed a two-minute silence as a final farewell to their commander in chief.[294] FDR was the citizens' beloved great leader who had

---

[293] Morgan, FDR, A Biography, pp. 764, 767-769; Black, Franklin Delano Roosevelt, Champion of Freedom, pp. 1109-1110, 1115, 1119-1122; Nathan Miller, F.D.R., An Intimate History (Garden City, NY: Doubelday and Company, 1983), pp. 509-510.
[294] Collier, Peter with David Horowitz, The Roosevelts, An American Saga (New York: Simon and Schuster, 1994), pp. 432-433.

brought Americans out of the Depression and was the champion of freedom and architect of victory over the Axis. FDR would remain the greatest presidential leader of the greatest generation of the Twentieth Century.

Americans and the Allied powers followed FDR's plan for ending the war and for establishing the peace. By July 1945 at the Potsdam conference the Allies warned Japanese leaders to surrender or face 'prompt and utter destruction'. The new president Harry S. Truman ordered the atomic bomb to be dropped on Hiroshima August 6 and on Nagasaki August 9 when there was no official response to the Potsdam conference's ultimatum to surrender. On August 8, 1945 the Soviet Union had formally declared war on Japan as promised earlier at the Yalta conference when the Allies believed they would need Russian aid in finishing the Pacific War. Stalin sent forces into Manchuria and would later demand concessions in the Pacific based upon his willingness to aid in this theater. After the bombing of Nagasaki, the Japanese officials pressed for peace, receiving assurances that the position of the Emperor would not be violated, and formally surrendered on August 14, 1945, named Victory over Japan Day [V-J Day]. General Douglas MacArthur presided over the formal signing of the unconditional surrender documents on the battleship the *USS Missouri* in Tokyo Bay on September 2, 1945.[295] The war was over.

Into Truman's hands scientists had placed the newly developed atomic bomb in July 1945. Truman decided between varying opinions on the bomb, evaluating whether it was 'the most terrible thing every discovered', or the device that 'would bring the war to an end'. Truman decided that it would save American lives, possibly end the war through a revolution within Japan or the Emperor's intercession and exclude Russia from any peace making role in Japan if the war could be ended soon enough. Moral arguments over the decision to use the bomb remained but it had the desired effect, it had ended and had certainly shortened the war.

America had won the war on the same basis as World War I, air power and armor. In both wars, America's entry turned the tide for the Allies with her superior industrial power, additional manpower, and control of the high seas. American casualties were relatively light when comparing 292,131 battle deaths with 7.5 million for Russia, 35 million Germans, 1.2 million Japanese, and 2.2 million Chinese. World War II also affected a new balance of power between the USSR and the United States precipitating the Cold War.

---

[295] Douglas MacArthur, Reminiscences; William Manchester, American Caesar: Douglas MacArthur, 1880-1964 (Boston: Little, Brown, 1978); Herbert Feis, Japan Subdued: The Atomic Bomb and the End of the War in the Pacific (Princeton, NJ: Princeton University Press, 1961).

The United States emerged from World War II a relatively unified, powerful, and confident nation. Victory had given Americans pride in the prowess of their armed services, confidence in the American mode of productivity, and in the endurance of the American way of life. One of the truly positive gains to come out of World War II was the United Nations. FDR had planned mightily for the postwar period. Early in 1942 FDR had gained agreement of twenty-six nations, including the allied powers, for a United Nations Declaration.[296] This affirmed the Atlantic Charter and solidified the warm aims. As the war was winding down, FDR convened the United Nations Monetary and Financial Conference at Bretton Woods, New Hampshire, where the International Monetary Fund was established and the International Bank for Reconstruction and Development was launched. These two institutions would stabilize the world's currencies and begin to rebuild a war-torn globe. The United Nations charter was drawn up and signed at Dumbarton Oaks, in Washington D.C. providing a permanent world peace-keeping organization that had been so coveted by President Roosevelt.

The world after World War II was a world fashioned by Franklin Delano Roosevelt with its emphasis upon international peace-keeping through the United Nations, the victorious nations who had fought in the war on the side of the Allies. It was a white and black world where morality and righteousness had vanquished evil with the defeat of the Axis. The U.S. would remain in the center of world power and ultimately triumph further after the fragmentation of the Soviet bloc, and the eclipse of the once grand British Empire.

FDR made the position of the U.S. President into a post of respected world leader and mentor to smaller developing nations. Of the Big Three, Roosevelt's image would shape the new world in the post-1945 decades rather than the image of Churchill or Stalin. FDR died a hero. Perhaps it was merciful that he died knowing that the Allies would win the peace as well as the war through the formation of the UN.

The legacy of FDR was the New Deal political coalition composed of intellectuals, the urban working and middle classes, the former unemployed, the poor, southern and western farmers, women, blacks, and mainstream Democrats [and many Republicans] who used the new liberalism of the New Deal to secure the gains advanced by the early political progressives. This coalition, working often on a bi-partisan basis, would sustain the Democrats in power for a generation and continue to move liberal views forward. Structurally the New Deal created new institutions

---

[296] Melvyn Leffler, A Preponderance of Power: National Security, The Truman Administration and the Cold War (Stanford, CA: Stanford University Press, 1992); William E. Leuchtenberg, In the Shadow of FDR: From Harry Truman to Ronald Reagan (Ithaca, NY: Cornell University Press, 2001).

which greatly expanded the federal government and ideologically sustained the view that the government should intervene in the economy for social betterment of its citizens rather than stand on the sidelines as an umpire. FDR's presidency developed governmental guarantees for assistance to the unemployed, the elderly and the poor, while protecting the rights of labor to organize and collectively bargain. His presidency had established a minimum wage law, abolished child labor, established the forty-hour workweek, and combated monopoly power to 'distribute wealth and products more equitably'. FDR's New Deal had stabilized banking, insured deposits, regulated financial markets, subsidized agriculture, generated public power, lower utilities rates, and built low-income housing. President Roosevelt cultivated close relations with the Washington Press Corps and used his Fireside Chats to inform the public of his policies, a tradition that continued by recent presidents. The depression had ended during the war due to massive government spending on armaments and defense. To ease the transition to peace FDR had crafted the 'G.I Bill of Rights' or the Servicemen's Readjustment Act of 1944 and this went into effect at war's end. FDR's view of seeking to reform society for the betterment of all citizens would resonate in the future with the New Frontier and the Great Society. FDR conducted an A+ presidency that established the U.S. President as the world's greatest leader and America as the world's greatest power.

FDR was a *truly great man and a truly great president* because he had restored faith in America's insitutions to the doubters and downtrodden, saved the U.S. economy from the throes of international Depression, and guided the coalition led by the U.S. to victory over Nazism, Fascism and militarism. He had practiced restraint in not claiming for the U.S. a supreme position as victor, but strove for a temperate peaceful position for long lasting security through collective international forum with the UN and international policies like the Good Neighbor. Like George Washington, FDR stood the test of the presidency and had not claimed any additional *imperium*. FDR showed the world how democracy was the best solution in government, and acting as a preserver of spirit and hope, protected liberty and freedom and all else that is dear to Americans today.

ACKNOWLEDGEMENTS

Nova Science Publishers has been dedicated to educational excellence in producing this *First Men, America's Presidents* book series for university students, public libraries, and the general public. I wish to thank Maya Columbus at Nova for her guidance of the entire series to fruition and the numerous contributing authors for their commitment to educational excellence and to producing a world class collection of biographical books on the U.S. presidents. I want to thank Jeannie Pappas in production at Nova Publishers as well.

The Library of Congress has generously reproduced photos used in this volume and the library services at Stanford, Harvard, Princeton and Yale Universities are greatly appreciated. My thanks extends to the libraries locally at Oregon State University, Portland State University, Lewis and Clark College, and Reed College and also the Tigard and Tualatin Library systems for their fine collections and resources utilized in my research. Overseas the documents and correspondence collections of the British Museum, the University of British Columbia and the University of Victoria were employed especially for letters between President Franklin D. Roosevelt and Winston Churchill. The Franklin D. Roosevelt Presidential Library at Hyde Park, New York proved an invaluable source for President Roosevelt's presidential papers, speeches, fireside chats, campaign interviews, and personal letters. I want to thank the staff of Firestone Library at Princeton University and Hoover Library at Stanford University for their helpful recommendations. I want to thank the personnel of the Archives of Hawaii for allowing me to access their materials on FDR in Hawaii and on historical Pearl Harbor, and the librarians of the Hawaii-Pacific Collection of Hamilton Library at the University of Hawaii at Manoa, and of the Hawaiian Historical Society.

I am indebted to the Council for the International Exchange of Scholars and the Fulbright program for sending me overseas so that I could more clearly evaluate the contributions of America in world history. I was a Fulbright Scholar to Japan (1967) and to The People's Republic of China (1988-89) and from these experiences have learned more of what is distinctive and enviable about the U.S., those traits other nations desire to incorporate into their own cultures. I am especially grateful for my former post on an Adjunct Fellowship at the East-West Center in Honolulu, Hawaii where I was associated alternately with the departments of Culture and Communication and Education and Training as this federally supported institution is famed for its commitments to international education and training of scholars for duties throughout the Pacific. In the postwar period the East-West Center has been a beacon of light in promoting peaceful relations around the Pacific Rim and across the ocean. The East-West Center's Library proved invaluable for Pacific documents both in English and Chinese and I wish to thank the current president of the East-West Center Dr. Charles Morrison, former presidents Everett Kleinjans, Victor Li and Kenji Sumida, and colleagues Tu Weiming, Richard Baker, Godwin Chu, Mark Valencia, Betty Buck, and Larry Smith. Additionally James A. Kelly, Assistant Secretary of State in the federal administration, and John E. Lundin at CINPAC are thanked for supporting Fulbright public programs to spotlight international education and cultivate harmonious world relations.

I wish to thank my husband Dr. Frank L. Peterson, Emeritus Professor, SOEST, University of Hawaii at Manoa for his unstinting support and encouragement in all my intellectual endeavors as we have always attempted to guide our students toward a brighter future. Through our overseas teaching experiences and our semesters spent as faculty members of Chapman College (1974), University of Colorado at Boulder (1978), and the University of Pittsburgh (1999) on the Semester At Sea shipboard education program we have both cultivated global viewpoints and advanced cross-cultural harmony. I wish to thank Dr. John Tymitz as Director of the Institute for Shipboard Education for involving us in such a dynamic program for international understanding. Fellow colleagues, present and past, at the University of Hawaii I wish to thank for years of friendship and professionalism are Presidents Albert J. Simone and Kenneth Mortimer, Stuart Gerry Brown, Richard L. Rapson, James McCutcheon, Paul Varley, Rex Wade, Paul Hooper, H. Brett Melendy, Idus Newby, Jim Connors, Jerry Bentley, David Chappell, Mark Helbling, Wilhelm G. Solheim II, Ned Shultz, Doris Ching, Miles Jackson, Sarah K. Vann, Gertraude Li, Robert Wilson, Rhoda Hackler, Pauline King, Craig Howes, Marie-José Fassiotto, Noel Kent, Cornelia Moore, Judith Hughes, Carol Eastman, Sally Kanehe, Larry Zane, John

Baker, Mona Chock, Ralph Moberly, Roger and Lea Hadlich, Alfons Korn, and Douglas Hilt. Stuart Gerry Brown, one of the early founders of the American Studies Department at the University of Hawaii at Manoa, was instrumental in my publishing an article titled "FDR's 'Quarterbacking' of U.S. Naval Policy in the Pacific 1933-1939" in *The Pacific Historian* (Winter 1972-Summer 1973) that established my interest in doing a more lengthy biography of President Roosevelt. For nearly ten years I have served the University of Hawaii at Manoa Biography Center as a contributing editor to the Reviewed Elsewhere section of the professional journal *Biography* published by the University of Hawaii Press. I wish to thank everyone linked to that enterprise because their endeavors are so closely connected to my own research interests and writings of biographies. I have written brief biographical entries on FDR for various encyclopedias including *The United States in the First World War* edited by Anne Cipriano Venson. Several of my brief articles, biographies of Omar Bradley, John Foster Dulles, and Dean Acheson, as related to aspects of World War II appeared in *The Korean War, An Encyclopedia*. My article "The Progressive Period in Hawaii" appeared as a chapter in my book *America 19th and 20th Centuries* published by American Heritage, offering local perspective to national themes included in this volume. My appreciation extends to my colleagues at Hawaii Pacific University, where I served as an Adjunct Professor of History, including President Chatt G. Wright, Helen Chapin, Les Correa, Michael Pavkovic, Jerry Feldman, Jeanne Rellahan, Wayne Andrews, and Hunter Kennedy.

Recently I have retired as a courtesy Professor of History at Oregon State University 2000-2003 and from this opportunity I would like to thank Chairman Paul Farber, and colleagues Gary Ferngren, William B. Husband, and Robert A. Nye. Mentors from the past at OSU include C.K. Smith, R.D. Smith, and Leonard Adolf. I wish to thank too master teacher-mentor and friend P.O. Marsubian. I thank them for their excellent historical perspectives and wise counsel. Lately I have taught for California State University San Bernardino Palm Desert courses on the U.S. Presidency and American Colonial History and I want to thank Leticia Quezada for her dedication to the Osher Institute and Lifelong Learning for adults, a program for which I was a History Professor in 2004-2005.

Since my halcyon days in the graduate program at Stanford University in the early Sixties, I have expanded my enthusiasm for writing biographical history because people make events worth recording. Among my Stanford mentors I would like to thank Professors Thomas A. Bailey, Otis Pease, Don E. Fehrenbacher, George Harmon Knoles, Gavin I. Langmuir, and John C. Miller. My lifelong appreciation also extends to my family Colonel George W. and Hope H. Bennett, Rose Barclay and Carl Ernest Chatfield, Clarence and Ora Wright

Bennett, Carlyle and Yvonne Bennett, Clarence 'Cy' Bennett, Linda and Don McNeill, Janet Bennett, her children Jennifer and Will Eadie, Nancy Bennett Moore, Dick and Joanne Peterson, Patti and Jim Van Dyke and Mary Ann and Troy Rupp, and Burton Wayne and Linda Peterson, Erik Peterson, Larry and Candy Peterson, Holly and Daniel Rosos, Varonica and Steve Buchanan and lifelong friends Bruce and Karen Clark, Wendell and Anne Duffield, Carl and Carol Wentworth, Bill and Carolyn Wright, Mildred and Stuart Chapin, Elizabeth and Duane Duke, Ed and Carolyn Worth, and Gerhard and Hisako Frohlich for their considerate discussions of world events and of grand historical designs. Each of these people in their own way has given provocative answers as to why history matters.

Dr. Barbara Bennett Peterson
NOVA Series Editor *First Men, America's Presidents*
Professor of History (retired) Oregon State University
Emeritus Professor University of Hawaii
Former Adjunct Fellow East-West Center
Former Adjunct Professor Hawaii Pacific University
Professor of History California State University San Bernardino, Palm Desert

BIBLIOGRAPHY

Abbazia, Patrick, *Mr. Roosevelt's Navy: The Private War of the Atlantic Fleet, 1939-1942,* Annapolis, MD: Naval Institute Press, 1975.

Abbott, Philip, *The Exemplary Presidency: Franklin D. Roosevelt and the American Political Tradition,* Amherst, MA: University of Massachusetts Press, 1990.

Adams, Henry Hitch. *Harry Hopkins: A Biography,* New York: Putnam, 1977.

Ansel, Walter, *Hitler and the Middle Sea,* Durham, NC: Duke University Press, 1972.

Badger, Anthony J., *The New Deal, The Depression Years, 1933-1940,* Chicago: Ivan R. Dee, 2002.

Baer, George W., *The Coming of the Italian-Ethiopian War,* Cambridge, MA: Harvard University Press, 1967.

Barber, William J. *Designs Within Disorder: Franklin D. Roosevelt, the Economists, and the Shaping of American Economic Policy, 1933-1945,* Cambridge, England: Cambridge University Press, 1996.

Barnard, Ellsworth, *Wendell Willkie: Fighter for Freedom,* Amherst, MA: University of Massachusetts Press, 1966.

Barnes, Joseph, *Willkie: The Events He Was Part of, The Ideas He Fought For,* New York: Simon and Schuster, 1952.

Beaufre, Andre, *1940, The Fall of France,* New York: Alfred A. Knopf, 1968.

Bellush, Bernard, *The Failure of the NRA,* New York: W.W. Norton and Company, 1976.

Belot, Raymond de, *The Struggle for the Mediterranean,* New York: Greenwood Press, 1969.

Berkowitz, Edward D., *Robert Ball and the Politics of Social Security,* Madison: University of Wisconsin Press, 2003.

Berle, Beatrice Bishop and Travis Jacobs, *Navigating the Rapids, 1918-1971: From the Papers of Adolf A. Berle,* New York: Harcourt Brace Jovanovich, 1973.

Bernstein, Irving, *The New Deal Collective Bargaining Policy,* New York: Da Capo Press, 1975.

Bialer, Seweryn, ed., *Stalin and His Generals: Soviet Military Memoirs of World War II,* London and Washington, D.C.: Brassey's Defence Publishers, 1987.

Black, Conrad, *Franklin Delano Roosevelt: Champion of Freedom,* New York: Public Affairs and London: Weidenfeld and Nicolson, 2003.

Bland, Larry I., et al, *The Papers of George Catlett Marshall,* Baltimore, MD: Johns Hopkins University Press, 1981-1996.

Blum, John Morton, *From the Morgenthau Diaries,* 3 volumes, Boston: Houghton Mifflin, 1959-1967.

_____, *Roosevelt and Morgenthau,* Boston: Houghton Mifflin, 1970.

_____, *V Was for Victory: Politics and American Culture During World War II,* New York: Harcourt Brace Jovanovich, 1976.

Boaz, Harold Hinton, *Cordell Hull: A Biography,* New York: Doubleday, Doran and Company, 1942.

Bowen, Ezra, ed., *This Fabulous Century, 1900-1960,* New York: Time-Life Books, 1969.

Bracher, Karl-Dietrich, Manfred Funke, and Hans-Adolf Jacobsen, *Deutschland, 1933-1945: Neue Studien zur Nationalsozialistischen Herrschaft,* Bonn: Bundeszentrale fur Politische Bildung, 1993.

Breitman, Richard, Norman J.W. Goda, Timothy Naftali, and Robert Wolfe, *U.S. Intelligence and the Nazis,* Cambridge, England: Cambridge University Press, 2005.

Brinkley, Alan, *Voices of Protest: Huey Long, Father Coughlin, and the Great Depression,* New York: Vintage Books, 1983.

_____, *The End of Reform: New Deal Liberalism in Recession and War,* New York: Alfred A. Knopf, 1995.

_____, *Culture and Politics in the Great Depression,* Waco, TX: Markham Press, 1999.

_____, "Franklin Delano Roosevelt," in *American National Biography.* Edited by John A. Garraty and Mark C. Carnes, Vol. 18 New York: Oxford University Press, 1999, pp. 816-826.

Bullock, Alan, *Hitler: A Study in Tyranny,* Harmondsworth, England: Penguin Books, 1962.

Burns, James MacGregor, *Roosevelt: The Lion and the Fox, 1882-1940*, New York: Harvest/HBJ, reprint edition 2002 originally published 1956.

_____, *Roosevelt: Soldier of Freedom, 1940-1945*, New York: Harvest/HBJ Book, 2002 originally published 1970.

_____, *The Three Roosevelts: Patrician Leaders who Transformed America*, New York: Grove Press, 2002.

Calvocoressi, Peter and Guy Wint, *Total War: The Causes and Courses of the Second World War*, London: Allen Lane, Penguin Press, 1972.

Cannadine, David, ed., *Blood, Toil, Tears, and Sweat: Winston Churchill's Famous Speeches*, London: Cassell, 1989.

Carruthers and John Erickson, *Russian Front, 1941-1945*, London: Cassell, 1999.

Chace, James, *1912: Wilson, Roosevelt, Taft and Debs, The Election That Changed the Country*, New York: Simon and Schuster, 2004.

Chapman, Guy, *Why France Collapsed*, London: Cassell, 1968.

Charles, Searle F. *Minister of Relief: Harry Hopkins and the Depression*, Syracuse, NY: Syracuse University Press, 1963.

Churchill, Winston S., *Great Contemporaries*, New York: Putnam, 1937.

_____, *The Second World War*, 6 Vols. London: Cassell and Boston: Houghton Mifflin, 1948-1954.

Churchill, Winston S. (grandson), *Never Give In! The Best of Winston Churchill's Speeches (Selected and Edited by His Grandson Winston S. Churchill)*, New York: Hyperion, 2003.

Clark, Alan, *The Fall of Crete*, New York: Morrow, 1962 and London: Cassell, 2001.

_____, *Barbarossa: The Russian-German Conflict, 1941-1945*, Harmondsworth: Penguin, 1965.

Collier, Peter, *The Roosevelts, An American Saga*, New York: Simon and Schuster, 1994.

Cooper, Dan, *Enrico Fermi and the Revolutions of Modern Physics*, New York: Oxford University Press, 1998.

Conrad, David E., *The Forgotten Farmers: The Story of Sharecroppers in the New Deal*, Westport, CT: Greenwood Press, 1965.

Craig, Gordon A. and Felix Gilbert, eds., *The Diplomats, 1918-1939*, Princeton, NJ: Princeton University Press, 1994.

Cross, David F., *Sailor in the White House: The Seafaring Life of FDR*, New York: Naval Institute Press, 2003.

Dallek, Robert, *The Roosevelt Diplomacy and World War II*, New York: Holt, Rinehart and Winston, 1970.

_____, *Franklin D. Roosevelt and American Foreign Policy, 1932-1945,* New York: Oxford University Press, 1979 republished in 1995.

Dallin, Alexander, *German Rule in Russia, 1941-1945: A Study of Occupation Policies,* London: Macmillan and New York: St. Martin's Press, 1957.

Davis, Forrest, *How War Came, From Fall of France to Pearl Harbor,* New York: Simon and Schuster, 1942.

Derber, Milton, *The American Ideal of Industrial Democracy, 1865-1965,* Urbana: University of Illinois Press, 1970.

Dickinson, Matthew J., *Bitter Harvest: FDR, Presidential Power and the Growth of the Presidential Branch,* Cambridge, England: Cambridge University Press, 1999.

Dugan, James and Laurence Lafore, *Days of Emperor and Clown: The Italo-Ethiopian War, 1935-1936,* Garden City, NY: Doubleday, 1973.

Erickson, John and David Dilks, eds., *Barbarossa: The Axis and the Allies,* Edinburgh: Edinburgh University Press, 1994.

_____, *Road to Berlin,* London: Cassell, 2003.

_____, *Road to Stalingrad,* London: Cassell, 2003.

Eubank, Keith, *The Origins of World War II,* New York: Crowell, 1969.

_____, *Munich,* Westport, CT: Greenwood Press, 1984.

Facey-Crowther, David and Douglas Brinkley, eds., *The Atlantic Charter: Retrospect and Prospect,* New York: St. Martin's Press, 1994.

Farley, James A. *Behind the Ballots: The Personal History of a Politician,* Westport, CT: Greenwood Publishing Group, reprint edition 1972, originally published 1938.

_____. *Jim Farley's Story,* Westport, CT: Greenwood Publishing Group, reprint edition 1984 originally published 1948.

Feiling, Keith, *The Life of Neville Chamberlain,* London: Macmillan, 1946.

Feis, Herbert, *China Tangle: The American Effort in China from Pearl Harbor to the Marshall Mission,* Princeton, NJ: Princeton University Press, 1953.

_____, *Churchill, Roosevelt, and Stalin: The War They Waged and the Peace They Sought,* Princeton, NJ: Princeton University Press, 1957.

_____, *Japan Subdued: The Atomic Bomb and the End of the War in the Pacific,* Princeton, NJ: Princeton University Press, 1961.

Fischer, Ovie Clark. *Cactus Jack: A Biography of John Nance Garner,* Houston: Texian Press, 1978.

Foner, Philip S., *Franklin Delano Roosevelt Selections from His Writings,* New York: International Publishers, 1947.

Freidel, Frank, *Franklin D. Roosevelt*, (4 volumes, *The Apprenticeship, The Ordeal, The Triumph, Launching the New Deal*), Boston: Little, Brown and Company, 1952-1973.

_____, *America In the Twentieth Century*, New York: Alfred A. Knopf, 1965.

_____, *Franklin D. Roosevelt: A Rendezvous with Destiny*, Boston: Little, Brown and Company, 1990.

Friedman, Max Paul, *Nazis and Good Neighbors: The United States Campaign Against the Germans of Latin America in World War II*, Cambridge, England: Cambridge University Press, 2003.

Gardner, Lloyd C., *Economic Aspects of New Deal Diplomacy*, New York: Beacon Press revised edition 1971 originally published 1964.

Gellman, Irwin F., *Good Neighbor Diplomacy: United States Policies in Latin America, 1933-1945*, Baltimore, MD: Johns Hopkins University Press,1979.

_____, *Secret Affairs: Franklin Roosevelt, Cordell Hull, and Sumner Wells*, Baltimore, MD: Johns Hopkins University Press, 1995.

_____, "Cordell Hull" in *American National Biography*. Edited by John A. Garraty and Mark C. Carnes, Vol. 11 New York: Oxford University Press, 1999, pp. 445-450.

Gilbert, Martin and Richard Gott, *The Appeasers*, Boston: Houghton Mifflin, 1963.

_____, ed., *The Churchill War Papers*, New York: W.W. Norton and Company, 1995.

Glennon, Lorraine, ed., *The 20th Century, An Illustrated History of Our Lives and Times*, New York: JG Press, 2000.

Goodwin, Doris Kearns, *No Ordinary Time: Franklin and Eleanor Roosevelt: The Home Front in World War II*, New York: Simon and Schuster, 1995.

Graff, Henry F., ed., *The Presidents, A Reference History*, New York: Charles Scribner's Sons, 1996 and 2002 editions.

Graham, Otis L., Jr.and Meghan Robinson Wander, *Franklin D. Roosevelt: His Life and Times: An Encyclopedic View*, New York: Da Capo Press. 1990.

Graybar, Lloyd J., "John Nance Garner," in *American National Biography*. Edited by A. Garraty and Mark C. Carnes, Vol. 8 New York: Oxford University Press, 1999, pp.733-735.

Great Britain, *Parliamentary Debates*, House of Commons, Vol. 339.

Groueff, Stephanie, *Manhattan Project: The Untold Story of the Making of the Atomic Bomb*, New York: Little, Brown and Company, 1967.

Groves, Leslie R., *Now It Can Be Told: The Story of the Manhattan Project*, New York: Da Capo Press, 1983.

Hawley, Ellis W., *The New Deal and the Problem of Monopoly,* Princeton, NJ: Princeton University Press, 1966.

_____, "Hugh Samuel Johnson," in *American National Biography.* Edited by John Garraty and Mark. C. Carnes, Vol. 12 New York: Oxford University Press, 1999, pp. 82-83.

Hayes, Grace Person, *The History of the Joint Chiefs of Staff in World War II,* Naval Institute Press, 1982.

Heinrichs, Waldo H., *Threshold of War: Franklin D. Roosevelt and American Entry in World War II,* New York: Oxford University Press, 1988.

Higgins, Trumbull, *Winston Churchill and the Second Front, 1940-1943,* New York: Oxford University Press, 1957 republished 1974.

_____, *Hitler and Russia: The Third Reich in a Two-front War, 1937-1943,* New York: Macmillan, 1966.

_____, *Soft Underbelly, the Anglo-American Controversy Over the Italian Campaign, 1939-1945,* New York: Macmillan, 1968.

Hinton, Harold Boaz, *Cordell Hull: A Biography,* New York: Doubleday, Doran and Company, 1942.

Hoddeson, Lillian and Paul W. Henriksen, Roger A. Meade, and Catherine Westfall, *Critical Assembly: A Technical History of Los Alamos During the Oppenheimer Years, 1943-1945,* Cambridge, England: Cambridge University Press, 1993.

Holden, Robert H., *Latin America and the United States: A Documentary History,* New York: Oxford University Press, 2000.

Hoopes, Townsend and Douglas Brinkley, *FDR and the Creation of the U.N.,* New Haven: Yale University Press, 2000.

Hopkins, June, *Harry Hopkins: Sudden Hero, Brash Reformer,* New York: St. Martin's Press, 1999.

Hughes, H. Stuart, *Contemporary Europe: A History,* Englewood Cliffs, NJ: Prentice-Hall, 1966.

Ickes, Harold, *The Secret Diaries of Harold L. Ickes: The First Thousand Days, 1933-1936,* New York: Da Capo Press, 1974 reprint edition originally published 1956.

_____, *Back to Work: The Story of the PWA,* New York: Da Capo Press 1973 reprint edition originally published in 1935.

Irons, Peter H., *The New Deal Lawyers,* Princeton, NJ: Princeton University Press, 1982.

Jackson, Robert H., *That Man: An Insider's Portrait of Franklin D. Roosevelt,* New York: Oxford University Press, 2003.

Jacobsen, Hans Adolf and J. Rohwer, eds., *Decisive Battles of World War II: The German View,* New York: Putnam, 1965.

James, Marquis. *Mr. Garner of Texas,* New York: Bobbs-Merrill Company, 1939.

Jayne, Catherine E., *Oil, War, and Anglo-American Relations: American and British Reactions to Mexico's Expropriation of Foreign Oil Properties, 1937-1941,* Westport, CT: Greenwood Press, 2000.

Jenkins, Roy, *Franklin Delano Roosevelt,* New York: Times Books, 2003.

Jordon, Killian, *Our Finest Hour, The Triumphant Spirit of America's World War II Generation,* New York: Time Inc., 2000.

Josephson, Matthew, "The General," *New Yorker,* 18 (Aug. 1934): 21-25.

Kennedy, David M., *Freedom from Fear: The American People in Depression and War, 1929-1945,* New York: Oxford University Press, 2001.

Kennedy, Susan Estabrook, "Frances Perkins" in *American National Biography.* Edited by John A. Garraty and Mark C. Carnes, Vol. 17 New York: Oxford University Press, 1999, pp. 339-341.

Kennon, Donald R., ed., "John Nance Garner" in *The Speakers of the U.S. House of Representatives: A Bibliography, 1789-1984,* Baltimore, MD: Johns Hopkins University Press, 1986.

Kimball, Warren F., ed., *Churchill and Roosevelt: The Complete Correspondence,* 3 volumes, Princeton, NJ: Princeton University Press, 1984.

Kingdom, Frank, *As FDR Said, A Treasury of His Speeches, Conversations, and Writings.* New York: Duell, Sloan and Pearce, 1950.

Kirkendall, Richard, "A.A. Berle, Jr.: Student of the Corporation, 1917-1932," *Business History Review* 35 (Spring 1961): 43-58.

_____, "Henry Agard Wallace," in *American National Biography.* Edited by John A. Garraty and Mark C. Carnes, Vol. 22 New York: Oxford University Press, 1999, pp. 531-534.

Kogan, Norman, *Italy and the Allies,* Westport, CT: Greenwood Press, 1982.

Kogon, Eugen, *The Theory and Practice of Hell: The German Concentration Camps and the System Behind Them,* London: Secker and Warburg, 1950.

_____, Hermann Langbein and Adalbert Ruckerl, eds., *Nazi Mass Murder: A Documentary History of the Use of Poison Gas,* New Haven: Yale University Press, 1994.

Korb, Lawrence J., *The Joint Chiefs of Staff: The First Twenty-five Years,* Bloomington: Indiana University Press, 1976.

Koven, Seth and Sonya Michel, *Mothers of a New World: Maternalist Politics and the Origins of the Welfare States,* New York: Routledge, 1993.

Laflin, Patricia, "Coachella Valley During World War II," *The Periscope,* Indio, CA: Coachella Valley Historical Society, 2001.

Lafore, Laurence, *The End of Glory: An Interpretation of the Origins of World War II,* Philadelphia: J.B. Lippincott Company., 1970.

Langer, William L. and S. Everett Gleason, *Undeclared War, 1940-1941,* Gloucester, MA: P. Smith, 1968, originally published 1953.

Larrabee, Eric, *Commander in Chief: Franklin Delano Roosevelt, His Lieutenants, and Their War,* New York: Naval Institute Press, 1989 republished 2004.

Lash, Joseph P., *Eleanor and Franklin: The Story of Their Relationship Based on Eleanor Roosevelt's Private Papers,* New York: W.W. Norton, 1971.

_____, *Roosevelt and Churchill, 1939-1941, The Partnership that Saved the West,* Franklin Center, PA: Franklin Library, 1976.

_____, *Dealers and Dreamers, A New Look at the New Deal,* New York: Doubleday, 1988.

Lear, Linda. *Harold L. Ickes: The Aggressive Progressive, 1874-1933,* New York: Garland Press, 1981.

Leffler, Melvyn, *A Preponderance of Power: National Security, The Truman Administration and the Cold War,* Stanford, CA: Stanford University Press, 1992.

Leuchtenberg, William E., *Franklin D. Roosevelt and the New Deal,* New York: Perennial, 1963.

_____, *The FDR Years: On Roosevelt and His Legacy,* New York: Columbia University Press, 1995.

_____, *The Supreme Court Reborn: The Constitutional Revolution in the Age of Roosevelt,* New York: Oxford University Press, 1996.

_____, *In the Shadow of FDR: From Harry Truman to George W. Bush,* Ithaca, NY: Cornell University Press, 2001.

Levine, Lawrence W., ed., *The People and the President: America's Extraordinary Conversation with FDR,* New York: Beacon Press, 2002.

Liddell-Hart, Basil H., *Other Side of the Hill: Germany's Generals, Their Rise and Fall, With Their Own Account of Military Events, 1939-1945,* London: Cassell, 1948.

_____, ed., *The Red Army,* New York: Harcourt Brace, 1956.

_____, ed., *The History of the Second World War,* New York: Exeter Books, 1980.

Liu, Xiaoyuan, *A Partnership for Disorder: China, the United States, and Their Policies for the Postwar Disposition of the Japanese Empire, 1941-1945,* Cambridge, England: Cambridge University Press, 2002.

Madison, James H., "Wendell Lewis Willkie," in *American National Biography.* Edited by John A. Garraty and Mark C. Carnes, Vol. 23 New York: Oxford University Press, 1999. pp. 40-541.

_____, ed., *Wendell Willkie: Hoosier Internationalist,* Bloomington: Indiana University Press, 1992.

May, Dean L., *From New Deal to New Economics: The American Liberal Response to the Recession of 1937,* New York: Garland Publishers, 1981.

_____, "Henry Morgenthau, Jr." *American National Biography.* Edited by John A. Garraty and Mark C. Carnes, Vol. 15 New York: Oxford University Press, 1999 pp. 863-865.

McCann, Sean, *Gumshoe America: Hard Boiled Crime Fiction and the Rise and Fall of New Deal Liberalism,* Durham, NC: Duke University Press, 2000.

McCraw, Thomas K., "In Retrospect: Berle and Means," *Reviews in American History* 18 (Dec. 1990): 578-96.

McElvaine, Robert S., *The Depression and the New Deal: A History in Documents,* New York: Oxford University Press, 2000.

McJimsey, George T., *Harry Hopkins: Ally of the Poor and Defender of Democracy,* Cambridge, MA: Harvard University Press, 1987.

_____, *Documentary History of the Franklin D. Roosevelt Presidency,* Bethesda, MD: University Publications of America, 2001.

_____. "Harry Lloyd Hopkins," in *American National Biography.* Edited by John A. Garraty and Mark C. Carnes, Vol. 11 New York: Oxford University Press, 1999. pp. 172-174.

McNeill, William Hardy, *America, Britain, and Russia: Their Cooperation and Conflict, 1941-1946,* New York: Johnson Reprint Co., 1970.

Meacham, Jon, *Franklin and Winston: An Intimate Portrait of an Epic Friendship,* New York: Random House, 2003.

Michel, Henri, *The Shadow War: The European Resistance, 1939-1945,* New York: Harper and Row, 1972.

Milward, Alan S., *The German Economy at War,* London: University of London, Athlone Press, 1965.

_____, *The New Order and the French Economy,* Oxford: Clarendon Press, 1970.

_____, *Fascist Economy in Norway,* Oxford: Clarendon Press, 1972.

Moley, Raymond, *After Seven Years,* New York: Da Capo Press, reprint edition 1972 originally published 1939.

_____, *The First New Deal,* New York: Harcourt Brace and World, 1966.

_____, *Realities and Illusions, 1886-1931: The Autobiography of Raymond Moley,* New York: Garland Press, 1980 edited by Frank Freidel.
Moore, Deborah Dash, *GI Jews,* Cambridge, MA: Harvard University Press, 2005.
Morgan, Ted, *FDR: A Biography,* New York: Simon and Schuster, 1985.
Moscow, Warren, *Roosevelt and Willkie,* Englewood Cliffs: Prentice-Hall, 1968.
Namorato, Michael V., *Rexford G. Tugwell: A Biography,* New York: Praeger, 1988.
_____, ed. *The Diary of Rexford G. Tugwell: The New Deal,* Westport, CT: Greenwood Press, 1992.
_____, "Rexford Guy Tugwell" in *American National Biography.* Edited by John A. Garraty and Mark C. Carnes, Vol. 21 New York: Oxford University Press, 1999, pp. 923-925.
Neal, Steve, *Dark Horse: A Biography of Wendell Willkie,* Lawrence, KS: University Press of Kansas, 1989.
_____, *Happy Days Are Here Again,* New York: HarperCollins Publishers, 2005.
Nourse, Edwin, Joseph Davis, and John D. Black, *Three Years of the Agricultural Adjustment Administration,* New York: Da Capo Press reprint edition 1971 originally published 1937.
O'Donnell, Patrick K., *Operations, Spies and Saboteurs: The Unknown Story of the Men and Women of World War II's OSS,* New York: Free Press, 2004.
Ohl, John Kennedy, *Hugh S. Johnson and the New Deal,* Dekalb: Northern Illinois University Press, 1985.
_____, "General Hugh S. Johnson and the War Industries Board," *Military Review* 55 (May 1975): 35-48.
Parmet, Herbert S. and Marie B. Hecht, *Never Again: A President Runs for a Third Term,* New York: Macmillan, 1968.
Patenaude, Lionel V., "Garner, Sumners, and Connally: The Defeat of the Roosevelt Court Bill in 1937," *Southwestern Historical Quarterly* 74 (July 1970): 36-51.
Perkins, Frances, *The Roosevelt I Knew,* New York: Viking Press, 1946.
Persico, Joseph, *Roosevelt's Secret War: FDR and World War II Espionage,* New York: Random House, 2002.
Peterson, Barbara Bennett, *America In British Eyes,* Honolulu: Hawaii Chapter Fulbright Association, 1988.
_____, "FDR's 'Quarterbacking' of U.S. Naval Policy in the Pacific 1933-1939," *The Pacific Historian,* Vol. 16 No. 4 (Winter 1972): 4-53

(part one); Vol. 17 No.1 (Spring 1973): 61-72 (part two); Vol. 17 No. 2 (Summer 1973): 60-73 (part three).

Pickersgill, J.W., *The Mackenzie King Record*, 4 vols. Toronto: University of Toronto Press, 1960.

Pike, Frederick B., *FDR's Good Neighbor Policy: Sixty Years of Generally Gentle Chaos*, Austin: University of Texas Press, 1995.

Pratt, Julius, *Cordell Hull, 1933-44*, New York: Cooper Square Publishers, 1964, part of *The American Secretaries of State and Their Diplomacy* series edited by Robert Ferrell.

Renouvin, Pierre, *World War II and Its Origins: International Relations, 19129-1945*, New York: Harper and Row, 1968.

Reynolds, David, *Creation of the Anglo-American Alliance, 1937-1941*, Chapel Hill: University of North Carolina Press, 1982.

_____, *Rich Relations: The American Occupation of Britain, 1942-1945*, London: Phoenix, 2000.

_____, *From Munich to Pearl Harbor: Roosevelt's America and the Origins of the Second World War*, Chicago: Ivan R. Dee, 2001.

_____, *In Command of History: Winston Churchill and the Second World War*, New York: Random House, 2005.

Rhodes, Richard, *The Making of the Atomic Bomb*, New York: Simon and Schuster, 1995.

Rich, Norman, *Hitler's War Aims*, New York: W.W. Norton and Company, 1973.

Robertson, Esmonde Manning, *Hitler's Pre-War Policy and Military Plans, 1933-1939*, New York: Citadel Press, 1967.

_____, ed., *Origins of the Second World War: Historical Interpretations*, London: Macmillan, 1971.

_____, *Mussolini As Empire-builder: Europe and Africa 1932-1936*, London and New York: Macmillan, 1977.

Roosevelt, Elliott, ed., *F.D.R., His Personal Letters*, 4 vols. New York: Duell, Sloan, and Pearce, 1947-1950.

_____, *Untold Story, The Roosevelts of Hyde Park*, New York: Putnam Sons, 1973.

_____ and James Brough, *Rendezvous With Destiny: The Roosevelts of the White House*, New York: Putnam Sons, 1975.

Rosen, Elliot A., *Hoover, Roosevelt and the Brains Trust*, New York: Columbia University Press, 1977.

_____, "James Aloysius Farley," in *American National Biography*. Edited by John A. Garraty and Mark C. Carnes, Vol. 7 New York: Oxford University Press, 1999, pp. 716-717.

_____, "Raymond Moley" in *American National Biography*. Edited by John A. Garraty and Mark C. Carnes, Vol. 15 New York: Oxford University Press, 1999, pp. 665-667.

Rosenman, Samuel I., *Public Papers and Address of Franklin D. Roosevelt*, 13 vols., New York: Macmillan and Harper & Brothers, 1938-1950.

_____, *Working With Roosevelt*, New York: Harper, 1952.

Salmond, John A. *The Civilian Conservation Corps 1933-1942: A New Deal Case Study*, Durham NC: Duke University Press, 1967.

Schewe, Donald B. ed., *Franklin D. Roosevelt and Foreign Affairs, January 1937-August 1939*, New York: Garland, 1979.

Schlesinger, Arthur Meier, *The New Deal in Action, 1933-1938*, New York: Macmillan Company, 1939.

_____, *The American as Reformer*, Cambridge, MA: Harvard University Press, 1950.

Schlesinger, Arthur M. Jr., *The Age of Roosevelt*, 3 volumes, New York: Houghton-Mifflin, reprinted 2003 originally published 1957-1960.

_____, ed., *History of American Presidential Elections, 1789-1968*, New York: Chelsea House Publishers, 1985.

_____, *War and the Constitution: Abraham Lincoln and Franklin D. Roosevelt*, Gettysburg, PA: Gettysburg College, 1988.

_____, *Crisis of the Old Order: The Age of Roosevelt, 1919-1933*, New York: History Book Club, 2002.

_____, *The Coming of the New Deal*, Boston: Houghton Mifflin, 2003 originally published 1958.

_____, *The Politics of Upheaval, 1935-1936*, Boston: Houghton Mifflin, 2003.

Schlup, Leonard C. and Donald W. Whisenhunt, *It Seems to Me, Selected Letters of Eleanor Roosevelt*, Lexington: University Press of Kentucky, 2005.

Schwarz, Jordon A., "John Nance Garner and the Sales Tax Rebellion of 1932," *Journal of Southern History* 30 (May 1964): 162-80.

_____. *Liberal: Adolf A. Berle and the Vision of an American Era*, New York: Free Press and London: Collier Macmillan, 1987.

_____, "Adolf Augustus Berle" in *American National Biography*. Edited by John A. Garraty and Mark C. Carnes, Vol. 2 New York: Oxford University Press, 1999, pp. 657-659.

Sherwood, Robert E. *Roosevelt and Hopkins, An Intimate History*, New York: Harper, 1950 originally published 1948.

Shirer, William L., *The Rise and Fall of the Third Reich*, New York: Simon and Schuster, 1960, republished 1990.

_____, *The Collapse of the Third Republic: An Inquiry into the Fall of France, 1940,* New York: Simon and Schuster, 1969.
Sitkoff, Harvard, *A New Deal for Blacks,* New York: Oxford University Press, 1981.
Smith, Bradley F., *The Shadow Warriors: OSS and the Origins of the CIA,* New York: Basic Books, 1983.
Snell, John L., ed., *The Meaning of Yalta: Big Three Diplomacy and the New Balance of Power,* Baton Rouge: Louisiana State University Press, 1956.
Sowden, J.K., *The German Question 1945-1973: Continuity in Change,* London: Bradford University Press, 1975.
Speer, Albert, *Inside the Third Reich: Memoirs,* New York: Collier Books, 1970 and republished 1981.
Stoler, Mark A., *Allies and Adversaries: The Joint Chiefs of Staff, The Grand Alliance, and U.S. Strategy in World War II,* Chapel Hill, NC: University of North Carolina Press, 2000.
Strawson, John, *Hitler's Battles for Europe,* New York: Scribner, 1971.
_____, *The Italian Campaign,* New York: Carroll and Graf Publishers, 1988.
_____, *Churchill and Hitler: In Victory and Defeat,* New York: Fromm International Publishing Company, 1998.
Synder, Louis L., *The War: A Concise History,* New York: J. Messner, 1960.
Syrett, John, "Roosevelt vs. Farley: The New York Gubernatorial Election of 1942," *New York History* 56 (January 1975).
_____, "Jim Farley and Carter Glass: Allies Against a Third Term," *Prologues* 15 (Summer 1983).
Szalay, Michael, *New Deal Modernism: American Literature and the Invention of the Welfare State,* Durham, NC: Duke University Press, 2001.
Thomas, Evan, *The Very Best Men: Four Who Dared: The Early Years of the CIA,* New York: Simon and Schuster, 1996.
Thompson, Neville, *Anti-Appeasers: Conservative Opposition to Appeasement in the 30s,* Oxford: Clarendon Press, 1971.
Timmons, Bascom Nolly, *Garner of Texas: A Personal History,* New York: Harper, 1948.
Trattner, Walter I., *Crusade for the Children: The National Child Labor Committee and Child Labor Reform in America,* Chicago: Quadrangle Books, 1970.
Trevor-Roper, H.R. (Hugh Redwald), *The Last Days of Hitler,* New York: Collier Books, 1962.

Troy, Thomas F., *Donovan and the CIA: A History of the Establishments of the Central Intelligence Agency,* Frederick, MD: Aletheia Books, 1981.

_____, *Wild Bill and Intrepid: Donovan, Stephenson, and the Origin of the CIA,* New Haven: Yale University Press, 1996.

_____, ed., *Wartime Washington: The Secret OSS Journal of James Grafton Rogers, 1942-1943,* Frederick, MD: University Publications of America, 1987.

Tugwell, Rexford, *Puerto Rican Public Papers of R. G. Tugwell, Governor,* San Juan: Service Office of the Government of Puerto Rico, Printing Division, 1945.

_____, *The Stricken Land,* New York: Greenwood Press, 1947.

_____, *A Chronicle of Jeopardy 1945-1955,* Chicago: University of Chicago Press, 1955.

_____, *Democratic Roosevelt, A Biography of Franklin D. Roosevelt,* Garden City, NY: Doubleday, 1957.

_____, *F.D.R., Architect of an Era,* New York: Macmillan, 1967.

_____, *The Brains Trust,* New York: Viking Press, 1968.

_____, *In Search of Roosevelt,* Cambridge, MA: Harvard University Press, 1972.

_____ and Thomas E. Cronin, *Presidency Reappraised,* New York: Praeger, 1974.

_____, *Art of Politics, As Practiced by Three Great Americans, Franklin Delano Roosevelt, Luis Munoz Marin, and Fiorello H. LaGuardia,* Westport, CT: Greenwood Press, 1977 originally published in 1958.

_____, *Enlargement of the Presidency,* New York: Octagon Books, 1977 originally published 1960.

_____, *Roosevelt's Revolution: The First Year, a Personal Perspective,* New York: Macmillan, 1977.

_____. *To the Lesser Heights of Morningside, A Memoir,* Philadelphia: University of Pennsylvania Press, 1982

Tully, Grace G., *FDR, My Boss,* New York: Charles Scribner's Sons, 1949.

Tuttle, Dwight William, *Harry L. Hopkins and Anglo-American-Soviet Relations, 1941-1945,* New York: Garland Press, 1983.

U.S. Department of State, Publication 1983, *Peace and War: United States Foreign Policy, 1931-1941,* Washington, D.C.: U.S. Government Printing Office, 1943.

Utley, Jonathan G., *Going to War with Japan, 1937-1941,* Knoxville: University of Tennessee Press, 1985.

Ward, Geoffrey C., *Before the Trumpet: Young Franklin Roosevelt, 1882-1905,* New York: HarperCollins, 1985.

_____, "Eleanor Roosevelt," in *American National Biography.* Edited by John A. Garraty and Mark C. Carnes, Vol. 18 New York: Oxford University Press, 1999, pp. 812-815.

Watkins, T.H., *Righteous Pilgrim: The Life and Times of Harold L. Ickes, 1874-1952,* New York: Henry Holt and Company, 1990.

_____, "Harold LeClair Ickes," *American National Biography.* Edited by John A. Garraty and Mark C. Carnes., Vol. 11 New York: Oxford University Press, 1999, pp. 626-628.

_____, *The Hungry Years: A Narrative History of the Great Depression in America,* New York: Owl Books, 2000.

Weinberg, Gerhard L., *The Foreign Policy of Hitler's Germany: Diplomatic Revolution in Europe, 1933-1936,* Chicago: University of Chicago Press, 1970.

_____, *A World at Arms: A Global History of World War II,* Cambridge, England: Cambridge University Press, 1995.

_____, *Visions of Victory, The Hopes of Eight World War II Leaders,* Cambridge, England: Cambridge University Press, 2005.

Weiss, Nancy J., *Farewell to the Party of Lincoln: Black Politics in the Age of FDR,* Princeton, NJ: Princeton University Press, 1983.

Wheeler-Bennett, John W., *Munich: Prologue to Tragedy,* London: Macmillan, 1966.

White, Graham J. and John Maze. *Harold Ickes of the New Deal: His Private Life and Public Career,* Cambridge, MA: Harvard University Press, 1985.

Wicker, Elmus, "Roosevelt's 1933 Monetary Experiment," *Journal of American History* 57 (1970): 864-79.

Willkie, Wendell L., *An American Program,* New York: Simon and Schuster, 1944.

_____, *One World,* New York: The Limited Editions Club, 1944.

_____, *This Is Wendell Willkie,* New York: Dodd, Mead, 1940.

Wilmot, Chester, *The Struggle for Europe,* Westport, CT: Greenwood Press, 1972.

Wilson, Daniel J., *Living With Polio, The Epidemic and Its Survivors,* Chicago: University of Chicago Press, 2005.

Wilson, Theodore A., *The First Summit: Roosevelt and Churchill at Placentia Bay, 1941,* Boston: Houghton Mifflin, 1969.

_____, *D-Day 1944,* Lawrence, Kansas: Eisenhower Foundation published by University of Kansas Press, 1994.

Winfield, Betty H., *FDR and the News Media,* New York: Columbia University Press, 1994.

Wood, Derek and Derek Dempster, *The Narrow Margin: The Battle of Britain and the Rise of Air Power, 1930-1940,* London: Arrow Books, 1967.

Wright, Gordon, *The Ordeal of Total War, 1939-1945,* New York: Harper and Row, 1968.

Zieger, Robert H., *The CIO 1935-1955,* Chapel Hill: University of North Carolina Press, 1995.

ABOUT THE AUTHOR AND SERIES EDITOR

Dr. Barbara Bennett Peterson is the NOVA Science Publishers' Series Editor for the *First Men, America's Presidents* book series and wrote the first book *George Washington, America's Moral Exemplar* in addition to this volume *Franklin Delano Roosevelt, Preserver of Spirit and Hope*. Professor Peterson has spent her career writing historical biographies and using those works in university classrooms all over the world. She is an Emeritus Professor at the University of Hawaii, serving there for thirty years before retiring, and was an Adjunct Fellow of the East-West Center in Culture and Communication and Education and Training. Dr. Peterson served as a Research Associate at Bishop Museum 1995-1998. She has recently been a Professor of History at Oregon State University from 2000-2003 and also at California State University San Bernardino Palm Desert 2004-2005 where she taught adult classes on the U.S. Presidency and American Colonial History. Dr. Peterson received her B.A. and B.S. from Oregon State University, M.A. from Stanford University, and PhD from the University of Hawaii. She has been a Fulbright Scholar to Japan, 1967, at Sophia University and The People's Republic of China 1988-89 teaching American History and graduate seminars in Historiography and American Thought and Culture at Wuhan University. While teaching in China she received Wuhan University's Outstanding Teacher of the Year award in 1989. She was awarded the University of Hawaii Board of Regents' Medal for Excellence in Teaching in 1993. She was the Founding President of the Hawaii Chapter of the Fulbright Association and in 1997 was selected a Distinguished Alumni of the University of Hawaii.

Earlier books by Professor Peterson are *George Washington, America's Moral Exemplar,* 2005, *Emalani, Queen Emma Kaleleonalani* with Alfons L. Korn 2003, *Sarah Childress Polk, First Lady of Tennessee and Washington,* 2003 a volume in NOVA's First Ladies series, *Hawaii in the World* 2000, *Notable*

Women of China 2000, *John Bull's Eye on America* 1995, *American History 17th, 18th, and 19th Centuries* 1993, *America 19th and 20th Centuries* 1993, *The Pacific Region: Change and Challenge* with Wilhelm G. Solheim II 1990, *America In British Eyes* 1988, and *Notable Women of Hawaii* 1984. Additionally Dr. Peterson was an Associate Editor working with Professors John A. Garraty and Mark C. Carnes on the *American National Biography* published in a 24 volume collection in 1999 which won the Dartmouth Medal from the American Library Association for the best library reference work of the year. Three of her biographical works have been nominated for the Pulitzer Prize in History or Biography.

Professor Peterson has written numerous biographical entries in encyclopedias and special collections including *Notable American Women, A Biographical Dictionary Completing the Twentieth Century* (Harvard), *American National Biography* (Oxford, New York), *American National Biography Online* (Oxford, New York), *Encyclopedia-USA* (Academic International Press), *New Dictionary of National Biography* (Oxford, England), *Encyclopedia of Eastern Europe, From the Congress of Vienna to the Fall of Communism* (Garland), *Europe Since 1945* (Garland), *Women in World History* (Gale Group), *Notable Women of China* (M.E. Sharpe), *Scribner's Encyclopedia of American Lives* (Scribner's), *The Global Encyclopedia of Historical Writing* (Garland), *The Korean War, An Encyclopedia* (Garland), *Encyclopedia of World War I* (Garland), *Encyclopedia of Twentieth-Century Britain* (Garland), *U.S. Women's Groups: Institutional Profiles* (Greenwood), *Dictionary of American Biography* (Macmillan), *European Immigrant Women in the United States, A Biographical Dictionary* (Garland), *Statesmen Who Changed the World* (Greenwood), *St. James Press Guide to Biography* (St. James), and *Notable Women of Hawaii* (University of Hawaii Press).

Essentially a biographer, Dr. Peterson represents the United States as a Deputy Director General of the International Biographical Centre in Cambridge, England, and as a Deputy Governor of the American Biographical Institute. She believes biographies are important for students and adults offering role models for lives well-lived. Her writings have been featured in the *Journal of World History, Journal of American History, Presidential Studies Quarterly, Pacific Historical Review, The Pacific Historian, Journal of the Australian Association for Maritime History, Current Development in World History Research, Hawaiian Journal of History, Educational Perspectives, Historical Journal of Literature,* and *Fiction International.*

Professor Peterson has taught several semesters for the Institute for Shipboard Education's Semester at Sea administered by Chapman College, Spring 1974,

University of Colorado at Boulder, Fall 1978, and the University of Pittsburgh, Fall 1999.

Active in worldwide causes benefiting children, Dr. Peterson gives a large portion of her royalties from her publications to children's charities and is married to Dr. Frank L. Peterson former chairman and now Emeritus Professor of Geology and Geophysics University of Hawaii at Manoa. She has dedicated this biography of FDR to what Tom Brokaw called the 'greatest generation' of Americans that experienced the Depression and won World War II.

INDEX

#

18th amendment, 41, 71
19th amendment, 41

A

accelerator, 48
acceptance, 44, 79, 192
access, 13, 74, 86, 92, 102, 114, 137, 138, 164, 165, 244, 273
accumulation, 15, 50
accuracy, 265
achievement, 36, 81, 89, 230, 264
activism, 118
adjustment, 165, 230, 231
administrators, 62, 84, 114
adults, 3, 275, 294
advertising, 48, 50
Advice and Consent, x
advocacy, 21, 42
affect, 195
Africa, 21, 33, 129, 132, 150, 177, 185, 186, 206, 207, 208, 216, 245, 247, 256, 257, 287
age, xii, 3, 4, 5, 11, 17, 19, 31, 50, 52, 54, 58, 77, 78, 102, 106, 110, 113, 232, 251
aggression, 86, 128, 131, 136, 143, 147, 149, 151, 154, 165, 169, 171, 172, 179, 203, 215, 254, 255, 259
aggressiveness, 213
agriculture, 96, 122, 201, 206, 271
Albania, 209
alcohol, 100
alternative, 24, 74
aluminum, 49, 163
ambassadors, x
American embassy, 6, 161
American Revolution, 1
American Woman's Suffrage Association, 41
antagonism, 117, 173
Anthony, Susan B., 41
antitrust, 97
anxiety, 109, 135, 171, 178
appeasement, 135, 139, 152, 214
applied mathematics, 5
arbitration, 191
Argentina, 86, 117, 168
argument, 41, 207
arithmetic, 168
armed forces, 141, 147, 159, 176, 178, 192, 213, 215, 224, 227, 243, 250, 251, 254, 259, 260
Asia, 35, 136, 149, 150, 153, 172, 174, 177, 190, 215, 223, 254, 256, 257, 262, 265
aspiration, 145
assassination, xii, 10, 262
assets, 59, 140, 141, 172, 173
assignment, 86
association, 49, 97, 107, 191
assumptions, 101
asthma, 25

asylum, 86
atrocities, 241, 253
attachment, 30
attacker, 167
attacks, 4, 170, 171, 172, 177, 186, 205, 240
attention, 8, 24, 28, 40, 43, 55, 57, 75, 96, 101, 189, 195, 222, 245
attitudes, 5, 43, 214
Attorney General, 54
Australasia, 150
Australia, 58, 185, 186, 221, 223, 227, 228, 242, 254, 266
Austria, 124, 131, 136, 152, 177, 205, 209
autarky, 130
authoritarianism, 116
authority, 19, 24, 36, 72, 83, 101, 112, 120, 136, 178, 213, 216, 236, 265
automobiles, 38, 39, 52, 155
autonomy, 41
awareness, 7

B

backlash, 86
Balkans, 178, 205, 209, 253
bank failure, 63
bankers, 61, 63, 71
banking, 17, 36, 37, 46, 67, 78, 79, 81, 82, 93, 103, 119, 148, 270
bankruptcy, 122
banks, 17, 36, 37, 63, 65, 67, 68, 93, 120
bargaining, 101, 106, 211
baths, 15
batteries, 34
behavior, 203
Belgium, 138, 139, 151, 178, 196, 262
bending, 154, 185
benign, 103
beverages, 41, 100
bi-partisan, 20, 27, 35, 58, 77, 90, 91, 140, 270
black tea, 20
Black Thursday, 61
blood, 16, 139, 201, 202, 226
bloodshed, 152

body, 22, 47, 49, 51, 53, 73, 108, 128, 134, 138, 145, 146, 215, 268
body weight, 47
Bolivia, 168
bonds, 9, 30, 132, 180, 226, 231, 242, 246, 252
boys, 4, 5, 31, 46, 94, 191, 260
Brazil, 150, 206, 209
breakdown, 98, 200
breakfast, 4
breathing, 268
breeding, 3, 4, 12, 18, 253
Bretton Woods conference, 242
Britain, 28, 88, 101, 125, 129, 133, 135, 137, 139, 140, 141, 142, 147, 148, 149, 154, 156, 161, 163, 164, 173, 182, 184, 186, 204, 207, 208, 210, 211, 215, 227, 240, 241, 243, 254, 292, 294
Brooklyn Navy Yard, 29
brutality, 181, 212
buildings, 95, 99
Bulgaria, 209
bullying, 137
bureaucracy, 73, 115, 119, 121
Burma, 188, 223, 242, 249, 250, 254, 256
burning, 54, 137

C

cables, 217, 229
campaigns, 45, 70, 71, 120, 138, 160
Canada, 56, 58, 64, 141, 196, 205, 210, 212, 213
candidates, x, 51, 121, 262
capitalism, xviii, 16, 39, 66, 74, 95, 99, 126, 163
Caribbean, 29, 121, 143, 171, 207, 254
carrier, 178, 228, 235, 266
cartel, 59
cast, 12, 18, 65, 79, 81, 128, 202
Caucasus, 162, 182
Central Europe, 253
central planning, 14
cerebral hemorrhage, 268
certificate, 12

channels, 57, 217, 241
chaos, 109, 138, 238, 242
charm, xvii, 3, 5, 14, 64, 108
chicken, 66
Chief Justice, 113, 263
children, 4, 7, 11, 13, 15, 16, 25, 30, 37, 40, 41, 42, 46, 48, 52, 54, 72, 73, 111, 114, 116, 148, 153, 169, 181, 182, 196, 206, 207, 220, 222, 226, 230, 244, 260, 263, 267, 276, 295
Chile, 117
China, 2, 45, 58, 118, 127, 128, 136, 147, 173, 185, 186, 187, 188, 192, 203, 204, 205, 207, 213, 223, 227, 242, 249, 250, 254, 255, 256, 257, 262, 265, 266, 267, 274, 280, 284, 293, 294
CIA, 122, 217, 289, 290
civil liberties, 118, 126
civil rights, 20, 114, 118, 119, 243
civil service, 17, 115
civil war, 214, 266
Civil War, 7, 8, 36, 43, 129, 131, 136
classes, 4, 5, 12, 104, 270, 293
classroom, 78
classrooms, 293
Clayton Anti-Trust Bill, 37
Cleveland, Grover, xi, 5, 16
coal, xvii, 7, 19, 20, 88, 112, 230, 231
coercion, 128
Cold War, xiii, 269, 284
collaboration, 76, 164, 165, 177
collective bargaining, 97, 99, 106, 201, 205
Colombia, 168
coma, 44
commitment, 37, 41, 44, 76, 115, 174, 273
commodity, 96, 108
communication, 179, 185, 186, 187
communism, 99, 103, 122, 130, 131, 163
community, 4, 10, 57, 66, 74, 75, 90, 152, 236, 253, 263
compassion, 92
compensation, 15, 49, 58, 105, 251
competition, 9, 37, 97
compliance, 97
complications, 103

composition, 22, 113
concentration, 59, 107, 152, 153, 252, 253
conception, 190
conciliation, 191, 211
conduct, 30, 81, 87, 147, 185, 214, 215, 219, 233, 238
confidence, xvii, 6, 17, 49, 64, 65, 80, 81, 93, 102, 110, 120, 125, 137, 156, 163, 176, 177, 189, 191, 201, 211, 220, 233, 254, 259, 261, 262, 264, 269
conflict, 131, 133, 134, 176, 184, 213, 214, 215
confusion, 14, 112, 119, 179, 201
congruence, 38
conjecture, 213
consciousness, 83, 213
consensus, 77, 106, 140
consent, 37, 44, 153
conservation, 16, 17, 18, 22, 25, 42, 50, 57, 87, 89, 96, 114, 123, 124, 201
conspiracy, 103, 168
constitution, ix, xii, xvii, 2, 23, 24, 41, 83, 110, 113, 145, 146, 212, 238, 263, 288
construction, 27, 29, 30, 56, 70, 89, 104, 243
consumers, 50, 77, 98, 201
consumption, 41, 59, 60, 61, 67, 89, 108
continuity, 201, 262
control, x, xii, 1, 8, 14, 23, 24, 26, 30, 34, 36, 38, 44, 45, 56, 58, 59, 72, 73, 78, 85, 89, 91, 94, 96, 99, 100, 114, 116, 117, 140, 142, 149, 150, 167, 168, 169, 182, 187, 188, 190, 198, 206, 207, 210, 217, 223, 229, 237, 240, 256, 269
conversion, 190
conviction, 110, 156, 222, 254, 264
Coolidge, Calvin, xi, 43, 50, 51
coping, 66
copper, 173
corn, 114
corporate finance, 77
corporations, 17, 19, 36, 59, 64, 77, 199, 239
corruption, 6, 9, 13, 14, 16, 41, 43, 54, 56, 72
cost of living, 154, 201, 225, 227, 235, 236, 237, 241
costs, 55, 170, 197, 198, 201, 211, 241, 249

cotton, 67, 96
counsel, ix, 201, 275
covering, 3, 14, 105, 225
crack, 246
credentials, 26
credit, 28, 31, 58, 60, 76, 81, 85, 118, 216, 248, 251
crime, 15, 56, 76, 80, 100
criticism, 102, 112, 226
cronyism, 16
crop production, 3
crops, 64, 67, 87, 96, 114, 226
Cuba, 29, 117, 121, 142
culture, 102, 107, 222
currency, 68, 82, 93, 103, 121, 123

D

damage, 175, 178
danger, 128, 148, 150, 169, 170, 176, 182, 183, 202, 204, 207, 208, 209, 211, 225, 237, 240
death, xvii, 3, 10, 15, 35, 48, 50, 74, 118, 124, 133, 152, 190, 202, 231, 240, 243, 266, 268
debt, 60, 68, 107
debtors, 120
debts, 225
decision making, 92, 106
decisions, 23, 74, 76, 112, 125, 132, 173, 216, 240, 256
defense, 88, 117, 136, 140, 141, 144, 146, 147, 149, 151, 154, 155, 156, 160, 161, 163, 166, 170, 171, 173, 176, 179, 180, 181, 185, 186, 187, 188, 196, 197, 200, 201, 202, 203, 204, 207, 209, 210, 211, 212, 213, 215, 219, 222, 244, 247, 249, 271
deficit, 85, 87, 116, 119, 125
delivery, 55, 210
delusion, 205
demand, 38, 59, 62, 72, 82, 83, 100, 104, 112, 153, 180, 191, 245, 260, 269
democracy, xi, 7, 44, 66, 84, 88, 101, 106, 109, 110, 111, 112, 132, 137, 144, 145, 146, 147, 152, 154, 155, 172, 177, 189, 190, 191, 198, 210, 211, 213, 238, 243, 263, 271
Democrat, 5, 16, 18, 22, 24, 44, 51, 59, 76, 90
Democratic Party, 14, 22, 23, 25, 26, 27, 43, 48, 51, 52, 55, 70, 74, 78, 85, 87, 90, 91, 103
denial, 206, 224, 225, 226
Denmark, 7, 116, 138, 139, 152, 178, 204, 209, 226, 253
Department of Defense, 215
deposits, 93, 270
depression, 59, 60, 62, 64, 67, 68, 71, 73, 78, 88, 102, 105, 108, 110, 115, 119, 123, 271
Depression, v, 49, 55, 58, 62, 64, 65, 66, 68, 70, 71, 72, 76, 78, 84, 87, 93, 94, 99, 100, 101, 103, 104, 106, 119, 220, 245, 268, 271, 277, 279, 283, 285, 295
designers, 199
desire, 16, 29, 117, 127, 135, 150, 151, 164, 165, 274
destruction, 165, 169, 190, 202, 203, 206, 208, 214, 228, 261, 267
devaluation, 68, 121
diet, 47
disaster, 62, 109, 111, 170, 178, 206, 207, 225, 238
discipline, 83, 84, 130, 134
disclosure, 179
discrimination, 37, 144, 243
disposition, 247
dissatisfaction, 22, 64
distortions, 47
distress, 81, 105, 196
distribution, 59, 62, 96
divergence, 22
division, 18, 48, 51, 55, 116, 219, 250
divorce, 30
doctors, 47, 253
dogs, 263
Dominican Republic, 117
draft, 23, 35, 78, 97, 115, 216
drainage, 94
dream, 7, 64, 110, 138
due process, 23
duration, 179, 226

dust storms, 67
Dutchess County, 1, 14, 42, 86, 124

E

early warning, 141
earning power, 71
earnings, 7, 129, 226, 244
earth, 230
East Asia, 86
Eastern Europe, 138, 294
economic boom, 57
economic crisis, 236
economic policy, 102, 225
economic problem, 65, 119, 122, 237, 265
economics, 26, 75, 76, 87, 93, 104, 110, 225, 227
egg, 201
Egypt, 161, 186, 206, 246
elderly, 56, 58, 270
election, x, xi, 12, 14, 17, 18, 19, 21, 22, 24, 26, 27, 29, 30, 35, 37, 40, 42, 43, 45, 48, 51, 53, 65, 70, 79, 80, 85, 87, 89, 90, 91, 95, 103, 104, 107, 108, 114, 117, 120, 121, 123, 124, 141, 143, 147, 148, 262
electricity, 27, 55, 105
electrons, 218
Ellis Island, 7
embargo, 84, 128, 129, 130, 173, 204
emergency management, xiii
empathy, 65
employees, 28, 35, 88, 105, 155, 201, 231
employment, 50, 82, 94, 97, 100, 103, 107, 115, 199, 200, 201, 251, 259
encouragement, 120, 244, 259, 274
endorsements, 125
endurance, 188, 227, 269
England, 2, 7, 11, 65, 86, 94, 97, 137, 138, 150, 165, 216, 228, 231, 253, 255, 261, 277, 278, 280, 281, 282, 284, 291, 294
enlargement, 199
enslavement, 152, 190
entanglements, 127, 129
enthusiasm, 14, 220, 275
environment, 18, 250

Equal Rights Amendment (ERA), 42, 115
equality, 8, 20, 41, 43, 57, 138, 227, 243, 246
equipment, 156, 163, 179, 184, 197, 198, 199, 246, 247, 250
Eritrea, 130
erosion, 89, 120
Estonia, 138
ethics, 81, 179
Europe, 2, 11, 30, 31, 33, 34, 35, 40, 41, 45, 50, 68, 90, 106, 117, 118, 119, 120, 129, 133, 135, 136, 137, 138, 139, 149, 150, 153, 160, 161, 163, 168, 173, 177, 190, 195, 197, 198, 199, 203, 205, 206, 207, 210, 215, 216, 219, 222, 226, 230, 240, 241, 242, 243, 244, 245, 246, 253, 254, 257, 258, 260, 261, 262, 263, 265, 282, 287, 289, 291, 294
Everglades, 89
evidence, 9, 167, 213, 262
evil, 103, 109, 110, 114, 144, 150, 151, 182, 184, 191, 205, 210, 216, 260, 270
evolution, 52
exaggeration, 150
examinations, 5, 73
excuse, 74, 110, 151, 156, 195, 213
execution, ix
exercise, 11, 52, 107, 110
expenditures, 68, 108
expertise, 91
experts, 154, 155, 180, 190, 227, 258
exploitation, 12, 18
exports, 68, 173
exposure, 44
expression, 145

F

fabric, 101, 206, 232
failure, 50, 71, 73, 76, 81, 98, 102, 119, 139, 154, 155, 162, 174, 197, 237, 262
fairness, 19, 85, 196, 252
faith, 6, 9, 62, 72, 109, 116, 145, 146, 147, 213, 233, 255, 259, 260, 264, 271
false belief, 53, 81

family, 1, 2, 4, 10, 11, 12, 13, 15, 16, 20, 21, 26, 30, 39, 47, 49, 53, 75, 91, 102, 111, 202, 242, 247, 257, 268, 275
family environment, 4
family income, 102
family members, 242
farmers, 20, 22, 24, 55, 66, 67, 70, 75, 76, 81, 85, 87, 96, 120, 122, 226, 229, 236, 238, 239, 242, 270
farmland, 123
farms, 67, 82, 96, 224, 242, 247, 250
fascism, xviii, 103, 122, 130
fat, 19, 201, 253
fatalism, 120
fear, 43, 80, 84, 111, 141, 149, 150, 155, 164, 165, 177, 178, 211, 214, 216
Federal Reserve Board, 36, 106
Federal Reserve System, 36, 46, 85, 93
feelings, 214, 232
feet, 4, 61, 62, 67, 110, 112, 167, 235, 267
fever, 6, 27
Filipino, 223
finance, 70, 76, 77, 87, 141
financial crisis, 93
financial markets, 271
financial soundness, 93
financial system, 67
financing, 241
Finland, 138
fire fighting, 94
fires, xviii, 54, 157
firms, 37, 59, 98, 140
First World, 28, 30, 208, 275
fish, 46, 49, 132
fisheries, 100
fishing, 3, 49
fission, 218
Five-Power Pact, 46
flame, 235
flexibility, 59
flight, 52, 228, 235
flood, 94, 100, 206
flooding, 99
fluctuations, 238
focusing, 53

food, 26, 41, 104, 123, 159, 166, 181, 184, 186, 196, 206, 231, 236, 237, 239, 246, 250, 251, 252
food production, 26
Ford, Henry, 98
foreclosure, 82
foreign exchange, 93
foreign investment, 50, 68
foreign policy, xvii, 86, 116, 121, 124, 125, 127, 139, 160, 247
forest management, 18
forgetting, xvii
Four-Power Pact, 46
France, 13, 31, 34, 35, 45, 88, 125, 128, 133, 135, 136, 137, 138, 139, 141, 143, 152, 161, 173, 178, 179, 195, 196, 203, 204, 222, 226, 240, 241, 245, 253, 260, 261, 277, 279, 280, 289
fraud, 58
free will, 183
freedom, 78, 107, 126, 137, 143, 144, 145, 146, 147, 149, 151, 152, 153, 156, 160, 164, 165, 167, 169, 170, 171, 172, 177, 184, 185, 191, 192, 196, 203, 207, 208, 211, 212, 213, 227, 233, 242, 244, 247, 257, 258, 264, 268, 271
freezing, 141, 173
friends, 2, 9, 10, 11, 12, 13, 15, 25, 27, 28, 29, 30, 31, 40, 43, 44, 46, 48, 51, 54, 66, 70, 86, 108, 114, 119, 122, 151, 168, 220, 242, 253, 254, 267, 276
friendship, 25, 30, 49, 76, 121, 205, 256, 274
fruits, 247
fuel, 19, 89, 250
fulfillment, 82, 109, 190, 202
funding, 95, 116, 124
furniture, 50, 65, 104

G

Galbraith, Kenneth, 65
garbage, 15, 72
gasoline, 55, 70, 89, 142, 173, 226, 247
generation, v, 81, 115, 131, 143, 146, 160, 169, 191, 202, 220, 268, 270

genocide, 219
geography, 34, 185, 227
Georgia, xii, 47, 99
Germany, 3, 26, 28, 29, 35, 41, 44, 45, 88, 124, 129, 131, 132, 135, 136, 137, 138, 141, 142, 143, 147, 149, 150, 151, 154, 161, 163, 164, 165, 166, 167, 169, 171, 172, 174, 182, 183, 184, 186, 190, 205, 207, 208, 210, 212, 214, 222, 233, 239, 240, 242, 243, 244, 245, 246, 253, 256, 257, 258, 259, 260, 262, 264, 265, 291
gift, 36, 84, 106, 125
gifted, 78
girls, 5, 221
goals, 16, 20, 26, 43, 64, 74, 98, 120, 160, 184, 190, 203, 220
God, 7, 81, 84, 103, 113, 137, 139, 147, 152, 160, 176, 183, 202, 206, 212, 213, 233, 260, 261, 263, 264
gold, 39, 45, 65, 84, 93, 100, 121, 253
goods and services, 104
government, x, xii, xvii, 14, 15, 19, 22, 24, 25, 26, 29, 37, 45, 49, 50, 62, 64, 66, 69, 72, 73, 75, 77, 78, 79, 80, 81, 83, 88, 95, 96, 97, 99, 100, 102, 103, 105, 106, 107, 108, 109, 111, 112, 114, 115, 118, 119, 120, 121, 125, 126, 127, 130, 131, 133, 135, 136, 138, 139, 140, 144, 146, 147, 149, 150, 156, 164, 168, 169, 172, 174, 183, 184, 189, 204, 218, 222, 244, 245, 246, 251, 253, 255, 270
government intervention, 25
grains, 41
gravity, 150, 171
Great Britain, 51, 105, 135, 137, 150, 153, 156, 160, 204, 207, 254, 257, 281
Great Depression, xvii, 1, 59, 60, 61, 94, 104, 278, 291
Greece, 161, 178, 209
greed, 8
grief, 134
gross national product, 50
Groton Missionary Society, 4
groups, 7, 38, 40, 41, 44, 50, 51, 104, 115, 147, 151, 200, 201, 213, 258

growth, xii, 7, 59, 123
guidance, 70, 71, 84, 112, 172, 273
guilty, 162
Guinea, 242, 249, 266
Gulf of Mexico, 207

H

Hamilton, Alexander, 2
hands, 36, 44, 69, 74, 101, 111, 137, 141, 146, 151, 167, 182, 217, 223, 260, 265, 269
happiness, 109
harm, 78, 199, 230, 274
harmony, 78, 199, 274
Harvard, 2, 5, 9, 10, 11, 19, 20, 56, 58, 62, 69, 74, 75, 76, 77, 88, 94, 95, 99, 114, 123, 129, 273, 277, 285, 286, 288, 289, 290, 291, 294
hate, 136, 232
Hawaii, xv, xviii, 7, 20, 88, 101, 139, 151, 173, 174, 175, 178, 187, 210, 214, 254, 266, 273, 274, 276, 286, 293, 294, 295
headache, 268
health, 14, 15, 26, 47, 49, 56, 95, 119, 120, 123, 206, 262
health care, 14
health insurance, 119
heart attack, 118
height, 38, 72, 142
helium, 48
hemisphere, 116, 146, 149, 150, 151, 155, 181, 183, 204, 207, 209, 212
heroism, 227, 229
highways, 89, 99, 208, 247
hip, 112
hiring, 95
hogs, 96
homeowners, 96
Hong Kong, 175
host, 41, 46, 81
House of Representatives, xi, 42, 85, 176, 184, 283
housing, 21, 104, 117, 123, 201, 206, 271
human dignity, 154
humility, 47

hurricanes, 109
husband, v, 10, 115, 160, 231, 274
Hyde Park, 1, 2, 3, 5, 12, 13, 40, 44, 52, 54, 56, 65, 84, 112, 147, 164, 165, 172, 202, 268, 273, 287
hydroelectric power, 56, 64

I

idealism, 66
ideas, 6, 46, 55, 76, 78, 79, 87, 108, 123, 218
identity, 166, 167
illusion, 181, 186, 205
illusions, 169, 171, 196, 221
imagery, 214
immigrants, 7, 50, 115, 242
immigration, 7, 50, 137
Immigration Act, 50
incentives, 49, 56
income, 7, 17, 36, 59, 60, 65, 69, 81, 82, 85, 95, 96, 105, 117, 120, 123, 206, 226, 239, 271
income tax, 17, 36, 69, 85
independence, 1, 46, 48, 54, 117, 148, 170, 174, 203, 206, 209, 212, 213, 222, 258
India, 58, 185, 186, 223, 242, 248, 250, 254
indication, 108
individualism, 68, 73
individuality, 21
Indonesia, 173, 242
induction, 80, 215
industrial sectors, 97
industry, 15, 19, 40, 50, 54, 69, 97, 104, 105, 106, 112, 114, 115, 117, 120, 148, 155, 180, 198, 199, 200, 201, 230, 244, 251
infection, 47
infinite, 47, 145
inflammation, 47
inflation, 28, 38, 103, 237, 239, 250, 252
influence, 15, 21, 41, 85, 152
inheritance, 52, 85, 106
inheritance tax, 85, 106
innocence, 31, 62
inspections, 28
inspiration, 259

instinct, 80, 109
institutions, 8, 13, 23, 88, 101, 123, 144, 185, 241, 270
instruments, 111, 128
insulation, 120
insurance, 49, 68, 78, 84, 237, 251
integrity, ix, 45, 117, 146, 209, 216, 266
intellect, 9, 76
intelligence, 11, 77, 122, 213, 217, 220, 231, 243, 252, 266
interdependence, 82, 83
interest, 14, 19, 24, 52, 57, 67, 78, 93, 96, 105, 111, 119, 127, 129, 163, 218, 275
interest groups, 119
interest rates, 67, 93, 96
International Bank for Reconstruction and Development, 270
international law, 142, 162, 166, 167, 169
International Monetary Fund, 242, 270
international relations, 257
international trade, 82, 86
International Woman Suffrage Alliance, 41
internationalism, 38, 119
intervention, 69, 78, 117, 128, 150
interview, 44
intuition, 249
investment, 78, 199
investors, 65, 199
Iran, 186
Iraq, 186
Ireland, 151
iron, 107, 264
isolation, 183, 186, 206
isolationism, 44, 127, 128, 129, 184, 186
Israel, 117, 124, 241
Italy, 7, 13, 34, 45, 130, 133, 135, 141, 143, 149, 152, 172, 177, 182, 183, 184, 186, 190, 214, 216, 222, 242, 245, 246, 247, 252, 253, 254, 256, 260, 283

J

Japan, 45, 128, 129, 136, 139, 143, 147, 149, 161, 172, 173, 175, 176, 177, 179, 180, 182, 183, 184, 186, 187, 188, 190, 214,

Index

219, 222, 224, 233, 240, 242, 244, 246, 250, 255, 256, 259, 265, 266, 269, 274, 280, 290, 293
jobless, 104
jobs, 7, 28, 38, 49, 59, 64, 65, 66, 94, 95, 102, 103, 125, 220, 244
judicial branch, 119
juries, 43
justice, 8, 113, 183, 185, 236, 237, 250
justification, 60, 133, 146, 152

K

Keynes, 94, 108
Keynesian, 87, 93
knowledge, 5, 14, 28, 31, 34, 46, 135, 146, 195, 208, 209, 214, 217, 254, 255
Korea, 190

L

labeling, 52
labor, 6, 15, 19, 25, 28, 29, 37, 69, 73, 76, 90, 97, 101, 102, 106, 114, 115, 124, 151, 155, 165, 190, 201, 205, 211, 212, 224, 226, 231, 241, 243, 244, 247, 270
labor force, 244
labor relations, 28, 124
land, 3, 20, 60, 71, 82, 87, 96, 110, 112, 122, 139, 143, 145, 146, 154, 165, 166, 167, 169, 172, 174, 182, 188, 191, 199, 200, 202, 207, 208, 226, 239, 243, 245, 246, 249, 255, 256, 264
land use, 123
Latin America, 86, 101, 116, 122, 127, 128, 141, 205, 210, 213, 281, 282
Latvia, 138
laws, ix, 15, 27, 42, 55, 57, 58, 75, 85, 114, 119, 123, 139, 168, 201
layoffs, 28
lead, 1, 26, 59, 90, 129, 149, 220, 223, 256
leadership, ix, xiv, 4, 23, 44, 58, 62, 64, 73, 76, 80, 81, 83, 84, 102, 113, 115, 122, 126, 130, 140, 159, 198, 248, 249, 256

Leadership, vii, 5, 73, 159, 216
League of Nations, 35, 38, 42, 44, 45, 50, 100, 128, 130, 136, 138
learning, 17, 199
legislation, xi, 8, 14, 20, 25, 27, 36, 54, 58, 62, 63, 78, 84, 91, 96, 97, 106, 113, 114, 115, 120, 121, 129, 131, 140, 142, 147, 173, 227, 236, 237, 251
leisure, 38
leisure time, 38
lending, 36, 81
liability, 58
liberalism, 21, 122, 270
liberation, 163, 222
librarians, 273
library services, 273
lifetime, xvii, 25, 48, 135, 144
limitation, 101, 226
links, 22, 36, 217
liquidate, 67, 102
listening, 21, 69, 166, 191, 196, 229, 235
Lithuania, 138
livestock, 226
loans, 25, 60, 68, 96, 104, 129, 233
lobbying, 17, 24, 42
local government, 60, 82
location, 36, 209
long run, 110, 179
Louisiana, 265, 289
love, 11, 13, 28, 34, 156, 192, 232, 233, 260
lower prices, 56
loyalty, 118
lying, 67, 168, 187

M

machinery, 22, 49, 59, 68, 140, 198, 211, 225
magazines, 8, 121
Mainland China, 173
major decisions, 101
malaria, 99, 253
management, 3, 14, 19, 28, 35, 38, 78, 87, 88, 97, 106, 154, 212, 219, 241
mandates, 46, 91, 217
manipulation, 251

manpower, 94, 142, 169, 204, 206, 250, 251, 269
mantle, 27, 50, 62
manufactured goods, 225
manufacturing, 50, 206
market, 38, 57, 60, 61, 70, 76, 100, 244
marketing, 25, 85, 96, 122
markets, 59, 81, 86, 96, 116, 253
marriage, 3, 12, 13, 31, 42
married women, 115
mass, 61, 103, 105, 107, 148, 186, 200, 228
mastery, 220
materialism, 43, 50, 53
mathematics, 225
measures, 15, 18, 19, 25, 63, 67, 82, 83, 84, 88, 95, 104, 105, 112, 120, 123, 125, 145, 165, 172, 174, 176, 203, 208, 210, 222, 225, 238
meat, 20, 39
mediation, 191, 211
Mediterranean, 34, 186, 206, 221, 222, 240, 245, 254, 257, 277
membership, 5, 11, 36, 42, 44, 107, 244
memory, 227, 260
men, 7, 16, 29, 35, 39, 41, 43, 61, 62, 63, 64, 69, 72, 81, 84, 92, 94, 109, 110, 111, 112, 118, 132, 144, 145, 146, 148, 153, 154, 155, 156, 160, 162, 165, 178, 180, 184, 185, 186, 188, 189, 190, 191, 192, 196, 197, 200, 201, 202, 209, 211, 214, 220, 222, 223, 224, 227, 228, 229, 230, 233, 236, 240, 244, 247, 248, 250, 251, 252, 254, 255, 259, 260, 261, 263, 264
mental capacity, 220
mentor, 17, 24, 55, 57, 270, 275
mentoring, 27
metals, 181
Mexico, 29, 58, 117, 196, 218
middle class, 39, 41
Middle East, 35, 221, 240, 253, 254, 262
military, ix, xii, 6, 33, 35, 44, 89, 98, 117, 125, 127, 128, 132, 135, 136, 137, 139, 141, 142, 147, 150, 153, 154, 155, 156, 161, 162, 163, 169, 174, 175, 176, 177, 179, 182, 184, 185, 189, 196, 198, 199, 200, 201, 203, 204, 206, 208, 210, 211, 212, 213, 214, 215, 216, 217, 219, 220, 222, 223, 227, 229, 231, 235, 240, 242, 243, 246, 247, 250, 254, 255, 256, 257, 258, 259, 260, 264, 265, 266, 267
military aid, 141, 242
military dictatorship, 132, 136
military spending, 127
milk, 15, 72, 96, 258
minimum price, 239
minimum wage, 54, 97, 112, 120, 270
mining, 58, 68, 206, 230
minorities, 138
minority, 23, 107, 150, 196, 201
minority groups, 196
missions, 231
mobility, 48
mode, 46, 269
models, xiv, 15, 38, 294
modern society, 68
modernization, 120
mold, 25
momentum, 41, 195
money, 2, 8, 13, 29, 30, 36, 42, 44, 48, 58, 65, 67, 68, 71, 81, 82, 87, 93, 95, 102, 104, 105, 114, 141, 148, 154, 180, 196, 197, 198, 199, 224, 225, 226, 233, 239
money supply, 36
monopoly, 60, 100, 101, 102, 270
monopoly power, 270
Monroe, James, xi, 29
mood, 74, 137
moral standards, 206
morale, 48, 191, 200, 202, 211, 223, 231, 246, 249, 262
morality, 3, 43, 110, 112, 169, 270
moratorium, 68
Morocco, 182
Moscow, 73, 118, 125, 162, 163, 192, 255, 286
mothers, 42, 44, 259, 260
motion, 216
motivation, 116
motives, 258
mountains, 247, 260

Index

movement, 7, 8, 15, 18, 20, 37, 41, 77, 101, 106, 131, 137, 200, 244
murder, 169
music, 40, 220
musicians, 95

N

NAACP, 20
National American Woman Suffrage Association, 41
National Association of Colored Women, 20
National Consumer's League, 12
national income, 60, 101, 104, 119
National Negro Business League, 20
national parks, 89
national security, 148, 201, 219
National Security Council, xiii, 215
nationalism, 20, 51, 119, 130, 172
nationality, 167
natural disasters, 99
natural gas, 88, 105
natural resources, 16, 17, 22, 57, 82, 111, 201
Navy Department, 29, 30, 35, 37, 90, 165
Nazi Germany, 130, 204
Nazism, xviii, 90, 99, 117, 118, 120, 131, 139, 147, 152, 161, 163, 170, 214, 219, 222, 242, 243, 253, 257, 271
NCA, 162
needs, xiv, 14, 16, 25, 28, 57, 74, 77, 79, 83, 104, 145, 154, 155, 180, 190, 195, 198, 199, 200, 204, 231, 232, 233, 239, 247
negativity, 43
neglect, 114, 240
negotiating, 107, 245
negotiation, 35, 136
nerve, 80
Netherlands, 45, 138, 139, 152, 178, 188, 223, 226, 249
network, 17, 23, 31, 48, 70, 87, 103, 122
neutrons, 218
New Deal, vii, xvii, 6, 8, 15, 18, 21, 25, 27, 28, 36, 37, 43, 54, 56, 57, 59, 63, 66, 69, 75, 78, 79, 84, 87, 88, 90, 91, 92, 93, 94, 96, 97, 98, 99, 101, 102, 103, 104, 105, 106, 107, 108, 112, 114, 115, 116, 119, 120, 121, 122, 123, 124, 125, 126, 130, 167, 223, 231, 262, 270, 277, 278, 279, 281, 282, 284, 285, 286, 288, 289, 291
New Zealand, 185, 186, 223, 240, 256
newspapers, 8, 10, 57, 67, 72, 179
Nicaragua, 27, 117, 128
nickel, 40
Nine-Power Pact, 45
nitrates, 100
Nobel Prize, 218
North Africa, 118, 125, 161, 171, 186, 206, 209, 215, 216, 241, 242, 245, 247, 250, 254
North America, 166, 185, 186, 195
Norway, 116, 138, 139, 152, 161, 177, 182, 196, 204, 209, 226, 253, 285
nucleus, 131
nurses, 47

O

obligation, 69, 83, 112, 171, 179, 181, 251
Oceania, 174
oceans, 149, 150, 165, 168, 169, 177, 180, 185, 222
oil, 45, 48, 51, 88, 108, 117, 130, 142, 154, 162, 173, 206, 224
old age, 57, 105, 120, 200
older people, 103
operator, 229
oppression, 147, 153
optimism, 38, 48, 62, 79, 252
ores, 138
organ, 4, 20
organization, 16, 26, 51, 102, 115, 122, 154, 166, 180, 215, 217, 219, 265, 270
organizations, 15, 20, 28, 57, 89, 90, 140, 217, 241, 246
outline, 35
output, 50, 67, 82, 159, 190, 208
overseas aid, 140
overtime, 221
oxygen, 229

P

Pacific, 27, 46, 70, 132, 149, 150, 157, 159, 164, 169, 173, 174, 175, 177, 182, 183, 187, 188, 189, 190, 195, 196, 205, 213, 224, 239, 240, 242, 246, 249, 255, 256, 258, 265, 266, 269, 273, 274, 275, 276, 286, 294
pain, 47, 268
Panama, 27, 117, 167, 168
paralysis, 47, 201
parents, v, 4, 5, 87
partnership, 46, 56, 97, 143, 192, 244
paternalism, 21
pathways, 170
peace treaty, 35, 45
Pearl Harbor, 88, 117, 128, 140, 143, 164, 172, 173, 174, 175, 178, 179, 181, 183, 184, 188, 189, 195, 203, 205, 213, 215, 216, 217, 219, 221, 224, 240, 242, 265, 267, 273, 280, 287
penalties, 75
pensions, 54, 102, 104, 105, 120, 200, 251
permit, 201, 206, 243, 246
personality, 17, 52, 65, 92, 220
perspective, 4, 275
persuasion, 9
Peru, 86
pessimism, 252
Philippines, xii, 22, 88, 117, 174, 178, 187, 188, 228, 242, 265, 266, 267, 268
physical aggression, 160
physics, 26, 218
pigs, 253
planning, 53, 71, 78, 82, 86, 99, 116, 123, 126, 154, 162, 248, 250, 259, 260, 262
plants, 107, 155, 180, 190, 199, 200, 236, 244, 249
pleasure, 3, 5, 13, 40, 70
pneumonia, 34
poison, 189, 202, 262
Poland, 88, 137, 139, 152, 161, 177, 204, 215, 226, 241, 262
police, 17, 63, 72
policy making, 130
polio, 47
political leaders, 71, 112
political parties, 32, 43, 120
politics, 14, 16, 19, 21, 22, 25, 27, 30, 44, 46, 49, 51, 62, 76, 80, 84, 87, 90, 108, 122, 140, 192, 247
Polk, James K., ii
pools, 47
poor, xvii, 7, 12, 15, 21, 26, 57, 66, 70, 77, 87, 115, 123, 270
popular vote, xi, 24, 118, 262
population, 7, 50, 59, 74, 82, 111, 227, 229, 257
ports, 117, 139, 172, 208, 244, 247
Portugal, 45, 151, 206
poverty, 7, 20, 76, 99, 111, 143, 146
power, x, xi, xii, xvii, 5, 14, 16, 17, 19, 20, 22, 23, 28, 29, 32, 37, 38, 41, 50, 55, 56, 59, 60, 62, 64, 67, 70, 71, 73, 76, 77, 78, 79, 82, 83, 84, 99, 101, 102, 105, 106, 109, 110, 115, 119, 132, 136, 137, 138, 139, 142, 149, 150, 153, 154, 168, 172, 174, 186, 187, 191, 197, 200, 205, 206, 207, 208, 212, 213, 217, 221, 222, 223, 227, 233, 236, 238, 240, 241, 245, 249, 252, 256, 257, 264, 267, 269, 270
prayer, 171
prejudice, 20, 243
preparation, 28
preparedness, 28, 85, 118, 140, 141, 147, 159, 160, 172, 196, 203, 216
presidency, ix, x, xi, xii, xvii, 15, 16, 17, 18, 23, 34, 41, 48, 51, 52, 54, 58, 59, 62, 66, 70, 72, 73, 74, 76, 79, 85, 104, 108, 119, 121, 123, 124, 140, 270, 271
pressure, 61, 102, 111, 161, 243, 250, 256
prestige, xii, xvii, 24, 113, 136
prevention, 26, 170
prices, 59, 60, 61, 62, 67, 68, 76, 87, 95, 96, 97, 106, 114, 120, 122, 154, 225, 226, 236, 237, 238, 239
priming, 87
principle, 58, 147, 166, 213, 216, 263
prisoners of war, 260
prisons, 57

privacy, 63
private banks, 63
private ownership, 38
privation, 154
producers, 96
production, 25, 28, 37, 39, 49, 55, 56, 59, 62, 64, 67, 76, 95, 97, 99, 104, 107, 119, 122, 140, 154, 155, 156, 159, 179, 180, 184, 187, 190, 192, 199, 200, 203, 204, 211, 212, 221, 225, 231, 237, 243, 248, 253, 267, 273
productive capacity, 155, 198
productivity, 7, 60, 174, 269
professionalism, 274
professions, 115
profit margin, 50
profits, 60, 81, 106, 120, 129, 180, 190, 205, 211, 225, 226, 237, 239
program, xvii, 15, 22, 28, 67, 69, 79, 82, 94, 95, 99, 102, 103, 104, 118, 121, 122, 124, 141, 149, 154, 156, 161, 181, 198, 199, 200, 201, 202, 204, 208, 225, 226, 237, 274, 275
Progressive Era, 41, 42
Progressivism, 8, 16, 24, 25, 36, 41, 43
Prohibition, 41, 71, 100, 120
propaganda, 129, 166, 178, 191, 202, 211
property rights, 123
prosperity, 6, 20, 59, 67, 71, 73, 77, 100, 110, 111, 165, 201, 223
public administration, 28
public debt, 50
public health, 14, 37, 103
public housing, 119
public opinion, xi, 81, 107, 121
public policy, 21, 57
public support, 42, 118
public welfare, 14
Puerto Rico, 88, 123, 290
punishment, 178, 182
purchasing power, 59, 67, 94, 103, 201, 236, 237

Q

qualifications, 80
quality of life, 88, 105
quarterback, 79
quotas, 96, 123

R

race, xvii, 12, 14, 16, 20, 23, 39, 53, 114, 152, 153, 172, 177, 183, 192, 218, 255
racial differences, 162
racial minorities, 115
racism, 89
radio, 35, 50, 52, 57, 61, 115, 118, 125, 148, 160, 177, 179, 184, 189, 195, 219, 229, 233, 253
rain, 63, 221
range, 16, 99, 150, 167, 168, 170, 187, 198, 203, 255, 264, 265
raw materials, 155, 164, 165, 180, 185, 186, 199, 224, 225, 253
REA, 105
reading, 8, 20, 47
real estate, 60, 87
realism, 8, 77, 148
reality, 20, 40, 195, 243, 250
reasoning, 152, 259
recall, 8, 23, 144, 191
recession, 59, 60, 62, 87
recognition, 82, 107, 191, 255
reconcile, 149, 154
recovery, xvii, 68, 78, 82, 86, 87, 91, 93, 99, 103, 116, 117, 119, 120, 235
recreation, 28, 111
recruiting, 55, 82
recycling, 35
redistribution, 82
reduction, 22, 36, 68, 86, 121, 160
reflection, xi, 216
reforms, 12, 15, 17, 19, 22, 38, 50, 53, 55, 78, 88, 98, 113, 122, 125, 130
refugees, 34, 117, 241
regenerate, 94

regionalism, xvii
regulation, 15, 17, 19, 26, 38, 54, 57, 63, 75, 78, 79, 96, 120
regulations, 37
rehabilitation, 49
relationship, 30, 120, 210
relationships, 109
relatives, 10, 11, 73, 178, 267
relaxation, 10, 51, 267
religion, 153, 169, 172, 192, 206, 247
remembering, 191
rent, 65, 104, 226
reparation, 100
repo, 83
repression, 253
Republican, 12, 14, 16, 17, 18, 22, 28, 29, 43, 51, 53, 54, 56, 57, 58, 64, 65, 71, 79, 85, 88, 90, 100, 108, 117, 121, 127, 132, 140
Republican Party, 22, 79
Republicans, 1, 6, 18, 22, 23, 27, 28, 44, 45, 49, 50, 59, 90, 103, 108, 118, 140, 244, 262, 270
reputation, 23, 28, 56, 64, 72, 74, 75, 77, 84, 216
reserves, 30, 45, 52, 78, 162, 174, 198, 261
resilience, xvii
resistance, 151, 152, 153, 163, 206, 223, 248, 258, 262
resolution, 19, 117, 127, 155, 171, 176
resources, 18, 88, 94, 116, 146, 149, 150, 151, 155, 168, 176, 184, 185, 188, 199, 203, 206, 209, 210, 243, 249, 273
responsibility, xvii, 15, 56, 63, 106, 120, 131, 171, 179, 190, 200, 220, 224, 230, 238, 259
responsiveness, 43
retaliation, 68, 173, 252
revenue, 55, 72, 100
rhythm, xviii
rice, 114
rights, 21, 23, 64, 83, 85, 98, 99, 107, 115, 117, 129, 154, 162, 164, 168, 170, 185, 207, 210, 255, 257, 270
risk, 144, 153, 259
rods, 60
Roman Catholics, 51

Roosevelt, Eleanor, 2, 8, 11, 12, 42, 47, 55, 74, 77, 95, 115, 244, 281, 284, 288, 291
Roosevelt, Theodore, ii, xi, 1, 5, 6, 8, 9, 11, 12, 16, 17, 18, 20, 21, 23, 24, 27, 31, 33, 34, 35, 49, 58, 74, 97, 132
Russia, 58, 136, 138, 142, 147, 154, 161, 162, 172, 174, 178, 182, 185, 186, 222, 231, 239, 240, 243, 244, 249, 253, 254, 257, 262, 269, 280, 282, 285

S

sacrifice, 83, 127, 146, 154, 155, 177, 180, 191, 192, 193, 227, 229, 233, 246, 249, 251, 252, 254
sadness, 195
safety, 15, 19, 25, 27, 28, 87, 109, 165, 169, 175, 181, 196, 206, 208, 210, 238, 241, 258
sales, 50, 72
sanctions, 131
satellite, 253
satisfaction, 62, 83, 110, 230
savings, 59, 63, 81, 148
scandal, 51, 89
Scandinavia, 195, 203
scheduling, 219
school, xvii, 3, 4, 6, 13, 15, 17, 19, 20, 57, 60, 65, 77, 89, 130
scores, 8
search, 67, 105, 206, 251
Second World, 131, 139, 140, 142, 147, 208, 214, 243, 266, 279, 284, 287
Secretary of the Treasury, 16, 51, 67, 71, 86, 241
securities, 38, 61, 78
security, 36, 57, 58, 103, 109, 118, 120, 132, 134, 143, 144, 146, 148, 153, 154, 159, 160, 163, 165, 181, 185, 202, 204, 209, 212, 218, 231, 246, 255, 257, 261, 271
segregation, 243
seizure, 130, 205
self, 3, 20, 39, 43, 66, 81, 101, 105, 107, 109, 110, 111, 127, 130, 146, 153, 164, 166, 174, 186, 192, 193, 204, 224, 225, 226, 227, 249, 255

Index

self-employed, 105
self-esteem, 3
self-interest, 110, 111, 204
self-organization, 107
Senate, x, 20, 22, 23, 24, 26, 29, 36, 42, 52, 85, 90, 129, 176, 184
separation, x, 78, 98
Serbia, 182
series, ix, xiv, 4, 25, 45, 167, 204, 266, 273, 287, 293
services, 4, 16, 27, 30, 45, 77, 109, 143, 162, 212, 215, 217, 231, 236, 250, 251, 268, 269
shame, 97, 181, 221
shape, 9, 88, 121, 125, 199, 206, 246, 270
shaping, 78, 85
shares, 179
sharing, 4
shelter, 196
shock, 102, 144
shoot, 108, 165
shores, 7, 149, 151, 171, 208, 248
shortage, 19, 181
sign, 22, 97
signals, 217
silver, 36, 53, 103
Singapore, 223
sites, 94, 218, 264
skills, 3, 10, 20, 28, 46
skin, 104
slaughterhouses, 7
slavery, 144, 150, 160, 212, 222
slaves, 247
smoke, 138, 202, 235
social change, 27
social fabric, 16
social group, 43
social ills, 8
social justice, 16, 41, 110
social responsibility, 12, 90
social security, 165, 259
social services, 49
social structure, 172
socialism, 74, 99, 116, 120, 130
solidarity, 16, 20, 86, 142, 212
South Africa, 187

South Pacific, 186, 221, 266
Southeast Asia, 164, 173, 242
sovereignty, 46, 130, 170, 172
Soviet Union, 118, 123, 125, 147, 163, 174, 243, 262, 269
Spain, 129, 136, 161, 206
species, 132
speculation, 60, 82
speech, 20, 43, 51, 52, 56, 73, 76, 78, 79, 128, 143, 152, 160, 172, 189, 192, 196, 203, 205, 212, 247, 267
speed, 39, 71, 109, 137, 154, 155, 180, 200, 209, 228, 232, 248
sports, 4
stability, 93, 97, 154
stabilization, 69, 226, 236, 237
stabilizers, 120
standard of living, 8, 111, 205, 244, 257
standards, 37, 81, 111, 145, 165, 200
Stanton, Elizabeth Cady, 41
stars, 231
starvation, 44, 69, 72, 246
state intervention, 66
state reform, 14
statistics, 7, 8, 235
Statue of Liberty, 7
statutes, 43, 137
steel, 48, 49, 107, 154, 256
stock, 40, 57, 60, 61, 71, 120, 144, 146, 226, 232
stock exchange, 120
stock price, 60
strain, 220
strategies, xvii, 34, 161, 187, 266
strength, xi, 9, 47, 48, 52, 68, 132, 139, 154, 156, 161, 163, 171, 173, 179, 184, 185, 190, 196, 197, 200, 201, 204, 207, 209, 212, 239, 248, 249, 252, 259, 261
stress, 4, 17, 83, 190
stretching, 101
stroke, 44
strong force, 221
students, 4, 274, 294
subsidy, 115
subsistence, 7, 111

suffrage, 14, 41, 42
sugar, 1, 6, 123, 226, 249
suicide, 209, 265, 267
summer, 10, 11, 12, 13, 19, 36, 40, 46, 57, 63, 108, 130, 132, 133, 136, 141, 142, 165, 172, 184, 192, 228, 243, 245
superiority, 136, 185, 240, 246, 261
supervision, 36, 82, 88, 106, 134, 217
supply, 36, 47, 61, 76, 81, 96, 136, 147, 162, 170, 174, 185, 186, 199, 204, 215, 218, 224, 232, 247, 250
Supreme Court, x, 37, 75, 96, 98, 112, 113, 114, 116, 123, 241, 284
surplus, 64, 155
surprise, 175, 188, 215
survival, 95, 132, 203
survivors, 105, 167
sweat, 7, 139
Sweden, 138, 154
symbols, 170
sympathy, 73, 75, 103, 134
symptoms, 111
systems, 8, 14, 89, 200, 273

T

Taft, William Howard, xii, 19, 21
takeover, 137
targets, 243, 265
tariff, 17, 22, 36, 49, 50, 68, 78, 84, 101, 121
tax cut, 67
tax rates, 50
taxation, 100, 127, 226, 236, 239, 241
taxes, 17, 49, 54, 55, 81, 105, 127, 180, 205, 225, 226, 239
teachers, 4
teaching, 32, 75, 274, 293
teaching experience, 274
technology, xiii, 28, 101, 243
teeth, 253
telephone, 56, 247
tension, 232
tenure, 18, 124
terrorism, 169, 172
textile mills, 7

Thailand, 178, 187, 242
theory, 23, 52, 64
thinking, 67, 137, 151, 167, 251, 259, 260
Third Reich, 131, 132, 161, 162, 253, 264, 265, 282, 288, 289
threat, xiii, 103, 104, 113, 118, 147, 148, 149, 152, 156, 162, 175, 201, 206, 219, 238, 244, 264
threats, 122, 135, 150, 156, 165, 203, 213, 258
timber, 88
time, ix, xiii, xviii, 1, 4, 5, 6, 8, 10, 13, 15, 20, 26, 27, 28, 29, 34, 37, 38, 43, 45, 47, 49, 50, 52, 54, 56, 58, 60, 62, 63, 66, 68, 78, 80, 82, 83, 87, 89, 99, 101, 108, 109, 113, 120, 121, 124, 125, 126, 130, 132, 134, 135, 136, 137, 141, 143, 144, 145, 148, 149, 151, 156, 160, 163, 166, 167, 169, 170, 172, 173, 175, 178, 179, 185, 186, 190, 191, 192, 199, 201, 202, 204, 205, 210, 211, 213, 216, 224, 225, 228, 232, 233, 236, 237, 238, 239, 240, 241, 244, 246, 247, 249, 250, 251, 252, 254, 255, 258, 259, 263, 265, 267
timing, 48
tin, 66
tobacco, 59, 96, 114
tonic, 10
torture, 47
trade, xvii, 2, 19, 37, 49, 50, 81, 82, 85, 97, 98, 101, 116, 143, 152, 164, 165, 173, 204, 205, 206, 208, 251
trade war, 152
trading, 61, 127
tradition, 57, 79, 81, 112, 231, 271
Tragic Tuesday, 61
training, 198, 199, 200, 229, 230, 242, 247, 251, 274
traits, ix, 3, 274
transactions, 68, 93, 103
transformation, 47
transition, 55, 271
transmission, 56, 105
transport, 35, 52, 188, 235, 260
transportation, 8, 15, 27, 37, 82, 96, 187, 200, 211, 224, 244

Index

Treaty of Versailles, 44, 50, 100, 132, 210
trees, 94
trend, 189, 263
trial, 47, 131, 134
trust, 10, 13, 34, 81, 83, 178
Turkey, 186
turtle, 186, 210
typhoid, 27
typhus, 253

U

U.S. economy, xviii, 78, 87, 106, 120, 126, 243, 271
U.S. Treasury, 121, 125, 231
UN, 270, 271
uncertainty, 137
unemployment, 59, 62, 69, 78, 99, 105, 114, 119, 120, 200, 251
unemployment insurance, 62, 69, 105, 200, 251
uniform, 30, 244
unions, 37, 97, 106, 115, 120, 205, 243
United Kingdom, 164
United Nations, 118, 125, 184, 187, 188, 190, 191, 192, 222, 240, 241, 246, 249, 250, 257, 261, 265, 269, 270
United States, ix, xi, xiv, xvii, 1, 7, 9, 18, 19, 28, 30, 43, 45, 61, 63, 68, 72, 79, 82, 84, 86, 98, 100, 102, 104, 105, 109, 111, 112, 116, 118, 128, 129, 130, 132, 133, 137, 139, 140, 141, 142, 144, 145, 146, 147, 148, 149, 151, 152, 153, 154, 156, 160, 164, 165, 166, 167, 168, 169, 170, 171, 172, 173, 175, 176, 177, 178, 179, 180, 181, 182, 183, 184, 185, 190, 195, 197, 199, 203, 204, 205, 206, 208, 209, 210, 212, 213, 214, 224, 225, 229, 230, 235, 238, 247, 249, 251, 252, 254, 255, 257, 258, 259, 266, 269, 275, 281, 282, 284, 290, 294
universities, 2, 13, 20, 57
university students, 273
uranium, 218
urban areas, 59, 72
urbanization, 8
Uruguay, 117, 168
USSR, 269

V

vacuum, 50
Valencia, 274
values, 20, 61, 69, 81, 82, 83, 102, 118
vehicles, 142, 248
vessels, 29, 33, 167, 171, 172, 178, 243, 261
victims, 47, 114, 152
village, 130
violence, 166, 167, 170
visas, 86
vision, 68, 81, 109, 111, 160, 202, 256, 264
voice, xi, 36, 52, 112, 220
voters, 14, 24, 44, 45, 51, 66, 70, 114, 130, 143
voting, x, xi, xii, 55, 199

W

wage level, 78
wages, 19, 25, 28, 44, 50, 59, 60, 67, 95, 97, 105, 106, 200, 205, 225, 226, 230, 236, 237, 239
waking, 202
Wales, 12, 52
walking, 52
war, xvii, 3, 6, 17, 28, 29, 30, 33, 34, 35, 36, 37, 40, 44, 45, 50, 53, 59, 68, 72, 82, 83, 84, 86, 94, 117, 118, 120, 124, 125, 127, 128, 129, 131, 133, 134, 135, 136, 137, 139, 140, 141, 144, 147, 148, 149, 150, 151, 152, 153, 154, 155, 156, 160, 161, 162, 163, 164, 165, 166, 167, 168, 169, 170, 171, 172, 173, 175, 176, 177, 178, 179, 180, 181, 182, 183, 184, 185, 186, 187, 188, 189, 190, 191, 192, 195, 197, 198, 199, 201, 203, 204, 205, 206, 207, 208, 209, 210, 211, 212, 213, 214, 215, 216, 217, 219, 220, 221, 223, 224, 225, 226, 227, 228, 230, 231, 233, 235, 236,

237, 238, 239, 240, 241, 242, 243, 244,
246, 247, 248, 249, 250, 251, 252, 253,
254, 255, 256, 257, 258, 259, 260, 261,
262, 263, 264, 265, 267, 268, 269, 270, 271
Warm Springs Foundation, 48, 49
Washington, Booker T., 20
Washington, George, ii
water, 7, 69, 89, 171
weakness, 214
wealth, xvii, 1, 3, 59, 62, 71, 73, 81, 87, 102,
106, 111, 143, 146, 151, 155, 270
weapons, 88, 135, 141, 153, 173, 185, 198,
199, 201, 203, 224, 225, 240, 241, 261, 264
wear, 12
welfare, xvii, 9, 56, 69, 96, 106, 109, 115,
116, 119, 120, 257
welfare state, 119
well-being, 68, 154, 263
West Indies, 1, 207
Western Europe, 59, 122, 132, 138, 195, 196
wheat, 67, 96, 114
White House, xiii, 4, 10, 18, 20, 24, 25, 31,
42, 58, 71, 72, 91, 108, 143, 148, 165, 192,
203, 219, 223, 224, 268, 279, 287
wholesale, 101
Wilson, Woodrow, xi, 22, 23, 27, 36, 41, 44,
51, 57, 58, 75, 85, 87, 97, 114
wind, 39
winter, xvii, 3, 19, 20, 66, 95, 138, 142, 163,
184, 239
wives, 42, 259, 260
women, 4, 14, 15, 16, 26, 37, 41, 42, 44, 51,
54, 69, 72, 111, 114, 115, 145, 153, 156,
180, 190, 196, 201, 202, 211, 220, 222,
226, 230, 231, 244, 250, 251, 254, 260,
263, 270
women's groups, 115
women's organizations, 41, 115
Women's Trade Union League, 15, 16, 41, 55,
88, 116
words, 20, 52, 102, 134, 146, 148, 149, 192,
205, 207, 211, 213, 248, 263

work, 6, 9, 11, 15, 16, 18, 26, 27, 28, 34, 42,
46, 47, 48, 54, 56, 57, 59, 65, 66, 69, 74,
75, 78, 81, 82, 94, 95, 99, 103, 105, 107,
111, 112, 115, 119, 122, 123, 125, 126,
131, 134, 135, 136, 151, 155, 180, 190,
191, 197, 199, 200, 210, 211, 213, 218,
225, 226, 229, 231, 241, 244, 251, 252,
258, 263, 294
work ethic, 74
workers, 7, 14, 26, 28, 37, 45, 50, 55, 67, 69,
77, 90, 95, 98, 104, 105, 106, 120, 143,
154, 155, 199, 200, 226, 229, 236
working conditions, 12, 37, 55
working hours, 25, 97
working women, 16, 54, 114
workplace, 106
World Bank, 242
world policy, 82
World War I, v, vii, xiii, xvii, 1, 19, 28, 31,
33, 35, 37, 39, 41, 42, 49, 50, 58, 60, 68,
77, 86, 87, 88, 90, 96, 97, 100, 118, 119,
122, 123, 124, 125, 126, 127, 128, 129,
130, 131, 136, 137, 139, 140, 142, 159,
162, 177, 195, 205, 210, 214, 215, 216,
217, 220, 231, 235, 241, 242, 243, 244,
261, 262, 269, 270, 275, 278, 279, 280,
281, 282, 283, 284, 286, 287, 289, 291,
294, 295
worry, 163, 220
writing, x, 5, 23, 48, 56, 71, 75, 76, 109, 124,
170, 214, 275, 293
wrongdoing, 81

Y

yield, 18, 155, 185, 190, 192, 201
young men, 11, 94
young women, 220
Yugoslavia, 161, 178

Index